CW01192346

ON TREK IN KORDOFAN

The Diaries of
a British District Officer
in the Sudan
1931–1933

ORIENTAL AND AFRICAN ARCHIVES · 2

ON TREK IN KORDOFAN

The Diaries of
a British District Officer
in the Sudan
1931–1933

by
C. A. E. LEA

edited by
M. W. DALY

Published *for* THE BRITISH ACADEMY
by OXFORD UNIVERSITY PRESS

Oxford University Press, Walton Street, Oxford OX2 6DP
*Oxford New York Toronto
Delhi Bombay Calcutta Madras Karachi
Kuala Lumpur Singapore Hong Kong Tokyo
Nairobi Dar es Salaam Cape Town
Melbourne Auckland Madrid
and associated companies in
Berlin Ibadan*

*Published in the United States
by Oxford University Press Inc., New York*

© *The British Academy, 1994*

*All rights reserved. No part of this publication may be reproduced,
stored in a retrieval system, or transmitted, in amy form or by any means,
without the prior permission in writing of the British Academy.*

*British Library Cataloguing in Publication Data
Data available*

ISBN 0–19–726128–0

*Typeset by J&L Composition Ltd, Filey, North Yorkshire
Printed in Great Britain
on acid-free paper by
Bookcraft (Bath) Ltd.
Midsomer Norton, Avon*

Contents

List of Plates	vi
Glossary	vii
Abbreviations	ix
Introduction	1
TREK JOURNALS	9
Chapter I: C. A. E. Lea's Explanatory Note	11
Chapter II: Soderi	17
Chapter III: A Trek in Dar al-Kababish	27
Chapter IV: The *Nazir* of the Hawawir	53
Chapter V: Among the Nuba, Kawahla, and Kababish	93
Chapter VI: A Trek in the Northern Hills	133
Chapter VII: A District Commissioners' Meeting	163
Chapter VIII: A Tribal Peace Conference; A Trek to the Nile	169
Chapter IX: A Homicide Case	218
Chapter X: The Governor of Kordofan Visits Soderi District	244
Chapter XI: Dar Hamid	259
Chapter XII: "The Biggest *Shaykh* in the Sudan"	272
Map of the Anglo-Egyptian Sudan	292
Map of Northern Kordofan	294
Appendix: Family Tree of Shaykh 'Ali al-Tum	296
Index	297

List of Plates

Between pages 36 and 37

1. 'Ali al-Tum Fadlallah Salim (1874–1938), *nazir 'umum* of the Kababish. Sudan Archive, University of Durham Library (S.A.D.) 587/2/132.
2. A tebeldi tree. S.A.D. 587/2/142.
3. View westwards from Jabal 'Atshan. S.A.D. 587/2/150.
4. *Hamla* camels on trek. S.A.D. 587/2/200.

Between pages 164 and 165

5. Kababish slave women. S.A.D. 587/2/212.
6. (l.-r.) Angus Gillan, J. A. de C. Hamilton, and Harold MacMichael at Soderi, 1929. S.A.D. 588/2/54.
7. Kordofan Province Police. S.A.D. 2/14/27.
8. Kordofan shaykhs at Bara. Far left, 'Ali al-Tum; to his left, his brother Muhammad and Muhammad Fadlallah, *nazir* of the Kawahla. S.A.D. 587/1/118.

Between pages 260 and 261

9. Kaja Saruj, 1907: (l.-r.) Ibrahim Fahayl; the 'old friends' Na'im Sirkatti and 'Ali al-Tum; and Harold MacMichael. S.A.D. 587/1/181.
10. Marakh Wells. S.A.D. 587/1/195.
11. C. A. E. Lea. Author's photograph.
12. C. A. E. Lea. Author's photograph.

Glossary

awaid (*'awayd*): fees.
awlad: pl. of *walad*.
bimbashi: Ar. colloquial for Turkish *binbashi*: major in Sudan Defence Force.
dar: homeland, land, country.
dia (*diya*): blood-money.
diafa: guest-gift.
dukhn: bullrush millet.
durra (*dhura*): sorghum.
effendi, effendia (*afandi, afandiyya*): "Mr." (used of educated townsmen).
farwa: fur, pelt, skin, hide.
feki, fiki (*faki*): Muslim holy man; religious teacher.
ferik, feriik (*fariq*): nomad camp.
gail (*qa'il*): noon; herein to stop at mid-day.
gebel (see jebel).
ghaffir (*khafir*): Sudanese colloquial: watchman.
gizzu (see jizzu).
goz (*gawz*): stabilised sand dune.
hakim, hakiim (*hakim*): wise man. In the Sudan, doctor. *Hakim sahha*: travelling doctor.
hamla: military transport; the baggage train of an expedition.
hareem (*harim*): women's quarters, private family-quarters.
heidan (*hidan*): water-troughs. (Sing: *hiyad*).
hukm: judgement, opinion, sentence; used herein as a verb: to sentence.
jebel, gebel (*jabal*): hill, mountain.
jizzu, gizzu (*jizzu*): waterless area where animals are put out for winter grazing.
kerib (*karrib*): land eroded by water channels.
khalwa: lit. place of retreat; in the Sudan, a Quranic school.
kharif, khareef (*kharif*): autumn; in the Sudan, rainy season.
khor (*khawr*): water-course.
khut (*khutt*): provincial subdivision.
kisra: fragment, chunk of bread; in the Sudan, flat cakes of unleavened bread made from *dhura*.
kurnuk: grass building.

lahad: bruise.
mak (*makk*): traditional title for a Sudanese ruler.
mamur (*ma'mur*): lit one who is commissioned. In the Sudan, a Sudanese district official.
mandub (pl.: *manadib*, herein rendered also as manadiib): deputy, delegate, agent, representative.
mejlis, meglis (*majlis*): council.
melik (*malik*): king.
merkaz (*markaz*): station, (police) post, headquarters.
meshra (*mashr'a*): water hole, drinking place, landing place.
mudir: governor. During the Condominium, governor of a province.
mudiria (*mudiriyya*): provincial headquarters.
muhanna, muhamma (*muhanna*): the courtesy extended between friendly tribes.
naga (*naqa*): female camel.
nashugh, nishugh (*nashugh*): rainy-season grazing.
nazir: head of a tribe or section of a tribe. *Nazir 'umum*: head *nazir* of a tribal confederation.
omda (*'umda*): head of a town or group of villages; omadia (*'umadia*): the unit of which he is head.
onbashi (*aunbashi*): corporal.
rajil: man; height of a man.
rasan, rasaan (*rasan*): head-rope of a camel.
reika (*rayka*): a basket: Sudanese measure of capacity; in Kordofan, 247.5 litres.
rial (*riyal*): silver dollar.
sagh: major in the Sudan Defence Force.
sagia (*saqiya*): water-wheel.
salatin (sing. *sultan*): rulers.
shartai (*shartay*, pl. *sharati*): Fur title for district chief.
shawish: sergeant.
sheikh (*shaykh*): tribal, religious, or other notable.
shidd: stage of a journey.
sid el meshra (*sayyid al-mashr'a*): "master of the watering place".
ushur (*'ushr*): one-tenth; the Muslim tithe.
wakil: deputy.
walad (abbreviation: wad): son of.
zeriba, zariba (*zariba*): cattle pen, corral, stockade.

Abbreviations

As used in the footnotes

BD: Richard Hill, *A biographical dictionary of the Sudan*, 2nd ed., London 1967.

BM: A. F. Broun and R. E. Massey, *Flora of the Sudan*, London 1929.

IT: K. C. Sahni, *Important trees of the Northern Sudan*, Khartoum 1968.

Massey: R. E. Massey, *Sudan grasses*, Khartoum n.d. [1926].

SNR: *Sudan Notes and Records*.

SPS: Sudan Political Service.

SPS: Sudan Political Service 1899–1956, Oxford n.d.

Tothill: J. D. Tothill, ed., *Agriculture in the Sudan*, London 1948.

Introduction

In 1930 C. A. E. Lea, a junior member of the Sudan Political Service, was appointed assistant district commissioner in Dar al-Kababish, Northern Kordofan. Although a sprawling semi-desert sparsely inhabited mainly by Arab nomads, Northern Kordofan was considered a plum appointment in the Political Service. The official's time was spent mainly on trek, not in the office, and either alone or with a few hardy nomads, not crowded on the velvet cushion of headquarters. To the Political Service this was the "real" Sudan, the lives of whose people changed only in response to the demands of nature; who seemed immune to the confusion of modernity Europeans had brought to the Sudan but wished to escape. For the next three years, until his transfer in 1933, Lea recorded in detail his experiences in administering this vast domain, at a time ironically of considerable strain and flux in the social and political life of its peoples.

The Anglo-Egyptian Condominium had been founded in 1899 on the ruins of the Mahdiyya, the revolutionary movement of Muhammad Ahmad al-Mahdi which had swept across the Nilotic Sudan in the early 1880s. The British, in occupation of Egypt since 1882, had deferred "reconquest" of these lost lands until 1896 when, in the last stages of the Scramble for Africa, European politics and imperial rivalries dictated a forward policy. The Egyptian Army, under British and Egyptian officers and with British regular units attached, launched an elaborate and expensive campaign that culminated in the battle of Omdurman (Karari) on 2 September 1898. Anglo-Egyptian forces inflicted a heavy defeat on the Mahdist army, occupied the capital, and proceeded to pacify the country. The Khalifa 'Abdallahi, the Mahdi's successor, was finally defeated and killed in November 1899. Rudimentary civil administration, which had accompanied the advance of Anglo-Egyptian forces, was gradually extended from the Nile and its tributaries to outlying regions.

The Condominium Agreement of 1899, by which Egypt and Britain established the regime that was to last until 1956, was itself the result of complicated political calculation. The British had entered the Sudan ostensibly to recover Egypt's lost provinces, and it was that claim that served to cover French withdrawal from Fashoda.[1] British annexation of

---

[1] For details, and for a general history of the early Condominum, see M. W. Daly, *Empire on the Nile: the Anglo-Egyptian Sudan, 1898–1934*, Cambridge 1986.

the Upper Nile was therefore precluded. But restoration of Egyptian authority, the abuse of which was seen as the main reason for the Mahdist revolt, would have brought with it the international machinery of the Capitulatory regime that so complicated British control in Egypt. Lord Cromer, agent and consul-general in Cairo, therefore devised a "hybrid form of government", by which Britain and Egypt would in theory rule jointly but which from the start was completely dominated by the British. Full executive authority was vested in a governor-general; every governor-general until independence in 1956 was British. His main advisers, department heads, provincial governors, and military officers were all British. Egypt's role was limited to financial subsidy of the fledgling regime, manning hundreds of lower-level positions in the bureaucracy, and garrisoning the Sudan.

Administration before the First World War was in theory "direct". The country was divided into provinces (sing.: *mudiriyya*), along the lines of the old Turco-Egyptian regime, each under a British governor (*mudir*). A province comprised a number of districts, each of which was served by a British *mufattish* or "inspector", who after 1922 was called district commissioner. The districts were in turn divided into *ma'muriyyat*, each under a *ma'mur* (in the early years usually Egyptian, but later Sudanese). The duties of these officials varied greatly from district to district. Although the *mufattish* was originally intended to "inspect" the administration of the *ma'murs*, in most districts he gradually assumed executive authority; *ma'murs* became, in effect, assistants to the D.C. and intermediaries between him and the people. In towns, in the absence of tribal authority and where social and economic change demanded more elaborate administration, the *mufattish* indeed ruled directly. In rural areas, however, where a degree of tribal authority had survived the Mahdiyya and where low population density and nomadism made direct rule impossible, the *mufattish* did in fact inspect rather than rule.

During and after the First World War, this system was challenged. Unrest in India, Egypt, and other British dependencies seemed a general indictment of "direct" rule, involving as that did the growth of an educated native bureaucracy imbued with modern political ideas antithetical to European rule. The Egyptian revolution of 1919 was followed in 1922 by Britain's unilateral declaration of Egyptian independence which, although qualified by four Reserved Points, nonetheless ended British administrative control. The Sudan became a battleground of Anglo-Egyptian competition, a symbol to Egyptians of their country's continuing subordination, and to the British a vital safeguard to the imperial chokepoint at Suez. Egyptian attempts to win Sudanese support for the Unity of the Nile Valley were thus seen by the British as a direct threat to their vital interests. These attempts were combated in several ways, including gradual but far-reaching changes in the administrative policy of the Sudan Government.

The statutory beginnings of the new policy occurred in 1922 with promulgation of the Powers of Nomad Sheikhs Ordinance. Justified by recommendations of the Milner Mission, which in 1921 called for administration to "be left, as far as possible, in the hands of the native authorities, wherever they exist, under British supervision".[2] The Powers of Nomad Sheikhs Ordinance was therefore intended to regularise authority traditionally wielded by tribal chiefs in rural areas. Under terms of the ordinance the judgements of tribal *shaykhs*, sitting alone or in *majlis*, would be recognised as lawful. Capital crimes were still reserved for Major Courts under British officials, and rights of appeal were granted. By 1923 some 300 *shaykhs* had been recognised and empowered under the ordinance.

Where traditional tribal authority had remained strong or even, significantly, where it had been strengthened during the first two decades of Condominium rule, the powers granted under the ordinance were much less than those actually wielded by *shaykhs*. Indeed it was regarding such tribes as the Kababish that *true* Indirect Rule had long existed. In remote areas with nomadic populations the lone British *mufattish* was a rare visitor rather than a ruler. He had not the time or even the knowledge to interfere with tribal administration. As late as the 1930s the internal administration of as prominent a tribe as the Kababish was largely unknown to the Sudan Government. This ignorance conformed with policy, as long as tribesmen raised few complaints, inter-tribal relations remained generally smooth, and government taxes were regularly paid. But by the early 1930s, ironically the heyday of official Indirect Rule (or Native Administration as it had come to be called) in the Sudan, the very autonomy of even these nomadic tribes of the Western Sudan was seen as inconsistent with the demands of a modern administration. Thus as Assistant D.C. Dar al-Kababish Lea was much concerned first with ascertaining the workings of tribal administration and then with preserving it within the framework of an evolving colonial regime and modernizing society.

The dilemma this posed is epitomised by Shaykh 'Ali al-Tum Fadl Allah, K.B.E., *nazir 'umum* of the Kababish, the "biggest *shaykh* in the Sudan". The very existence of what had come to be called the "Kababish tribe" was largely his achievement. During the Turkiyya the Kababish were a confederation of tribes loosely linked as circumstances occasionally demanded. The Turco-Egyptian regime, in its own necessary resort to indirect rule, created a hierarchy in which a paramount chief or *shaykh al-mashayikh* was appointed over the various Kababish tribes of Kordofan.

---

[2] *Report of the special mission to Egypt*, 1921, Cmd. 1131.

The extent of his powers, and indeed that of the *shaykhs* of the individual tribes, is unclear.[3] At the outbreak of the Mahdiyya the Nurab tribe of the *shaykh al-mashayikh*, al-Tum Fadl Allah Salim, resisted; he was executed by the Mahdists and his tribe forcibly removed to Omdurman. After the Anglo-Egyptian conquest in 1898, al-Tum's son, 'Ali, was recognised by the new regime as *shaykh* of the Nurab and, in a renewal and extension of Turco-Egyptian policy, as *nazir* of the Kababish. Consolidation of the various Kababish *tribes* into the Kababish *tribe* therefore occurred mainly under 'Ali al-Tum during the first decades of the twentieth century. The powers of this "nomad shaykh", like those of others, had not, it seems, been wielded "since time immemorial" (as government policy had it), but been assumed or usurped and extended and regularised during the early years of colonial rule.

The ability of 'Ali al-Tum and other nomad *shaykhs* of the western Sudan to consolidate their personal and clan authority was partly the result of the government's simple ignorance of their affairs. Until 1916, when Darfur was conquered, Northern Kordofan was the frontier of a vast, sparsely-populated country with an undermanned government. The cooperation of a tribal *shaykh* who seemed to exert local authority was valuable. 'Ali al-Tum was more: a bulwark defending the Sudan's borders against the sultan of Darfur and the marauding tribes of French and Italian territory beyond. The First World War greatly enhanced that role. The Sudan Government armed the Kababish, who supplied valuable irregular support during the 1916 campaign to conquer Darfur.

Until the First World War Dar al-Kababish had been virtually unknown territory to British officials of the Sudan Government. The first *mufattish* was posted there, at Soderi, only in 1913. Interference was largely restricted to applying the new Herd Tax Ordinance, which involved replacing the lump-sum payment of tribal "tribute" with an enumeration of individuals' flocks and payment of a per-capita tax on them.[4] In this exercise, as in the conduct of affairs generally, it was in the government's interest to maintain good relations with Shaykh 'Ali, whose authority within the Kababish sections was moreover steadily increasing. Extension of Indirect Rule through government legislation ironically helped him to break the vestigial power of section *shaykhs* by monopolizing for himself and his own extended family official recognition of judicial functions. Thus the period witnessed the assimilation of the Kababish *tribes* into a Kababish *tribe*, under the leadership of what now would be called a

---

[3] This description relies on Talal Asad, *The Kababish Arabs*, London 1970, 157–77.
[4] See Reginald Davies, *The camel's back: service in the rural Sudan*, London 1957, 60–66.

section, the Nurab, and its *shaykh*—from 1915 *nazir 'umum* of the Kababish.

When Lea was appointed assistant D.C. Dar al-Kababish in 1930 Shaykh 'Ali was universally recognised as the most important tribal leader in the Sudan. In 1919 he had been a member of the Sudanese delegation sent to London to celebrate the victory over Germany. In 1925 he was knighted: one of only three Sudanese to win this British honour during the whole period of the Condominium. While the *shaykhs* of neighbouring tribes had seen their powers recognised under government ordinances, 'Ali al-Tum had acted as the ruler of a state within a state. The other tribes of Dar al-Kababish—notably the Kawahla, but also the Nuba of the Northern Hills—and of neighbouring *dars*, such as the Hawawir, Dar Hamid, and even the Maydub, had to recognise his preeminence and to manoeuvre constantly to maintain their independence. Thus, as we shall see so clearly in Lea's account, when in the early 1930s the Sudan Government sought to bring the Kababish under the terms of the Native Courts Ordinance 1932, the main difficulty was in convincing Shaykh 'Ali that this would not diminish the powers he already wielded. The impression is inescapable of the Sudan Government's *negotiating* with the powerful *nazir*, not dictating to him.

In contrast to the apparent orderliness of Shaykh 'Ali al-Tum's regime, other Native Administrations of Kordofan presented the British with constant problems. To an extent, ignorance was bliss: the more the government knew of a tribe's internal workings, the less successful its administration seemed to be. Whereas *shaykhs* and even *nazirs* were disciplined, even deposed, for financial irregularities—illegal exactions, extortion, "eating" fines, and so forth—the Kababish exchequer was a mystery. Whereas, as we shall see, the Nuba of the Northern Hills openly defied rulings of their carpetbagging *nazir* (Na'im Surkatti), Kabbashi complaints never reached the ears of the British D.C. Lea himself comments on the fiasco of the *majlis al-muluk* in Darfur. And his trek notes offer in detail an example of how improvisational Indirect Rule was in practice: far from honouring a tradition of strong executive authority, the Nuba would change their *mak* from time to time, if the government would allow it; far from establishing a shaykhly dynasty among them, Lea foresaw no need for a *nazir* at all when the current incumbent died. Thus the Kababish administration, whatever tensions it experienced in its lower levels, seemed to the British the perfection of "traditional" tribal rule.

Inevitably, Lea's trek notes are not mainly concerned with matters of high policy or speculation on abstract principles. Indeed, "administration" itself occupied a very small part of his and similarly-placed D.C.s' time. Readers may wonder at the number of days and long periods of others spent wholly in travel, rest, and such time-killing recreations as reading fiction, hitting a golf ball, and writing private letters. Remarkable too is the apparent lack of contact between the travelling D.C. and his own entourage, the men of his *hamla*, who, although frequently mentioned in passing, are almost never named or described. The desert D.C.'s famous isolation was a function not only of his physical environment but also of his colonial role; when he wrote of being alone, he meant separation from other Europeans, not literal solitude. Life on trek therefore exerted the mind at least as much as the body; tedium was a greater enemy than terrain, introspection as dangerous as duststorms and disease: countless times Lea resorts to "pink pills" even after an exhausting day on camelback. In a district such as Northern Kordofan, the *mufattish* was truly an *inspector*, whose forays into active administration were usually limited to capital cases and inter-tribal mediation. Otherwise he moved among the Sudanese rather as a visitor than as a ruler.

Many of the attitudes that informed the Sudan Political Service's administration of the rural Sudan are epitomised in Lea's trek notes. (He himself has been mentioned by old hands as epitomising the desert D.C.; almost from the start of his Sudan career he was called "Shaykh Lea".) His disdain for the towns, especially Khartoum, with its expatriate social life, is clear and typical; he takes trouble to make his infrequent visits even to El Obeid and Bara as brief as possible. And not only the towns but the products of the towns were disdained: merchants, *affandis*, Egyptians, European clothes, "town" manners. Lea's unqualified belief in the evils of modern, "literary" education typified the attitude of the Service: contact with European ideas, indeed contact with Europeans, "ruined" the native; with that contact came adoption of foreign ways and rejection of the tribal heritage. Lea's visits even to local *khalwas* were dutiful, any enjoyment of them derived largely from the organised games that invariably followed dull recitations. A trained teacher assigned to the Kababish was a constant disappointment: while Lea enthused about the principles of Indirect Rule, the "product of Gordon College" was concerned with pay and prospects— wanting the impossible, a "modernised" *faki*, Lea inevitably found instead a depressed *affandi*. Likewise Lea's defence of slavery (and the pervasiveness of the institution in Northern Kordofan) may be shocking; to contemporaries in the Sudan Government it was pragmatic: abolition of the slave *trade* in the Sudan had resulted from concern with European, not local, opinion, and attitudes towards slavery itself were positive, not merely tolerant. Finally in his religious views Lea seems typical too: mild mistrust of the local *faki*, dislike of the growing influence of Mahdism, sensitivity to local belief and practice—these were hallmarks of the Political Service in the inter-war period. Here we see how remarkably little religion intruded into the relations of the Christian D.C. and Muslim populace.

It is, however, as a source for the history of Dar al-Kababish that Lea's trek notes are of most value. Although he was hardly privy to the mechanisms of Kababish administration (and this in itself is significant evidence of the colonial encounter in practice), Lea was an interested observer who, moreover, had the great benefits of linguistic skill and historical perspective. His experience across this huge territory provides important general information about inter-tribal relations, environmental change, the habits and customs of the nomads, the local impact of worldwide Depression, the degrees to which Northern Kordofan's people had by the 1930s been influenced by the urban culture of the Nile Valley and the wider world beyond. The by-now hackneyed description of 'Ali al-Tum as the beau ideal of the desert *shaykh* is in Lea's notes so fully fleshed out as to allow a just appreciation both of the realities of life in 1930s Kordofan and of the combination of pragmatism and romance with which the British viewed it.

Cyril Alexander Edward Lea was born in 1902. He was educated at Eton and at King's College, Cambridge. He joined the Sudan Political Service in 1926, arrived in the Sudan in 1927, and was stationed in Kassala province until 1929. During a brief tour in the civil secretary's office (1929–31) in Khartoum he evidently impressed Harold MacMichael, the civil secretary and doyen of the Political Service who, like so many others who rose to prominence in the Sudan Government, had had formative administrative experience in rural Kordofan. Partly as a result of Depression-era retrenchment, Lea was seconded from 1933 to 1935 to the Education Department as an inspector. He served in Kassala in 1935–40 and again in 1944–46, among the nomads of the Red Sea Hills. During the Second World War he saw service along the Abyssinian frontier and, in 1941–44, with the occupation forces in Libya. He concluded his Sudan career in the Finance Department, first as assistant director of establishments, 1946–49, and finally as director until his retirement in 1952.

As he explains in his own Introduction, Lea's trek notes were written in diary form and sometimes enclosed in letters home. The original notes and a typescript were deposited in the Sudan Archive, University of Durham, in 1979.

For this edition the following method has been used. Bearing in mind that these trek notes were never considered a polished memoir, I have corrected obvious slips in the spelling of English words, and in punctuation and grammar, and have organised very short paragraphs into longer ones. All omissions are indicated with . . . . All insertions are indicated with []. I have not tried to reproduce the occasional pen-sketches with which Lea illustrated his original notes, or the few handwritten Arabic words. The organisation into chapters, and the chapter titles and occasional route-summaries are mine. The few long gaps in the record are with one exception explained by annual leave.

Transliteration is always a problem, which would here be made worse by the absence from maps (and indeed from the memories of Sudanese informants) of some place-names. Some of these are not Arabic in origin. To facilitate the use of Lea's notes as a historical source I have retained his transliterations of all Arabic and African words. In many cases these are those in official use at the time (for example sheikh [*shaykh*], omda [*'umda*], mejlis [*majlis*], goz [*gawz*], mamur [*ma'mur*], and so forth). But in rendering place-names, flora, and some personal names Lea wrote what he heard, and his spelling was inconsistent. Thus, for example, sayal (a tree) is rendered also sayaal, seyaal, and sayala; kittir (a bush) as kittr and kitir; one of Lea's camels, a Bishari, as a Bushari and Beshari; the Hitan as Heitan and Heitaan, Sanaqir as Senagir, Sanagir, and Sanaagir; the I'aysir family of the Kawahla as Eaysir, Eyasir, Aeysir, and Aeyisir. Therefore in some cases, to avoid confusion, "[sic]" has been interposed, in a few others a standard spelling, in brackets (for example [Qurun al-'Ujaymi] after Gurun Abu Ajaama). Usually, however, the context makes clear that a variant spelling rather than a different entity is introduced, as, for instance, where Lea used Zayadia and Zeyadia interchangeably, Gumuiya and Gumuwiya; Guraan and Goraan (for Quraan); and so forth. The glossary lists some variant spellings used by Lea, the notes some others. All spellings of personal and tribal names are listed and cross-referenced in the Index.

C. A. E. Lea
Trek Journals
Northern Kordofan
1931–1933

Chapter I

[C. A. E. Lea's Explanatory Note][1]

I hope that these "trek journals" may be of some use to any person studying the development, among the nomadic tribes of the Northern Sudan, of what was called "Native Administration" or "Devolution". The Milner Report of 1920[2] recommended: "Having regard to its (i.e. the Sudan's) vast extent and the varied character of its inhabitants, the administration of its different parts should be left, as far as possible, in the hands of Native Authorities, wherever they exist, under British supervision." The government of the Condominium was trying to act upon this recommendation.

On my appointment to the Sudan Political Service at the end of November 1926, I was fortunate to be posted, as a probationer Assistant District Commissioner, to Kassala Province, and, by the governor of the Province, Mr. R. E. H. Baily,[3] sent to serve in the Butana District under Mr. P. D. D. Acland,[4] with whom I had been at school. The governor was then making this district the subject of an experiment to build up a "Native Administration" with its own small budget and police (called "muhafiziin") round the personality and prestige of the great Sheikh Awad El Kerim Abu Sinn,[5] head of the Abu Sinn family, traditionally chiefs of the Shukria tribe, whose "Dar" extended approximately from Rufaa to Khashm El Girba, having its southern boundary running east to west from about the confluence of the Setit River with the Atbara to the confines of the Blue Nile Province near Wad Medani in the west. In the north it extended to around Goz Regeb in the east and to the borders of Khartoum and Berber Provinces in the west. One of the difficulties in this project was that it was impossible, under the Powers of Nomad Sheikhs Ordinance 1922,[6] to provide the Nazir with adequate powers in civil and criminal cases. It was understood that a new ordinance was under consideration.

---

[1] Undated; written before Lea's papers were deposited in the Sudan Archive, Durham, in 1979.
[2] After the Egyptian revolution of 1919, a mission under Lord Milner recommended reform of the British administration in Egypt and the Sudan. See M. W. Daly, *British administration and the Northern Sudan, 1917–1924*, Leiden 1980, 45–47, 107–10; and John Marlowe, *Anglo-Egyptian relations 1800–1953*, London 1954, 237–44.
[3] SPS, 1909–33; governor of Kassala, 1926–33. *SPS*, 20.
[4] P. B. E. Acland, SPS, 1924–46. *SPS*, 43.
[5] 'Awad al-Karim 'Abdallah Abu Sinn (1877–1943), *nazir 'umum* of the Shukriyya from 1923. See *BD*, 63.
[6] See Daly, *British administration*, 173–77.

In 1929 I was transferred from Kassala Province to become Deputy Assistant in the Civil Secretary's office in Khartoum. I was not happy at this removal to the secretariat life in Khartoum. But I soon found that I was serving under a man of great charm and wisdom, Mr. Clive Young.[7] I also found that the Civil Secretary, Sir Harold MacMichael,[8] was one of the best trainers of civil servants imaginable. Drafts submitted to him returned covered with his amendments in the blue pencil he used, but one could see at once how he had improved the draft, making it clearer and more concise. Further, as I was in the "Native Affairs" branch under Clive Young, I was directly involved in plans for the development of Native Administration.

One day in the first half of 1930, Sir [sic] Harold sent for me and (since he was reputed to be a martinet) amazed me by saying that he proposed transferring me to Kordofan to be assistant district commissioner [in] Dar El Kababish, and, as the post was so solitary, he wished to be sure I felt that I could stand it. I knew the post was, for a very junior Assistant District Commissioner, prestigious, and just the kind I wanted, and so I said I thought that I could stand the solitary conditions.

In June of that year it was arranged that I go to Kordofan, meet the district commissioner of Northern Kordofan, Mr. J. A. de C. Hamilton,[9] and trek with him to be "put in the picture".

The journals, therefore, begin with the journey by lorry to take over from Hector Maclean Watt,[10] who had been stationed in Dar El Kababish for several years. Here the problem was entirely different from that in the Butana District of Kassala. Here there were five different peoples: four nomad tribes, Kababish (lords of all they surveyed, in their own opinion), Kawahla, Howawir and Meganiin, and the more-or-less sedentary Nuba of the Northern Hills. Customary "Native" administration had existed since before the Condominium started. The application to the five Nazirs of the "Powers of Nomad Sheikhs Ordinance" was so poor a reflection of the powers they customarily exercised as to throw no light on what went on.

It was a basic principle of administration that the Assistant District Commissioner of Soderi should use no intelligence agents or informers. The assistant district commissioner (known to all as El Mufattish—The

---

[7] F. T. C. Young, SPS, 1910–36; assistant civil secretary, 1930–32; governor of Kassala, 1932–4. *SPS*, 22.
[8] SPS, 1905–34; civil secretary, 1926–34; later governor of Tanganyika, 1934–38, and high commissioner, Palestine, 1938–44; knighted 1931. *SPS*, 15. For his influence see Daly, *Empire*, 273–4, 328–35, 351–3.
[9] SPS, 1921–46, stationed in Kordofan, 1928–32. *SPS*, 33.
[10] SPS, 1925–43, including service in Kordofan, 1925–31. *SPS*, 47.

Inspector) must be continually on the move, keeping his eyes and ears open to note any signs of injustice, lawlessness or discontent. He must behave as a guest among Arab hosts. A "bureaucratic" attitude to his job was firmly discouraged, office work reduced to the minimum of Code of Criminal Procedure forms, accounts, a monthly report and an Annual Report, and the minimum of correspondence. He was encouraged by a generous travelling allowance to spend at least two thirds of this time "on trek", visiting in turn each of the five Nazirs in his encampment, wherever that might be, or his village, listening to such complaints as the Nazir might make to him, and referring to the Nazir petitions and complaints brought to the "Mufattish" by tribesmen of the Nazir and others. The Assistant District Commissioner had to keep his ears alert for rumours or evidence of inter-tribal friction or inter-tribal fights over watering, grazing or cultivation rights. Thefts, or suspected thefts of camels, cattle or sheep by men of one tribe against animals of another, should receive the Assistant District Commissioner's attention as soon as possible. Sometimes, however, such incidents would have resulted in wounds or homicide before news reached the Mufattish, whose subsequent magisterial inquiry would receive such confused, contradictory or obviously false evidence, that no case could be brought before a court under the Code of Criminal Procedure. Then approval had to be obtained and arrangements made over long distances for an inter-tribal "mejlis" to agree payment of "dia"— blood-money—to avoid a continuing vendetta, and make an agreement for the restoration of "muhamma". The Legal Department of the Government was chary of "dia" settlements and sometimes made difficulties. . . .

In 1931–32, there was . . . serious trouble between the Kababish and the Zeyadia of Darfur, and between the Kawahla in Dar El Kababish and the Hamar in Western Kordofan, when the Kawahla moved south in the early rains to find new grass.

I was fortunate in the summer of 1931 that trouble between the Kababish and the Kawahla within Dar El Kababish had been settled recently by Watt and Hamilton. The Nazir of the Kawahla, Muhammad Fadlallah, recently appointed after the death of his father, Fadlallah El Eaysir,[11] was aged about 30 and still unsure of his position, especially vis-a-vis Sheikh Sir Ali El Tom, whose father[12] had been beheaded in El Obeid on the Mahdi's orders, whose tribe had been removed from their Dar in the Mahdia and reduced to penury. Sheikh Ali had restored the fortunes of the Kababish during the Condominium and become the hero

---

[11] Fadl Allah Ahmad 'Abd al-Qadir al-I'aysir (d. 1929). *BD*, 122.
[12] Al-Tum Fadl Allah Salim had led the Kababish in opposition to the Mahdi. He was executed in 1883. *BD*, 362.

of his people. He was illiterate, but his intelligence was of the highest order, and, as an advocate of his people's causes, he was brilliant. No wonder Sheikh Muhammad Fadlallah felt inferior.

I was less fortunate because the relations between the Kababish and the Northern Nuba, hitherto usually excellent, had gone awry owing to a personal dispute between Sheikh Ali El Tom and Sheikh El Niama Sirkatti, Nazir of the Northern Hills, about the right to take ushur (tithe) from cultivators, Kabbashi and Nuba, in lands by the Wadi Hamra north of El Wuzz. (The matter is described in detail under 18th December 1931 and following days.) An argument between the two Nazirs in February 1931 in Soderi during the Ramadan Bairam[13] ended with Sheikh El Niama Sirkatti calling Sheikh Ali El Tom a liar. This event caused the breakdown of "muhamma" (the Arab notion of mutual understanding and assistance between neighbouring tribes) and led even to an affray and culpable homicide in June 1931.

Sheikh El Niama Sirkatti was a very remarkable man. He was an Arab from Dongola (not a Nuba) who was said to have arrived as a young man among the Nuba of the Northern Hills and by sheer personality made himself paramount chief among them.[14]

The other two Nazirs also had distinctive and strong personalities. Hasan Khalifa[15] of the Howawir, now old and bed-ridden, had since the Mahdia been a greatly respected chieftain of a tribe which wandered by "muhanna" through Dar El Kababish, but also, when grazing was available there, to the far northwest to the Wadi Hawa, to the neighbourhood of El Atrun Oasis (approximately 15 degrees 40 minutes N. by 26 degrees 30 minutes E.). Some of their herds would wander as far as the borders of French territory and Ennedi. Hence their experience and fear of raids from Ennedi by the Quraan....

Usually to be found at or near Mazrub Wells, Feki Juma Sahal, Nazir of the Meganin, was a deeply religious and highly respected chief of his semi-nomadic tribe.

The government had under consideration a new ordinance to replace the Powers of Nomad Sheikhs Ordinance 1922, which was eventually promulgated as the Native Courts Ordinance 1932,[16] and the government was anxious at the same time to regularise and legalise the "unofficial" form of Native Administration which had existed among the tribes for many years, in so far as it was not contrary to justice, morality or order.

---

[13] *'Id al-fitr* or the lesser *bayram*, the feast marking the end of the Ramadan fast.
[14] Na'im was a Rikabi of the Dualib. *BD*, 290.
[15] d. 1931. *BD*, 156.
[16] See Daly, *Empire*, 368.

Therefore the Assistant District Commissioner had been instructed to try to add to the government's existing knowledge of the methods used by the Nazirs to rule their tribesmen.

There were two subjects on which the government and its District Commissioners could not see eye to eye with the nomads and their Nazirs: (1) unlicensed arms (2) slavery. As to (1), the government knew there were many unlicensed firearms among the tribesmen. In the case of the Kababish, Sheikh Ali El Tom had been asked to use his tribesmen to guard the northern flank of the British and Egyptian force which invaded Darfur in 1916,[17] and he was issued with a large number of rifles, mostly Remingtons, and ample ammunition. These rifles had not been withdrawn at the end of operations. The government now wished to reduce the number of rifles to a few only, the identification of which should be registered by the district commissioner. These duly registered rifles were to be kept by the Nazirs and used for administrative purposes.

As to (2), slavery, the vast increase of animal wealth of the tribes under settled government had made the task of watering the flocks and herds a great burden, especially, of course, in the dry season. (I have noted my surprise at seeing young girls helping at the wells.) For this reason the Arabs said they could not do without their slave herdsmen. John Hamilton had had the good idea of providing pulleys (mostly second-hand from the Public Works Department's pumping stations and other works) to be erected over well-heads. A long rope could then be attached to the "delu" (leather bucket), over the pulley to the pack-saddle on a camel or donkey. As the animal was walked away from the well-head, so the bucket came up without man power. Also a much bigger delu could be used. This idea was gradually "catching on". But it was no more than a palliative.

The government's instructions to District Commissioners were clear. When a slave, born in the tribe, complained to the D.C. against his or her master, the D.C. must carefully investigate the case, and, if no unlawful conduct by the master against the slave was established by evidence, do his best to effect a reconciliation and persuade the slave to remain with the tribe. Failing that, the slave must be given a certificate of freedom and the D.C. must decide whether it was safe to leave the freedman with the tribe or whether he must remove the freedman for settlement elsewhere. Cases of kidnapping with a view to sale into slavery, when proved, were very severely punished. Meanwhile, in the early 1930s a noble Ethiopian lady resident near the borders of the Sudan was found to be making much profit by slave trading. Lists of missing persons were sent to District Commissioners who had to try to trace them.

---

[17] See *ibid.*, 171–86.

Chapter I

Reference should be made to the effects in 1931 of the world-wide economic depression. The Sudan Government had to balance its budget. It received no subventions.[18] The value of cotton, the main export and source of revenue, had fallen disastrously, and likewise the value of gum arabic, hides and animals. Recent droughts had added to the hardship of low animal prices. Many Arabs resisted paying their herd tax. The government reduced the number of police in Northern Kordofan (never numerous) to such an extent that, in 1932–3 help from the Commander of the Camel Corps (Colonel—later Sir Hugh—Boustead)[19] in lending soldiers to help make up the District Commissioners' escorts on trek, was gratefully accepted. Also the government transferred Mr. John Hamilton to be Assistant Sudan Agent in Cairo and abolished one of the three District-Commissioner posts in Northern Kordofan, leaving two young Assistant District Commissioners, Charles de Bunsen[20] and myself, to do the work formerly performed by one senior District Commissioner with two assistants.

These journals were written with two purposes: first, to keep myself reminded about events, discussions held with sheikhs and others, and information collected on trek; and secondly to keep two ladies in England —my fiancee (wife from 7th July 1931) and mother—informed of what my work was and how I lived. The top copies were posted to one of them, as opportunity arose, for reading and passing to the other. It is amazing that so much of this manuscript has survived.

---

[18] In fact the Sudan Government was still subsidised by Egypt in the amount of £E750,000 annually.
[19] An autobiography, *The wind of morning*, was published in London, 1974.
[20] SPS, 1928–54, including Kordofan, 1929–36. *SPS*, 54.

Chapter II

Soderi

7.3.31 [El Obeid]

I spent this morning before breakfast riding Mayall's[1] horse, which he had kindly offered me. With his syce, I rode eastwards out of the cantonment past the Camel Corps lines, and then turned back and rode past the railway station and the native town to the wells at the extreme west of the town. We returned through the town and past the mosque and the market to the station to see Hugh Boustead off on leave (for a six months' course with his regiment before he takes over command of the Camel Corps). After we had said good-bye to him, the Mayalls (who had walked up) and I walked back to breakfast. After breakfast I did the necessary packing (Koko is by no means clever at packing clothes) and gave last order for sundry small stores (including a bottle of gin as I hear that Leicester,[2] the gallant marine, and his infantry company of the Camel Corps will be at Soderi soon after I arrive there). I then went to the office and (a) sent Koko to look for some lost pig-nets (for loading kit onto camels) at the station (b) gave a character [reference] to Muhammad Salih, the servant who had trekked Kordofan with me in the summer, and whom I gave to Lomax when he went to Darfur, and who has since apparently got into trouble over a lady and is without work. (I would not mind re-employing him myself, for he is a cheery devil, and, after all, boys will be boys at 20 years of age; and the story is so confused it probably isn't a lady at the bottom of it all.) (c) Met a young (19) elementary schoolmaster named Hasan Ahmad Nagila who is to go up to Sheikh Ali El Tom's to be tutor to his son. (It is this lad's arrival which has held me in El Obeid for 6 days.) He appeared pleasant-mannered, but a townsman and wearing European shoes!

I had intended to start about 3.30 p.m. and had asked for the lorries to be at Mayall's house at 2.30 in consequence. The "Western Transport Company" (an amalgamated syndicate of a Greek and a Syrian) with true oriental procrastination sent one lorry at 2.40. I sent it to fetch the schoolmaster. The second lorry arrived about 3.30 so we were not ready to start till about 4.15.

---

[1] R. C. Mayall: SPS, 1920–40; in 1931, DC El Obeid. *SPS*, 34.
[2] "Jumbo" Leicester, a British officer seconded to the Camel Corps, No. 1 Company.

Chapter II

Meanwhile the Governor[3] had arrived before lunch somewhat unexpectedly (because his small son whom he had attempted to take on his tour round the Nuba Jebels, had fallen sick—bronchitis) and had asked to see me in his house on my way out of El Obeid. I accordingly went there at 4.15. He was very kindly. He had seen my and Hamilton's notes on the questions of (a) my marriage (b) the possibility of taking a wife to Soderi. All is well: he agrees with what I wrote and consents to what I asked for. Praise be to God. I saw Mrs. Gillan for a moment and made suitable remarks of regret for the son's illness.

We then bumped out of the great metropolis of the central Sudan and took the western road towards El Gleit and Soderi. A fat flabby Egyptian driver (efficient however), the schoolmaster and I rode in one car, the servants in the other. Much bumping and rattling. I hope the stuff survives.

This journey I did with Hamilton last June and I've described it before. You go in second gear for two miles or so up a Goz (sand-hill), and, if you're lucky for two miles in top gear down the other side. Some gozes are 10 to 15 miles across or more and sometimes the sand is so loose on the camel-track that one tacks about among the bushes off the road to get the greater assistance of the dried grass. The countryside is composed of red sand covered with dried yellow "haskaneet"[4] grass (all burrs which cling all over and leave pricks and thorns in the skin). There is a fairy story of a princess who could not sleep because her delicate skin felt a pea below 7 mattresses. If the poor dear had had a haskaneet burr in her nightie she'd have been driven stark crazy. All northern Kordofan is covered with this grass and they say that it's much thicker in western Kordofan.

We passed Jebel Abu Sinun about 5.40. The gozes are covered also with scattered bush—mostly dark green "merakh".[5] Here and there a Rackham-esque "tebeldi"[6] tree stands up above the low bush. We passed a grass fire which was burning brightly along one side of the road and had eaten up a good deal of the countryside already. Dark fell but we went on, in order to enable me to pass the next mid-day at Mazroub wells where I had told a petitioner to await me. At 7.30 p.m we stopped in an old cultivation where there was less haskaneet and bedded down for the night. It was pretty cold. A neigbouring village which we had not seen in the dark started beating drums for a dance (the young schoolmaster said a "wedding", but two boys who came in the morning to look at the motors said, "No. Just for fun."). Later, after my dinner, I had the schoolmaster

---

[3] Angus Gillan: SPS, 1909–39; governor of Kordofan, 1928–32; assistant civil secretary, 1932–34; civil secretary, 1934–39. *SPS*, 21.
[4] *Cenchrus cartharticus*. Massey, 37–38.
[5] *Leptadenia spartium*. Tothill, 35, 684.
[6] *Adansonia digitata*: the baobab. *BM*, 124.

to drink tea and talked and tried to impress on him that he should not "throw his weight about" when he got to Sheikh Ali El Tom's and should try to drop his town ways a bit.

It was a very cold night. But it is pleasant to be out of towns and (though this sounds churlish) English sociability and hospitality. And the air off the sands is so pure and bracing and there are no flies (at this time of year).

8.3.31

The chaps all slept inside the lorries on account of the cold and the thorny grass. A bitterly cold morning. We arranged to get under way by about 7 a.m., passed Um Shidera and El Gleit jebels and increasingly frequent people on the road and arrived at Mazroub at 9.30. Here Nazir Juma Sahal's brother En Nil met us and a number of chaps besides, and someone was sent off to tell Sheikh Juma of my arrival. "Feki"[7] (Holy Man) Juma is the Nazir of the Meganin, whose country this is. I had met him last June in Khartoum on his way back from the pilgrimage to Mecca. I breakfasted, shaved and bathed. En Nil Sahal came to talk to me and was anxious for an order that certain Hababin should either pay "ushur" [tithe] or go away from his lands, and also for another order about cattle plague. I carefully avoided both, saying that I had not yet taken over from Watt and would consult him when I reached Soderi.

Sheikh Juma then arrived and one Muhammad Jad Er Rab and others. They drank much coffee and Sheikh Juma talked much of his tribe and of his own good qualities. In particular he emphasised his generosity by saying that he had spent about £E240 in going on pilgrimage last year. I suitably congratulated him on his holiness. I took note of certain things to refer to Watt. Juma ended our session, when the others had left, by offering me the present of a horse, which of course I politely declined. The camels I bought and sent to Soderi had impressed him, he said. Funny old thing! By the time he had done it was time for lunch. After lunch I had a chat with the schoolmaster and then again with Feki Juma. The Feki Juma was rather shaken at the idea of the government's sending a teacher to Sheikh Ali El Tom.

We set off about 2.30 p.m. After Mazroub the road became much less heavy sand for some way. Large Jebels (Katul for one) appeared on the horizon to right and left. Then an enormous ridge of a sand hill—the great dune before Soderi. It is at this point that one really gets the sense of space and infinity which the Soderi country gives one. I felt happy as if I were going home.

---

[7] *Faki*: religious teacher. In the Sudan, the roles of *faki* and *faqir* (*sufi*) tended to merge.

We reached Soderi about 5 p.m. Hector Watt welcomed me kindly and soon all the Effendia turned up and also Sheikh Niama Sirkatti (the Nazir of the Northern Hills). Everyone was cheery and I glad to see them again.

When they had departed, Hector and I sat talking and drinking for hours and hours (as always happens when a man has been some time alone). We did not dine until 11 p.m.! He talked of Soderi and Soderi tribes and politics. He talked of my engagement, which (as I knew already from other sources) had worried him a great deal. At last we got to bed at midnight: I was dead beat.

9.3.31

Rose at 6.30. A very clear and cold morning. I think I have already described the Soderi scenery—the big jebels to the west beyond the now-dry lake glittering in the morning sun, Jebel Katoul of the Nubas away to the northeast and more distant jebels on all sides with sand dunes in the foreground.

Watt talked much after breakfast and we discussed what of his furniture I should buy. I am taking most of it: except large bookshelves, as I have few books. He did not go to the office and we sat and talked and wrote letters for the returning lorries to take. In our efforts to get the various letters we wished to write sent by the lorries we went on writing until 3.30 p.m. The lorries, in charge of rotund George the Syrian and the curiously-trousered native who skippered the second lorry, left at 3.30 and Hector and I had lunch. We were both a little sleepy and we sat and read and talked till dusk and then sat and drank and talked till about 8.30, when we dined and went to bed. . . .

I slept profoundly.

10.3.31

The long-expected infantry company of the Camel Corps—or rather its commander, Leicester[2] (the gallant marine), arrived before we had got out of bed. The actual company arrived while I was getting dressed. It was a good sight in the early morning to see these chaps trudging along through the sand (they had covered about 400 miles since 1st January) with flags flying, mule transport behind, and singing a queer song with the chorus of "La Ilah ill' Allah".[8] They formed square and bivouacked in the depression between this house and the Merkaz. I like their big turbans with ostrich feather plumes better than those of the Eastern Arab Corps.

Hector gave a very magnificent breakfast for Leicester's benefit, producing a ham out of a tin.

---

[8] "There is no god but God."

Hector and I went to the offices where he showed me round. I had of course not seen the new offices since they were completed. Very pleasant. I then sat with him for a while and watched him deal with correspondence. It was amusing to see a circular turning up which I had drafted myself a few weeks back. After that I returned to the house and read and talked to Leicester—a very pleasant and intelligent soldier.

In the afternoon Leicester, whose march had started at 3.30 a.m., slept. Hector and I read. At 4.30 p.m. I went out with a mashie and two golf balls and walked out to the aerodrome, where I spent the time practising shots. Good fun. I am glad that I started trying to hit a golf ball. It will obviously be a good way of getting exercise and passing the time here. I hate sitting indoors all the afternoon and, unless I have some exercise, I shall soon become as spherical as Hector is. This place looks lovely in the evening. The hills to the west take on a purple colour, the sky turns a deep blue and then faint green. Jebel Katool [sic] to the N.E. turns pink in the setting sun and the village of Soderi stands out like a dark row of gnomes in pointed hats in the foreground. On my way back I overtook Hector and Leicester. Leicester had been paying his troops.

We drank whisky and Hector produced for our amusement some lines of a scurrilous nature which he had written and decorated (not for publication) to cheer up Hamilton when he was rather down-hearted a year or so ago. We talked continuously before, during and after a late dinner this night. There was a long argument on novels as to the merits or demerits of Galsworthy's *Forsyte Saga*, Priestly's two long-drawn efforts, Aldous Huxley, D. H. Lawrence, certain American authors whom I did not know, *Flamingo*, Anatole France. And so we went to bed at midnight.

11.3.31

I was the first man up, as Leicester had very kindly lent me his horses. I rode round the village to the south, out across the wadi westwards and so onto the aerodrome for a canter and home by the wells and the small government garden. Over breakfast we talked a good deal of Oxford and Cambridge and professional soccer (Hector had been an Oxford Association Football Blue), after which Hector went officewards, telling me not to go. So I spent the morning doing accounts, and reading files which Hector sent me.

In the late afternoon Leicester slept and we read until 4.30, when Leicester most kindly took me out for a ride. We rode through the market and out across the aerodrome to the country under the jebels beyond and then back, ending with a gallop over the aerodrome. We talked of hunting, horses and the H.A.C. [Honourable Artillery Company]. Leicester is an amusing companion.

The evening was as usual. There was much talk and rather good talk by Hector. After dinner I felt desperately sleepy; and when they had a long discussion on crime and punishment, Glasgow criminals and famous cases, and Marshall Hall and Edward Marjoribanks[9] (whom we called "Clarence" at school and whom I thought conceited and foppish) I fell asleep. And I fell asleep three times and ultimately excused myself and staggered to bed at 11 p.m. I don't know when they went to bed.

12.3.31

I went out for a ride on one of Leicester's horses while he paraded his troops, or looked at mules or something. I went out over the dry bed of the lake, galloped the aerodrome and returned by the wells. After breakfast I wrote letters and chatted with Leicester and read papers— Hector did not want me to go to the office. In the afternoon, Hector wrote letters, I read and Leicester slept till 4.30. We had tea and I went to hit a golf ball while they looked at the soldiers.

After dark a great conversation started. It began with school stories. I told of Tuppy Headlam who went to sleep while batting and of his "If anyone asks me to a house party and they say there's huntin' *or* shootin' *or* fishin' *or* tennus [sic] *or* golf I say, 're-fused'. But if they say there's nothin' at *all* to do I say, 'Accepted with pleasure'." Hector went on to tell of a cricketing master at Winchester who was so devoted to cricket he always talked in its terms, even, by absence of mind, in Divinity classes. By degrees the talk turned to religion, and a tremendous argument arose on the question of Faith versus Science. Leicester is a Roman Catholic; Hector was brought up Presbyterian by his father who was Moderator of the Church of Scotland, and I brought up C. of E., and goodness knows what I am cheerfully pagan, I suppose, with a profound admiration for the personality and teachings of Jesus Christ. Consequently the argument was profoundly interesting; but, even so, the sleepiness which the strong air of Soderi brings over me at about 10 p.m. proved too much for me. I fell asleep so many times that at length I made my apologies and went to bed supperless. They told me next morning that they dined at 11 p.m. and went to bed still arguing at 1 a.m.

13.3.31. Friday

We all rose late, but they much later than I. I read a long note by Maclaren[10] on the administrative policy of Soderi District and correspondence

---

[9] Edward Marjoribanks, M.P., Lea's contemporary at Eton, published *For the defence: the life of Sir Edward Marshall Hall*, in 1929.

[10] J. F. P. Maclaren, SPS 1922–35, had served in Kordofan in 1923–25 and 1927. *SPS*, 39.

on the Meidob-Kababish question. After breakfast we all read and I drew Hector on to many things I wanted to find out about: the way things are done here, how you should deal with murders, thefts, fights, when police should be used, and so on.

After lunch Leicester had to start with his merry men back to El Obeid. I suppose it will take them a week to march there via Bara. Hector took photographs of the company and him on his horse. And so the flags moved off and the company disappeared over the sand hills. We were sorry at their going. Leicester is one of the nicest soldiers I have met in some time. I hope I'll see him again.

After tea, Hector and I played golf. First hole a tree, next the petrol store, third a bramble fence surrounding an old field of cotton. (We lost both balls on the third and laughed while we were searching for them, thinking how ridiculous two British looked searching for golf balls in a cotton field in the middle of Africa, with dusky Rachels, water-pots on their heads, looking on shyly as they went to the wells.) We found one of the lost balls, put down another and played three holes homewards. The usual beautiful colours on the distant hills surrounded us when we went in to our whisky and water.

There are several pairs of very attractive little birds—about 4" long overall, with finch-like beaks, grey brown wings and light yellow throats. They nest in the thatch of the roof. I'd like to know what kind they are. We went to bed fairly early this night after talk on Soderi affairs.

14.3.31

Spent this morning in the office learning about the way taxes are collected, sugar controlled,[11] and the police run here. About 8 p.m. the previous evening we had heard a car and seen its lights arriving. We had feared that it might be John Simons (Medical Inspector) and Dr. Atkey[12] turning up suddenly. However it proved to be a Greek who arrived without a permit to enter a closed district.[13] He was brought into the office and mildly told off. He said that he was leaving the next morning. Consequently we spent the afternoon writing to try and catch an extra mail. However the Greek did not keep his word and pushed off in the afternoon before we were ready.

I went out late and hit a golf ball. As I was looking for my ball, which

---

[11] The import and sale of sugar were government monopolies.

[12] O. F. H. Atkey had joined the medical service in 1907. He was Director, 1922–33. See H. C. Squires, *The Sudan Medical Service*, London 1958, 10, 51.

[13] Under *The Passports and Permits Ordinance 1922*, districts could be "closed" to outsiders. Most famously applied in the Southern Sudan, the ordinance was used also in Darfur and parts of Kordofan. See Daly, *British administration*, 179.

I hit a goodish way into the setting sun, Sheikh Niama Sirkatti came by on his horse. He asked what on earth I was doing, and in two minutes he was off his horse and hitting a golf ball with my mashie, laughing like anything. We played together back to the house, where he refused to come in because, he said, he had guests. . . .

16.3.31

Hector did not want me in the office, so I sat in the house and read files on the Kababish-Kawahla disputes.

In the afternoon I had the young schoolmaster who came here with me to tea. We talked of geography and Darwin and so on for an hour, after which I dismissed him and went out into the compound to practice [*sic*] short mashie shots. I did quite well. We had two hot days and a hot night and I felt pretty weary. However, we talked late on Soderi politics.

17.3.31

To the office and discussed cattle plague and new houses for the Effendia, and made out the rough plans for my treks until the end of May.

A very hot and airless day after a poor night. The kind of heat that makes one's flesh creep.

In the evening the Effendia of the merkaz gave a farewell tea party to Hector. On our way to it Hector was furious that so many people had been invited. There were the usual stale cakes common to these functions—and speeches. I thought the speeches would never stop. I think Hector was amused by it. We went to bed fairly early.

18.3.31

Another hot day, which was spent by me almost entirely in reading and writing. There was another tea party in Hector's honour, this time given by the police, who themselves, however, did not partake. It is comic how they love these farewell tea-parties.

Our last whisky went this night. I ought to have brought more with me.

19.3.31

Hector did not want me in the office, and I spent most of the morning writing Arabic and reading various papers he sent me. He stayed in the office till 2.30 p.m. After lunch the lorry which was to take him to El Obeid arrived. We both wrote letters till 5 p.m. At 5.30 we had to go to the last of the tea parties given in Hector's honour—by the merchants of the village this time. Hector had arranged that there should be races for the children of the village beforehand. Small "Craig" appeared limping like a "gaffer". There were seven races—very amusing ones. Boys from the local holyman's school—big boys, little boys and very little boys. Then the little girls down to very tiny ones. Great enthusiasm. Hector gave small prizes of money, accepted very shyly by the little girls. He had a number of piastres and half piastres left over which he tossed to be scrambled for. The small boys made a wild rugger scrum for each coin. We then had tea and one of the merchants read an amusing speech mostly in verse.

I sat up writing letters very late—an enormous mail for me. I was under the impression that the camel post left Soderi on Friday and that I'd get an extra letter or two by posting one via Hector and another by the camel post. But I was wrong, the post goes on Thursdays and I missed it.

20.3.31

Rose feeling sleepy. It began to blow very hard at breakfast time and continued all day—distant jebels all obscured by dust and sand flying everywhere. Hector packed up. Over breakfast Hector told me a disturbing piece of news about illegal "dues" paid by the tribesmen of the Kababish to their Nazir. Apparently the Mamur in enthusiasm has been doing a bit of sleuthing indirectly. If Sheikh Ali El Tom finds this out there may be the devil to pay, for his confidence in us that we always play straightforwardly with him will be shaken. It is all very difficult. We had a confab. with the Mamur. Also I took over keys and files and Hector produced before me from the prison four rebellious men of the Robab Howawir whom he had arrested on various charges when he did his trek northwards to Dongola this year. Then Sheikh Niama Sirkatti arrived to talk about a gum dispute between his Nubas and the Hamar tribe southwest of here. We told him that I would try to arrange a date to meet him and the Nazir of the Hamar, and, if possible, Bill Henderson[14] (Asst. D.C. Nahud) at the place of the dispute in September or October. Sheikh Niama then talked of his recent "tiff" with his friend Sheikh Ali El Tom about a cultivation boundary. We will have to patch that up somehow. We got to lunch about 3 p.m.

At about 4.30 we set off with every local notability on camels, horses or donkeys to give Hector a send-off on his transfer from Soderi. His car had been sent on ahead. He refused to ride my camel and took the one (now sold to me) on which he had originally arrived in Soderi four years ago. When we had ridden about a mile and a half out to the car, we took leave of him. Sheikh Niama actually broke down and shed tears.

So here am I set to try not to make a mess of things by myself. I shall need some luck.

I read for the rest of the afternoon and went to bed early. The night was cold.

[14] K. D. D. ("Bill") Henderson: SPS, 1926–53. *SPS*, 49.

21.3.31

I did not rise very early—finished reading an American novel called *The Party Dress* (not recommended) and went to the office. Here I looked up certain papers; and talked to Sheikh Niama who, to avoid a quarrel with Sheikh Ali El Tom (who is his friend) over tribal lands in Wadi Hamra, wants me to delimit a boundary. I have not time to, but may be able to arrange for the Mamur to do it. I then heard my first case as a magistrate for 2 years and 3 months, which resulted in the accused being sentenced to 18 months' imprisonment. In the afternoon I read and then went out to knock a golf ball about. In the end I lost one of my two remaining golf balls. After that I read some poetry and wrote. And so to bed at 10.30 p.m.

22.3.31

A bitterly cold night so that I slept lightly and woke before dawn. A big grass fire was blazing to the northwest, lighting up the Jebels five miles away. We have had strong winds blowing from about 8 a.m. until dusk for the last two days and these have brought the temperature down. I felt rather sleepy. Went to the office at 10 a.m. and found a note from Watt at Mazroub and another from Feki Gumaa Sahal. A bunch of notes came in from Sheikh Muhammad Fadlallah (Nazir of the Kawahla). I checked the safe and returned to the house at 1 p.m. There I packed clothes for transport to Omdurman to go on leave. A cheering job, although leave is still a long way off. My stuff will have to go off by camel from here to Omdurman about the end of April. But I may as well get everything packed against dust and moth now. After lunch I finished the packing and read.

At 5 p.m. the Mamur came to tea—a pleasant tete-a-tete. He left about 6.30.

I must try to get an Arabic prose written before I go off tomorrow afternoon.

Corporal Tingle, who is self-constituted master of the D.C.'s camels, produced an urchin to be my camelman's mate. Whether the lad is going to help the camelman or the cook I don't know and shall not enquire.

Chapter III

A Trek in Dar al-Kababish

[Soderi—Umm Khirwa'—Abu Za'ima—Hamrat al-Shaykh—Gashta—
Umm Badr—Khawr al-Sunt—Jabal al-Sanaqir—'Idd Abu 'Ajaja—
Soderi]

23.3.31

Rose at 6.15 and finished some packing and putting things away. Mail arrived at about 7.30, brought to the house by Tingle. Read my letters over breakfast and then went through the official mail in the house to see if there was anything urgent. Went to the office and went to see some broken well-head pulleys which had been brought from El Obeid with a view to their being given to Sheikh Ali El Tom. Returned to the house and wrote letters and then back to the office about 1 p.m. to finish up.

I had told Tingle that the hamla should start about 2 p.m. knowing that they always delay on the first day. In fact they got off at 3.15, leaving me writing letters. I started at 4.30 complete with two out-riders with Egyptian and British flags and Tingle. It is customary in Soderi to speed the parting guest—consequently all the officials, Sheikh Niama and certain of the merchants variously mounted rode off with me for about two miles towards Jebel Kaja Soderi (westwards). They then turned back. Niama on taking leave was most insistent that, if I go to Hasan Khalifa, I must also pay him a visit at Haraza, where he will be then.

We rode on till 6.40 p.m. when we came up with the fires of our hamla, which had outspanned on the western slopes of Kaja Soderi. I gave the young schoolmaster tea and talked with him about stars, on the question "Is it wrong according to the Faith, to know about stars?" He was rather good on this subject, maintaining that it was good to know the stars and their courses but wrong to foretell the future by them. Certain feasts and duties of the Muslim can be timed only by astronomy; also the Prophet found people studying astronomy and did not forbid it. Further the Khalifa Haroun er Rashid was keen on it. But horoscopes—No!

I did not go to sleep for some time. It was pretty cold.

24.3.31

The hamla started about 4 a.m. I got off about 6 a.m. and rode till 8.45 a.m., when we reached the village at Um Khirwa (lit. "Mother of castor oil", a pleasantly unconstipated name). The new pure-bred Bishari camel which Hamilton purchased for me in El Obeid arrived by the mail yesterday and I have been riding him since (reserving my best smooth camel, which is rather thin owing to change of air). He's not too smooth but undoubtedly a good camel and a very good buy (cheap). After the pleasures of breakfast, a shave and a bath in a grass house at Um Khirwa, old men descended on me—to wit: Ibrahim Fereih, aged about 95 so they tell me, and retired sheikh of the village; his slightly younger brother; his younger-still brother (say 65) who is now sheikh, named Na'iim Fereih. Following points in the conversation:

(1) A stray filly has wandered in from the Baragna Kawahla and they are getting tired of feeding her. I suggested that they go and see the Baragna about her, but they appeared rather to prefer to send her to the merkaz. I said, "No objection".

(2) Sheikh Niama, some days ago, had brought to the office a messenger from Naim [sic] Fereih who said that there was cattle plague in the Kababish herds at Abu Zaima and Id El Edeid wells and now cattle from there had to be moved on to Um Khirwa. Accordingly at Hector's instructions I had written a diplomatic note to Sheikh Ali El Tom asking him to have the said cattle driven back where they came from, and sent it by a policeman. The policeman met me here this morning. Na'iim said that the cattle had not been moved yet. But on enquiry of the policeman it appears that he (the bobby) brought a note from Sheikh Ali to the latter's agent here (a slave called Belal) to turn them back, and Belal has gone off to do this. The cattle came from Id El Edeid. No plague at Abu Zaima.

(3) These Nuba say (Sh. Niama had warned me that they would) that they have been paying ushur (one tenth of the value of the millet crop) to Sheikh Ali for some time past (ten camel loads—23 reikas—last year) and now for the last two years they have been put on Poll Tax and have to pay that as well to Sheikh Niama. They say that after the time that MacMic (now Sir Harold MacMichael) came back from the taking of El Fasher (1917), for two years the government Ushur Boards came here and they paid ushur to government through Sheikh Niama. After that, because there is friendship between Niama and Sheikh Ali El Tom, Niama let Ali El Tom take the ushur off them (presumably he "eats" [that is, keeps] it, for the Kababish paid no usher to government—this needs verifying) and they have paid to him these last nine years. They are not annoyed with Sheikh Ali, they love him dearly, but they would rather not pay two taxes. (*N.B.* Talk to Sheikh Ali and to Hamilton.)

Old Ibrahim Fereih has the devil of a cough and says he has seen the local govt. hakiim (doctor) and had medicine; but it don't get any better. I gave him some cough cure and eight Gold Flake (for which he asked, but which will do his throat harm). I said I would bring him cough cure if I came this way again from the merkaz. A garrulous old boy and hard to understand.

The hamla started at 2.30 and I at 4. Rode till 6.45 on the Feki's camel I bought in Khartoum—very smooth. Most of the way over a big goz (sand hill). It is difficult to describe the beauties of this country. It is something like Sussex gone wrong—rolling country between low hills. But the rolling country is covered with low bush and yellow grass, instead of oak forest, and the hills are usually rocky and of the hues and shapes of the mountains in the backgrounds of Italian pictures. Probably it bears no resemblance to Sussex at all except in the feeling of pleasure it gives me. The sense of space is tremendous, and the colours immediately after sundown are amazing. It is astonishing how camels brisken their pace when they see a camp fire ahead, like a horse when you turn his head towards stables.

25.3.31

Hamla started at 3 a.m. I started at 5.30 and rode till 8.30 when we reached Abu Zaima wells. The hamla had got down under almost exactly those trees under which Hamilton and I set ourselves last year. After breakfast and a shave, I went along the wells. Some folk were shearing sheep. I chatted with a young man and some girls, and also at another well with a hearty old boy who had a lad at hand with a pipe (called zumbaara), sitting in the shade of a tree. He bade the lad pipe to me and he played a merry tune. I had hardly got back to my chair when one Sheikh Rahma Udeila of the Zanaikha of the Kababish (there are also Zanaikha with the Gumuiya in Khartoum Province—"cousins") turned up with his son and a sheep as a gift. I produced coffee and we talked for half an hour or more. There are also Nurab and Barara watering at these wells. Sheikh Rahma Udeila said he paid ushur on his small cultivation N.W. of here to Sheikh Ali El Tom. And so, he said, do all Kababish. He was not to be trapped, however, into any admission about the other Kababish dues to Sheikh Ali. I have been reading a *A High Wind in Jamaica*, a remarkable thriller.

The hamla moved off about 2.30 p.m. and then I sent for the young "prof.", Hasan Nagila, and had him read with me part of a collection of Kababish and Kawahla folk songs made by John Hillard's servant two or three years ago, which Hasan had copied out into legible Arabic for me. They proved rather good fun. A large number of them are love songs and one or two are rather sarcastic political rhymes.

We rode off about 4 p.m. I was on the Beshari [*sic*] again—he needs less driving than the other. The soil became gravelly and the country bush. By 6.15 we had reached the northern slopes of Jebel Um Dabi' where Hamilton and I had camped when I came here last time.

I completed reading with Hasan the collection of songs.

It took a long time to get to sleep. The night was warmer than nights have been lately and also I could not make up my mind which way the ground sloped and whether my feet were higher than my head or not.

26.3.31

Started at 5.45. When we had crossed over the ridge of a col in Jebel Um Dabi', the police lost the track of the hamla and were roundly ticked off by Corporal Tingle. After scouting right and left, Tingle came on it again. I took the opportunity, finding him alone and out of ear-shot of the rest, to tell him of Sheikh Muhammad Fadlallah's note saying that there had been a fight at Um Badr and indicating that relations between the Kawahla and the Kababish were a bit strained. I said I was anxious to find out whether it was "wolf! wolf!" or whether there was trouble brewing, and asked him to chat quietly with the veterinary policeman who is now in Sheikh Ali's ferik with the government stallion and find out how things stood. He told me that he had already heard at Abu Zaima that things were not serious and that Sheikh Muhammad El Tom[1] had gone off to Um Badr to put things right. If so, all is well and we have an easy trek ahead—touching wood.

I am never sure what the great attraction of this camel-grazing country is. Dark bushes, often shaped like umbrellas, against saffron-coloured grass. Lines of jagged rocky hills jutting up in the distance and a brilliant sky overhead. We passed through two herds of Kabbashi camels grazing. A small urchin who was walking was so surprised when I said, "How do you do?" that he was still staring at me when I had gone on 200 yards. Why does an old she-camel always remind one of a maiden aunt? . . . We saw two ostriches in the distance, who ran hard ahead of us looking like two slightly crapulous old gentlemen (of the figure of "the Colonel" in the Pop cartoons), running in a rather dignified manner after a bus, their hands under the tails of their black morning coats—but alas! they have absent-mindedly forgotten to put on their trousers. They look most indecently half-clad, ostriches do.

Feeling somewhat above myself this morning and reflecting how much happier I feel than I did in Khartoum a month ago. Who would miss this kind of thing to sit in an office, or strap-hang every day to business, or teach in school?

Arrived at 9.15 a.m. near Hamra sainas (wells) to find camp made in a pleasant wadi (dry watercourse) under large trees.

---

[1] Muhammad al-Tum Fadl Allah Salim (c. 1868–1938), Shaykh 'Ali al-Tum's elder brother. *BD*, 277.

I read one or two articles in *Truth*, which journal is very sarcastic about the split in the Conservative party and about Mr. Lloyd George's scrimshankings. I tried translating a piece out of *Islam*, Lammen's book,[2] into Arabic—which passed the time very well.

The hamla went off at 2 p.m. . . . We set off at 3.30 p.m., I riding the Feki's camel (the smoother one). After about an hour's ride, as we were coming up the side of a goz, the Sheikh and his party suddenly appeared on the top of it. I was riding entirely at ease—tunic and hat hung over the back of my saddle—sun glasses and shirt open. There is a Civil Secretary's circular saying one must always be properly dressed to meet important natives. I had intended having tie and tunic on when that gentle knight Sir Ali El Tom appeared. As it was, his retainers and family had mounted and were galloping hard at me (as is their custom in welcoming one) as I struggled into my tunic. And when I dismounted to shake hands, I found that buttons and studs were still undone. The C.S.'s circular can go hang in future: I refuse to ride semi-asphyxiated in tunic and collar through a hot afternoon.

When we arrived at the feriik [*sic*] (camp) we were greeted with drums, song and dance as is Sheikh Ali El Tom's custom. A deuce of noise—slaves and slave-girls beating drums and singing to the base accompaniment of the Nazir's three war drums. And it went on for about three quarters of an hour while Sheikh Ali and I drank coffee.

Then he let me rest from 5 till about 7.30, when he came and talked over coffee. We discussed (1) The schoolmaster, hoping that he would be a success. Sheikh Ali El Tom had not heard that he (A.T.) had to find the lad's pay. But he agreed. As to his leave, A.T. and I suggested that he go not later than the end of Dahia II,[3] or before then if the Arabs move off to their rainy-season grazing ("Nishugh") sooner. Sheikh Ali wants the teacher to teach any tribesmen's sons who come—excellent.

(2) Sheikh El Niama Sirkatti and Wadi Hamra cultivations. A.T. is really rather annoyed about this dispute (an old one), the reason being, he says, that Feki Dardiri[4] arranged an agreement about this particular cultivation and Niama has encroached on the terms thereof. I dunno. Anyway A.T. won't agree to sending a representative to meet Niama and the Mamur on April 13 for the Mamur to make a boundary. He wants me to do that myself. God forbid. Thank goodness I cannot get there before next winter. So we agreed that I should write an order that Kababish and Nuba in that wadi should each cultivate only in their old lands and not in any new patches. It is all very difficult.

---

[2] Henri Lammens, *Islam: beliefs and institutions*, London 1929.
[3] *Al-dahiyya al-thaniya*, the Sudanese name for the Muslim month of *Muharram*.
[4] Possibly Shaykh Dardiri Muhammad al-Khalifa of the Tijaniyya *sufi* order.

(3) The Kababish cattle at Um Badr. A.T. said that Muhammad El Tom had just been there to settle up differences and found no cattle plague among the Kababish cattle. The cattle are still there. Now Hamilton had ordered that all Kababish cattle should go away and not water there. A.T., sly dog, has taken the order as being "all infectious cattle must go". Dirty dog. I said we would talk about that in the morning.

(4) "Jufar" (trypanosomiasis) in camels, which A.T. says is very bad this year. Muhammad El Tom and Ali El Tom have been very busy isolating infected animals from the herds. Talked on "Jufar el Lahm" and "Jufar el-Adom" (i.e. in the flesh or in the bones—from the latter type camels do not recover, i.e. it is malignant). I drew a parallel between benign and malignant malaria and we chatted about the causes thereof. (What is the Arabic for "germ"?) I also talked of Naganol,[5] which the vets. inject for tryps.

(5) The well Um Meiroos, which has fallen in.

(6) The misdeeds of the Meidob from Darfur. A.T. says there have been thefts on the way back from Omdurman quite recently.

After the gentle knight had gone I wrote a letter and then went to bed. Didn't sleep very well—too much coffee and too many dogs barking.

27.3.31

Rose 6 a.m. and had the luxury of a bath. Sheikh Ali arrived about 8.30: but previously Tingle had come to me and said that the news was that there is no trouble between the Kawahla and the Kababish—only the question of the cattle at Um Badr. Sheikh Ali and I dealt with nearly all outstanding business, I keeping back one or two slave cases and the question of the govt. stallion. We got onto Um Badr again. Sheikh Ali said that Muhammad Fadlallah had agreed with El Tom Ali[6] that, as there was no cattle plague among the Kababish cattle, they might continue watering. I hate upsetting any arrangement the Arabs make for themselves, but (a) in view of Hamilton's direct order, which he would not have made without good cause; (b) because there can only be less water than before at Um Badr now; (c) because the Kababish have misunderstood Hamilton's order (I think deliberately); [and] (d) because of Tingle's news, I determined to tell A.T. that I considered that Hamilton's order ought to be carried out in full, and El Tom's arrangement thereby upset. He took it very well. *N.B.* Sheikh Ali El Tom says Muhammad Fadlallah has not written to him about the cattle or anything else. It will be interesting to

---

[5] Suramin sodium, an antiprotozoal used specifically against trypanosoma. *The Merck Index*, Rahway, N.J., 11th ed., 1989, para. 8986.
[6] Al-Tum 'Ali al-Tum (1897–1945) succeeded his father, 'Ali al-Tum, as *nazir 'umum* of the Kababish in 1938. *BD*, 361.

see what Muhammad Fadlallah's version of the affair is. A.T. asked for time to move them, which was granted.

Talked about slavery. A.T. objects to slaves who have run and taken freedom papers being settled at Soderi. The government does not want this either. But what is one to do? A.T. would prefer their removal from the district and settlement elsewhere. How? Where? And with what funds?

A.T. says that, in spite of all the fuss in the world, he does not see how the way of life of the Arabs will ever be changed. I agreed. He went on to expatiate on how financial depression leaves the nomad unaffected: for his wealth is animals, not money.

He then went away and I slept; and read a book called *Equestrian Portrait* (rather a good romantic novel); and wrote an Arabic translation out and a note to Ferid Bey (my tutor in Arabic language), and lunched and dressed.

Then about 4.30 came Sheikhs El Tom Ali and Muhammad El Tom and chatted. We discussed all that had happened on Hamilton's trek to the Meidob and the muddle that has arisen about payment to the Kababish of the price of their strays sold by auction at Meidob. Muhammad El Tom rumbled along and his great fat face broke into a grin every now and then and he laughed like anything in describing Mrs. Ewan Campbell[7] trekking on a horse in Jebel Meidob. I asked El Tom what he had done at Um Badr. They left just before sunset.

At 8 p.m. Sheikh Ali turned up and drank coffee. We talked grasses and grazing and colours of camels (he says the best are "sofar", "ghabash" and "dabas"—Akhrash is a bad colour and so is Akhrar. "Dabas" I don't know, nor "Akhrash" but "sofar"—yellow—I recognise, and "ghabash" which is grey with yellow in it).[8] Then we started talking about the history of the Kababish and Sheikh Ali got going upon the story of what happened to his father and the tribe in the Mahdia and of his father's death (beheaded in El Obeid). Sheikh Ali, at all times vivid in speech, became dramatic as he narrated. The story was considerably better than most novels. I went to bed at 9.30 and slept sound.

28.3.31

At 7.30 a.m. Sheikh Ali turned up with Muhammad El Tom and horses to take me to see the well at Um Meiroos being dug. We had a pleasant ride out, talking of the Guraan raids, and of horse racing in England

---

[7] Ewen Campbell: SPS, 1921–48; stationed in Darfur, 1928–34; governor of Kordofan, 1938–47. *SPS*, 35.
[8] *Dabas*: deep "pinkish fawn"; *akhrash*: possibly "dirty white". See P. B. E. Acland, "Notes on the camel in the eastern Sudan", *SNR* XV, 1, 1932, 148.

(which Sheikh Ali has seen). I met again the well Osta [foreman] whom I saw last year and we went to the well. The well mouth has now been built up 80 cms. thick, masonry all round, to a depth of 10'. . . . Below is solid rock.

[The] working party (mostly slaves) are now digging out sand washed in by heavy rains when the well fell in last year. The Osta says about 8 days' work will get them down to the water. Sheikh Ali says that there are great caverns below and the water like a lake.

After standing and watching amid the noise of singing as the men pulled on the ropes and others (singing a chanty with a different tune) dug and filled the buckets below, we ascended and sat under trees, and the Osta brought us tea made with kurkadai[9] (a herb, red in colour, which, made into a beverage, one part kurkadai to two parts tea, gives a drink red in colour, which tastes like tea with lemon in it).

We talked of the well, of the Berberines of Halfa, of Wad En Najumi[10] and how the English conquered him, of cotton and the unfortunate effects of the economic revolution its cultivation in the Sudan has caused, of the Awlad Ugba at Um Inderaba and how proximity to the city of Omdurman and to the river is corrupting them. A pleasant and amusing bucolic Sheikh, Hammad of the Awlad Tereif, turned up with camels bringing rock for the well building. The Osta has a poisoned finger and I promised him iodine and bandages. Also he wants a "character" from me.

Then we got up off our sheep skins under the tree, unhitched the horses and rode back, talking of Hamilton and what he did in the war at Kut and Baghdad and in Persia; and A.T. questioned me of all the history of my life (far duller than Hamilton's). And I told him, and it appeared to amuse him, that I had failed to become a "professor" (Ustaz) and to please him that I had found that I could not bear the "office stool" in Birmingham and London, having been brought up "zol khalla" (his expression), i.e. a countryman.[11]

Breakfast and bath. The returning hired camelman who brought the schoolmaster will take my mail tomorrow. I wrote letters until 2.30, lunched and wrote again and at 4 Sheikh Ali appeared. We chatted over tea a while—about Reid's[12] being made governor of the White Nile, and about gazelle hunting during the rains.

Then he produced Sheikh Ibrahim Faheil and two slaves and their master. The usual slave case which we dealt with in the usual way. We

---

[9] *Hibiscus sabdariffa*: the roselle hemp. Tothill, 947.
[10] 'Abd al-Rahman wad al-Nujumi, a leading Mahdist *amir* killed at the battle of Tushki in 1889. *BD*, 17.
[11] Literally, a person of the open country.
[12] J. A. Reid, SPS, 1914–38; governor of the White Nile Province, 1931–37. *SPS*, 26.

could not reconcile the parties, and the parties could not prove ill-treatment on one side, or theft on the other. So I warned the slaves that they were free in the eyes of the government anyway, and I was willing of course to give them a paper to that effect; but they knew the life of the Arabs if they stayed in the tribe with their freedom papers, but, if they went away, how would they gain a living? Better the devil you know than that you don't. They departed to think it over.

Then we talked and talked. I explained income tax, as far as I understand it, and Sheikh Ali commented. I explained the old Radical economic theory and how now-a-days men wanted there to be neither rich nor poor in England—but all a government and servants thereof. Sheikh Ali made sarcastic comments. I went on to talk of the Marxian theory and the Bolsheviks—and Sheikh Ali took refuge in God from misfortune and said they were clearly afflicted of God. Then we fell to talking of slavery. Sheikh Ali's comment was, "This government does not agree with us over slavery, but it has spoken plainly and agreed to disagree. It has not done us down in the matter, for it is not of its own that it is abolishing slavery —but because all the governments of the earth have agreed together to abolish slavery, and it is doing the thing gradually." I told stories of Huskisson[13] and his friends and of the American Civil War and its after-effects to show the wisdom of the Sudan Government in freeing slaves gradually.

By now it was dusk and they went away to pray. After my supper, Sheikh El Tom Ali came to see me and talk about the Kawahla. He, of his own, volunteered that he would like to come to Um Badr with me. I jumped at it.

More letter writing and so to bed.

29.3.31

I spent the morning talking slaves and rifles with Ali El Tom, and then writing letters for the mail to go off with the returning camelmen at noon. A very awkward situation has arisen as a result of a note from D.C. Eastern Darfur to Sheikh Ali, which he handed to me yesterday evening.

Um Kedada[14] merkaz has arrested two Kabbashi slaves with unlicensed rifles. The slaves said (a) they were Ali El Tom's own slaves [and] (b) the rifles are A.T.'s part of government-issue rifles. The D.C. (Guy Moore)[15]

---

[13] Lea appears to mean Thomas Clarkson, the abolitionist. See *Dictionary of National Biography* IV, 454–57.
[14] Headquarters of Eastern Darfur District.
[15] For sketches of Guy Moore as district commissioner and governor see Wifred Thesiger, *The life of my choice*, London 1987, 192–203 *et passim*.

wrote politely to A.T., saying if he wanted his rifles, would he please send a note through me. Very neat—shifts the responsibility.

A.T., of course, supports the slaves' statements (I think with entire truth—but it won't necessarily look like it to the Darfur authorities). As I am trying to enlist A.T.'s aid to clear up the rifle question by finding out how many government rifles A.T. has in his charge (I don't think even he knows exactly), it would be very awkward to put him off by letting two rifles be forfeited to government and his slaves punished. So I had to scratch my head what to do and determined—longest way round, shortest way home—on a note to George Bredin[16] at El Fasher through Hamilton, rather than send an Arab in to Um Kedada with a chit from me. I hope it will work the oracle and deliver the goods.

It was a very hot day: real hot—woodwork inside the tent hot to the touch.

Later in the morning Sheikh El Tom Ali came with Ali Salih of the Awaida (the Kabbashi *wakil*—agent—at Um Badr). Also three Remington rifles were sent for me to see. I took their numbers and branded them L. Sheikh El Tom says that he will come to Um Badr.

At lunch time I started reading a book of Hector's called *Mosaic*, a sort of *Forsyte Saga* on a Jewish family, but considerably more entertaining when one gets into it.

Ali El Tom came round in the afternoon and we finished off that slave case, and he drank tea and talked about King George and his sons and Democracy. I said all forms of government boiled down to one man in the end: whether you had a king or whether you elect a bloke by a more or less complicated process. Then we went for a walk to see the stallion, but the stallion was out.

There had been a high wind blowing all afternoon and everything was dusty. I was very sleepy and went to bed at 8.30.

30.3.31

The night became cooler and the morning was cold. I went to see the stallion before breakfast. At 10 a.m. the schoolmaster called. About 10.30 Sheikh Ali appeared with others and a number of rifles. I spent some time checking them. Later A.T. sent his son Muhammad to summon me to his tent where I was given a spread: camel's meat, camel's milk, doughnuts, chicken, eggs, tea, coffee. We talked of Ali Dinar,[17] Sultan of Darfur,

---

[16] SPS, 1921–48; in 1931 stationed at El Fasher. *SPS*, 35.
[17] 'Ali Dinar Zakariya Muhammad al-Fadl, sultan of Darfur from 1898 until his death during the Anglo-Egyptian conquest of his country in 1916. See A. B. Theobald, *Ali Dinar, last sultan of Darfur 1898–1916*, London 1965.

PLATE 1

'Ali al-Tum Fadlallah Salim (1874–1938), *nazir 'umum* of the Kababish

S.A.D. 587/2/132

PLATE 2

A tebeldi tree S.A.D. 587/2/142

PLATE 3

View westwards from Jabal 'Atshan

S.A.D. 587/2/150

PLATE 4

Hamla camels on trek

S.A.D. 587/2/200

and of Slatin Pasha[18] and of the conquest of Darfur, and then I went home.

After lunch I read most of the afternoon until I was tired of novels, having finished *Mosaic*, and took to the *Arabian Nights* and *The Times*. I went to bed early. Sheikh Ali in his evening talk with me about rifles [had] also prevailed on me to stay another day, because he wanted to spend all next day at the well in the hope of reaching the water, and consequently he would not be able to see me off properly. I consented readily.

31.3.31

Felt rather idle in the morning and wrote to James Bevan (a letter promised three months ago). Then I read *The Times* and the *Arabian Nights* and Sheikh El Tom arrived. I talked about the various divisions of the Kababish—in order to learn them—and their watering places, and about the state of the Kababish before Darfur was conquered. He said the Kaja Nubas used to have many rifles and apparently had that *feu de joie* custom (also found at Kufra and in the Western Desert) of loosing off their guns at the feet of a pretty girl at a dance. El Tom said the Kababish had never had that custom. A rifle appeared and soon after El Tom went away.

In the afternoon I became tired of sitting indoors and went for an hour's walk to the top of a neigbouring hill to the east to look at the country round. Marvellous view. Um Dabi [*sic*] to the east, Gashda [Gashta] and Um Badr to the south and Ummat to the north. On the way back I saw a small bird which may have been a red start, but I think not. Finch-shape, brown with darker lines on the wings. White belly becoming red at the stern.

On my return I found that El Tom was waiting for me. Meanwhile that terrible old slave woman Bakhita turned up and ranted again. I don't think that she has any grouse really, so far as I can find.

El Tom talked camels and herding. He says the utmost manageable size of a herd is 100 nagas [female camels] and their young. Apparently, unless there is "jizzu" grass, nagas drop foals alternate years—not every rains. (Of course some drop foals in the winter: there is apparently no time when a naga cannot be in season, and the stallion will come on heat according to the state of the grazing, not necessarily during the rains). Names and ages are as in the Butana:

---

[18] Rudolf (von) Slatin (1857–1932), Austrian officer and official of the Turco-Egyptian regime, a prisoner during the Mahdiyya, and Inspector-General of the Sudan 1900–1914. See Richard Hill, *Slatin Pasha*, London 1965.

1st.	rains, when born	——————	Howar
2nd.	″	——————	Mafruud
3rd.	″	——————	Wad Lebuun
4th.	″	——————	Hig
5th.	″	——————	Jeda'a
6th.	″	——————	Tinny
7th.	″	——————	Roba'a
8th.	″	——————	Saddiis
9th	″	——————	Naib, Ta'an[19]

We talked of the best camels to import for riding. El Tom says: Bushariaat from El Damer. . . .

El Tom went away and after sunset Sheikh Ali appeared, rather tired —they had not got to water yet, but the sand had become damp. Over coffee I talked about Audas.[20] Sheikh Ali said that, years ago, when Audas came with MacMic, Audas had camels better than any that A.T. had seen. I told the story of the buying of my riding camel from the Feki, which amused A.T. A slave turned up—the lad Farajallah, who had come before—a nice boy. I told him he must wait for his master, who had been sent for, and, if Sheikh Ali cannot reconcile them, he shall catch me up.

It is noticeable that all slaves say they will stay with A.T. but not with their masters. After the lad had gone, A.T. gave me another long lecture on the difficulty caused to the Arabs by our freeing slaves, and hoped I would in time understand the ways of the Arabs. I excused myself that, even if a D.C. understood all, he could not help the situation much, for he is "under authority".

And so another day over and another month. It is comic how staying with A.T. is like staying in a country house. Your host comes daily to see how you are getting on. But it is much better than a house party for (a) one has a suite to one's self and one's own cook and valet [and] (b) there is no one to badger one into doing anything.

1.4.31

A cool night. The full moon was so brilliant that one could see colours plainly. This morning El Tom Ali appeared with an old man who has a case about a slave, who, he says, has run away with a camel, seven pounds, and a sword worth a tenner.

El Tom produced another Remington. Later Sheikh Ali El Tom came from the well, where apparently work is going on at great pace. He talked

---

[19] *Wad labun*: literally, "child of a milk-giver"; *rub'a*: literally, of medium size or height.
[20] Major R. S. Audas.

(1) about sending his khalwa feki (now out of job because the schoolmaster has nobbled the children) to Soderi to learn a little simple wound-dressing and leeching. Hamilton had suggested that someone do this at £E1 per mensem. I am to make sure about the money. The feki appeared—a young man, a bit obsequious but otherwise all right. (2) the well. It appears that one of the reasons he wants the cattle to stay at Um Badr is that it will release more people for the work. (3) how long does one take to get to England now-a-days? leading to his visit to Paris and London—the Underground! (4) how is England governed—how do we tell that such-and-such a big man has brains? (Very difficult questions these—I tried hard to describe the British Constitution and not to say that some leading politicians seem to have addled pates). (5) *Ali Wad Belal*: A.T. says he should go to El Obeid and asks me particularly not to leave him in Soderi when I go on leave. (6) Education—its advantages and disadvantages in the Sudan . . . .

I had lunch soon after he left me, and the hamla moved off at 2.30. As it was warm I slept a little, and, when I woke, found a scorpion in the blanket on which I had been resting my head. I chased him away but could not catch him. About 3.30 Sheikh Ali and all the others came to put me on my way. Sheikh Ali and Muhammad El Tom admonished me on the subject of Um Badr. I listened attentively and said I hoped Sheikh El Tom would reach an agreement with Sheikh Muhammad Fadlallah. They all rode with me a considerable distance—down to the wells and beyond—in all about two miles. There must have been over 20 people in the cavalcade. Then we said good-bye and Sheikh El Tom and I rode on.

The country between Hamra Wells and Gashda (our next wells on the road to Um Badr) is very pretty: pleasant large trees, hills in the distance and good going for camels. We came upon the hamla at sunset by the side of a pleasant dry watercourse.

I spent the evening talking to Sheikh El Tom about the Pilgrimage and about Ibn Saoud in the Hejaz, reading *Death comes for the Archbishop*, and watching my camels being fed by firelight. The full moon was *some* moon.

2.4.31

We got away at 5.30—a cool morning. The country became rather more open as we neared El Gashda. There are here by the wayside extraordinary rock formations like fingers sticking out of the ground. El Tom calls the place "El Gamad El Afin" (I don't know what this means). Several large buck gazelle crossed our path. We reached El Gashda at 8.30 and got down under the trees there. Sheikh El Tom rather overdid things and insisted on producing a sheep for us. I protested: hospitality should not be overdone. An Arab came and asked for medicine for his child which had whooping cough.

A very strong and dusty wind got up from the north and of course got hotter as the day wore on. It made our stay in Gashda (a pretty place in the midst of hills, when the weather permits one to admire it) very dusty and uncomfortable. Writing was quite impossible and I developed a headache. I spent part of the morning trying to sketch camels' heads, with poor success. I must have another shot at the full-face pose which gives the maiden-aunt effect.

We went on at 3.30. The Sheikh of the Barara Kababish turned up just as we were starting and I gave instructions that, if he comes down to water at Um Badr, the master of that mischief-making old crone Bakhita should come and see me.

The road from Gashda to Um Badr is very stony and amongst red rocky hills—like Bishariin country—as I explained to El Tom.

Sheikh Muhammad Fadlallah and a number of Kawahla sheikhs rode out to meet us from the hills just round Um Badr. We met in formal style and filed along into Um Badr over the last rocky defile. Um Badr is an amazing sight. Last year when I was here it was dry—now all of the hollow among the hills is full of water with a forest of trees standing out of it. The lake is still a mile long and several hundred yards wide, and, of course, no rain has fallen since September. When it was full this year it must have been an enormous lake—about the size of the Tarns above Coniston Water and about 20 feet deep. Thousands of camels, sheep and cows come down to water every day and the dust rises in clouds and the galumphing young camels canter down the last few hundred yards to water and the herdsmen shout "Ha! Ho! Ha!" And then, as the camels reach the basins of mud (which the Arabs make by the side of the lake to prevent the camels fouling the water or breaking their legs in the mud), the herdsmen say "Trrriim—Trrriim" and the camels snuffle the water. But it is all much better described in Doughty (*Arabia Deserta*).[21] Camels here water every 9th day, and when they water, they stand in the water and go on drinking at intervals from early morning till noon, or, if it is hot, till late afternoon.

I got down in one of the grass huts of last year's locust dump. Of course the door is open to windward. It had blown all day and proceeded to blow big guns all night, and the sand whipped into one's eyes and covered everything.

Sheikh Muhammad Fadlallah told me of a thief he had caught (there had been a fight between the thief and a herdsman and both [had been] wounded). I said I would see them as soon as possible in the morning and

---

[21] *Travels in Arabia Deserta*, London 1888.

take the accused in charge. I chatted and then led the conversation round to his appointment and talked to him like a father, repeating almost exactly the words Hamilton had used when Muhammad was first appointed Nazir. He had himself brought up the question of the Kababish watering here and I said he should discuss it with Sheikh El Tom.

Sheikh Muhammad had produced a vast mail for me which his retainer had brought from the merkaz. It included, apart from letters definitely hoped for, a long screed from Tom Bofeld on the grimness of farming in England . . . . Also Hamilton had written me a helpful letter and very kindly sent me three books. A rather pathetic letter arrived from Martin Blake saying he had been "axed".

I tried to sleep outside, but it could not be done: too much wind and dust. I removed inside where the dust made one like to choke (these grass walls hold it powdered and it comes out at every gust of wind, as if someone were shaking an enormous powder puff), but there was shelter from the wind. There was a total eclipse of the moon.

3.4.31

I've thought all today that this was the second of April. Now I find it's the 3rd, and Good Friday. Praise be to God.

I woke filthy and removed the mud from my eyes and reflected gloomily over a muddy cup of ovaltine that I simply did not understand how any English ladies ever married men in this service, and, if they rashly did, and ever got let in for this kind of thing (trekking), as some of them must have been, why they had not arranged divorces. My dirty clothes revolted me and the sheets of my bedding were like a gravel pit. I put on grey flannel trousers, a clean shirt and Russian boots, and left my hovel for a blow on the top of the sand dune outside, whence I surveyed Um Badr. It was a cool morning, and, if it had been May instead of April, I'd have said it looked like rain.

After breakfast Corporal Tingle and I were rapidly converted into a field dressing station. The thief and his captor turned up and, though I have seen a few wounds in the Sudan, I've seldom seen more revolting ones. The thief had received a sword cut on the napper which had gone to the bone (and would have killed him if he had not broken his left arm warding off the blow). The captor (a slave) had been stabbed in the forearm. The native treatment of wounds is either grease (as in the case of the head wound) or smoking over a wood fire (as in the case of the forearm). The result is easily imagined when they arrive for treatment anything up to 20 days later. I shall not feel easy (for fear of the spread of gangrene) till I can get those two off on the road to the doctor (i.e. "Hakiim sahha") at Soderi. I don't want a murder case. I must try to push them off tomorrow. I've had no time to take their statements today and there are other witnesses to come from near by.

Talk with Sheikh Muhammad and the usual chat with sheikhs and usual stream of slave cases and the usual camel-theft case (another bloody coxcomb involved—almost healed now) took up the morning until 2 p.m. Lunch and more slave cases. Haj Saiyid [*sic*], my friend of last year, turned up and wanted to know where was the photo of him I took.

About 3.30 p.m. Sheikh Muhammad produced a horse and he and I and Sheikh El Tom and a slave retinue went all round the lake to see the arrangements made for the Kababish to water. We ended up with taking tea with Sh. El Tom and then rode off to inspect the aerodrome where we had a few gallops.

After dark Sheikh Muhammad Fadlallah brought sheikhs to see me who: (1) Said they could not stand for the Kababish cows any more— largely because they have a custom of appointing a Melek El Mashra (King of the Watering place) who directs operations and "aggers" animals, and the Kababish won't obey him. (2) Made long complaints against the Nuba of Kaja Seruj of theft and harbouring camel thieves. I said that Sheikh Muhammad and I would make a list of complaints and perhaps during the rains I might meet Asst. D.C. Nahud (I hope Bill Henderson) and see what we could do. It has blown hard and sandy all day.

Slaves in important positions

Yesterday over coffee I talked to Sheikh El Tom about Kababish slaves in high positions. I had noticed when we left his father's camp that he was accompanied by two or three men very well dressed and riding good camels, with swords on their saddle pommels and carpets hanging below their "farwas" (sheep-skins used as prayer mat hung over the saddle to sit upon). I asked him who these were and he said "Slaves of long standing and pedigree". Their features had, it is true, something of the negro. He said such men among the Kababish themselves own property, marry according to the customary Muslim rites, and bequeath their property to their heirs. If their masters demanded a sheep or a camel they would not refuse, but otherwise their property is their own. Sheikh Ali, says El Tom, uses them a good deal for tax collection. The tithe of the crop from Kababish lands is always measured and checked at the matmurra (pit in the ground for storing grain) by a slave. So here are the *Arabian Nights* still in our midst! I went on from this subject last night, again over coffee, to discuss, and question him about, the Kababish Customary Dues: a-legal taxes paid to Sheikh Ali El Tom. Hamilton suggested I should do this. Sheikh El Tom admitted, of course, tithe of crops, and the sheep from each herd every year—but nothing more.

It appears that part of the trouble between Sheikh Muhammad Fadlallah and the Dueih tribe (who are independent but live in the territory of the Kawahla) is due to refusal to pay the tribute of sheep.

I saw Sheikh El Tom before dinner and told him I thought the Kawahla would refuse to let the cattle stay here. He didn't seem upset and said we would see finally in the morning. I asked him to speak firmly to the Awlad Tereif and Awlad Awad Es Sid[22] that they must mind their p's and q's here.

Sat up writing and bed at 11 p.m.

4.4.31

This was a very busy day. The morning was taken up with hearing the case in which the thief and another had been so badly wounded, and then with a stream of complaints—mostly from slaves. This slavery question is one that has always worried me dreadfully: it does every D.C. in Arab countries. I know the general line of policy but must talk to Hamilton to get tips as to how to deal with particular cases. The most difficult one of this day was raised by a girl called Howa (which may mean either wind or passion), a pretty little piece and obviously well looked after. She appeared and said she had a man to whom she was married (a slave is rarely married) and her master wanted to divorce her from the lad and marry her by force. Her lover appears—O G! a most unattractive black man—and her master, who asserts she is his legal concubine and a naughty girl: and he swears to that on a holy man's book. Who is lying? The holy man on whose book the Arab swore is very holy. A man who swears falsely on that book may easily die. I don't know. They shouted at each other in front of me at intervals and I said to the Arab at last, "What's the use of a concubine who's as unwilling as that, the little shrew?" But he wouldn't give her up.

By sunset I was dead tired. Muhammad Fadlallah was so tired that he said, "I think it would be better if the government took these slaves who won't remain contentedly in the tribe and dumped them somewhere else." Yes—but, if government does that, where is it to settle them, and, when they're settled, who is to be responsible that they don't all take to thieving or over-stocking the place with harlots? I suppose Lady Simon[23] and company and such sentimentalists would say we're very wrong to try and solve the slavery problem gradually, and try to settle the serfs within their masters' tribes. The serfs have known no other life than tribal life, no other discipline than tribal discipline, and are quite unfitted for anything but herding, rough cultivation and manual labour.

---

[22] *Sid*: Sudanese colloquial for *sayyid*: master.
[23] President of the Anti-slavery Society.

By "serf" is meant a slave born in the tribe or bought so long ago that he can remember no other life. This term covers practically all slaves in this district. Slaves not serfs are freed and repatriated at once and the kidnapper is put in prison for a very long spell. In which connexion, the last kidnapper in this district was captured by Sheikh Ali El Tom's son Salim two months ago.

Sheikh El Tum Ali said his camels were coming down to water tomorrow, and would I then ride round with him and drink a little milk?

5.4.31

Business opened as briskly as yesterday. About 10 a.m. Sheikh El Tom came and took me along to visit his camels along the western shore of the lake. It took about 1 ½ hours and entailed drinking any amount of milk. The whole of the western side of the lake, bar where the hills come right down to the water, was crowded with camels—a mile long and to a depth of about 150 yards back from the waterside. I met Salim Ali El Tom and others. I have never seen more camels in one place. I tried distinguishing colours, without much success. The difference between "dabsi" and "khurshi"[24] is very difficult.

After my return to the Locust Post, more complainants came. Later, Sheikhs Muhammad Fadlallah and El Tom Ali came and said they had come to an agreement about the watering: the cattle might stay, but individual men objected to by the Kawahla were to be removed.

After lunch I went on working until 5 p.m. At dusk, Muhammad Fadlallah brought his sheikhs for me to exhort them to list the animals for herd tax properly. Then El Tom Ali arrived and I impressed upon him that camels suffering from tryps. [trypanosomiasis] must be removed as part of the agreement. Business ended about 6.30 and I went to bed at 8 p.m. No wind for once.

N.B. Post and prisoners left for Soderi yesterday evening.

6.4.31

After breakfast, Muhammad Fadlallah came and said that his camels were down to water and would I come and look at them. We went out to find the east and south of the lake even more crowded than the west had been yesterday. Camels and dust and the peculiar sharp smell of camels everywhere, the nagas lowing and others crowding the mud troughs, most of which had had salt put in them. (Salt is good for camels and always given them.) We drank much milk. At one point we found two most

---

[24] That is, between deep "pinkish fawn" and "dirty white" with dark tail and hump. See Acland, "Notes", 148.

amusing old cronies one of whom was clearly a great character—deaf, a bucolic wit, and a man who loves his camels, they say, more than anything on earth—name of Abdallah Abu Chieyba. The other was also a cheery bird. Muhammad Fadlalla explained that that was in spite of life rather than because of it. The man at one time had had a frightful fight with certain thieves and his wounds had rendered him, as Muhammad F. naively put it, "so that the ladies had no more use for him". He did not seem to mind: no doubt the memory of a well-spent youth sustained him. A merry pair of grigs. But I have not their taste for asses' milk, which they pressed upon us. A little further along the water's edge we came to a place where the curve of the lake allowed one to see half the east side and the south end as well. It made an amazing picture—a serried rank of camels for about a mile, and behind them the red granite hills rising into a brassy blue sky. Unfortunately I had used up the spool in my camera and had not another with me. The rest of the morning was taken up with miscellaneous business and the day became very hot.

The hamla moved off at 2.30 and I lay on my farwa trying alternatively to read *Tom Fool* (sent to me by Hamilton—I'd read it before, but it is well worth a second reading) and to sleep. The chaps would not let me alone—always these last minute complaints and requests. Muhammad Fadlallah even woke me up, and that over a trivial affair which he had much better have dealt with off his own bat, as he has power to and I, strictly speaking, have not.

At last we got off. A large cavalcade rode over the dune eastwards to put me on my way. Sheikh El Tom Ali also came on his camel. The Kawahla did their usual turn of furious gallops ending in a dead pull-up. I took leave of Sheikh El Tom, and Muhammad Fadlallah rode on with me. We found the hamla at sunset encamped in a very lovely spot, between two hills called Gurun Abu Ajaama [Qurun al-'Ujaymi], behind which the sun was setting. It was a perfect evening and starlit night. Muhammad Fadlallah rode on to this home at Khor Es Sunt to make ready for my arrival.

Just after dark there was a rumpus in my camp and a wild galloping of a horse to and fro over the sand and the rocks. I thought at first that a horse was loose. It proved, however that the Arabs had found a stray camel and were trying to catch it. The rodeo continued for a quarter of an hour, at the end of which the horse fell and the camel escaped into the bush again.

I had a great sense of peace and beauty in this place, after the alternately dusty and hot and always crowded atmosphere of Um Badr. At Um Badr one was too much on top of the arguing Arabs all the time, which marred the beauties of the scene. I shall try and avoid those grass huts next time and pitch tent further back from the water.

7.4.31

A still night and a grand, cool, still dawn. We were riding before the sun rose, down a slope over firm soil and among bush. To the north was Jebel Sheikheib and to the south Sheikhab,[25] and away to the east in front the line of Abu Fas El Mufattih. By 6.30 we were near the Kawahla camp and were met by about 30 horsemen in the usual style, with the drums beating in the camp behind. Everyone was in great form, especially a certain sort of court jester who more or less acted as master of the ceremonies, Muhammad Jangay: and another old lad who is expert at the long luluing joy-cry usually made by the women, Ahmad Kabjerak.

Today has been rather amusing, although very hot at midday. I was offered a wife from the Beni Gerar tribe in jest by a sheikh, and, for the first time in my life, attended a race meeting organised in my own honour, and kindly consented to give away the prizes, presented by myself. Muhammad Fadlallah had put up a vast Arab tent for me in the same place as last year and furnished with all the leather camel trappings—beautiful work. Few people came to worry me and many to chat. Then, at 4 p.m. we went to the race meeting, which was grand. The course was, for the big race, about one mile over sand dunes. The character of the course was rather like the spring course at Newmarket, i.e. up and down and ending up-hill.

The rules of the Kawahla Jockey Club are similar to those of King's College Cambridge—there are none. There were three races, one for very good, one for medium, and one for bad horses. (Classification by local knowledge of horse form personified by a wild Arab on a white horse.) Prizes for 1st (6/-) and 2nd (3/-). I gave the prizes for the first race and the first prize for the second and Muhammad Fadlallah gave the rest. The grandstand consisted of my folding chair under a sunt tree, up which small boys climbed for a free seat. The race meeting was well attended by an enthusiastic crowd—top hats and binoculars were conspicuous by their absence. No ladies attended. At one point a camel got on to the course. The jockeys merely went round him. The crowd shouted like mad at the finishes. It was all rather a familiar party. At the end Muhammad Fadlallah and I gave the prizes and then we went away, while slaves went on beating the drums for fun for quite a while. Several sheikhs gathered round outside my tent and I had tea brought and served in glasses. One of my sheikhs was Ali El Nur, the Omda of the Dueih. He asked me was it true that I was called "The Sheikh" and I said, "Yes—by the English". Everyone was much amused. When the others left, Ali El Nur stayed behind and

---

[25] Lea mistook one for the other: Jabal Shikhab lay to the north, Jabal Shikayb to the south. Sudan Government map, "Umm Badr", Survey Office, Khartoum 1940.

talked for some while. His very small tribe have lived with the Kawahla here for a number of years. Muhammad Fadlallah has complained to me that this year for the first time Ali El Nur has refused to pay ushur on crops to him and has also refused to pay sheep for the privilege of watering at a Kawahla well here. I tried to draw him out about this. He merely denied having ever paid. I went to bed very early.

8.4.31

The night was quite cool. I woke about 4.30 but slept again till dawn. The day rapidly became very hot. There was very little business. Ahmad Gismallah, exact first cousin of Muhammad Fadlallah, came to call on me. All business was over by 11 a.m. I tried reading Arabic, but the inside of the tent was so hot and there were so many flies that I gave it up and lay about in pyjamas reading old newspapers, flapping at flies and dozing till 4 p.m., when I had tea and a wash. About 4.30 Muhammad Fadlallah turned up with horses to take me to see the wells. He put me to ride on his horse, the race winner. It proved a nervous animal needing exercise. It would be a grand horse, had it been English-bitted and trained when young. After we had seen the wells, we rode around a bit. Muhammad Fadlallah drank tea with me and went on again about the shortcomings of Sheikh Ali El Nur. He retired soon after sunset. I wrote until 10 p.m. and then went to bed. It was quite a cool night again.

9.4.31

The early morning was cool, but by 8.30 a.m. it was roasting. The real hot weather has come. I abandoned the tent for a tree in the wadi outside to get some breeze. The morning fairly stoked up. There was no work to do. Muhammad Fadlallah came and chatted for a while and produced a very awkward complaint by a slave herdsman of the Kawahla who had hired himself to the Kababish and now says they refused to pay his wages (2 young camels) and, when he complained to Ali El Tom, A.T. awarded him one young camel only.

Talked to Muhammad Fadlallah about Nigeria and Liberia. I then tried reading Arabic and got sleepier and sleepier and watched a fly-catcher (grey with black line on eyes to bill) eat a grasshopper. Meanwhile the breeze began from the south and suddenly, while I was using the dictionary, became a hot wind and took all the papers of one file off the table and sent them at a brisk pace over burnt grass in the direction of cooler weather and the North Pole. Police arrived at the double and rescued them. If there is a hot wind there are no flies. If the wind drops, the flies bother one. All the time ticks crawl up the legs, which is one good reason for wearing shorts—you can tell when the blighters have got half-way up and blow the whistle for half-time. The wind blew even more strongly and, when Koko arrived with lunch, I retired to the tent and had one side of it opened. This was as well, because a large dust-devil came by soon after and went straight through the grove of trees in which I had been sitting.

The afternoon was too hot for one to do anything but lie on a bed in pyjamas, or half a pyjama, and read desultorily Clarence Marjoribank's *Life of Marshall Hall*[26] (very good). About 4 p.m., when I felt I could breathe again, Koko brought tea, and the Sheikh Gismallah Ahmad came to talk.

We talked of horses—the Kawahla method of breaking a horse (breaking is the word) and the English method, of Kawahla marriage customs, and how a Kahli wife is too modest to complain of her husband. Then we talked of wells and I explained how a block and tackle can be worked to lessen the trouble of drawing water in deep wells.

Just before sunset, Gismallah came back with Haamid Hamaad [sic], the fellow whom I had met at Um Badr (and who had said that he had been wounded in the back presumably through the prostate), and a slave girl carrying a very small non-negroid-looking child at the breast. The slave girl started shouting at me, so I calmed her down and made faces at the baby while I got the story out of the men. Gismallah explained that Haamid had divorced a wife on account of this concubine who has now four children (one boy already a herdsman), and she now says none of the children are his—but all children of slaves (in particular of one slave) and she wants to take them from Haamid. Haamid claims them all—what about his wound story then?—the child brought to me was no more than 2: and the fight took place four years ago. I laughed like anything to myself, sent them away and explained to Gismallah what had been told me at Um Badr. He was immensely tickled. As I am neither King Solomon, nor Daniel, nor a jury of matrons, nor a midwife, I shall do my best to avoid giving any decision. Haamid must be a fool about women for the girl is a shrew if ever there was one. And he must be foolish, for, if her children have an Arab father they are free and inherit with his other children; if their father is a slave, they are slave and have no rights in Arab custom.

When they had all gone and I had chatted with Sheikh Muhammad Fadlallah and he had gone too, I was at last able to read a mail which had arrived at tea-time. A tremendous number of flying insects arrived round the candles as if rain had already fallen. The night cooled down a bit.

---

[26] See above, Chapter II, note 9.

10.4.31

The main thing about this day was the heat. I abandoned the idea of going under a tree. The Arabs were feeling the heat too and only desultory business was done in the morning. I spent the noontime on my bed in pyjama trousers and a singlet reading Clarence Marjoribank's *Life of Marshall Hall* when I felt strong enough, and then writing when I could not face lying down any longer.

At about 5 p.m. the Arabs turned up with the witnesses in a case which Sh. Muhammad Fadlallah had asked me to try against a slave for pinching and slaughtering his master's she-camel. I found however that Muhammad's father had given a customary judgement in the case nearly two years ago. The slave's masters had agreed to pay his fine and then refused because the slave had later left them to live on his own. I therefore did not hear the case but asked the Nazir to enforce his father's judgement in what way seemed best to him.

Muhammad Fadlallah and certain elders then read me a long lecture on the thievish propensities of the Kaja of Seruj.

11.4.31

This day started cooler. I had arranged to leave Khor es Sunt in the afternoon. In the night there had been the noise of a rifle shot and much shouting and beating of drums. None of this disturbed my peace of mind; but in the morning Tingle appeared to report that the commotion was caused by the birth of a son to a daughter of the ruling house of El Eaysir. The rifle shot was the customary *feu de joie*. I made the appropriate congratulations.

There was very little to do this morning. But although it was much cooler—the wind had gone back to the north again—I felt very tired and had a nauseous head, whether from the heat or from too much coffee I don't know.

We started about 4.30 with an enormous cavalcade and rode eastwards till we came to the hills called Zolot Um Khusus, which are rather pretty. There we camped for the night.

This morning I had had the Omda of the Dueih to see me and asked him, "Was it not true that there had been a great friendship between himself and Fadlallah El Eaysir (the late Nazir of the Kawahla), and that it was by his kindness the Dueih had been settled at Khor Es Sunt?" He said, "Yes". I went on to say that I hoped friendly relations would not change, but that I had heard that the Dueih had slightly departed from the custom of the Arabs about little acknowledgements of privileges in the way of lands to cultivate and wells to water at: it was not of course my business to interfere or say what he should do—I'd merely heard that. He, of course, said, "Did Muhammad Fadlallah tell you that?" I said the news had come to me. It appeared clearly from his talk that what was rankling in his mind was the fact that his herd-tax lists had been sent by mistake to Muhammad Fadlallah with those of the Kawahla, and the little man took this as an affront to his independence. I hope that my talk did no harm.

12.4.31

A cool night and a cool morning. Wind still in the north. Started by 5 a.m. and rode to Sanaagir, arriving about 7 a.m. A pleasant ride. On arrival Muhammad Fadlallah took me to see the well that is being built up (after digging down to the spring of water). We descended about 50 ft. by a rope ladder. He has an ancient builder and two frightful townee assistant builders who wear Bombay bowlers.

The hamla had put me on top of the sand hill east of the wells and the lake (now dry), where there is a grass rest house. This is a magnificent situation, whence one looks west at the Sanaagir hills and then all round the country for miles and miles. Muhammad Fadlallah took me to see the remains of R. Davies's[27] post (the fort is now no more than a vallum and foss on the top of the hill), where he and 25 police and 200 armed Arabs had watched for any of Ali Dinar's troops or raiders in June-July 1916, the summer of the expedition which took Darfur. Davies dug one well here; but west of this there was no known water except for rain pools in those days. They all went off from here to Jebel Meidob, while the expedition went farther south to El Fasher. Davies must have had an interesting time then. His nearest supports were in Bara, over 200 miles away. The old fort wall is full of broken potsherds—old blow-pipes used by Bronze Age men in working copper, the ore of which they dug out of a hill just to the north.

There was a pleasant breeze all morning. I dropped asleep over an Arabic book and tried again after lunch; but became rather restless. *N.B.* Muhammad the cook stung on the face by a scorpion last night.

The camels watered here this morning so we do not move until tomorrow morning. Tingle's camel has become exhausted. It is Watt's old riding camel and never had time to recover from his trip to Dongola.

Consultation with Muhammad Fadlallah about a theft of camels traced to Gaili, south of here. The Kawahla say they've found the remains of their she-camel buried there. I am to leave a bobby to go and investigate . . . .

Before I left Sanaagir, it was arranged that Sheikh Abd El Gadir Awad Es Sid should go and look in the White Nile Province for one of his chaps who owes 10 years' arrears of taxes and has disappeared for nearly all that

---

[27] Reginald Davies, SPS 1911–35, had been stationed in Kordofan, 1912–20, and Darfur, 1920–24. See *The camel's back*.

time. Muhammad Fadlallah says Jad Es Sid Muhammad of the Gima has gone to the river contrary to orders with all his shaykhship.

Query: Should a well be built with walls sloping inwards towards the top for strength (as the expert here says) or not, if the materials are stone and cement mortar only? If the diameter at the top is smaller than at the bottom, does the pressure of the earth filling tend to strengthen the masonry (cp. and arch) or to make the well fall in sooner? The cement mortar is being made 1:9: cement : sand. Query proper proportions (Muhammad F. says 1:7).

13.4.31

Left at 5.30 am, taking leave of Muhammad Fadlallah. A cold morning. Rode east over those tiring sand-hills in the direction of Abu Ajaja. Up and down all the way. I was riding "The Feki" and he began to tire towards the end. Passed a large tawny (?) owl sitting with a raven in a tree (owl had a very fine pair of ears—ochre colour—rest of him french grey). We found the hamla camped in a hollow between the two sand hills.

I felt idle and did nothing but sit under a tree, read the *Life of Marshall Hall*, and remove ticks and camel flies from various parts of myself at intervals. Went on at 3.30, continuing over sandhills. By 5 we were emerging from sandhills down towards Abu Ajaja wells. In the evening light there was a particularly fine view of hills to the east of us on the plain — Bakalai (which looks like a mediaeval castle and was a natural fortress in the past), and behind it Kaja Soderi to the north and hills in ranges to Kaja Hofra in the southeast. We passed the place where I *qail*ed[28] last year in the rain.

Abu Ajaja (the dusty place) is so called because of the friable soil there. Any wind raises an appalling dust storm. John Simons and John Hillard[29] were once sitting there, a dust storm came on suddenly, John Simon's hat blew off, he jumped up and ran 20 yards to find it, and by so doing lost John Hillard and himself. We crossed the valley and came upon the hamla camped on the slopes to the north on the way to Bakalai. There is a salt scrub here called "khreit" which the camels love.

Tingle told me the Omda Tichu (good name) of [the] Hofra Nubas was close by and he had told him to come and see me. (Tingle had been over to the Nubas' camp for milk.) After my supper Tichu and friends appeared. They had just been having a funeral. Tichu apologised for not having come to pay respects in Soderi—he'd lost his camel. I gave him an opening about gum tapping, and he had a few sly digs at Nadeef (another

---

[28] Arabic: *Qail*, noon; so, to pass the noon-time.
[29] SPS 1925–53; stationed in Kordofan, 1925–29. *SPS*, 46.

Nuba Omda), whose chaps, he said, had refused to tap any gum this year near Jebel Gaili because Nadeef had asked too high a rate of rent. As soon as they had gone I turned in.

14.4.31
It was a cold night, and the hamla moving off at 2.30 woke me and I slept only lightly thereafter. It was really very cold from just before dawn until 7.30. Rode from 5.30 till 8.15, when we reached the Nuba village among hills. Pretty place—stayed the night here last year. So this evening we'll be in Soderi and there is my first trip over, and, if I am lucky, 40 more days only until I leave Halfa.

I have come to the conclusion I read too many books. Also they are heavy to carry. Next trip I shall take two heavy English books and Arabic books only. The thing to do is to try and draw whenever there are no chaps wanting to talk, and reading becomes boring and sitting makes one restless.

The hamla left at 2.30 and we at 3.30. At one point as we rode, Corporal Tingle became eloquent and exceedingly interesting about the customs of the local Nubas here. Nubas eat rats and coneys, although they say they are Muslims. Arab fathers feel very strongly about their wives having children by other men. Nuba husbands, apparently, don't care a hoot, will go off on a journey for a year and then bring up a child conceived in their absence, making no difference between the child of joy and their own children. The Nubas here, Tingle says, have wizards all right. They have a snake [that] lives up on the top of a hill near Soderi to which, if there is a drought, they sacrifice and the old women go and anoint its head. If they have a bumper year, they likewise sacrifice to it; and you can see the fire blazing on the mountain top from afar off. Many other queer things they do, such as slaughtering a bull on a man's grave and burying the bones after a feast on the flesh. Later they return to the grave and hold the deuce of a blind on beer. And yet, says Tingle, they say they are Muslims.

We reached the merkaz about 5.15 and were met by Akib (returned early) and the Effendia. I found a mail waiting for me.

Chapter IV

The *Nazir* of the Hawawir

[Soderi—Umm Sunayta—'Idd al-Marikh—Hamrat al-Wazz—Al-Safiya—Abu 'Uruq—B'ir Rabda—Habisa—'Idd al-Khala—Umm Indaraba—Omdurman]

26.4.31

From 14.4.31 till 25.4.31 I spent at Soderi. The 15th and 16th April were more or less uneventful. I prepared papers to consult Gillan (Governor Kordofan) and Hamilton (District Commissioner Northern Kordofan). The 17th I spent, so far as the afternoon was concerned, in writing a letter in Arabic to Ferid and in waiting for Hamilton and Gillan to arrive. They failed to do so until the middle of the following morning, when I was suddenly told cars were approaching. One of the amusing features of Soderi is the look-out man, when any important visitor is expected. A prisoner is sent onto the thatched roof of the merkaz where he sits perched like a stork.

Gillan was a sick man—has been having malarial complications. But he was very pleasant and most easy. Micky, Hamilton's dog, was also sick—a much sicker man than Gillan. Next day, moreover, Hamilton had a chill on the stomach. However, it was very pleasant to have them and they gave me much advice and help. I think that Gillan's visit did him good—he certainly looked much better when he went away.

Gillan was quite amazing on the subject of getting married. He said he doubted if Khartoum were prepared to go as far as he was.

Gillan and H. left on the morning of Monday 20th, and the succeeding days were one long struggle to get through a murder case, two other big cases, a lesser one, and a large amount of correspondence. The weather also was very hot. The summer is with us and the deuce of a wind blows every day at Soderi, covering everything with sand. By yesterday I was thoroughly tired and had to go on drafting letters up till the time of riding out almost.

I left Soderi on 25th April at about 4.30 p.m. with the local doctor and Sheikh Muhammad Musa, who is Sheikh Ali El Tom's representative attached to me for my trip. Took a fond farewell of the Mamur, translator, Abdel Gadir the police officer, and assorted sheikhs and merchants. We rode northwest and by 7.15 reached the Nuba village of Sheikh Muhammad Ali.

This old gentleman talked of MacMic and talked of his own part in the conquest of Darfur under Osman Adam[1] during the Mahdia.

I sent more papers (brought away by mistake) back to the merkaz and slept quite extraordinarily badly. It was hot and the Nubas had many barking dogs.

We started just before dawn and by 7.30 were down in a pleasant wadi (I under a large sayal tree)[2] for the heat of the day. I slept on my bed in pyjamas for some time, thanking God that there [was] nobody who need be talked to and then read some of [*The*] *Star-Spangled Manner*, which is most amusing but very obviously the work of a "clever young man". I'm sure I should hate America.

We started again about 4.30 and rode for two hours over gozes until we came at 6.30 upon the hamla out-spanned in a very pleasant sandy wadi —one of those which flow down from Jebel Shaw [Shau]. When we had rested awhile the hakim and Sheikh Muhammad Musa came down and drank tea with me and we had a chat which ranged over many subjects, largely the history of the Sudan. It was a cool night—slept well.

27.4.31

I came to the conclusion yesterday on working things out that I must abandon all hope of catching the train from Khartoum on 24th May, as I shall only skimp work and probably ruin my camels if I try to catch it, and even then I should quite likely miss it. I have therefore 5 days extra to spend en route, to avoid being too long in Khartoum at the end. The five days will be needed to rest at various points, especially if it is going to be as hot as this.

Started 5.30 and by 7.30 reached the wells of Darwil, the way lying over rocky rises which finally fell away into a basin among the ridges in which are the wells surrounded by a wood of very fine trees. There are a few Ruahla Kababish here with their sheep. The water is not very plentiful. An old man named Ali came and drank tea with me and said that they had had a good deal of sickness among the sheep this winter, a running at the nose combined with splitting of the hoof (foot and mouth?). I walked down to the wells where blokes were watering our camels. One or two good looking women about. Sheikh Muhammad appears to have clicked with one of them.

The doctor has found one patient only, so we will go on this afternoon.

---

[1] 'Uthman Adam Janu (d. 1889), Madhist governor of Kordofan. He suppressed revolt in Darfur in 1887–88 and took charge of the whole West. *BD*. 367; Holt, *The Mahdist State*, 156–65.
[2] *Acacia tortilis. IT*, 60–63.

Had a chat with him about the Gordon College and how it ruins lads, and so, he says, does the Army ruin those who become Native Officers.

A pleasant tree to sit under: but the beauties of the wood are marred by occasional whiffs of the effluvium of a dead camel or sheep which must be somewhere near.

Did the Creator make these waterless places as a last refuge for the quiet-minded from the inanities of progress?

There is little doubt that this trip is likely to be pretty trying owing to the heat. Yesterday was hot, today as hot as could be—a real inferno. I should think that the shade temperature must have been up to 110 degrees and over. It was so hot at mid-day that sitting or lying still was extremely uncomfortable. One's legs began to twitch—nerves of course. Even reading was too much of an effort. I lay a long while watching a brilliantly coloured bird with a long bill, which I think must have been a species of bee-eater—green above and russet below—at work, and wondering how the devil it raised the energy to catch bugs in this heat. I also tried, without success, to draw a sayaal tree.

About 4.30 it was slightly cooler—a difference great enough to make one no longer feel as if one's head would burst, and we started to ride. We went on and on and on over treeless country covered with tufts of grass with yellow sand below. There was hardly a tree to be seen nor a jebel for hours. Then we saw a wadi with bushes in the distance, and, as it got dark, the light of a big fire which the chaps with the hamla had lit to guide us into camp.

On the road I had a long talk with the doctor about various sects of Islam, with particular reference to Ibn Saoud, El Afghani, Soufism, and Muhammad Abdu (the modernist).[3] I rode the government Howari camel to try him out and found him quite smooth and a very good ride. When we got into camp, I found that the heat had so exhausted me that I lapped my cold tea too fast and had to lie down on my bed to avoid being sick.

The night was cool and pleasant.

28.4.31

The sergeant started the hamla early enough, but failed to get me up till after 5 a.m. I had no idea of the distance we had to go—but he had and should have managed better. He apologised later, but that won't make the riding camels less tired. We rode over the same sandy soil from 5.45 to 9.15. A cooler day.

---

[3] 'Abd al-'Aziz al-Sa'ud (1880–1953), king of the Hijaz and Najd; Jamal al-Din al-Afghani (1839–97), pan-Islamist and reformer; Muhammad 'Abduh (1850–1905), student of al-Afghani, reformer, and *Mufti* of Egypt.

Chapter IV

We reached the forest surrounding Um Soneita about 7.45, but had to go on through it for over an hour till we got to camp by the wells. A strong wind blew in our faces from 7.30 onwards, very tiring for camels. Dust haze everywhere.

The doctor very kindly lent me his bell tent to have a bath in the morning. Inside the bell tent it was hot as the hotter rooms of a Turkish bath. However, I felt much better for the wash.

They say the water of the wells here is exceptionally good.

Wind blew all the morning. I was very tired and slept a bit. Sheikh Muhammad Musa came and I tried to talk Meidob business. He was not very helpful. The Sheikh of the Shileywab Kababish here is one Muhammad Ahmad. It appears that the Shileywab, or rather some of them, are nearly always here. But Muhammad Musa says no one would take on the job of Kababish wakil here except he was compelled to do so. *N.B.* Passed a shrub of dark leaves and long spines one foot high, bearing blue flowers, named "kurraaj" in Arabic. The plant that looks rather like sea lavender on the sand hills is said to be "dobbeij" in Arabic.

Muhammad the cook produced a dreadful pink cornflower concoction as a sweet for lunch. [I] made them open a tin of peaches which took the taste away and were very good after nothing but dried fruit etc. for some time. Today is distinctly cooler but still pretty trying. We shall sleep here tonight and also rest here till tomorrow afternoon.

Sheikh Muhammad Musa was rather amusing about the Seligmans' visit to the Kababish some years ago. Seligman and his wife (Brenda even to the Arabs, apparently) are well-known anthropologists.[4] According to Reg Davies, who reviewed[5] what they wrote of the Kababish, Muhammad Musa and Muhammad El Tom had stuffed them up with a lot of nonsense as a joke. I taxed Muhammad Musa with this and he said, "Well I was only a boy at the time of the Mahdi's rising, how should I remember accurately, and the customs of the Arabs are many and varied—how should we know them all?" Hmm! Apparently they liked the Seligmans, when they had got over Seligman's habit of sitting down and asking things like, "What are your customs on the bridal night?" and such-like intimate questions and then pronto writing down the answers in a note book like a policeman at an accident.

Today is the big feast day—Kurban Bairam.[6] I asked what the Arabs

---

[4] C. G. and B. Z. Seligman visited Kordofan in 1911–12. See, e.g., their *The Kababish, a Sudan Arab tribe*, Cambridge, Mass., 1918.
[5] *SNR* III, 4, 1920, 281–86.
[6] The Turkish term for the *'Id al-adha*.

did to celebrate it. It appears that they have a three days' do on meat, kisra and merissa[7] with slaves dancing and a certain amount of horse show.

In the afternoon I tried to read. A young lad driving sheep came by and paused in great astonishment. I talked to him and found he had never seen an Englishman before in his life. He wanted to know what my table was and what my bed, and what was my fountain pen. He had a good look at everything, and then said, "Where is your motor car?" "Haven't got one". "Where's your gun?" "Haven't got one—left it in my house." "Ah! ha! cigarettes?" So I pointed him to an old Gold Flake tin in which I carry Matossian for such few sheikhs as smoke. But I had no matches, so I had to send him to the police for a match.

Later a woman riding a donkey came by and stopped as she greeted me and turned a bold and boyish face towards me, instead of veiling her face as is usual. By which hangs a tale.

By 4.30 it was fairly cool again. I had tea and went up the sandhill to the west to hit a golf ball. My language became abominable and my hands blistered but the view from the top was good. After dark I went and visited the doctor's camp and talked. Sheikh Muhammad Musa had rammed a tree somehow and split his head rather badly, so that it had to be stitched. We had an extraordinary conversation which began about date palms in Dongola and went on to the woman who had greeted me. Apparently she is a freak and refuses to have anything to do with men, but spends her time with the herds and even going to market in Omdurman. I expressed surprise that the complete "bachelor girl" should exist among the Arabs.

Talking of masculine women, the doctor spoke of Miss Wolff,[8] the Government midwife, who is a very remarkably efficient lady. The Arabs (said the doctor) refused, from her figure, to believe that she was a woman for a long time; especially were they doubtful of her bona fides on account of her slight beard and moustache. They now, he says, acknowledge the benefits of her work and a woman who has had a government trained midwife won't go to an old-fashioned one again.

N.B. Kababish economics. Muhammad Musa said, talking of MacMichael, that MacM. had proved a true prophet because he continually said, when he was D.C. here, that the railway and motor cars would cheapen camels and that Arabs would be wise to buy and breed more cows and sheep. Muhammad Musa says that the Arab who formerly used to sell one fat naga for about £E18 and pay therefore his taxes and dues and buy his year's supply of clothes (one suit only for himself and

---

[7] *Marisa*: beer, usually brewed from sorghum.
[8] Probably Mabel Wolff who, with her sister Gertrude, was instrumental in founding and expanding midwifery training in the 1920s and 1930s. See Daly, *Empire*, 448–49.

one for his wife), corn, sugar and tea, now has to sell three or four (unless she is very fat, a naga may fetch only £E5). Sheep will now fetch £E1 apiece at Omdurman. As to the Meidob sheep, he says they reach Omdurman in good condition, taking 17 days from Um Soneita to the river, as follows:

Um Soneita to Id El Merkh	5 days
Id El Merkh to Safia	3 ″
Safia to Ribda or Id El Kheil	5 ″
Thence to the river	4 ″

The marching is done largely by night, one party of the drovers going ahead by day and lighting a big guiding fire after dark.

29.4.31

Slept well but awoke tired. A hot morning. Walked round the wells with Muhd. Musa. Good cows—no sheep down yet and practically no camels. They enclose the heidan here with a zeriba, which usually also contains a grass hut for the slaves, and the animals drink inside the zeriba.

He showed me where they used to divide up the meshra—wells for the Awlad Tereif, Awaida, Serijab, Shileywab, Awlad Suleiman, Rawahla and a few Ribeygat. For the last three years, he said, the wells had been much less populated. This year Um Badr had taken off most of the camels. The previous year, the Awaida had been in Jebel Meidob . . . .

The simoom[9] blew very hot. I tried writing a letter for a while to relieve the depression. I also tried drawing a tundub[10] tree without success. Meanwhile the lads and slave girls of the Arabs were celebrating the Feast with clapping of hands and song and dance. How they do it in this heat Allah knows, to whose glory it is done. I had forgotten my young friend of yesterday returned while I was at breakfast and sat down.

He: "Where is that doctor?" I: "In that tent over there." He: "Will he give me an injection?" I: "You ill?" He: "Will he give me an injection for that cold in the bones?" (Present temperature of the air 108 degrees.) I: "What, cold in the bones after malaria?" He: "Yes, and has he got any purges?" I: "My God, you must be ill." He (broad grin): "By God, I am. I went to see him, but there were so many there I didn't wait." I: "You'd better go and wait." He: "Might do." I then sent for a tea cup: but meanwhile he got up and buzzed off—*not* to the hakim. The masculine lady also came past again.

After lunch Muhammad Musa brought me a certain Fadl Es Sid Ali

---

[9] (Elsewhere simoon.) Arabic *samum*: hot wind, sandstorm.
[10] *Capparis decidua*, a leafless shrub. Tothill, 954.

Hashim of the Shileywab who wanted a note to Muhammad Fadlallah about a slave who, he said, had fled and sold two camels without leave and is now with the Kawahla (name Zubeir). I wrote him a note telling Muhammad F. either to make voluntary agreement between them or to send the slave to Soderi. Fadl Es Sid also wanted an order to prevent cattle from infected well centres coming to water at Um Soneita. I improved the shining hour by pointing out that if there was no Kabbashi at Um Soneita capable and willing to become Sheikh Ali El Tom's agent to check the Kababish (in their misdeeds against the Meidob), there was no one it was worth my while to leave an order with for it to be carried out. However, after I had twisted their tails for a bit I wrote an order for Muhammad Musa to sign. (Fadl Es Sid is blue eyed—very rare in Arabs.)

Started about 4.30. Country now becomes very like the Butana—kittr[11] bushes and short grass and rocky stretches. Talked about Dongola and said I would like to go there later. The doctor says there's no work to do there, to which I said that that was no objection. We also talked about poetic metaphors and similes. (The moon was visible and I asked why the Arab poets likened a young man's face, if beautiful, to the full moon; and a girl's eyes to those of a gazelle. Muhd Effendi admitted the former to be a bad simile not to be used in good poetry; but said that the latter was permissible because there is a true likeness.) We passed on to Hamza Eff. El Melik (known to the Political Service as the gigolo) and his poetry and literary turns.

We got down in a wadi which I think must be a branch of Wadi Abu Laot [La'ut]. The doctor and Muhammad Musa took tea with me. I had produced John Hillard's collection of songs and the doctor read one or two. I did not realise that the originator of the Dobai form of song (to be sung when riding a camel) was Hardello, father of my friend Sheikh Ahmad El Hardello.[12] The poems started Muhammad Musa off with the question, "Do folk have love affairs in your country?" Any embarrassment which this question might have caused was nipped in the bud, for I had only time to say, "Oh, Yes", before he launched out about people dying of love. Both he and the doctor agreed that many Arabs had done so, but fewer nowadays than formerly. Nothing would now stop Muhammad Musa who proceeded to hold forth about his five-year-long passion for a lady who lived in the Um Soneita neighbourhood. "And then there was that little girl at Gabra—and another time that one at Bara" (the latter lady appeared from the story to have been mercenary and rather a cheat).

---

[11] *Acacia melliflora*, a thorny shrub or small tree. BM, 172. See glossary for variant spellings.
[12] Muhammad Ahmad Abu Sinn (1830–1917), Shukriyya notable and poet. *BD*, 248–9. See Sa'd Mikhail, *Shu'ara' al-Sudan*, Cairo 1923.

At all events Muhd. Musa made it quite clear that he had been no end of a lad in his day. One of the better remarks was, "Of course Arab tents help these affairs—when they hear the husband coming, the lover can slip out the back and then come round to the front and say 'good evening' to hubby all cool and collected." The doctor, who is, as he should be, rather a "pie" little man, took a somewhat "not amused" attitude during much of the telling of Lothario's tale and, as soon as possible, brought the talk round to religion in the approved Victorian style. Slept very soundly.

30.4.31

Hamla started at 2 a.m. Rose at 3.45. Cool night. Rode from 4.15 till 6.45. Much better ride because earlier and cool breeze. The way this morning led over country not unlike the Butana but with yellow sand underneath; otherwise kitir[13] and gufala[14] bush with mukheita. Grasses tufted for the most part: a considerable amount of ajaraab where there are outcrops of rock. A line of hills appeared in the east as soon as we had scrambled in the half-dark out of a wadi, onto a ridge and it was light enough to see. By a quarter to seven we had come up to the hamla on the slope of a hill. They had set my table and chair under a sureeh[15] bush. The usual wind had sprung up in time to make the conveyance of porridge to one's mouth a risky business. Shaving, of course, is a race between oneself and the wind—can one get the razor over half the dial before the wind has dried the soap?

I had Muhammad Musa along and talked Meidob without success, and then animal breeding. It appears that Sheikh Ali's statement that the best stallion ousts the rest is qualified by the fact that Arabs do geld camels here. (The Shukria did not, as far as I know.) Bulls and rams, according to Muhammad Musa, are selected as with us. Slept on the ground a bit. Tried writing but it was very difficult and I was too sleepy to read much.

Rode again about 4.30 till 6.30. The country did not change much except that the sand became red. We found the hamla in a wadi with large trees. I had intended to sit up reading to make up for my idleness of the day but my idleness was too much for me and I went to sleep by 9 p.m.

A party of three Arabs came by about 8 p.m. going west and spoke to Muhd. Musa.

1.5.31

Rose with the morning star and rode at 4.15 a.m. Saw two small gazelle just after dawn and remarked to Muhammad Eff. that, since leaving Um

---

[13] See above, n. 11.
[14] Possibly *Commiphora africana*. BM, 229.
[15] Possibly *Maerua crassifolia*. *IT*, 12.

Soneita, we had seen of living things (apart from two thin stray she-camels just by the wells) one wild cat, the party of three Arabs, one camel and one donkey, and the two gazelles. Even birds have been rare.

We found the track of the hamla, after scouting, at about 6 a.m. just before entering a stretch of "kerib", a nightmarish piece of country [the Karabat al-Sarir]. This "kerib" consists of low hills of black rock split into squarish lumps like coal. The hills rise all over the place like bizarre-shaped peaks, some like Aztec pyramids, some like table tops, some like sugar loaves. Here and there the path crossed dry torrent beds and where the path climbed the rocks they were worn smooth by the passage of animals.

This country is very like that seen from the train as one goes through the Red Sea hills on the way to Port Sudan, and is very adequately described as "wilderness and solitary place". I walked most of the way through it. At 7.45 we had come out of it and found the hamla in a wadi —to the north Jebel El Turk [Turuk] and to the south Jebel Erbit [al-Arbad].

That perishing Greek in El Obeid has sold us bad tinned milk. Put on pyjamas, read the tale of the Berber's Six Brothers, and went to sleep. An Abyssinian Roller—a lovely bird, large and blue, came and perched on a neighbouring bush, balancing himself against the gale. This bird is lucky —so the Shukria told me. Certainly a feather of a roller brought me luck on one occasion.

Rode again at 4.30 and approached the wadi of Merkh. Large hill on the south, and beyond it El Erbit and other hills. The country here is exactly like the central Butana. By dusk we had descended to the wadi and saw camels and cattle and one or two tents. Guinea fowl were seen, and the little Doc. got down to pot at them. How he does it in the dark I don't know, but he always gets some. He sent one to me later on.

About a quarter of an hour later we saw a beacon ahead of us and crossed a deep water course and were in camp. Ahmad, son of Sheikh Jabir wad Tugga of the Howawir, came and greeted me. His father had a fall from a camel 7 months ago, and, although no bones were broken, his right leg is still useless. He wanted the doctor to see him. Sat up late writing.

2.5.31

At 6 a.m. I went over and called on Sheikh Jabir, whose tent was not 100 yards away. A fine-looking old boy—blue-eyed. The doctor and Muhammad Musa were drinking tea with him. I stayed about ten minutes. Then we rode on to the wells, arriving there about 7.

The water course here is very wide, with deep cliff-like banks sometimes 10 feet high. There are large trees on the banks and the hamla had got down under trees on the south side, the wells stretching away to the East. Bizeigli had arrived on Thursday with my mail and our delay had caused him to think that I had changed my plans. However, he had not, thank goodness, moved.

Meanwhile a strong wind got up and a dust storm resulted. The doctor had kindly lent me his tent for a bath and it kept out sufficient of the sand to permit of my getting clean. . . .

Merchants (four) appeared with a sheep, for which they refused to take a price, and, as Sheikh Muhammad Musa said they had brought it for him as much as for me, there was nothing to be done about it but take it as a guest's gift (diafa). I don't like "diafa" from merchants. One of them was an amusing bird with a very sad and solemn face. He is a Dongolawi—all four came from Dongola originally, but one is a Shaigi by tribe. They produce most of their goods—sugar, tea, pepper, salt and a small amount of white and blue cotton cloth—from Omdurman, a month there and back (transport about £E1 a camel); and also buy from the Arabs fat and semen [*sic*] (butter), and sometimes camel and goal hair and wool from sheep (these last three the Arabs don't often sell). (*N.B.* Make Muhammad Musa repeat details of differences in price.)

I sat and wrote with a screen of blankets and my biggest ground sheet set on poles and tied with loading ropes, to keep off the driving sand. The dust continued to blow until evening. I decided that, as I had promised Sheikh Jabir to leave one policeman (Ahmad Doweina, our crack shot) behind to cope with hyenas by poison, and as Muhammad Salim Bizeigli is not (as I thought) supernumerary but attached to the doctor, I could not spare a bobby to take mail. Will make a plan to send mail to Bara by help of Niama Sirkatti.

The doctor appeared about 5 p.m. and drank tea and talked, partly about the case of an unfortunate girl whom he had sent to me, as the disease in that form is rare here. (The people are most reluctant to travel to distant hospital.) The doc. will stay at Id El Merkh a few days and rejoin me at Safia. He will visit Hamrat El Wuzz on the return journey. He and I and Muhammad Musa went for a walk round the wells in the bed of the wadi. Muhammad Musa [said] . . . that more Arabs used to make their summer quarters around here than now. At present there are a few of the following: Howawir Khomasiin, Kababish Dar Omar, Shileiwab, Ribeigat, Sirajab. He also talked about how the Howawir first came to Id El Merkh.

I then asked how a stranger would proceed if he came and wanted to water at one of these wells, since there is no "Sid Meshra", no well-known Sheikh and no wakil of the Kababish here. He said he'd go up to any of those slaves there and they would not deny him but give him a "delu" (leather bucket). Would there be a charge? (The Meidob say they have been overcharged lately for watering.) "Oh *No! No!* Sell water which is from God? Oh! Oh! what a shame!" (Yes?) "Not a ram from the flock as dues or guest-gift?" "Good gracious no!" When we got back to my windscreen, I sent for tea and Muhammad Musa said I had tired him out (but apparently not his tongue—so soon as he had drunk water and tea). He carried on for a while about Kababish taxes and the change over from Tribute to Herd Tax (see R. Davies's letters in file). The people had said at the time, "Rather Saalim's exactions" (Saalim was chief under the Turks).[16] I then tried to trip Muhammad Musa into admissions about present exactions of the ruling family, but he was not to be caught out.

The wind had died down by 7 p.m. and the night was quite cold after the gale.

3.5.31

At 2.30 a.m. the roaring of one of Nur Ed Din's brother's young camels woke me while the hamla was loading and I could not get to sleep again properly. Rose at 4.30 and we rode at 5. Quite cold and no wind yet. The doc. was probably still asleep—at any rate he did not show a leg. Went due east out of the meshra into lovely country like that round Bereisi in the Butana, gravelly soil covered with saffron "go'" [*sic*][17] grass and tufts of haskaneet. To the south we saw the two jebels called the Nuhuud[18] from their shape. No Arab going westwards will drive his flocks between these hills on his way to the rainy season grazing for fear lest one of his party die. The legend is of giants—that the rocks were like those clashing rocks Odysseus so narrowly escaped. Muhammad Musa asked what English pastures were like and English wool. Mindful of my excellent Tutor Honest John Clapham's lectures in days gone by, I held forth on the wool trade in mediaeval England and expressed regret in proper Arab manner that customs in my country had changed and things are not what they were in my forebears' times. Reached the hamla in a wadi at 8 a.m. The wind began to blow but it is cool. Sent a bobby on with a note to Niama Sirkatti. Wrote, read and slept, and read the Accountant of Kutum's Arabic *History of the Kababish*. Rode on at 4.30. We crossed a long stretch of kerib at a walk and then descended into a wadi. Beyond this after dark we saw the fire lit by the hamla and came to it at 7 p.m.

It became very still and cold: bright moonlight. Sat up writing until 10 p.m. When I got to bed there appeared to be something alive in my pillow, buzzing like an approaching motor—searched everywhere and inside

---

[16] Salim Fadl Allah, d. 1840.
[17] *Aristida funiculata*. Massey, 40.
[18] *Nuhud* (sing. *nahd*): breasts.

pillow cases, no luck. However, it subsided after a bit and nothing bit me in the night.

4.5.31
Rose 4 a.m. Rode 4.30 a.m. When we had passed over the top of a goz we saw the sun rise away over Jebel Haraza—a very good sight. The jebel looked long and low, but it was about 15 miles away and is very big. On our right was another jebel, Abu Hadid, turned pink and purple by the rising sun. In front of Jebel Haraza appeared a long line of a sand hill of red sand which at certain times of day throws up the dark blue of the jebel.

We came to Wadi El Wuzz about 7 a.m., were met by Niama Sirkatti and an entourage on camels, and rode across the well-field in the wadi through the trees to the Locust Dump (of poison bran) of last year, now a sort of rest house: all very well kept up. Niama chatted and left me to breakfast and a bath.

Hamilton had sent me the Bara Howawir files, a letter from himself, mainly about a proposed Court for the Meganin, and a bottle of black Munich Beer.

Niama returned later and we briefly disposed of two theft cases and then went off to see the local market. He was keen for me to go as it was market day (Mondays and Fridays are market days). The shops are grass huts—long shape (kurnuk); there is one mud house only. A Greek, the inevitable khawaja,[19] has just arrived. We went round and then to the grass booth in which Niama rests when he is here. There we drank coffee and Niama produced from the Greek a tin of fruit which we shared with avidity as we squatted on the ground, sharing one bowl. Niama has a Governor-General's presentation rifle which always jams after one shot. I promised to take it and get it repaired in Khartoum.

Then an old man of the Doalib came in, ex-Omda of Um Durag, whom MacMic had found in Darfur, when Ali Dinar had been killed, and sent home to be Omda. This old lad had been sent by the Khalifa[20] to Rejaf, where he had fought disease and the Niam-Niam[21] (who eat men, he said) for years with the Amir Arabi.[22] After that the remnant of them, 25,000,[23] marched through the Bahr El Ghazal with slave carriers to Darfur. It took

---

[19] Sir; Mr.: foreigner. In the Sudan, a white Christian foreigner other than an official.
[20] 'Abdallahi Muhammad (1846–99), successor of the Mahdi.
[21] The Azande.
[22] 'Arabi Dafa'allah (d. 1916), Mahdist commander and governor of Equatoria from 1890. See Holt, *The Mahdist State*, 219–21; *BD*, 58.
[23] *Cf. BD*, 58.

7 months he said. Ali Dinar made them *Mulazimiin*,[24] or some of them, and when the English came to El Fasher 5 only were left. El Haj Khidr El Dokri also came in and he told his yarn of Slatin Pahsa's escape from the Khalifa. El Haj Khidr was apparently present and in [on] the secret.

Niama and I visited the carpenter's shop and the blacksmith's.

In the afternoon before sunset more business was done outside my hut, looking towards Jebel Haraza, now with the rays of "the great setting flame" on it. I went to bed early and slept very deeply until 5.30 a.m. Hamilton's beer went down awfully well, and, it being my mother's birthday, I drank her health in it.

I suppose it is Niama's eternal boyishness and air of mischief which makes him so attractive an old man. He always cheers me up.

5.5.31

Rose 5.45. Niama came in for half an hour and pushed off to see about lists of cattle which had died of plague. I read the Howawir files, wrote and spent more time than I ought to have done deciding not after all to accept Travers Blackley's car for leave.

It was a fairly cool day. Niama did not turn up again till 3.15, when we talked about cattle plague and whether we could let any blokes off tax in consequence; and about that infernal bicker between him and Sheikh Ali El Tom about the Wadi Hamra here. Four Nuba Omdas appeared with the deuce of a petition about it. I looked innocent and said, "Please God, when Sheikh Ali or a specially-appointed agent of his is here I will see the wadi and the case—perhaps next winter?"

As I was going out to play at golf on the aerodrome, Niama came back and said people had come to say that his brother Muhammad Sirkatti (who has been ill 7 months) is dying. So I told him he must on no account stay here to see me off tomorrow, and he has now ridden away. He refused to let me send a messenger to Muhammad Effendi, the doctor, to bring him from Id El Merkh. He said his brother appeared to be past doctors.

Muhammad Musa came and chatted after dark, mainly about the wadi case, and also about Kababish who come here with cows, damage Nuba cultivation and then say, "If you want to complain, go to Sheikh Ali El Tom"—ten days away. I must write to Sheikh Ali. Query? ask for a wakil?

A rather interesting case occurred yesterday, illustrating the effect of the English (and service in their Sudan Defence Force) upon the native. A terribly out-of-place-looking fellow clad in a long silk gallabiya[25] over a waistcoat and wearing below European brogues, socks and sock-suspenders,

---

[24] Attendants, guards.
[25] Long, loose, shirt-like garment.

had fetched me a Royal-Marines-pattern salute as I was walking through the market. Later my police sergeant came and said an ex-soldier had a complaint to make. This same bloke then swaggered into my hut, near knocked the roof off with his salute, grinned first in a cock-sure manner and then in a self-conscious one (when he saw that I was not impressed by his military acrobatics). I asked him to be seated (i.e. squat on the floor like a decent Arab or Nuba), which he did, in a surprised manner. He then said that his Omda was oppressing him. This was the story: he, Muhd. Ahmad, was, two years ago, a serving corporal in the Camel Corps, No. 1 Co. (Leicester's men), and had cattle on trust with his brother Ali, a Nuba of Um Darag [sic], where his home is. An injured husband accused Ali (most unjustly of course) of committing adultery with his wife. The Omda had in consequence taken and eaten two of Muhammad's bulls which were in Ali's herd.

Had Muhammad complained to the Nazir? No. Had he not done anything about it when he came on leave last year? No. So I pushed him off to fetch his brother and got them before the Omda and Niama. The Omda said, "Yes, it is mostly true. Ali was fined £E4 by me for adultery, and those present in the mejlis at the time begged him off £E2. Then Ali produced two calves which were priced at £E2 and actually fetched 180 PT when sold." Ali admitted that he had brought those calves himself and that the Omda had not sent and taken them.

Now here is a tribesman spoiled by contact with us English and our ways, our individualism and our codes, and turned into a local sea-lawyer. His brother's property and his are no longer practically one, when it comes to getting either of them out of a hole. "Any man who goes off to the army and comes back discharged comes as if he were a D.C. or at least a Mamur, and anyone who goes off to prison comes back with his nose in the air, proud as a peacock."

6.5.31

I sent off the mail to Bara early this morning. Constable Ibrahim Adam was reported by the sergeant for having spent the night on the tiles without leave. He saddled his camel and went off "to see an aunt"—one of Autolycus's aunts I should think. Chap has a good character—severely reprimanded. Heard that Muhammad Sirkatti is dead, sent a note. Read for most of the morning.

Muhammad Musa of course did nothing about producing a responsible Kabbashi to answer for Kababish whose cattle eat Nuba cultivation.

After the hamla had gone, Omda Ajab of Abu Hadid and 3 of his sheikhs, who had been over to Haraza to attend Muhammad Sirkatti's funeral, came to talk. Pleasant of them. The conversation mainly concerned itself with their asking "Where is (1) MacMic (now Sir Harold MacMichael—Civil Secretary) (2) Reid (now Governor White Nile) (3) Maclaren (D.C. in White Nile) (4) Davies (Asst. Civil Secretary) (5) Young (Asst. Civil Secretary) and Ah ha! Hall now? and where is Watt going to? MacMic always knew all our pedigrees, Young had bells on his camel trappings, Reid knew us very well, and Watt would always have his joke. Reid and Watt were cousins, weren't they? Yes, you know Watt was quite thin like you (!) when he first came here." Extraordinary district this.

Sent mail to Soderi. Started about 4.45. Hasan Doleib and his son Ahmad go with us to try to bring home a charge of theft of camels by the Howawir.

When we mounted the goz north of Wuzz, I tried to make out the division of the wadi described in Maclaren's ruling on the case, and as described by (a) Niama and (b) Sheikh Ali El Tom. I failed to reconcile the points even with Ahmad Hasan Doleib's help.

Rode till 6.45 over barish sand with small bushes and tufts of haskaneet and ajarab. My Bushari is going much more smoothly now, getting used to work.

7.5.31

My watch must have gone wrong. The hamla apparently went off at 3.30 and we at 5. We were late in starting. Cool night but hot day to come. Rode mounting a goz northwards. All Jebel Haraza appeared to the east and, after a while Kol Zurga and Merafa'ib jebels showed up. We found the hamla in Wadi Masariin (which means "tripe"—why it is so called I don't know), next to a providential herd of sheep: we'd run out of milk. That accursed Greek not only sold me bad tinned milk but sold me tinned cream instead of tinned milk. Sat under a tundub tree which hummed with insects. Started to try to write a translation of the Kuttum history of the Kababish. A hot day.

Started again 4.30. As soon as we got out of Wadi Masariin we climbed a goz and trees became very scarce. As we came up to Merafi'bat [Marfa'ibat] and mounted the ridge, Jebel Nasb [Nasib] El Husan appeared miles away to the northeast. To the west of this jebel Hasan Khalifa's tents are at present. Further west on the horizon appeared Teraabiil, a very much serrated range of rocks. On our right front in the distance was the wadi which runs down to Safia. We passed the summer encampments of Nuba from Haraza, miserable booths and lean cattle.

We reached Safia after dark, and found there Muhammad Effendi, who had just arrived. He very kindly gave me tea for which I was most grateful. My hamla must have taken a wrong turning for it arrived after me. Slept early.

8.5.31

When the light came I found I had been set down quite close to the wells in one of the dirtiest spots I think I have ever known. All the cattle of Haraza seemed to have passed that way. The ruined buildings of the old Police Post and rest house were behind to the south about 100 yards. Sheikh Muhammad Musa and I walked round the wells where herds were already collecting for watering. There were a certain number of Howawir, and Shileywab and Ribeygat. Most animals looked in poor condition. No milk was to be had. Muhammad Musa bought a halter for an exceptionally small quantity of snuff. Water is very near the surface here—about 8 feet. The police moved me under a tree (foliage rather spoiled by the eating of camels), which bred a phenomenal quantity of very large-sized ants. I notice that some of these ants stick their sterns out and some wear them in a less conspicuous manner—in fact rather like humans.

Four merchants came to call upon me, all of whom, especially El Haj Saiied [*sic*], who wore his Mekkawia,[26] looked more like fekis than merchants. I gave them tea.

After breakfast the weather began to become baking hot. Even the ants took a siesta. Hasan Doleib produced one of his wanted men, and I sent a summons for one other, and a note to Hasan Khalifa (with my message of arrival) for the third. A Howari rode off to the Nazir for me. Muhammad Effendi came to talk and he borrowed the Kababish history to read. Meanwhile Muhammad Musa produced a most mixed case between a Maagli and a Kabbashi with a Magnuuni in the middle. It looks to me as if the Kabbashi has pinched the camels. . . .

I had a talk with Yasin Muhammad Gaili, merchant and debtor, about the civil claim against him. An Arabian-Nights tale of the young merchant who wasted his substance in the great and wicked city (El Obeid). Yasin to come with me to Hasan Khalifa.

There are hundreds of sand grouse here. They came down from 6 a.m. till 9.

Muhammad Effendi and I had a long talk on various subjects, including circumcision. In his view the argument that circumcision of women[27] is necessitated by their natural licentiousness is not one maintained by most of the older men in the Sudan. The townsmen, he says, and his own people have taken very largely to the mild form (the Sunni), e.g. the daughter of Sagh Ahmad Okeir married to Nazir Ibrahim Musa Medibbo. The licentiousness argument, he says, does not work, for the nomads of Kordofan, who practice a most brutal form, are meanwhile exceptionally

---

[26] *Sufi* headress.

[27] That is, clitoridectomy and infibulation, practised in varying degrees in the Sudan.

lacking in chastity. I asked why, then, one never heard of illegitimate children among the Arabs. He said that the reasons were (a) the circumcision itself (b) the mothers of the girls, who get them married quickly if they have any suspicions that they have been playing around, and (c) as to married women, their own craftiness in passing off children as their husbands'. He said that the Sunna prescribes circumcision in the mild form for male and for female in hot countries, but the extreme form is quite unorthodox and he does not know how it originated in Sudan tribes. After he left I slept a little.

After lunch a man called Dokeir of the Shileywab, a hot-tempered, slightly deranged devil, came up and complained that a Gerayati, who had been in prison with him at Soderi, owed him £E1 given as "bushara".[28] I pushed him off to Muhd. Musa—no luck: Muhammad Musa is too idle for that sort of thing. So he and his adversary appeared. A great scene with one or two looking on, especially one downward-looking Arab who kept catching my eye and grinning. They both admitted they were thieves and I told them I should be pleased if they would fight it out with knives, as I could then have the pleasure of their company and assistance in drawing water and performing sanitary service at Soderi. They laughed and went away still arguing.

N.B. P.C. Ahmad Doweina whom I left behind at Id El Merkh at the request of Ahmad, son of Sheikh Gabir Tagga [sic] reported on the night of 7.5.31 that he had been unable to perform what he had been set, because the Arabs had made a mejlis as to who was to provide an animal for slaughtering so that the meat might be poisoned and used as bait for hyenas. The Howawir and Kababish agreed to purchase a bull, but then fell out as to the division of the price. The Howawir said they were few and the Kababish many and that they, the Howawir, should therefore pay only a small part of the price. The Kababish wanted half and half. It was then suggested that the Howawir should produce a sheep of their own and the Kababish be dealt with separately. But they would not agree. There is, said Ahmad Doweina, no sheikh of the Kababish at Id El Merkh who can hold them. I pointed out the moral to Muhammad Musa. Another instance of the "bloody Etonian" attitude of the Kababish.

Ahmad said that the following sections were represented at Id El Merkh: Shileywab (but their Sheikh Khor Es Sumiit is at Um Dam); Awlad Ugba (but Sheikh Haamid Ali is at Um Dam): (a) Gajaja (b) Dar Omar (but very few of these latter, most of whom are at Hamrat El Wuzz).

Rode on at 4.30 after talking to Muhammad Effendi about the Abyssinian Coronation.

---

[28] Literally "good news", thus a reward given to the bearer of good news.

Muhammad Sadig, the cook, suffers, like his master, from constipation and had complained that the doses given him by Muhammad Effendi did not work. Muhammad Effendi therefore prepared for him this morning apparently a depth charge to sink the world's biggest submarine, and just before the hamla started, Muhammad Sadig had made certain he was dying. Everyone else was rather amused.

A very hot afternoon ride across the wells and into country alternately sand with tufted grass and tracts of blackstone. A jolly countryside which explains the thinness of the animals on the wells. We passed Jebel Nasb Es Sunugh [Sumugh] and marched on Nasb El Husan.

N.B. With the Maagli's law suit arrived one of the "Muta-Nurab", i.e. the blokes who, some free and some slave, live with and upon Sheikh Ali El Tom and his family. This lad was a thin old adventurer of the swashbuckling type with the deuce of an outsize in turbans and in drawers. He looked like a Hadendowi. His name was Gabak Allah ("God brought you": and I bet he comes down on the unhappy Kabbashi like the wrath of God too). These are the Pretorian Guard and the "legati a latera" of Sheikh Ali's government for tax collection and summonses and general discipline. I remember the wild Fuzzies Ahmad Kerar used to keep in the same way on a smaller scale.

A very hot simoom blew from noon to dusk. We now followed a wadi which becomes Khor Abu Urug later, in a northeasterly direction. We came upon the hamla just before dark, beside the wadi. Very poor grazing. The heat had knocked me up a bit. However I had the doctor to tea.

9.5.31

Started 4.30 a.m. Same kind of country, same direction. I felt tired and unsociable. Got down in the wadi again. Simoom sprang up before I had finished breakfast. Very hot. Very poor grazing. Are my camels going to stand 19 more days of this? The old temper not good this morning. So much wind it is difficult to read or write and impossible to sleep. Lay down for some while and then wrote the above. . . .

N.B. On the evening of 7 May Nur Ed Din reported the Giheimabi camel sick. Symptoms: stopping, raising the head, and constipation. The Arabs said it was "khila", which they attribute to a "duud" (worm) in the head. Cure: atroon[29] (tar) to which I suggest adding Epsom Salts. Took on the second of his brother's camels from 8 May.

Mid-day of this 9th May was very trying and hot. The merchant Yasin Muhamd. Gaili had failed to come with my hamla—sent a policeman back to Safia to fetch him. The afternoon ride started late (about 5) because the

---

[29] Natron.

Shawish said the shidd was a short one. It was a very hot ride. By 6.15 we had found the hamla near a few small Arab tents—evidently the wells of Abu Urug were fairly near. The heat had made me very limp. The next hour and a half was devoted entirely to satisfying gradually a terrible thirst.

10.5.31

Rose late—4.30 a.m., and felt desperate. Rode at 5.15 feeling like death. Before we had gone half a mile, I had fully resolved to resign at all costs, and I reflected gloomily upon all the discouraging things that had been said in my first confidential report. It is at times like this that I feel even more than usually useless at making conversation with Arabs.

We went down into the wadi again and crossed over the wells which are there and which were crowded. The soil is all very sandy and there is little grass. When we came out beyond the wells, we saw Sheikh Nimr and his folk drawn up ahead on camels and we met in the usual manner. After reflexion, I have come to the conclusion that Sheikh Nimr is the typical king in a fairy-story book illustration. His figure is perfectly pear-shaped. He wears his turban a little on one side and his moustache and imperial resemble those of the Second Empire. It takes four men to get him onto his camel and the sight is worth seeing, provided one can refrain from smiling.

So we came into the ferik and I was taken to pay my respects to the old Nazir.[30] A magnificent partiarchal figure—about the size of his son. He is bed-ridden. Muhammad Musa had been imitating old Sheikh Hasan Khalifa yesterday afternoon—a goodish imitation, and also had been poking fun at the Howawir tents, said to be poor. They are.

The ferik is on the slope of a stretch of red sand not far from Jebel Ez Zakhofa. There is some grazing a little further over beyond a rocky ridge to the northeast. Before we had finished drinking tea and making salutations, the wind began to blow from the northeast and the sand rose in clouds. The wind soon freshened to a gale and I had to have the "bait" I was in closed up. The heat became terrific. At 10 I went to see the Nazir and on the way I looked at the servants, the police and our companions. They were in extreme discomfort and could light no fires. The doctor's tent was blown down.

Hasan Khalifa talked about the Robab and said 16 of them had refused entirely to pay herd tax. The Sheikh, Adam Abdullah, is here. I said I wanted to go into the whole question of arrears and asked him to have his clerk make me out details. He said he would do so. I then talked about rifles, and then the doctor appeared and we left politics. The doctor

[30] Hasan Khalifa.

apparently was at school with Ali Hasan Khalifa in a khalwa at Korti. Soon after this I left, saying that I would come again in the evening.

The heat became infernal. The wind dropped at noon. I took off all clothes except a singlet and a towel and dripped as if I were in a Turkish bath.

By 4 p.m. it was just cool enough to bear a few more clothes (to wit a pair of shorts) and there was shade outside the tent. I had tea and sent for water to wash. When the bucket came the water out of the iron fantassies was too hot to bear one's hand in with any comfort.

At 5.00 I went to the Nazir. Hasan Doleib was there, complaining about his camels. Conversation was desultory. I think the Arabs were tired from the heat. I was dead beat. After some time, when he had sent others away, I plucked up courage to explain to him and Nimr the position in the case of Fait Ali the murderer. The Nazir appeared to understand. But I don't know.

I then left to inspect camels. We shall have to send back to Soderi the Giheimabi and the Miri (on which I was riding). A "Baseer"[31] turned up to look at Ibrahim Adam's lame camel. Has Watt ever noticed anything wrong with this camel?

N.B. Sheikh Hasan Khalifa stated that the customary dues in his tribe are: (1) Ushur, (2) a sheep a year per flock [and] (3) the "rial ed dho"; and that he never takes any others.

After dark Muhammad Musa and Nimr came and drank tea and date wine (which Nimr had produced). Later Muhammad Eff. came. I had noticed a terrible number of rotting eyes in his ferik, especially among children. Muhammad Eff. says he has treated over 30 today. . . .

The night did not cool down early, but, when it did, I slept like the dead. A poisonous day—even flies were so done one could kill them easily.

11.5.31

Awoke very tired. The sky was entirely overcast, whether with sand or mist or both. A southerly breeze sprang up and I expected a repetition of yesterday. Felt despondent until breakfast, after which I summoned up courage to send and ask to see Sheikh Hasan Khalifa. The breeze had kept cool and, on the way to the Sheikh's tent, his son Muhammad said that there must have been rain in the south a long way off. Indeed one could smell the damp in the wind.

I found the Sheikh brighter—the heat had evidently tired him yesterday afternoon. Talked (1) generally and of past district commissioners (2)

---

[31] Literally, proficient one; in the Sudan, bone-setter.

of Jackson Pasha[32] (3) rifles [and] (4) Herd Tax: the clerk produced a list of arrears. The Robab again. I then left with Nimr and Adam Abdallah to talk about the shortcomings of the Robab. Adam Abdallah says that the following have refused to pay last year's herd tax:

Hasan Kabja	Haamid El Hafian
Adam Muhd. Ahmad El Gusayr	Hamid Salah
Muhd. Abd er Razig	Muhd. Ali Tuweiyr
Saddiq Adam	Mahmoud Hasaballah
Johar Adam Muhd. Ahmad	El Hajj El Jezouli Ahmad
Hammaad Osman	Muhd. Muhd. Ali
Abdallah El Amin	Musa Miniallah
Bakhit Dakour	

I told him to have a detailed list of all his arrears made out and bring it to me. Nimr spoke of Ahmad Jibril and Mahi his brother (of whom Sheikh Hasan had spoken yesterday), concerning whom his clerk had produced a note from Soderi Merkaz saying that, if these men made a fuss again, the Nazir should send them to the D.C. It appears that these are the blokes who were complaining about the land at Um Jawasir and who came to me at Soderi and I, knowing nothing of their case, refuted them by means of Onbashi Tingle and sent them away (knowing also nothing of the merkaz note to Hasan Khalifa). Nimr says that these men have, since Hector Watt's trip north, complained at Khartoum and at El Obeid. This also I had not heard. Nimr spoke also of the tree at Gambir, mentioned yesterday by Hasan Khalifa. It appears that a Robabi named Ali Jerki Barcor burned it down to spite his sheikh and Nimr on the Id of Ramadan. This tree was famous and Nimr used to take care of it so that D.C.s and guests and he himself might sit under it. Nimr wants to "hukm" the bloke or for me to punish him. I said I would rather he saw the case providing that he made sure of doing it in due form.

Adam Abdullah's evidence is wanted in a theft case in Soderi. I promised to take it on commission to enable him to collect herd tax.

The breeze died away about 11 a.m. and it became very sticky. I took most of my clothes off and then the doctor turned up and talked until 12 of various things. I showed him a copy of *Punch* and explained as best I could what a Punch and Judy show is. He reminded me I ought to see the khalwa (Qur'an school) here. The sky was still overcast and there were heavy clouds to the south. Medicine I had taken together with the date wine brought by Nimr's son Hasan were having a very excellent effect on

---

[32] Sir Herbert Jackson (1861–1931), soldier and administrator; governor of Dongola, 1902–22. Upon retirement he lived at Merowe (see below, 212–16). *BD*, 188–89.

me but, combined with the extreme stickyness of the heat, made me very exhausted. I lay dripping till 4.30 and then went outside. After tea I had a bath and, still sweating slightly, went to call on the Nazir, whom I found very tired. He dismissed me pretty soon and then Nimr and his son came and talked to me till it was dark.

It was still very stuffy after sunset. I tried writing but gave it up and went stickily to bed about 8.30. In the middle of the night a wind like the steam from a kettle woke me.

12.5.31

Woke with eyes bunged up and a mouth like two nights of delight in Berlin. The sun got up like a Bessemer blast, but, after breakfast, thank goodness, a cool southerly breeze sprang up.

Ahmad Doweina has brought Yasin Muhammad Gaili, who calmly says that he was ready to go when my hamla started but, as I did not send a camel for him, he thought I had let him off. I hope he was hot on the way here.

The Nazir was in much better form this morning. Insisted on slaughtering a naga. I explained to him that I had consulted last night with Nimr about the Robab who were refusing to pay tribute and had concluded that the best thing would be for him to go with Sheikh Adam Abdullah and collect from them and all Robab who are in arrears. If they refuse to pay after he had visited them in person, then the government might step in.

The Nazir then raised the question of the men whom Watt put in prison and of Ahmad and El Mahi Gibril. He is insistent that these men should be brought before him and fined by him, that those who are in prison should be sent to him as soon as they are released. He said that this had been done in the case of the Solhab and the Fezarab before and that, as a consequence, all disobedience from them had ceased. If these men, he contends, are not punished by him as well as the government, they will merely come out of prison saying they care nought for the Nazir, and will go round the tribe stirring up trouble. (As indeed it appears from the Nazir and his son's talk, Ahmad and El Mahi Gibril are now doing.) I said I fully understood what he had said, but that my advice for the moment was "sobr" (patience). These men had been punished: let us wait and see if the punishment will have its effect. If it has no good effect, then on my return we could find a way against them. I said, "Give the thief enough rope and he will hang himself". After a little talk about Yasin, who has, the Nazir says, no animals, and is, indeed, bankrupt, and discussion about unlicensed rifles, I left. On the way to my tent I met the Khalwa Feki and agreed to visit the khalwa tomorrow morning. I repeated again to Nimr in my tent what I had said before him and the Nazir and added that, while

I wanted him to "osbir" [be patient] now and especially not to "hukm" (sentence) any of these people who are in arrears with herd tax, yet if, as we hope it will not, a "fitna"[33] should arise in my absence he should let Hamilton know direct to Bara. I hoped that, after the rains, he and I might trek together round his tribe. I then sent for Yasin Muhammad Gaili and arranged that he should pay £E1 every other month. If he fails a suit is started. Nimr then talked of Atroun Post days and the Goraan raids in the Western Desert. He described a rifle duel between himself and a Guraan, and his journey with 120 Howawir to Jebel El Akhdar in 1916. The Nazir had already told me that the Goraan have already raided again this year.

The noon and afternoon were excessively hot. A heavy cloud was away to the east and one could see rain and hear thunder. Rain fell on Nasb El Husan.

I went at 5 to Hasan Khalifa and found him a bit under the weather— he would hardly talk at all: so I left as soon as I could and took the numbers of 6 government rifles at my tent. Also I exhorted sheikhs to collect arrears. A boy came and complained that his brother had been killed by a merchant. They all left fairly early. I felt rather sick after dark and tried without success to make myself sick. The night was airless and hot.

13.5.31

I awoke entirely despondent and in the worst of tempers, not improved by finding that Koko had left my remaining bottle of bay rum in store at Soderi. However at 7.15 I went with Nimr to see the khalwa. The Feki said that most of the boys were still away ill with pink eye.[34] Khalifa, one of Nimr's sons, is one of the elder boys. I had one or two of them do sums on the ground before me, and others recite Suras of the Quraan [sic].

By breakfast time the atmosphere was think with mist. After breakfast I finished off Hasan Doleib's case. He has got no change out of Hasan Khalifa, and I agree that Hasan Doleib should swear his three accused on the tomb[35] of Ba Naga by Safia on Friday. If they fail to swear, they produce his camel or its price. The old boy went off this afternoon—nice old thing.

Yasin the merchant then turned up with a very pretty story about a brawl which took place in his shop between Meidob and Kababish and about the subsequent bribing of police who were sent from Khartoum

---

[33] Trouble, intrigue, discord.
[34] Conjunctivitis.
[35] In Sudanese popular Islam, an oath taken on a saint's tomb would have been especially solemn, more so even than one upon the *Qur'an*. See J. S. Trimingham, *Islam in the Sudan*, London 1949, 141–48.

North. I took his statement. Muhammad Musa tried to interrupt and Muhammad Effendi came in in the middle.

I then took the statement of the boy about his brother said to have been done in by cruelty of a merchant.

After that I went to see Hasan Khalifa whom I found in great form. The doctor was there and has given Hasan Khalifa smelling salts, which relieve his catarrh. (*N.B.* Might be a good thing to bring him back a proper bottle of smelling salts as a gift.) Chaps talked about the Mahdia and quoted a considerable amount of Hardello Abu Sinn's poetry. Hasan Khalifa reached the height of his form in describing the trials of a Pasha travelling from Halfa to Abu Hamid in the old days, in which Hasan Khalifa imitated the English pronunciation of Arabic and quoted the well-known "Baladdy Fool". Altogether a very encouraging and amusing session.

Nimr and the doctor then came and sat with me. Nimr wants to take the hyena-poisoning policeman, Ahmad Doweina, all round with him on his tax-collecting expedition. I don't like the idea of this and shall if possible get out of allowing it.

The doctor went on talking till 1.15. By this time the atmosphere was that of a steam bath. The doctor says the Howawir are much more chaste than the Kababish and therefore, apparently, have much less V.D. He has seen no primary-stage S[yphilis] and no G[onorrhea] at all. He saw over 200 people at Id El Merkh and about [the] same here. Nimr was insistent that the doctor stay longer than three days after my departure, but I explained that he could not: pressure of work elsewhere. *N.B.* The doctor's appearance here an unexpected success as the Howawir are feki-ridden.[36]

After the doctor had gone, I lay down and freely perspired until 3, when I had lunch. At 3.50 a violent storm broke from the east, followed by rain. The sons of the Sheikh appeared with great kindness to see that my tent should not be carried away and then sheltered with me from the rain. The tent seemed over-crowded with fat men (they are all fat . . .). When the rain had stopped and a cool breeze blew and I had seen Ahmad Doweina, who says his camel is not in good enough condition to go far afield, I went to see Hasan Khalifa at 5 p.m.

He was again in very good form. My "foot" is now "lucky", for I have brought rain in my train. Talked, amongst other things, of Feki Jumaa. Also of the dispute between Ali El Tom and Niama over Wadi El Wuzz. Hasan Khalifa says he has heard that El Tom Ali told his father, after the

---

[36] That is, ministered to by holy men who might be expected to resent or feel threatened by medical doctors.

row at Soderi, that he ought to let things rest and not stir up mud, because the Kababish and the Nuba had always been friends. This rather coincided with Hamilton's report that El Tom had chided Ali El Tom for being unreasonable. It would be a good thing perhaps to get El Tom as his father's representative for a settlement.

Nimr came back to my tent and sat and talked and asked about the Shukria until well after the hour of prayer. Rain came on again. At 8.15 it was still raining and cool outside the tent. At 9 p.m., however, an abominable huboob[37] arose and the dust continued to blow till midnight. I read till 11.15 the sad story of the Princess Ibriza, a portion of which, viz. her wrestling match with the Prince Shirkan, is clearly omitted from my cheap edition. Got to sleep badly after midnight.

14.5.31

Woke to a cool morning like an English summer day but felt despondent with lack of sleep. Having removed a large sand-hill from each eye, and had a bath, I felt better.

Wrote mail to Mamur Soderi. Camels drank yesterday and are being "howassh"ed.[38] Discovered that the nickname "Lawlaw" attached to Sheikh Muhammad Musa means a small boy who extorts things from his brothers. Shawish tells me Yusef Idris, Sheikh of the Atawia, is dead recently and his brother committed suicide on his death. Sheikh Ali El Tom has not yet heard of this. Arabs at Abu Urug are Howawir, Barara and Atawia.

The Nazir I found in rather good form. He produced another excellent English swear word, "Goddamain".[39] I told him I was sorry that the doctor could not stay longer, this visit, owing to calls elsewhere.

A hot wind sprang up and blew hard. Everything in my tent became dusty and I tried sitting outside with a handkerchief round my throat. Gileygha, my camel boy, came for pay and I took 25 PT from the cook to pay him.

After the hamla had gone, Muhammad Hasan Khalifa and El Tom Hasan came with another Remington and also with an old carbine of Nimr's which wants repair. I gave Muhammad Hasan a note to Muir (of Ordnance Dept. Khartoum North).

I then went to take leave of Hasan Khalifa and after about half an hour with him left at 4.30. Nimr, the Hakim (doctor), and others rode with us to put us on our way. The sky was murky with dust everywhere. As we

---

[37] Sandstorm.
[38] Arabic: *hawasha*, to round up.
[39] Or, "twice God damn!".

crossed the Wadi Abu Urug, a man came out of a tent to speak to Muhammad Musa. I was told he was Mekki, brother of Ali El Tom's clerk. I told Nimr before we parted that I was sorry I could not let Ahmad Doweina go all round the Howawir because (1) I had not asked leave to send a policeman into Dongola (2) his camel is very thin [and] (3) he has applied for early leave to see his wife who is eight months in child.

We rode southwest and found the hamla after dark. The wind then proceeded to blow a gale. Fortunately the ground there was hard and practically no dust rose. But the result for me was a second night of very inadequate sleep.

15.5.31

Started 4.30. The country has now much more grass in it, and is composed of sand dunes crossed by stony ridges which rise into small rocky hills occasionally. The two Jebels Kol appeared in front of us. We are leaving Hobagi to our left rear and giving it a miss, because there is said to be little water and few people there. We make for El Rasan.

Passed a tortoise on which Muhammad Mahmud, the Nuba policeman, who at present carries my Egyptian flag, pounced. The Nubas eat them. Later, just before we came to camp, we saw a young vulture on its nest atop a sumera bush.

This was a very trying day. Whether from sun or lack of sleep or food or all three, I had a headache all day, and did nothing but lie uncomfortably in a chair.

Second shidd from 5 to 7.30. Similar country—no animals or men. Wind at night again. But I was so weary I slept like dead till 4 a.m.

16.5.31

Shidd from 5 till 7.30. It appears that El Rasan also has very little water. The country is full of grass but empty of Arabs because, says Muhammad Musa, they have all gone to Habisa and Ribda where there is water. Country definitely pleasanter. Passed conically shaped sandhills.

Shawish Ahmad Ibrahim says that the Howawir are losing their formerly enormous herds through their extravagant expenditure on sugar and tea. He volunteered this remark, "a propos des bottes". He said the Kababish and others are not extravagant—their women and children do not drink tea: but the Howawir hareem do. Cool morning, extremely strong north wind. Cool and bracing.

Muhammad Sadig is finding it difficult to feed me because there is no milk. Tea is short because we have had so many Arabs drinking it.

Asked for Muhammad Musa to talk to him but he was asleep. Slept, more or less, myself and read "The Manners and Customs of the Ruwala".

Very hungry. The expert produced a horrible-looking but rather good souffle and stewed figs. Felt very well and viewed the distant hills with more satisfaction than before. Before the hamla moved off, Muhammad Musa came to talk for a while. He talked of the meshras in front of us and of the hills around and he repeated to me the verse about Kol Um Shenab which he had recited the evening before. . . . We chatted some more and then he went to pray.

Rode 5 p.m. till 7 p.m. The way was over sand dunes and stony stretches as before. The hamla had got down near a wadi in which was one Arab tent, hence milk.

On the point of starting our evening ride, Muhammad Musa suddenly asked if the Shukria sheikhs went around their Dar like this. I misunderstood his words, . . . thinking he meant "had they divisions of the tribe for which they are responsible". I said "The arrangement there is not like that Sheikh Ali El Tom has with you Nurab. There they have sheiks, Omdas and Sheikhs of Khut as well between the people and the Nazir". . . . Bad show! said he. I laughed and asked why. He said, "The sheikhs 'eat' and then the Omdas 'eat' and then the Sheikhs [of] Khut 'eat'—so where does the Nazir get his bite from?. . . . I laughed more and said, "Perhaps they don't eat", and got on my camel. "Don't eat? Of course they 'eat'", said Muhammad Musa. "They're just liars. Much better 'eat' and confess to the government that you do. I 'eat' of course, I 'eat', but only a little."

As we rode I asked him whether the arrangement was now that each of the Nurab notables had certain sections of the tribe for whose taxes, etc. he was responsible, or whether the arrangement was geographical, i.e. by meshras. He said, "Formerly or now?" I said, "Now", and it appeared that the arrangement was that Muhammad El Tom and El Tom Ali had certain sections of the tribe with which they more especially concern themselves and go round occasionally. He himself has no section.

We passed one flock of sheep and later two men, a donkey and a dog.

After we had reached the hamla and I had washed, Muhammad Musa came to tea and drank tea with much sugar and some Kia Ora lemon squash (which he liked). He became expansive (there was less wind than usual) and asked if I had father, brothers or sisters or mother. He thought it extremely hard that I should be the last man of my family and said I ought to marry. I said maybe I would, even soon, but that in our view Soderi is a hard place for an inspector to be married in. He jovially urged that I should marry, bachelordom being in no way a blessed state. I should, said he, marry a wife and leave her in my house in Soderi when I trekked. I said that would be considered by us as cruel [and] hard. He said, "Not so hard as leaving her in your own country so far away". Having got him mellow, I then went back to the talk at the beginning of our ride, and he repeated what he had said of the Shukria system, and instanced in support Dar Haamid [sic], where the Omdas and go-betweens have caused trouble. I then asked, "Did he mean 'eating' fines or eating taxes?" He said, "Fines", and I replied that maybe they did 'eat' over there but the Shukria "sultas"[40] forbade "eating" and said all fines should be paid to government. He went on to explain how Sheikh Ali El Tom's system works. The "Salatin"[41] like himself had varying powers delegated to them. All real fining power is with Sheikh Ali, who confirms each sentence and keeps the book. Thus he, Muhammad Musa, can hear cases up to £E4 in value, affrays, blows on the head, and so on. Anything more important he has to report to Sheikh Ali and any judgment Muhammad Musa gives on trek he has to report to Sheikh Ali on his return to him. All fines are payable to Sheikh Ali's chest and are not supposed to be "eaten" by the Nurab "sultan". And so with all the Nurab "Salatin" and "Manadib".

He went on to tell me how he is at the moment carrying a letter from Ali El Tom to certain men at Um Inderaba who had disobeyed Sheikh 'Ali's own orders, given when he was there in January, that they should dig no more wells without reference to Sheikh Ali Kheirallah, Ali El Tom's wakil there and lord of the meshra. He is to see the sheikhs. Each man is to be fined £E2: and if he has anything to say he can go to Hamrat Esh Sheikh to say it (10 days' ride or more). Had I any objection? Of course not. (*N.B.* Must get details and warn Khartoum in case the blighters go and complain to them.)

With that he went away, leaving me to reflect that, after all, one may be getting somewhere, in spite of confidential reports and inability to make small talk or side-splitting jokes all the time. I feel there is probably a great deal in the remark of that disease-rotten wreck of an Irish sailor (see *Tom Fool*) about birds, women and ships, that you can find out almost anything if you only sit quiet and watch. Anyway a sudden insight like that conversation is to me worth three days solitary, almost silent and very wearying riding.

Cool night with a strong breeze which turned definitely cold just about the time the morning star got up. Had to put on my saddle blanket then.

17.5.31

Rose 4.30, rode 5.15. Very short ride. We were within three miles of Ribda wells, which we reached at 6.15. A wide wadi runs all the way from Jebel Haraza under various names. The wadi is extremely sandy and full of ushur bush of great size.

---

[40] (Warrants of) authority or jurisdiction granted by the government.
[41] Literally rulers (sing.: *sultan*); those with authority.

The police set me under a mukeita tree. I talked to Muhammad Musa about the Kababish tents and how they are planned for a family to live in. (I was thinking of more things he had said to me last night: how he had married once in his youth and the girl proved barren, so he divorced her and married his present wife, by whom he had a daughter (since dead) and a son about my age. He had never, he said, taken a second wife—too expensive. Muhammad Musa is the sort of poor country-squire type—of the best family, but cannot afford to hunt, and shoots only his own few acres and when invited by friends. . . .

All tents have four "shei'bas"[42] in middle and in front. Big tents have 12 ropes instead of ten. When they move, the men help roll up the tent and load it on a camel (one load with the she'bas [sic]). The wife is responsible for her utfa (litter) once the men have saddled it onto the camel. When they reach the new camping ground, the women build the tent with the slave girls. The men never assist, unless slaves and sisters and daughters are entirely lacking to the women.

The cook then came to say the Arabs would give him no milk. "Should we buy?" I said, "Yes". But Muhammad Musa said, "God forbid! This is where I get up", and went off.

I wandered down to the wells and talked to Ribeigaat [sic] and Jaalin. There are also here Howawir. Camels and sheep on the wells were very fat, but cows in poor condition. There had been cattle plague here, they say.

Sausages for breakfast, first time since leaving Soderi. Had a bath under cover of wind-screen (ground sheet and blanket set up on branches by the police.) Cool but windy and good deal of dust till 10 a.m. Read, slept, had lunch. Had tea at 4 and then played golf up the wadi. Began badly, but later played a very good hole in 3. (Would have been 2 if I had not pulled slightly.) Further up, after the turn, I unfortunately lost a ball down a jackal's hole (remains one ball only).

Muhammad Musa came and drank more tea and lemon. I asked him if it was considered a bad thing among the Kababish to count men, animals, wells, etc. He said, "Very". (I had counted the wells this morning and then suddenly remembered.) He said many people's herds had suffered severely as a result of the herd-counting in 1917. We went on to talk of the evil eye, and the methods and signs for warding it off. (I haven't them all clear in my head yet.) Then I said, "Did the Nurab eat from taxes as well as from fines?" and he said, "No".

He said that he had sent word for Sheikh Musa Kurfees . . . of the Ribeigat to come and see me and perhaps be appointed wakil in this

---

[42] Arabic pl.: *shi'ab*, poles.

neighbourhood. We talked of Ali Kheirallah, who apparently has only one son (small boy). His daughter's son is now a young man (she married her cousin). After he had gone I went to look at the camels and then sat and read the Ruwala till 8.30, dined, and slept till 5.30. Cold night.

18.5.31

A very pleasant and cool morning. After bath [and] breakfast, Muhammad Musa and his companion came and drank tea. . . . In the Kharif[43] and derat,[44] when the camels have been long without salt and the owner has plenty, the camels are brought to water in the morning, stay all day on the water drinking salt, are haltered by the water, drink the rest of the salt next morning until "diha",[45] and then "Sadiran"[46] (go up from water). . . . At other seasons camels always come to water in the morning and go away in the afternoons.

Read more Ruwala and went to look at the wells. The Atawia were repairing one of theirs where sand had fallen in. Further over, certain Howawir were fairly chatty. They had some very fair wenches drawing water. This is an excellent cool day with a northerly breeze.

Sheikh Musa Kurfees is reported by his daughter to have a belly-ache and therefore to be unable to come and see me.

A rather "miskeen"[47] merchant here presented me with a bottle of honey. I gave him a tin of fruit in exchange with which he was greatly pleased. The afternoon passed rather slowly. I greatly perturbed the Shawish by attempting to draw a camel. Started riding at 5 p.m. and by 6.45 had reached Habisa. Very easy going all the way and rode quite fast. Poor grazing where we camped. Could not get to sleep. Tried translating one or two of the songs collected by John Hillard.

19.5.31

Pleasant cool morning. Went down to the wells before breakfast. Muhammad Musa caught me up on the way there and walked round with me. We found Sureih and some Barara. I talked to him about sheep shearing. Apparently the Arabs here shear twice a year—end of rains and about now. The wool is cleared of haskaneet and ticks after shearing, with combs. The women then spin, rolling the spindle on their thighs. Arabs sometimes sell or give wool to one another but never to merchants. A young Ribeygi was much amused at our conversation. The cows here

---

[43] Literally autumn; in Kordofan, rainy season.
[44] The rains.
[45] Forenoon.
[46] Arabic: *sadara*, to proceed.
[47] Poor.

looked better than those at Ribda, but I was told that cattle plague has appeared at Habisa three days ago. They tried to get me to make some declaration about re-listing cows as a consequence of the plague: but I said plague was still going on and I did not propose to do anything till it ended.

When we returned to camp, we found Sheikh Ahmad Es Sherif [sic] of the Howawir, who had come to get two gun licenses [sic] renewed. Adam Abdallah had gone off to Gambir to collect tax from the recalcitrant Robab, and Nimr will join him there in three or four days time.

Later an ancient called Adam Ed Dish of the Um Sureih turned up, closely followed by one of the oldest women I have ever seen. Adam had most kindly brought in a sheep. He is an "ajwad" (counsellor) of his section and a man with a great reputation for uprightness and generosity. A very nice old bloke. He suffers from lumbago. I suggested ironing (with a hot stone as there are no irons here) by his wife. This led the talk to the fact that he has no sons and his married daughters will not do anything for him, so that he is much busied with his flocks. Muhammad Musa suggested to him that he should marry again. But he said "No. No girls in the tribe [are] free and [all are] too expensive. They all want tea and sugar now-a-days." On which he turned to me and said that sugar was ruining the people, who will spend too much money on it.

He drank what I gave him without much relish. The old woman refused to drink, explaining (what I had forgotten) that it would be very bad form for her to do so in the presence of men.[48]

Later in the morning, about 1.30, when I was having a doze, Muhammad Musa came with two chaps who had a case and letters from Sheikh Musa Kurfees. A certain Fadlallah, a youth of the Shaigia, is serving as herdsman with Awad Es Sid Abd El Hadi of the Um Sureih Kababish. Fadlallah had a fight with the son of another of the Um Sureih, Abdallah Suleiman. Fadlallah and Abdallah went before Musa Kurfees, who made Abdallah pay Fadlallah one sheep (because Abdallah's son had split Fadlallah's crown). Musa also fined Abdallah £E5 for his son's misdeed. Musa, incidentally, so far as I can find out, has no legal right to fine anyone (I cannot even discover from Muhammad Musa that he has a natural right as sheikh of the Um Sureih). Fadlallah then again made a row with Abdallah and again appeared before Musa, who has now sent him to me. Such a pity Musa chose to have a belly-ache. I sent the two chaps to sit with the police. An awkward situation now arises. Muhammad Musa said that he recommended making Abdallah pay another sheep to Fadlallah, as one is insufficient blood-money for the wounds inflicted; making Abdallah produce the £E5 and give it to Muhammad Musa for Sheikh Ali

---

[48] See Talal Asad, *The Kababish*, 39.

El Tom, who alone is legally allowed to "eat" fines in Dar El Kababish; and sending Abdallah with a note from me to Musa Kurfees. . . .

Please God, Musa Kurfees and Abdallah will meet us at Id El Kheil tomorrow. I proceeded to write the note and Muhammad Musa to re-hear the case in part, because Musa Kurfees wanted to push Fadlallah and his quite blameless brother (serving with another Ribeygi) out of Dar El Kababish.

The letter went off at 4.15 and strict instructions were given to Abdallah that he was to tell Musa Kurfees not to have it read to him except in private; and, if he had not a feki handy, then to take the note and bring it to me unopened.

Started 5 p.m. Easy riding over sand hills. Direction E.S.E. Talked to Muhammad Musa, asking him was it the custom for a stranger among the Kababish to find himself an "Akhu",[49] a neighbour who should be responsible for protecting him. He said that was so [and] instanced the present case of this morning and said that all the Jaaliin in this neighbourhood were under the protection of the Ribeygat. We also talked sheep. Sheep lamb twice a year, at the end of the rains and beginning of summer. Summer lambs are looked after in the tents—do not go out to graze at first, for sheep, at this time of year, may be watering only every fifth day. He again alluded to MacMichael's advice to them a long time ago to breed sheep and cows rather than camels. Muhammad Musa was much surprised of my accounts of herding with Southdown or Collie sheep dogs. "Why would not I bring one out here?" I said that I thought that, as the dogs are long-haired, the heat and the haskaneet would be too much for them.

The hamla had not reached Id El Kheil but stopped in a pleasant wadi at 5.30. We reached them at 6.30. I was a little surprised, and finding after supper that the Shawish proposed to start at 5.30 a.m., and that therefore Id El Kheil must be near, I sent for him to inquire what was wrong. He said he had told them to stop on grass for the camels, and that there was not grass ahead. Cool night.

20.5.31

Reached Id El Kheil 6.30 a.m. Pleasant wadi.
(1) Abdallah Fadlallah Niama   is listed for 22 cows.
(2) Muhammad Zaid Muhammad ″   ″   ″   14 cows.
Both are Hamdab Awlad Ugba (Sheikh Musa Jelli). They state they have no animals except cows. (2) states that since the listing his cows have increased and that 25 have now died of disease and he has *10 left*. Abdallah states that he has only 2 left.

---

[49] Literally, brother.

Hamid Isa Fadlallah complains that one Abu Anga, a slave herding with Sheikh Salih Muhammad Araki, has stolen two of his sheep. Abu Anga is at Abu Ameira.

I went up the wadi to see the wells about 10 a.m. In front of me I saw Sh. Muhammad Musa and another and the policeman Ajeeb. They saw me and their companions came to salute me. The leader of them proved to be Sheikh Salih Gumaa El Bey, a Nurabi who lives here. Salih had married some years ago Ajeeb's sister and his sons resemble Ajeeb.

I went with Ajeeb to look at men digging wells and drawing water from wells in the khor of the wadi, which had run with the rain of the day and were at Hasan Khalifa's. Plenty of water. Cheery blokes and pretty girls—one a fizzer. Animals in fair condition. Returned to my tree and slept, then felt very hungry and sent for coffee.

About 1.30 p.m. (the worst time) Muhammad Musa turned up with the man Abdallah Suleiman, of the case concerning Musa Kurfees's probably illegal judgment, and others. . . .

Abdallah brought a letter from Musa Kurfees in which he said that he had permission from Ali El Tom to judge cases up to £E5 and he was too ill to see me. I sent them away, had lunch, and proceeded to write a letter to Musa Kurfees, acknowledging receipt of five pounds for Sh. Ali El Tom and saying that Musa could do what he liked about sending Fadlallah and his brother out of the Dar. I was in the middle of this when Abdallah Suleiman popped out, as it were, from the wadi, produced a pound of silver and said, "Sheikh Musa says 'Salaam'[50] and don't tell anyone". I said, "What? is this part of the five pounds?" "No", says he, "Sheikh Musa's salaams and don't say anything."

This was all very awkward and intensely annoying. I left the money on my table and pushed him off.

(1) The principle is that all Arabs must be shown that D.C.s don't take gifts or bribes secretly.
(2) Another principle is that one must save a Sheikh's face always, unless one is going to break him entirely.
(3) Arabs continually offer presents, it being their way of polite approach. We never accept presents, but we allow them to give us milk and to slaughter animals for our entourage when we are the Arabs' guests. What to them is the difference between a present of money and a present of a bowl of milk except in quantity and value?
(4) But, in (3), I speak of gifts offered openly, not secretly.
(5) Musa Kurfees has been sheikh since early after 1899. It may be true he has seldom seen Englishmen, but in thirty years of this government

---

[50] "Peace"; greetings.

surely he must have heard the astonishing news that the English don't take bribes and actually punish the givers of bribes.

(6) Was the one pound, then, a gift in lieu of Diafa—food offered to a guest (as I had not been to see him)—or a bribe? Musa, if charged, can easily say, "Intended as an open honest gift: but my messenger bungled it. I never told him to tell the D.C. not to say anything". If a bribe—motive? I had, in my letter, asked him to explain why he had "hukm"ed Abdallah (a) pointing out that Musa had no "sulta" (b) asking, "Had he permission from Ali El Tom?" If his answer to (b) is true, he should have nothing to fear, but (a) might have frightened him. If his answer to (b) was untrue, and I suspect from Muhammad Musa's attitude it is, then Musa Kurfees has every reason to try to bribe me to keep the matter from Ali El Tom and from the government. Then, why choose Abdallah, whom Musa had illegally "hukmed", as messenger? How was Abdallah to know why Musa was sending me one pound? And what other messenger could he find without being conspicuous? I was therefore pretty certain the one pound was intended as hush money. *But* this afternoon I failed, unfortunately, to be clear as to Abdallah's function as mere cat's paw.

I determined, rightly or wrongly, (1) that it was essential to leave no opening for Abdallah or Musa to say I had taken the money. Therefore I must have two witnesses to my handing it back to Abdallah. (2) It was essential that all the money must get back to Musa and as *inconspicuously as possible*, so as to save his face if necessary.

Therefore I must frighten Abdallah (and my witnesses) sufficiently to ensure that none of them "eat" any of the money on the way, and that a note from me to Musa reaches him immediately, saying I had refused and returned the cash. The question of what action to take as regards Musa I did not feel I could decide on the spur of the moment, with my hamla shidding up (as it then was), but I felt that strong action, even if necessary, should and could be taken only through and after consultation with Sheikh Ali El Tom. I thought of returning to Ribda to see Musa Kurfees, but (a) Muhammad Musa pointed out we could not now afford the time (b) If Musa proved not to be ill, things would be worse than they now are (c) If he is ill, it would be an abominable burden to him, my turning up. (d) It would make the thing conspicuous, and (e) I should have to decide whether government will punish him before seeing (and his guilt on the bribery charge somewhat depends on his guilt on the question of the "hukm").

I therefore talked to Muhammad Musa. He was at first astonished, indeed amazed, when he saw the money, and then, when I said it was a bad offence, he naturally began to excuse Musa (and rightly so from his point of view). Muhammad Musa said that Musa Kurfees had no right to "hukm", had done so before, and had been punished for it by Ali El Tom.

I then sent for Abdallah Suleiman and explained to him before Muhammad Musa the government law of bribery (a beastly business), pointing out that he was also liable as accessory. He was very frightened and swore that he would return the money before witnesses without saying what the money was (which was what I wanted). Then I handed back the money in the presence of Sh. Muhammad Musa and the Shawish, both of whom I requested to say nothing of the matter to anyone for the present, after I had explained what had happened. In talking of the penalties for bribery I may, in my vexation, have said too much. This occasion is the nearest I have come to losing my temper since I came to this district. I then concluded my letter to Musa Kurfees . . . which I gave to Muhammad Musa for Abdallah.

We rode at 4.15 over a good deal of stone and reached the hamla at 6.45. I felt very gloomy and worried. Muhammad Musa, like a gentleman, tried to cheer me up by talking to me of his own accord (which he does not usually do), of which parts of animals Englishmen will eat. Tripes? Yes.

Slept in mediocre fashion. Woke very depressed.

21.5.31

Rose 4.15. Rode from about 5.15 to 8.15, when we found the hamla in another wadi. Slept and decided that, if I came to the conclusion that no action need be taken about the bribe, I would send . . . a letter of pardon and explanation of the law and regulations governing bribes, gifts, and "diafa" dated 22nd May. . . . Then I wrote the foregoing four pages of this diary.

This morning's ride was most depressing—stony ground all the way, little grass and my mind revolving on yesterday's events, reflecting that I had probably made a mess of it and concluding I would never make a D.C.

Very hot noon. Rode 4.30 to 6.45. Much easier going. Found the hamla after we had crossed animal tracks leading to Um Inderaba meshra. I had Muhammad Musa to tea and, after a good deal of talk about stars and anything that came into my head, explained what I proposed to do in the case of Musa Kurfees. I explained, too, how Adam Hasan, Nazir of the Northern Gawamaa, had but recently been dismissed for taking bribes.

22.5.31

Started 5 a.m. The distance proved much longer than the guide had supposed. We did not reach Um Inderaba till after 8 and then found that the hamla had not yet unloaded, having disagreed as to where to set down under the trees.

By the locust poison dump we found a merchant named Ismain [*sic*] Hasan, a cheery bird, a Muwallad[51] of Berber. I went to look at the wells and then sat in the merchant's grass hut and chatted for a while. He said that Eric Penn[52] (D.C. Khartoum North) had come here to meet me about 8 days ago and then gone, leaving police, who also left after 3 days. Ali Kheirallah had not met him. Penn had brought Ali Nasir with him in his car. Ali Kheirallah is said to be ill with pains in the back; at any rate he was when Penn was here.

There was little shade and the wind got up, so I had the ghaffir of the poison-bait dump clear me a grass hut. There I had my bath and afterwards set up my table and chairs.

There is no grazing here. The trees have been grazed off, as to their lower branches by animals coming to water, and no grass. Our camels are, therefore, to be sent north about six miles to grazing near the tents of Id Beliila [*sic*], a serf of the Nurab who lives partly here and partly in Omdurman. Id will carry letters to Omdurman for me tomorrow. Ali Kheirallah may come in tomorrow if he is not ill. Spent the rest of the day until 4 writing letters.

After tea played golf—one good hole (ant hill) in two, but my last ball is now splitting. Started reading Hogarth's *Penetration of Arabia*.[53] To bed at 8 and slept till 4 a.m.

23.5.31

Rose 5.45. Stoutness exercises and bath (waist measurement appears no larger than when I left Khartoum—measurement by belt).

Muhammad Musa came and talked and I gave him the note for Musa Kurfees, after reading it to him and making quite clear what was intended. I do not think Muhammad Musa can possibly misunderstand. I said if, in his opinion, it would not damage Musa K.'s prestige to have this letter read to him, then Muhammad Musa is to send it now. If otherwise, then Muhammad Musa shall go and see Musa K. on his way back from Omdurman. There is of course a risk that Muhammad Musa or the Shawish may blackmail Musa K. But I have had to take that risk.

Ahmad El Aisar came and we three drank coffee. Then I had breakfast.

Ali Kheirallah has arrived in person. About 10.30 Ali Kheirallah came

---

[51] One born in the Sudan but of foreign or mixed ancestry.
[52] A. E. D. Penn, SPS 1925–51. *SPS*, 47.
[53] London 1904.

to see me together with Sheikhs Musa Fadlallah, Bakhit Jadallah and Abdallah Muhammad (of branches of the Awlad Ugba) and El Amin Rabih El Amin (Barooda), Ali Kheirallah's daughter's son, who is his agent. This last seemed a nice lad—very quiet, of course, in the presence of his grandfather. Ali Kheirallah's back seemed very sore and stiff. After prolonged salutations he spoke (1) of the Hassania cultivators alongside the Awlad Ugba in the White Nile Province. About this I have already written to Humph. (John Humphry[54] of the White Nile) (2) The wood at Um Inderaba, which he says is like a garden to his tribe, for the products of its trees, edible by man and beast. He complains that people from the river are cutting fire wood and damaging trees, and he wants me to order that no such cutting take place. Products are: alleif, nabak, meikah, mukheita.[55] He says people also steal the timber used by the Arabs and left standing by them when they move out in the rains (3) The Gumuiya agreement, of which he wants a copy. Arranged that the merchant come and make one tomorrow.

The Arabs then talked generally of distances and camel marches, and, as Ali Kheirallah's back seemed to be paining him, I closed the meeting. They left about 11.50. The noon was very hot and sticky and heavy clouds appeared to the east and south. I found it too trying to do anything except make a pretense of reading till 5 p.m. I then went out and played golf from ant-hill to ant-hill.

Went to bed early but could not get to sleep for a long time owing to the heat. Nor could my following sleep. They talked long into the night.

24.5.31

Rose very weary at 5.30. Went to see the wells. Muhammad Musa joined me and soon the three sheikhs I had met yesterday. Saw a very pretty girl of 14 or 15 who was drawing water with her young brother at one well. . . .

Some wells here are particularised. At some the "dimi" alternates. And this is the case also with wells of the strangers—Gumuiya and Kawahla. I specially went around the southeast side of the well-field where most of the strangers are. Bakhit Jadallah incautiously pointed out a newly-dug well (evidently contrary to Sheikh Ali El Tom's orders). The sheikhs said that the well-known old associates with the Kababish from the Gumuiya and the Kawahla come every year nearly always to the same well. Men

---

[54] J. N. Humphry, SPS 1920–46. *SPS*, 33.
[55] *Nabak: Ziziphus spinachristi.* (a shrub or tree with edible fruit, branches used for thatching, and wood for building and fuel). Tothill, 950; *maykah: Dobera roxburghii.* BM, 219; *mukhayt: Boscia octandra.* BM 50. See Glossary for variant spellings.

who behave badly come once or twice and are turned away by Ali Kheirallah. Returned to breakfast.

Later, Ali Kheirallah and the rest turned up and the merchant, Ismain Hasan, copied (rather badly) the text of the agreement which I read to him. The others soon after left and I chatted with Ali Kheirallah about a case (now finished by him) and the Gumuiya. He seemed quite pleased with Ali Nasir for saying during his recent visit to Ali Kheirallah, "If any Gumui breaks the agreement, do not hesitate to send him to me". Ali Kheirallah said that relations between the tribes are now happy.

Then we talked slavery (raised by him). He asked, "Would it be possible to let the slaves who want to run stay in the tribe apart from their masters?" I said that was just what the government wanted and instanced cases where this is being done. The trouble here is, says Ali Kheirallah, they can run to Omdurman or the Gezira Scheme and they never come back. For this, of course, there is no remedy. . . . We talked also of the price of sheep and present fall of all prices, especially cotton, and the collapse of the Howashat[56] (i.e. the Gezira Cotton Scheme). He left at 10.30. It was already very hot.

By 11 it was apparent that this was going to be the hottest day we've had yet, and so it was. I gave up the ghost from 11 to 5—could manage only a little reading and about half an hour's attempt at writing. At 4.30 it was still blazing hot. At 5.15 I played a round of golf (the cover of the ball is now half off). And, at 6.15 rejoiced in the sunset and had a bath.

Warm evening. Remarkable to think that in 15 days I may be in England and not sitting outside an overheated durra-stalk hut with the noise of a slave girl grinding corn behind me. Muhammad had ruined the soup. Dined on little. Read some more of Hogarth until 9.30 and then tried to get to sleep. Very warm night. What is a "sabara",[57] is it a mongoose?

25.5.31

Rose at 5. At about 8.30 our camels arrived from the grazing to go to water. So I left my hut to go and see them watered on the wells. A wind had sprung up about 7 and by 8.30 a fair dust storm was blowing. I wandered about the wells for half an hour with El Amin Barooda, Muhammad Musa and others. I remarked a very fine bull at one well. This meshra, they say, is 40 years old but the wells at Um Sidr are 70 years old.

---

[56] Colloquial: a land-holding; in the Gezira Scheme, a tenancy. The Depression-era crash of the world cotton market and Sudanese yields left the debt-ridden scheme a liability for the Sudan Government and forced severe retrenchment in government expenditure. See below, pp.

[57] A type of fox.

On my way back to my hut, I found "my aged uncle",[58] Ali Kheirallah, sitting on a sheepskin under a tree with the police and Arabs all round. I prevented him from rising (on account of his back) and sat and talked with him for a few moments.

The wind made the day much cooler than yesterday. I sat and read in fair comfort. After lunch, and after the hamla had left, Ali Kheirallah came with others to say "Good-bye" to me. He paid the usual Oriental compliments saying, as he had said before, that the Arabs, like cattle, shy from a man of loud voice and harsh temper, but like their District Commissioners to be quiet mannered. This led him to speak of the fight with the Gumuiya 6 years ago (referred to by Ali Kheirallah as. . . . "the year of the areoplanes") when, he said, government came down on him with aeroplanes and motor cars with 40 police in them and effendis. He took fright and flight to Sheikh Ali El Tom and so to El Obeid.

Sheikh Bakhit brought me samples of the fruit of the Meykah [sic] tree and Ali Kheirallah showed me how to break the cortice, eat the red lining and then break the kernel and expose the green seed, which smells like French beans and is eaten when the Arabs have a famine year.

We then talked of MacMic's statement to Ali El Tom that all Arabs who did not come from Dongola are not real Arabs, and Ali Kheirallah expatiated on the ancestry and origin of the Awlad Ugba, and I upon the ancient kingdom (Christian) of Dongola. After that he took his leave.

Bakhit stayed to ask if there were any government method of stopping a fool from wasting his wealth, and I said I knew of none and recommended him to resort to Ali El Tom.

At 4.30 we rode. Easy going over hard sand through scrub over more or less featureless country. Camels, well-watered, went fast and showed no fatigue. We passed Wadi Abu Kitr at 6.30 and found the hamla beside Golaat El Jihadi. *N.B.* The lemon-scented trees near Gashda are called Um Rueihiin—the women use them for scenting themselves.

Cool night but did not get to sleep for some time. Sheikh Muhammad Musa was singing and the men talking in anticipation of the journey's end. I heard some Arabs driving cows come up and pass near by.

26.5.31

Rose 4.30. Rode 5.15 till 7.15. Shawish says we are making short shidds because Omdurman is not 4 more shidds away and we don't want to get in before 28th. morning. We passed the cow herds we had heard in the night, on the road. Evidently they were going to market. Gailed in a wadi (rather pleasant with sammar and merkh trees) just south of a Jebel called,

---

[58] An allusion to Edward Lear's "Incidents in the life of my uncle Arly".

they say, Garamrueih. Sardines for breakfast. Felt lackadaisical and wrote a letter to Tom Blofield. Comparatively cool day.

After the hamla had left, Muhammad Musa came to talk to me. He had not, he said, completed the business of "hukming" the blokes who dug wells contrary to Ali El Tom's orders. They appear to be somewhat bolshy; having refused Ali Kheirallah's orders and Salim Belal's, they are now disputing with Muhammad Musa. Muhammad Musa says that Ali Kheirallah has "sulta" from Sheikh Ali El Tom, but is afraid to use it now on the Awlad Ugba. We both lamented the influence of proximity to Omdurman on the Awlad Ugba and the Robab.

Rode 4.30 to 6.30 and found the hamla on the south of Fattasha wells. Passed sheep going to market. Muhammad Musa drank tea; but I was too tired for much talk.

From here the lights of Omdurman are visible in the northeastern sky.

27.5.31

Woke when the hamla went off at 3.30. Rode until 7 through Fattasha wells with Jebel Barok in front. After passing the wells we came out onto the motor road to Mageru and Um Inderaba: and then gailed in some grass huts in Wadi Barok.

From here Jebel Abu Marawi west of Omdurman is visible. Sausages for breakfast. Last bangers.

Chapter V

Among the Nuba, Kawahla, and Kababish

[Soderi—Abu 'Ajaja—Sanaqir—Khawr al-Sunt—Umm Badr—Umm Qawzayn—Abu Bassama—Umm Khirwa'—Soderi]

26.9.31

The day of starting on a trek is always one on which I wish I could temporarily disappear. This one, however, was remarkably orderly, because no one had been rushed at all and preparations had gone on for some days beforehand. I had slept pretty heavily the night before thanks to dope. But felt not too grand in the tummy—due to the weather, or lime juice, or quinine or something.

The morning passed very rapidly—lunch was vilely cooked and beastly, and rapidly dealt with. Then of course the Omda Nadif managed to produce a case at the last minute, a bloke who had threatened another bloke over a woman. Nadif wanted him to swear to keep the peace, but he would not accept the merkaz Koran as good enough. Altogether Nadif was a bit unreasonable, but I backed him up and said the man (a stranger from Kaja Seruj) had better live in Soderi and go to his cultivation from there and see me in two months' time. I hate being plumped with anything at the last minute. Wrote various notes.

Started at 4.15, seen off by Abdalla [*sic*], the accountant, Yasin, the translator, Omda Nadif Mukhawi, Omda Rabah Safi, a couple of merchants and old Sheikh Soghayroon. Passed through several swarms of hopping "kaboora" locusts. It was hot: felt pretty bored.

The big migratory storks, which are here in great numbers, are called, says Tingle, "Kaljoo" here in Kordofan, but "Simbir" on the river. The Arabs say this bird and one other only migrate across the "Salt Sea", i.e. Mediterranean. They're wrong of course. Nadif said today, "pity you don't bring your wife out—then you wouldn't move about so much." Hum.

Arrived at dusk at Sileya, a village—Sheikh El Mahi Ahmad. Calm evening. Sheikh came and chatted. There is due to be an eclipse of the moon tonight and it is nearly full.

Slept pretty badly and therefore had a fine view of the eclipse.

Chapter V

27.9.31

Hamla started about 3 a.m. and I at 5.45. It was quite cool but I hated getting up. Passed four swarms of small kaboora—mostly less than a week old. Third swarm, by Jebel Bakalai, was the largest in numbers.

Found the tent pitched by the small Nuba village (before one comes to Abu Ajaja wells) where I met the Omda Tichu in the night last April on my way back to Soderi. The village belongs to one Id Sumain, wakil of the Omda, who appeared at the tent to greet me.

After breakfast I went out and found more small locusts. They appear to be hatching out in this neighbourhood. Had a shave and felt better.

Id Sumain came to talk to me. He himself and his family are Kaja Aried, but owing to locality have been joined onto the Hufra Omodia. His son Muhammad is Sheikh. His son Muhammad Ahmad (second son) had just died when I arrived last April. Id talked long about this son and his last illness and said that he had been a better man than either of the other two. I made suitable comments. He has a third son, Muhammad Ali.

Id spoke regarding the Poll Tax due on his dead son, that he had requested the Mamur to strike the name off. Memo.: see what the answer is.

We went on to talk of local sources of cash and to comment how bad this year is. The Kaja here have three sources of money: gum, sale of cattle, [and] sale of corn. The price of gum dropped to nothing a year ago. Just here they are short of grain, having had a bad season last year and little rain this. (Hufra has had more rain than fell here.) Bullocks are now fetching 41 to 60 PT only, whereas last year they would fetch 80 PT to £E1. The Nubas here sell mostly to Hamar and Meganin who want bulls for "karama" (i.e. slaughtering for weddings, funerals, births and circumcisions etc.). But these tribes also are hard up for money now. Otherwise Nuba sell in El Obeid. Id could not quote me El Obeid prices. He said no one had sold there lately.

He said folk are all afraid of cattle plague infection and the only animal which will fetch a price is a cow which has recovered from the disease—which may fetch £E2. Cattle plague has broken out at Hufra afresh. Id says he hears there is an order in Nahud that Northern Kordofan cattle shall not be sold in that market. I asked (1) If the Kaja kept sheep. He said, "A few. They used to keep large herds, but they became fed up with looking after them, especially at night, and so turned them all into cattle, which", he said, "was foolish because sheep sell readily and don't have so many diseases". Price of goats, he says, is down to 6 PT. True? (2) . . . "Did Kaja from here hire themselves out to Arabs much as herdsmen, when they are hard up?" He said "No, not from here, but people of Um Darrag [*sic*] and Haraza do". I asked why—did the Arabs dislike Hufra people? Oh no! he said, merely Hufra people don't go herding: if hard up they cultivate.

After he had politely sipped three cups of coffee, he went off saying that, when my hamla started, he would bring a bucket and get a boy to give us water from Abu Ajaja wells.

I arranged for the Veterinary policeman who is with me and has serum for about 96 cattle, to go to Hufra and rejoin me later.

N.B. Id, commenting on Omda Tamar Agha's death, said people of Katul differ among themselves as to which one of his two sons they wish to succeed him.

Read and wrote. At 1 p.m. a thunderstorm broke and a sharp shower fell on us for 20 minutes. Had lunch. Rain returned. At 3 p.m. we were between two storms to east and west and large drops were falling. So I decided we had better stay for the night. No more rain fell on us (of course) but storms went on all around us. The thunder atmosphere induced in me great depression but at 4.30 I pulled the body together, started translating for myself some of the evidence in the kidnapping case, and called for tea. The Cow and Gate ("Babies Love It") was opened for the first time—great success —much better than tinned milk. About 5.30 p.m. I looked out and saw a magnificent storm cloud over towards Soderi. I tried to draw it and stuck in Jebel Bakalai to give it a dark foreground. The result looks like nothing on earth, but it was amusing to do. I wish there was someone here who could paint the colours of these clouds—very transparent gold turning to [a] crimson lake in the sunset and extraordinary mauves and greys below.

The night was cool. Rain was falling to the west, and occasionally lightning showed in the east. I read, after taking my supper, till about 8.30 and then slept extremely well till 4.30 a.m.

28.9.31

We were on the road by 5 a.m. [and] crossed the depression in which the Abu Ajaja wells lie by moonlight, and the sun came up before we were mounting the sand-dunes on the far side. The saltish shrub the camels like so much here is called "Ikhreit". We rode on over the sandhills very bumpily till 8.20, when we reached camp. The sun had become quite warm, so that I threw off everything but a vest (it had been cool enough for a great coat early). But so soon as we got in, the sky became overcast and I wore my greatcoat at breakfast in the tent. The weather became sticky though fairly cool by 11, and small black flies in great numbers were a ticklish nuisance. No wind. That grass which was so annoying in the cars on the way to Soderi is called "same'na".[1]

---

[1] *Aristida plumosa*. Massey, 41.

N.B. Referring to certain men whom Tichu sent to have summonsed to be made to pay their fines, Id said, "They aren't disobedient, they merely have nothing to pay with." A point to keep in mind this year. Might be worth warning sheikhs with powers to make their fines light.

The new camel bought from Hamilton is certainly swift but not quite so smooth as I had hoped. However, it had little chance of showing smoothness today, the ground being up and down and very rough.

Read files and put papers in order. At lunch time the small flies became pestilential and remained so after the tent had been taken down and the hamla had left me under a tree about 3 p.m.

Rode at 4.15 and reached a point not far from Sanagir just before sunset. Many bugs and a hot night. Dreamed, among other things, that I was playing cricket and fielding on Agar's Plough between three pitches —always dreaded I'd have to do that—and woke with a caterpillar crawling on my cheek.

29.9.31

Rose 4.30 a.m. rode at 5. When I arrived at Jebel Sanagir I took a look at the well which had been in building when I was last here. It is finished, and also another less deep one just close to the old locust huts. Everything is very green and there is a considerable amount of standing water, from which our camels drank. We then crossed one of the passes over the jebel. When we had descended the other side there appeared no sign of the hamla's track. By this time, however, it was getting pretty warm, and I soon stopped the leading bobby and waited to see if Tingle would come up. He didn't, but by good fortune we heard one of those long-pitched screams the folk use to attract attention, rode towards it and found the camp. Tingle did not appear—others were sent searching for him and he arrived after 11 a.m., having been goodness knows where back-tracking. I had arrived at 9 a.m. The hamla had crossed the jebel at a pass lower down towards the south, and hence we had missed the tracks.

Camp in among large trees. In view of the accident of the morning which will have tired the police camels, I decided not to go on till morning.

Whether from overdose of Plasmoquin[2] or sun, I have had a head the last two days. I think it's Plasmoquin, so I shall reduce the dose from the standard quantity, for this is almost as bad as having the malaria instead of the prophylactic. Only bits of the "head" left by lunch time. Lying down had done it good. This is a sticky day but there is some breeze.

An Arab this morning at the water in Senagir [*sic*] said Jumaa Sahal's

---

[2] Pamaquine naphthoate, an anti-malarial. *The Merck Index*, para. 6953.

sheep are beyond Jebel Gaili. On the other hand two Arabs met yesterday evening said Jumaa is at Um Kuhl, a long way off.

The day closed pretty sticky. There was standing water in pools close by, so that the mosquitoes were very numerous. Muhammad Sadig has malaria already—he is always the first to get it.

Slept early (8 p.m.) and well until the hamla starting woke me at 2.45 a.m. It was quite cool then and there was a heavy dew.

30.9.31

Started 5.15 and rode over Zolot Um Khusus to a wadi on the far side. Arrived 9 a.m. My camel nearly trod on a black snake about 5 feet long.

There is much "bigheil" grass here. It is like a low Scots thistle and has a deep blue flower which is out just now. There is a creeper which has a brilliant orange-red fruit, something like the Japanese lantern plant. They call it "maghed". It is eaten raw and said to be very sweet. There is also a grass like bracken in appearance. Pleasant N.W. wind today. Weather felt more like the approach of winter. Two Arabs of the Ribeygat arrived and asked for quinine. They said the rains were good but that there was much disease among animals: cattle plague had done a lot of damage, and a sheep disease (foot rot I think). They also said one Hasan Abdullah of their clan had had money stolen by a Magnuni and had gone to Jumaa Sahal to complain. A pleasant north wind all the morning and afternoon.

Looked at papers and noted the dreadful state of the Herd Tax. How are the nomads going to pay with the prices of animals down by 50% and often no sale for camels at all?

Muhammad Sadig's fever is no better.

Hamla left at 3 p.m. I then tried drawing some "bigheil" grass for the blue flowers. A dismal failure, mainly owing to the paper on which I tried drawing. In future I'm going to use government stuff. It is the only smooth paper I have, owing to stupidity in mislaying S.'s sketch book.

Started 4.15. No sooner started than we found a pool and in it geese, but also sacred ibis. I mustn't shoot the ibis. However, luck was with me and two geese singled themselves out of the ruck, and I potted them—mere 'browning" I'm afraid, but meat for the police anyway.

The new camel *is* smooth—very. Arrived Khor Es Sunt about 5.30. The cultivations very poor and full of small hopping locusts. Old Sanduk (Box), Muhammad Fadlallah's slave left in charge of the place (only 9 slaves or so here where the big Arab summer encampment is), came to meet us. I found myself put down in almost the same spot as that where I was lodged in April when we had the horse races.

Muhammad's temperature is 102.

Many flies of all kinds by night here. Went to bed at 7.45 p.m. on that account but was still awake at 10.45. That's September done—thank God.

1.10.31

Rose 4.30 a.m. Sanduk came to see us off. A slave called Bakhit Mait (master Ahmad Jangai) came to ask for a freedom paper. Said a woman, Saida, whom he brought with her freedom paper, was his woman and he wanted his own name and her daughter's added to the paper. He said he was not "muwallad" but he remembers no other people than the Arabs. He does not want to leave Khor Es Sunt.

Apparently (evidence of Sanduk and Tingle) the Kawahla leave these slaves behind all the rains with no arrangement for them to eat at all. These are living on wild melons. (Someone produced milk from somewhere, however.) N.B. Use this to Muhammad Fadlallah, if opportunity occurs, to point out how bad his tribe are with slaves.

Reached camp at 8.30. Nothing of interest occurred. I tried another drawing of "bigheil". Not too hot a day. Hamla started at 3 p.m. and I at 4.30 approx. We reached Um Badr towards sunset. The grass is all green here still and there is much green corn standing. I had seen more "kaboora" locusts on the way.

The lake is filled to the brim and so are the two subsidiary lakes—Um Dabiib and El Wakil. The local people, slaves of the Kawahla, say there has not been such a filling for years, not even last year. So Allah has had some slight mercy in this most difficult of years. I passed through the Ababda Kawahla's summer quarters (now of course deserted except for a few recalcitrant slaves left behind when the Arabs moved west in the rains), and over the rocky hills, past the lake to the sandhill on the other side, where the camp was pitched. The Ababda slaves had welcomed me with beatings on a drum in imitation of their masters.

I arrived in camp after dark and slept early. Mosquitoes extremely bad here.

2.10.31

As I had arranged to stay the morning here I did not rise till 5.30 and at 6.30 got on a camel to look at the slaves in their villages and their cultivation. Um Badr is approximately Lat. 14 degrees 15' N. and Long. 27 degrees 57' to 28 degrees E. It has been already mentioned in this diary as the big Kawahla watering centre for the summer and such of the winter as rain water farther west in pools will not suffice for. At the moment the place is deserted except for about 200 serfs of the Kawahla who have refused to work as household slaves and herdsmen for their masters and are more or less settled around Um Badr in grass huts. The Arabs, when they are here for the summer, settle on the same spots as their serfs and set up their hair tents and build to the sunny side grass rectangular huts to give shade and coolness. These grass shelters are now left derelict. The serfs left behind have their own "sheikhs", one in each of the several villages dotted about among the hills, and there is an agent of the Nazir, also slave by birth, who is called a "Shartai"—name Farajalla.

I rode round the villages and cultivations on the west side of the lake between 6.30 and 8.30 and saw a number of the serfs. By 8.30 it was pretty hot; all the people were cultivating and so I returned to camp.

Previously I had not met and greeted Sheikh Jaafar, son of the Holy Man of Bara, Dardiri,[3] who had been staying with Ali El Tom and the Kababish. He had fever and I gave him quinine. After breakfast, one of the local merchants, who has a shop near where my camp was, came to see me. Name: Saiid Abd El Bagi, a quiet, pleasant little Dongolawi, originally from Bara. I pumped him about the economics of the Kawahla.

Tribal economics: Saiid says the Kawahla have found in the last two months that a Wad Lebun (2-to-3 year-old camel) will sell for up to £E3 in El Fasher District to Arabs (not in the town market), which is a better price than they can get in Nahud at present. In Nahud there is no sale for camels just now.

This year the carrying trade is no good. The Kawahla in past years have some of them made money on the El Obeid-El Fasher road—but this year there is nothing doing. For instance, four Ababda went from El Obeid to Nyala recently and came back empty-handed on account of the high price of grain in Nyala District.

Moreover this year there is very little merchandise on the road owing to economic depression. The price of camel hire used to be about £E1 a camel from El Obeid to El Fasher. From Um Badr to El Obeid via Soderi it is also £E1. The sack of sugar costs 23 to 25 PT for transport and a camel carries four sacks. N.B. Remember to check statements against those of Kawahla and possibly Abd El Bagi Muhammad (Saiid's father). The Kawahla, says Saiid, have not yet sold camels this year. They were waiting for the Egyptian merchants who usually come.

Saiid has a complaint that last month the Mudiria altered the plan of allowing sugar to come direct from El Obeid to Um Badr, and ordered that all sugar should go via Soderi for merchants in the west of Soderi District and be counted in Soderi. This naturally greatly increases the cost of transport and also causes his monthly allotment of sugar to arrive very belated. He said that the cause of the order is that certain merchants of Nahud and Fasher and Bara, who have agents in El Obeid have, owing to

---

[3] Dardiri Muhammad al-Khalifa, local *shaykh* of the Tijaniyya order. *BD*, 109.

hard times, been leaving part of their stock to be sold in El Obeid by their agents. Thereby El Obeid became overstocked, to the detriment of the El Obeid sugar contractors.

The rest of the morning and (bar half an hour for lunch at 3 p.m.) until 4.45 p.m. was taken up with hearing the complaints of a number of serfs.

At 4.45 p.m. I rode off to the east of the lake to see the villages and cultivations on that side. It was pleasant among the hills, but there was not time to visit all the hamlets. Farajalla went with Ahmad Beni Jerar (the lance corporal) and myself. I also looked at the Landing Ground, which must be hoed. Farajalla was asked to arrange. N.B. Farajalla, on his own account, said that nobody had been paid for the work they did on it last year. Beni Jerar said, "The money was paid to the Nazir". Farajalla rather looked down his nose. I dare say Muhammad Fadlalla, the Nazir, pocketed the cash—a mean trick if so.

Arrived back in camp after dark. A mail had come in in the morning which I hadn't had time to read properly. It contained the first letters posted since I left England. Apparently my mail has been messed up by the Khartoum Post Master, for bits of it were forwarded by John Madden.[4]

Enormous numbers of bugs of all kinds prevented either reading or writing. Got to sleep about 11.30 and was wakened by the hamla moving off at 3 a.m. Birds sang like nightingales (as at Soderi recently). I must enquire their name.

3.10.31

Rose 4.30, rode 5 a.m. We are now making for El Gadab on the Darfur frontier 27 degrees 27' E. by 14 degrees 5' N., and then Um Gozein about 12 miles farther N.W. Um Gozein is a rain lake said to be amazingly full this year. The morning was cool. Sky overcast until 11 a.m. Reached camp at 8 a.m. Very easy ride—only cool one we have had. Spent all the morning and afternoon writing mail, official and unofficial. Then, when it came to be time to ride on, I found that Tingle had sent the mail runner on with the hamla without letting me know. A little hard.

We now rode over a sand hill and then into the very thick bush known as [the Saddat] Um Kuhl. There is only one way through this: at all other points it is impenetrable (rather like the bush at Kasamor in the Butana where there were always lions). Most of the trees in Um Kuhl are maarab, which has no thorns and gives a sweet-smelling gum. It is amazing how the police find their way through. I saw no landmarks, except towards the end one Rackhamesque Tebeldi tree.

---

[4] J. F. Madden, SPS 1924–51. In 1931 he was deputy assistant civil secretary (personnel). *SPS*, 44.

We rode for about ¾ hour after getting out of the wood, over broken ground and sand hills considerably cut up by water-courses. Tingle's camel fell with him at one of these, but no damage was done. He spent some time describing to me rather amusingly the shortcomings of Skander Effendi Tadros, camel-buyer and correspondent of the "Moqattam",[5] who was in these parts buying camels two years ago. We found the camp just after sunset among thickish bush on a hillside. I finished the mail. Could not get to sleep for hours.

4.10.31

Tingle overslept and so we did not start till 6 a.m. The mail runner bobby's camel is very thin and had developed two "lahads" (bruises on the back which may lead to sore back—or not with luck). Query: was this one of the camels suspect of worms which I said should not be worked?. . . .

A cool ride through fairly thick bush. I had awakened dead beat but cheered up with the fresh air. Camp at 8.30 on fairly open ground. A big Tebeldi for the blokes to sit under. I felt excessively weary, but did an hour's work making out what men are "wanted" from the Kawahla and Kababish. Dozed a little after the hamla had gone on.

Rode at 4 p.m. We soon passed out into more open bush country with wide views on all sides of rolling plain—red sand dunes covered with bush and grass. There is very much "bigheil". . . . About 5 we came upon a herd of sheep of the Kawahla and then passed the tents of their owners who greeted me. Camp was only 300 yards further on, on the slope of a decline with Wadi El Gadab at its foot half a mile away. Muhammad Fadlallah is now only about 15 miles away at Um Heimi.

We were in camp before the sun went down, and after it had got dark, the sheikh of the ferik, one Suleiman Arbab, a very aged gentleman, came on an ass to pay me the compliments of the season. We drank tea and talked of the state of the grazing and the price of animals, and of cattle plague and of the two current cases of homicide. I said frankly that the government didn't think the Kahli had died of a blow given by the Arifi but much later and of fever.

The old man had been having fever. I gave him some quinine. He had produced a sheep for us and the police proceeded to gorge.

I went to sleep fairly [early] and slept very well. Many bugs here. Those beetles which ceaselessly push lumps of muck around and round in circles seem to me to typify in a magnificent symbol human life.

---

[5] A Cairo newspaper.

5.10.31

Started late (6 a.m.) for a short shidd. Rode over Wadi El Gadab and through fairly thick bush. The police lost the trail. Then we came upon the first herd of camels seen since I started. After some wandering, we took the direction of a camp of Arabs from a herdsman and soon came to it and the hamla together. Two Kawahla of Dar Hamid (the Nazir's section) came to meet me at a gallop on horses (one bareback) and they and another (who had recently returned from the pilgrimage to Mecca) chatted for a while pending the erection of my tent.

It was a cool morning—breeze but cloudless. I had a bath and arranged for a policeman to take on letters to Muhammad Fadlallah, the Nazir, who is at Um Heimi. They say, however, the water there is bad and drying up (i.e. it will be completely putrid), so I shall await his reply as to where to meet him.

One Ali Ezeyri of the Dar Hamid came to talk to me and drank much tea. He said among other things that the price of camels now is about 7 rials up to 13 or 14 rials. No sale at Nahud for nagas. The Kawahla are sending off camels and sheep to Omdurman for sale (25 days' march for sheep). I had my first drink of camel's milk since I set out, this morning. Ali Ezeyri said camels had decreased in number—cause for one thing fall in price—[and] an Arab has to sell more to get the money for taxes, clothes, sugar, etc.

After he had gone, I wrote notes to Muhammad Fadlallah and Omda Thabit Murgab of the Beni Jerar who is said to be with him. I read a number of notes on the district by Maclaren, had lunch, and tried painting and drawing. It is extraordinary how bored one can become with trekking through deserted country. It is a relief to be on the fringe of the Arabs and it will be better still when people turn up and I have to be busy.

Fairly cool all today. Finished reading *Montrose* and read the Arabic newspaper. Much amused by a portion of a leader which exclaimed against the immodesty of women on Tendelti platform and their showing off of their attractions. Never noticed any attractive ones there myself. Tried reading in bed under the mosquito net, with candles outside propped in my hats on top of tripods. Fell asleep and slept well till 4.30.

6.10.31

I always rejoice on the mornings when I don't have to rise before dawn and ride before breakfast. Got up at 6.15.

The Bishari camel I ride on is "Haij" (on heat) and they've tied him up on account of herds in the vicinity. I strolled out to look at a passing herd and found Nur ed Din driving our camels away from it. The Anafi has an old sore which has broken out again. The flies have been at it with the usual result. I shall have to cut it, clean and stop it: dirty job.

After breakfast there arrived Ahmad Ezeyri and talked over tea. (1) He says that camels have increased for some men and decreased for others of late. Jufaar (trypanosomiasis) has been bad the last three years or so. (2) *Tribal economics.* Talking of sheep they are sending to Omdurman, he asked how prices ran there and I said I'd heard they were better. Camels for slaughter I know nothing of. He said corn had been very dear in Nahud —9 rials' worth would not load a camel this summer. I talked of clothing and, after much hedging, got out of him (a) that people like "dumoor"[6] because it is hard-wearing (b) a suit of clothes lasts hardly a year and you can reckon a man has to buy two a year. As to food, the Kawahla don't want corn except in summer and at the end of winter when camels' milk is scarce. (Corn mainly from the Hamar villages, I think.) They have no use of cows' or sheeps' milk compared with camels'.

Camels vs. sheep. A naga is in foal 13 to 14 months and the foals dropped in winter are not usually nearly such a success as those dropped in the rains. . . . Sheep on the other hand produce young twice a year. He says this rains nearly all lambs died owing to great dampness of soil. He also said that, while sheep come in season almost as soon as they have lambed, camels take much longer. Is this correct? Apparently the Kawahla do not allow more than one stallion on heat in the herd at once. Or is it that not more than one will come on at once? At any rate the other camels are then herded apart from the nagas. You tell when a naga has conceived by the way she lifts her tail. . . . Horses among the Kawahla drink milk in the evening and are watered early morning and, if working, mid-day also.

Q.: Do Kawahla sell "samn" [clarified butter]? Said Abd El Bagi said what they sold was no use for export to El Obeid as it always went rancid on the way.

After he had gone away I read a file and the Arabic newspaper and became thoroughly bored and stupid. It was a warm day.

About 4.15 Nur ed Din turned up with the camel for dressing its sore. After that the two brothers Ezeyri both appeared and drank tea and talked especially of how camels were decreasing in numbers through tryps. and wire-worm, and many foals dying this year. Prices of two and three-year-olds only run to 4 to 8 rials—don't fetch £E2 whereas last year they would fetch £E3. And a young camel . . . will fetch £E4 to £E5 only.

Then I went to look at the horse Ahmad says he will sell me. Young, might fill out, not much to look at. Appeared sound.

---

[6] Coarse cotton cloth; homespun.

Chapter V

The younger police have been roaring with laughter most of the day. There being nothing to do they have been playing a local variety of draughts and teaching it to the cook. Wrote after dark and slept early and well.

7.10.31

Cool morning. Dressed the wound on "Grazin" (name of the small Anafi). Did some Arabic after breakfast until Ahmad Ezeyri, Sheikh Jadalla [*sic*] Abu Quran of the Kibeyshab Kababish, and a Kahli called Muhammad Ahmad Salih, who had recently been on the pilgrimage, came to talk. Jadallah will take a note for me to Sheikh Ali El Tom. They mentioned two stray Awlad Ugba nagas which Ahmad has found. One is dying and they want to slaughter her and save the meat. I enquired what the custom is. They said that, as between Kawahla and Kababish, and in the case of known brands, when animals arrive stray: (1) If you're not afraid of their being infected with disease, you take them into your herd pending the owner's arrival. (2) If you are afraid they are contagious, you hire a lad to herd them apart, pending the owner's arrival. (3) If one gets ill or breaks a leg to the point of having to be slaughtered, you slaughter it among witnesses and portion out the meat for money. When the owner arrives, you tender to him the price of the meat, and call upon the witnesses to prove your good faith.

If you don't recognise the brands on the strays, you should tell your sheikh and he, after an interval, should send the animal to the government.

They lamented the price of camels (£E1 for a full grown camel) and asked where all the money had gone to. I said, "God knows."

I talked about slaves.

The Hajj then talked about Mecca and about Ibn Saoud's government and especially his short way with thieves (decapitation), which the Arabs much admired and suggested as a good example to this lenient government. I spent the rest of this morning reading a little Arabic and the afternoon writing a note to Ali El Tom and reading a file about Jebel Meidob. A dull day.

Tingle said in the evening that there was news that Muhammad Fadlallah might arrive in the morning. I hope so: then we can move on and get busy.

Lightning to the south.

8.10.31

Slept well till about 1 a.m., when a hot wind and clouds sprang up. It felt like rain but none fell.

In the morning there arrived to see me Fadil Murjab, brother of the

Omda of the Beni Jerar, and six others. They said all was going well about the blood-money, and that the Omda and Muhammad Fadlallah (Nazir of the Kawahla) should arrive in the afternoon. The morning was overcast and muggy. Sheikh Jadallah also arrived and took Sheikh Ali El Tom's mail. In course of conversation he expressed his surprise at the conduct of the Amara in the recent fight with the Barok (a) for not telling Muhammad Fadlallah they had a man dead [and] (b) for denying knowledge at first of all givers of blows and then accusing two. I agree it's a fishy business.

About 4.15 p.m. Muhammad Fadlallah arrived with Omda Thabit Murjab of the Beni Jerar. We talked compliments only. He expressed surprise at my looking thin after my leave. When they had gone I went out and finished at attempt at a drawing.

Muhammad Fadlallah came to see me later, about 7.30, and I took the opportunity of putting it to him that he had done thoroughly badly in concealing from Hamilton that the man killed in the Barok vs. Amara fight was a Jerari. He admitted he'd been at fault and I read him a pi-jaw.

Prisoners had arrived just after sunset in charge of Onbashi Adam Muhd. El Hajj from Soderi. Consequently there was a busy scene round the camp-fires: the usual fire-lit silhouettes of camels and Arabs and police moving to and fro—much talk and laughter until the fires died down and men fell asleep, camels ceased to roar and there was nothing to see but stars and nothing to hear but chewings of the cud and rumblings of the beasts' bellies. Slept well.

9.10.31

Started at 6 a.m. for Um Gozein. Muhammad Fadlallah and Thabit Murjab rode with me and we went a fair pace. (My Bishari always goes faster in company.) The country became more open and we rose onto the higher ground so that one could see far and wide all round. The small hill of Um Gozein appeared in front, and far away to the south Jebel Sikanju, one of the Kaja Seruj group. We then dipped down into Wadi El Gadab (which bends round in a horseshoe to the south), which here was large and full of big trees, and found my tent pitched on the side of Um Gozein hill. A pleasant breezy spot with a view. We were dismounted by 7.45.

In passing the wadi I heard guinea fowl and flushed a partridge. I shall go down this evening and look for supper.

I dressed the sore on Grazin's rib and had breakfast.

The Omda Thabit was then sent for and I talked about the blood-money and expressed a hope that the dead man's people would accept £E150 of it in camels (they have been paid £E72 in money and are taking the rest of the first £E100 in camels). He said he didn't think they would but he would see. Then I did certain rifle business for him. His brother Faadil [*sic*] also appeared.

After he had finished I sent for Muhammad Fadlallah and saw the two men accused of causing the death of the man of the Omaara. (*N.B.* Thabit had also expressed his disgust at the Omaara for accusing two men of the same tribe as themselves after all the fuss had died down. "Shame", he said, "to wish to bury another Kahli on top of the Kahli killed". It was not, after all, murder, but a fight with sticks, and one fellow's cracked pate happened to fester long after he had been seen by the doctor and discharged—pure bad luck.) Both denied having hit anyone.

Talked to Muhammad Fadlallah:

(1) Rifles. Hoping we would finish with the "government issue" rifles this time. He said, "What about ammunition?" and I said I expected the governor would agree to an arrangement similar to that made for sheikhs in Bara District (i.e. 5 rounds per Remington) so soon as I had seen all the rifles (52).

(2) From this the talk went to the Darfur campaign of 1916 and to the watering of the Kawahla from of old in the Kheiran (Dellim, Adeik, Beshiri etc.) and to the numbers of their herds.

(3) Muhammad F. says that, on the whole, Kawahla camels are not so numerous now as they were in 1907 and later in 1917. (Can this be true?) Each listing shows fewer (*n.b.* check this at Soderi). Some individuals' herds have increased, e.g. those of our friend Ali El Ezeir [*sic*], but most have decreased. It is noticeable, he says, that the herds of men who herd them themselves have increased, whereas those of men who leave the herding to slaves and hired men decrease because the slaves and hirelings won't be so careful about isolating tryps. cases etc. and about rounding up stragglers. (N.B. Muhammad F. said to me yesterday that certain of the Kawahla have been bartering camels for sheep in recent years—just now he left Meidob in his camp exchanging sheep for camels. Query—how far true or general among Kawahla?)

(4) This last remark (re herding) gave me a text on which to preach about slaves, that they are not an economic proposition. I did so and went on as usual to the "settle them as cultivators" theme, and said I thought the condition of those left behind by himself at Khor es Sunt a bit scandalous and ditto that of the slaves at Um Badr. He said (a) at the time the Arabs left for nashugh they had no corn to leave behind (b) that if they had left any animals, they would not have stayed or lived in Khor es Sunt owing to "fly" (N.B. Ask someone else if there is "fly" at Khor es Sunt); he himself had left a cow for Sanduk and it had run (c) that the slaves could save their own corn if they want to, but will sell it to merchants

for tea and sugar. The Arabs do not take it from them—so Muhd. F. [says] (stuff and nonsense).

(Now Ali Ezeyr had been much more blunt with me and had said what is the ordinary Arab point of view: "These slaves refuse to go to work with their masters, their masters are not allowed to take the old-fashioned methods to compel them to, so the slaves have to be left behind and in that case they can damned well fend and forage for themselves".)

Muhammad F. said further that those who have slaves have to spend a lot to feed and clothe them and keep them "good", and that no Kahli ill-treats his slaves. Here I showed him that I knew a different story and went on to preach that the only way for them to keep slaves by them is good treatment, and went on to quote Solomon (Ecclesiasticus XXI): "If thou has a servant entreat him kindly. If thou wrong him and he fly from thee, whither wilt thou go to seek him?"

Muhd. F. said he had no news of where his people had got to and he proposes to reconnoitre this evening. Good. While he does so I will imitate the little man who had a little gun—or else sketch. I told him we wanted the landing grounds cleared. I wonder if he did pocket the money we paid out last time—he says he paid it to the slaves who did the work.

By the time I had written the above it was 2.30 p.m. so I had lunch. After lunch I felt like a rest but, having left the tent and being on my way back, I saw a bloke arrive and look in. I therefore waited behind a bush until he had gone and then went in and promptly fell asleep. The bloke returned and refused to let me sleep, which was annoying. He accused Muhd. F. of killing one of his slaves and carrying off two more. I told him to fetch Muhd. F. and went to sleep again. A little later the relatives of the slain Jerari arrived to talk about the blood-money. They did not seem so satisfied about the situation as Thabit Murjab.

After they had gone, there came a pause and I sent for the gentleman who had wakened me up (I knew Muhd. F. had gone off to ride round the countryside). The bloke's speech was so confused and silly that I had to get a policeman (whom his speech also confused) to untangle the tale. An old one of course, regarding three sons of a slave woman who had complained to me that her sons did not support her, and her master (i.e. my present complainant) didn't either. I had ordered the sons to hire themselves out as herdsmen and thereby earn her keep. One has died meantime—the complainant says "killed by the Nazir by ill-treatment". He can't produce evidence of this.

After him arrived Sheikh Muhammad Awad es Sid and Sheikh Ahmad Gismallah to chat. *Herd Tax*: Muhd. Awad es Sid said the camels in his list had decreased £E26 in all. Causes: Worm, tryps., decline in price leading to selling more to get money, and expenditure on tea and sugar.

I asked about sheep, but did not gather from these two sheikhs that the Kawahla are taking sheep in preference to camels.

Hence my hope of shooting or sketching went.

After dark, which brought with it extraordinarily large mosquitoes in prodigious quantities, Muhd. Fadlallah arrived while I was dressing "Grazin's" sore. He stayed talking till 8.15 p.m., both of us getting well-bitten by mosquitoes. He talked of theft by the Hamar. I said that, in the cases of both Hamar and Kaja Seruj, the Kawahla were always letting us down by screaming and failing to produce evidence.

He went on to say that the Nazir Naasir [sic] Muhammad Esh Sheikh of the Hamar Ghereysia had [been] fined two Kawahla camels for going into Dar Hamar in the early rains. This must either be bosh or mean that they were doing damage or had gone ill-manneredly too far south without asking anyone's leave.

To turn the subject he expressed a hope that I should marry soon. I said his hope was already fulfilled. He went on to talk of his own affairs. His father married him off to his cousin young and she died in childbirth and the child afterwards. He waited three years and chose another cousin for himself, who still goes strong and has one son aged 3. I expressed surprise that he had not married more than one wife. He then said that Kawahla women object strongly to rivals in the home and most Kawahla do not marry a second wife until the first has grown old and her sons grown up, and she has grown tired of her man. He said he had had quite a row when he took a mere concubine not long ago. The discussion then turned to the marriage customs of the English, viz. that they marry only one woman at a time and not another during that one's life-time or so long as she is the wife, and that divorce is difficult and viewed differently by the Law and by Religion.

A perishing mosquito inside the net—most annoying. Killed him as soon as it was daylight.

N.B. Told Muhd. F. that he *must* clear off the first £E100 of blood-money before I leave him this visit.

10.10.31

Reflecting on the way the recent kidnapping case has been handled (i.e. by direct government action), I think I should write to D.C. N[orthern] K[ordofan] pointing out (1) Maclaren said all summonses for Kababish go through Ali El Tom (who has not yet been informed of this case). (2) The administration of the Kababish is indirect and Ali El Tom has (e.g. in 1926) been heavily fined for not helping produce *murderers*. (3) If we want his cooperation in future hadn't we better act through him in all cases, however serious? At least he should be informed what action is being taken.

An uneventful morning followed. Ahmad Gismallah brought two Hamar who had held a Kahli's camels on trust for the last six years and been accused of stealing them and [been] punished by mistake by one of the Hamar Nazirs.

After lunch one El Zein Fadl El Mula turned up. He, it appears, is a dish of long standing with an everlasting complaint about a mare and her foal. I sent for his adversary, Sheikh Muhammad Awad Es Sid, who came with Sheikhs Ahmad Ibrahim and Hammaad [sic] Muhammad. Hammaad had a man who said he had lost all his camels. I swore him on my Koran after he had made his purifications. His Sheikh would not swear to support his testimony.

Herd Tax. I looked through the lists of Ahmad Ibrahim and Hammaad Muhammad. Ahmad says his herds are about the same as in the old 1927 list. Hammaad's list has decreased. These sheikhs and Gismallah all say that they don't think sheep have increased much by exchange against camels. All say that camels have declined owing to (1) disease (tryps. and worms) (2) fall in price of camels and consequent selling in greater numbers to obtain the same purchasing power in money [and] (3) increased extravagance of the Arabs (sugar and tea) leading to still further selling. I delivered a lecture on the necessity of pulling themselves together and getting this year's tax paid off. Meanwhile a mail had arrived. The sheikhs left just at sunset and I had time to open it before dark. Wrote and then read a little under the mosquito net.

11.10.31

Woke very early (3.30) and didn't get to sleep very deeply again. At about 6.30 I went out down the wadi from the hill with a gun to look for guinea fowl. I came on them in large numbers and shot four, but could retrieve only three of them on account of thorns and long grass. I had been filled with melancholy meditations since the early hour when I woke, and the slight "chasse a pied" cheered me up—as also did the prospect of good meat at lunch (a thing I've not tasted since Soderi). Mutton here is so poor and one gets so tired of it. I sent one of the birds to Muhammad Fadlallah. Saw a fox down there too.

After breakfast I sent for Muhd. Fadlallah and talked to him about various people who say he has oppressed them. He had good explanations for all the cases.

After he had gone, Omda Thabit Murjab came with other Beni Jerar, and the man Muhd. Salih (who had been accusing Muhd. Fadlallah of taking away his slaves and causing the death of one) now withdraws his accusation. Was it false originally? Who can say? But peace between men of different tribes and the removal of suspicion is worth a great deal. They sat and drank tea and talked about Bara for a while. After they had gone I wrote a letter to Charles de Bunsen until lunch arrived.

We are to move today to the other side of this hill (where, please God, there may be rather fewer mosquitoes), and Muhammad F.'s people will arrive and camp round us tomorrow.

A drum has been beating this afternoon at intervals in the bush away to the north. Tingle says that the news is Sheikh Ali El Tom is moving south and they are sending to enquire if this drum is his people.

I read the Sunday paper of a month ago after my tent was taken down and then tried desperately to explain to Muhammad F. the cause of the "present financial stringency". I dunno. However, I impressed upon him that although the price of camels is down to £E2 and £E1, his people pay 3/- per camel in their herds while we have to pay 1/4 of our incomes. It was easier when we got onto camel-breeding (the subject being raised by a bobby's having to rush out and stop my Bishari, who is on heat, making for some nagas a little way off). Muhd. F. says that only one camel comes on heat in a herd at a time—he then drives the other camels out. The owner of the herd will keep one specially as stallion. As this animal is never ridden and does no work, it tends to come on heat quicker than the others. Thus good breeding is ensured. Muhd. F., contrary to Maclaren's information, said that the stallion does not stick to one naga. He will take one and cover her two or three times . . . and leave her and find another. . . . It would appear that nagas have no definite "season": their coming on depends on grazing and condition, not on the time of year. And their being liable to take from the stallion is a matter of periods of a few days. Naturally, nagas are most liable to conceive in the rains when the grazing is at its best.

We rode down to the lake and through one arm of it to look at the northeastern side. There is a great deal of water, fine big trees and many varieties of birds. They say the water (a watercourse filled by three wadis) runs north for half an hour's ride. We returned to the new camp on the western slope of the hill. I went to look for more guinea fowl but found none.

It proves that the drum is Sheikh Ali El Tom's. It has come steadily nearer and he is now settling down on the other side of the lake. Rather a nuisance. I had hoped he would fall back on Abu Ressama [*sic*] farther north. Muhd. F. now says he will halt his people where they are, a bit farther away from the Kababish. So we move tomorrow morning. Conversation on English marriage customs with Muhd. Awad es Sid. Surprise expressed at their not usually marrying cousins.

I had supper and went to bed shortly after they had left. The night turned quite cold in spite of three blankets.

12.10.31

Rode at 5.30 for about an hour and a half through usual bush sloping slightly to the west—direction of our riding till we came to Sheikh Muhammad Fadlallah's camp, where we were met and welcomed with the usual cavalcade and drums. The Feki Fadl El Mula looked very resplendent in his "Mekkawiya" cap and reflected much holiness.

Hardly had I sat down and been given tea and started talking to the Feki's son, when Sheikh Ali El Tom was announced and I had to put on my best party manners and hat and welcome him and his son and his brother. They were all in very good form. I hope that their arrival in the Kawahla camp means better relations and not trouble.

We talked of the weather and the crops and they congratulated me on my marriage. It appears that the mail sent by Gadallah Abu Qurain has not yet reached Sheikh Ali El Tom. After his retinue had drunk my tea and withdrawn, I told Sheikh Ali about the Quraan raid (he said he had not heard of it) and about the kidnapping case (all the details of course he knew really; but government had unfortunately not yet informed him or asked his cooperation). He took the news pretty well but expressed great wrath at the Hamar for leading the innocent Kababish to buy the kidnapped children, and wrath at the Kababish too, saying that he thought his tribesmen had realised the uselessness of trying those games now. (Wrath, I think, well simulated.) I endeavoured to soothe him and said I knew we could rely on him for his help to deal with the case. (Fortunately as one offender of his tribe is in the jug and has confessed, we haven't to rely much on that help.) Then he talked at length about the Nuba-Kababish blood-money settlement of a homicide case. I said I wanted to propose that, in view of the hard times, the payment should be in animals. He said he was willing to be helpful, but thought that 100 camels would be difficult for the Nuba to produce—or did I mean that the animals were to be assessed at a price? I said, "Either one or the other, whichever we could get the parties to agree to".

He turned to the case of the Kabbashi boy murdered by the Zeyadi and broke into a declamation against settlements by mejlis. (*N.B.* This is a repetition of his remarks to Maclaren in 1926 after the Meidob cases.) I attempted to demur and said that if there were no majalis how were we to get settlements? I went on to say that, with regard to homicide, there were two sides to each case—the government's and the Arabs'. The government regarded such homicides as crimes, sometimes as very heinous crimes, and, where there was evidence to prove the latter, demanded the death of the culprit; the Arabs demanded either "blood" or "blood-money". If the government's action by its Code gives them the first, well; if not, surely settlement by blood-money in an Arab customary mejlis is best. He said that in general he did not want majalis without a D.C. present and that, in the present case, he understood the Zeyadia themselves disowned the culprit and the relatives of the deceased did not want mejlis. I said they had better go to Kuttum, and he said they would go willingly if I sent them with a letter to the D.C. there. I pointed out I had hardly the time to go there to hold their hands and that Asst. D.C. Kuttum, so I had been informed, was single-handed at present and could not come to meet me.

After Sheikh Ali had gone (it was by then 10 a.m.) I had breakfast, a shave and a wash and proceeded to write mail. No one much came near me all day, as they were all occupied with their visitors. That inveterate complainer Niama Suleiman and his blind father appeared, but that was about all.

At 4 p.m. Tingle came to tell me that Sheikh Ali was about to go and I rode with him for about a quarter of an hour and then returned. . . .

13.10.31

Woke very early, and felt rather bung-eyed. A busy day ensued. Before I had had my breakfast there appeared one Muhammad Abu El Qasim, brother of Ahmad, whom Muhd. Fadlallah says he fined £E13 for concealing 63 nagas at the time of the herd listing. (Ahmad says Muhd. F. took six camels from him by force and unlawfully confined him.) He put some awkward questions to me with intent to show that Muhd. Fadlallah had (1) illegally collected money for "locust work" (2) also for well-digging, and (3) was in the habit of taking 10 PT per man over and above Herd Tax. Muhd. Abu El Qasim said he could produce 13 witnesses. I rashly told him to do so, and it looked as if they were materialising when Muhd. Fadlallah turned up with another horse for me to see and they faded away. I hope they don't materialise again—very awkward. (N.B. To watch for any other signs of illegal exactions, and note Muhd. Abu El Qasim had a cause to bear Muhd. Fadlallah a grudge.)

Saw Muhd. Fadlallah's case book and upheld two of his decisions against appeal (including case of Ahmad es Saddiq Abu El Qasim referred to above).

Hajj Saiyid [*sic*] Hamid and his friend the other Hajj, with whom I travelled on my first journey to Soderi, came to see me. I talked herd tax. They said, "How can you pay when grown camels fetch 7 rials?" Hajj Ahmad, who is a very rich man, said that, a year ago, he had to sell 14 camels to pay £E70 herd tax—what on earth would he do this year? The meeting appeared to be of the opinion that camels had sharply declined in numbers since the last listing. But Kawahla had not increased the number of their sheep: (1) this countryside is no good for sheep (2) there are not the herdsmen to look after them as well as camels.

Hajj Saiyid, after a pause in the conversation, said very solemnly, "I have a mare and she reared and fell over backwards and broke her tail so that now it won't work and she is much worried by flies—can you do anything about it?" I replied, "I suggest you fix her up with some ostrich feathers behind", and the meeting burst into roars of laughter.

Later Sheikh Thabit Murjab came to me and later still that awful pair Niama and his father.

N.B. Muhd. Fadlallah had brought another horse in the morning which I shall I think buy.

Mail left this afternoon. Note arrived from Vicars-Miles[7] at Nahud by an Onbashi.

After sunset. Feki Fadl El Mula (uncle of the Nazir) came to talk with me. He talked until 8.45 p.m., mainly about the Hejaz. He told me the well-known Nigerian holy man who lived in Medina—Alfa Haashim[8]—is dead. He had much to say by way of description of the pilgrimage.

Cold night again. Woke again very early.

14.10.31

Dressed "Grazin's" sore. *N.B.* The camel I have bought from Hamilton has been named "Zurzur", i.e. the little bird, on account of its being small, light and swift.

Muhammad Fadlallah came to talk and I told him that I had decided to turn the case of the death of Murah Ribah, as a result of the fight between Awlad Barok and Awlad Omara, over to him for native settlement on payment of a fine of £E10. His youthful uncle, Muhammad Ahmad, came to see me and Gismallah Ahmad. Muhd. Ahmad has been very ill with malaria and looks washed out. After they had gone I dropped large hints about going easy with judgements and not ever getting hot under the collar. I also suggested that Feki Fadl El Mula is a better adviser than Muhammad Awad es Sid.

Later the people concerned in the matter of the man killed between Omara and Barok came and I announced that in no circumstances would I hang a man over the case, and I demanded a fine of £E10 for the fight and the sheikh of the tribe could settle the matter of the death according to custom. The father of the dead man objected strongly and demanded a life for a life. Feki Fadl El Mula said that would not give him back his son —he said neither would blood-money. I said I was sorry, but in no case would the government hang a man over this fight. They left. And they

---

[7] A. L. W. Vicars-Miles, SPS 1922–45. *SPS*, 40.
[8] *Khalifa* of the Tijaniyya order. *Cf.* J. Spencer Trimingham, *Islam in West Africa*, Oxford 1959, 86.

continued in mejlis all the rest of that day, for not a soul came near me. I tried drawing some trees to kill time.

At evening Muhammad Ahmad Fadlallah brought me a bowl of milk and we sat and chatted over coffee about horses. (The horse I am buying drinks milk in the evening and has one drink of water a day, unless it is very hot or there is hard work, when he is given a short drink about 11 a.m. I want to keep to that.) He chatted also about his uncle Feki Fadl El Mula, and his own marriage, and when a boy becomes a man, and so on. After he had gone I sat reading the *Arabian Nights* till 10 p.m. It had been a hot day and the night was warm. I had difficulty in getting to sleep.

15.10.31

The mejlis still goes on. Ahmad Gismallah came to talk to me and said they were near the end of it now. I drew him out about the Awlad El Feki Saddiq who made the row two days ago. He said their father Abu El Qasim was a merchant in animals: hence probably their "sea-lawyer" outlook. . . . I asked Ahmad G. if there were any customary dues to the Sheikh in the Kawahla and he said, "No—except the sheep per flock and a rial at herd listing".

Muhd. Fadlallah appeared and said the mejlis was resting and that the contention of the dead lad's father was he ought to have £E350 blood-money. Muhd. F. is rightly sticking out for £E250, paid in animals. The mejlis had considered the old custom of 100 camels and refused it.

Talked of pulleys and of traps for hyenas. I showed him how a double pulley works on a well to shorten the distance the draft animal must walk. It was extremely hot in the middle of the day and I fell asleep in my chair from 1.30 to 2.30, to wake up with a bad taste in my mouth and all of a sweat.

At about 4.30 there came to me Tingle who asked for £E2 loan for the police to buy sugar and tea. I found I couldn't manage more than £E1.500. Had they warned me to bring more money I would have done so.

After him came Sheikhs Abdallah Gismallah and Awad es Sid El Kabis and talked about certain cases of people they wanted altered in their herd-tax lists. Also slaves they talked of. Then came Muhd. Fadlallah and produced 5 sheikhs whom I lectured on the necessity of producing herd tax before the end of the year.

Tribal Economics: Abdallah Gismallah and Awad es Sid El Kabis both said the number of camels in their lists had decreased, that herds were decreasing and had decreased every listing. How was one to pay herd tax with prices of camels at £E1.400–1.600 or less and a prize fat animal fetching under £E3? Later, talking to Muhd. Fadlallah, he complained that sugar and tea are the undoing of the nomads. I asked how much he thought the average man would spend on sugar a month—£E1? He said at least that. Muhd. Awad es Sid, who has a number of daughters and women about, was recently breaking a new loaf every day, i.e. spending £E3–4 on sugar a month. Muhd. Fadlallah said that a man who paid £E10 in herd tax would often be spending £E20 on sugar a year.

I asked about the normal, e.g. clothes. He said clothes cost very little, a man can dress himself in 'imma, sirwal, jibba and tob[9] for 50 PT or less. His wife has 3 robes—two for day wear and one for night. A normal small household is dressed, so he says, for £E3 a year. (*N.B.* Two suits of jibba and sirwal for my camel boys cost me 40 PT only.)

Corn: The nomads eat grain at most 5 months a year, usually 4 months: at the end of winter and during the summer until the rains come. Muhd. Fadlallah said so far as I recollect that £E10 to £E12 at present grain prices, i.e. last year's, would suffice a household for corn for a year.

He said he had left the discussion on the dead man at the point of offering the relatives either £E250 paid in camels or 100 camels, and given them till morning to think it over. His brother came and talked to me for a short while, mainly about Meidob and Fasher.

The evening was warm. I read till 10 and probably was asleep by 11.

16.10.31

I have failed to write this diary for two days and now remember little of what happened on the 16th.

Sheikh Muhammad El Tom turned up to retrieve a slave boy of his who had run away and come to me yesterday. It is the same little boy who appeared before Hamilton at El Gashda in June 1930, having run from the camels. I sent him back under Sheikh Muhd's guarantee. Where else should he go? He has no people. I must see him after my arrival at Sheikh Ali El Tom's.

Last night, it appears, a thief came through the camp and stole a camel from a Kahli camp near by. The Kawahla say he is a Kabbashi slave.

I tried two of the prisoners I had brought from Soderi for attempted theft (as one of the witnesses had arrived and one of the accused had confessed).

In the afternoon I tried to draw some camels and also sent a man to tell Sheikh Ali El Tom I would arrive on the morning of the 18th.

While Muhd. Fadlallah and various sheikhs were talking to me about an unfortunate old man (also present), whose concubine had left with another man who proceeded to marry her, a policeman arrived with mail. He had done the journey from Soderi in $4\frac{1}{2}$ days—pretty quick going.

---

[9] '*imma*: turban; *sirwal*: drawers; *jubba*: long shirt; *tub*: robe.

17.10.31

Muhd. Fadlallah staged a shock for me this morning which failed to come off. He came all hot in the collar because another alleged theft by Kababish had occurred. While we were talking, in rushed the losers of the camel in question and said to have been stolen. But I remained quite unmoved and told them that they hadn't any proofs against anyone and had better shut up until they had some evidence.

Muhd. Fadlallah then began to open up an old, old sore about a man called Hamid Ajur who had caused much trouble between the Kawahla and Kababish in 1926. I listened, and looked the case up afterwards and spent the day thinking about these things and the evening calming down Muhd. Fadlallah's uncle Fadl El Mula about them. I hope they may refrain from making fools of themselves and trouble with the Kababish. Put myself to sleep early.

18.10.31

Started about 6.30, with everyone turned out on horses as usual to see me off. The ride to Sheikh Ali El Tom's camp was a short one, not more than ¾ hour. But by bad luck and a little mismanagement we missed him and his party who had turned out to greet us and, on arriving at his camp, I rode back a bit so as not to disappoint him by arriving without meeting him. His maternal uncle has died recently and as a result of the consequent mourning no drums were beaten. Muhd. Fadlallah had informed me of the death yesterday when Feki Fadl el Mula said that they proposed soon to return Sheikh Ali El Tom's visit.

After my arrival I expressed surprise at seeing Sheikh Ali here when I expected him much further north. I doubt if he saw the hint but he may have done. Sheikh El Tom, his son, said the grass had dried up further north. I hope to go to see for myself, for otherwise I think that Sheikh Ali is unduly cramping the Kawahla.

After my breakfast, stoutness exercises and bath, I sent for Sheikh Ali El Tom and we talked from 11 a.m. until nearly 2 p.m. on: (1) His schoolmaster and his complaints. (2) "dia" from the Nubas for the man killed at Nihid in June (when my caravan returning from Omdurman stopped a fight). (3) The Zaghawa of Kajmar and their evilness. A.T. suggested a meeting between D.C.s Bara and Soderi and himself, and I suggested about December 26th, for the date. (4) The Meidob agents of A.T. at those northern well-centres which I visited in the summer. He said he would name 5 to me. [(5)] The Meidobi's camel seized by a Kabbashi recently as one stolen by Meidob 5 years ago. I extracted a promise from A.T. that, if it had not died meanwhile, he would send it back. The answer of course will be that it is dead. *N.B.* Muhd. El Tom guaranteed it. (6) Rifles.

(7) Slaves. I explained my objection to having runaway slaves in Soderi, as I know the Nazirs hate their being there, and explained my wish to settle outstanding slave cases by 10th November. Just as he was going away, A.T. suddenly started saying that he wanted to get all he had to say off his chest and began saying he was old and afraid. Then my servant interrupted. I think A.T. is going to say again that he wants to retire.

Spent the afternoon writing letters—seeing one Sheikh Muhammad Eid from Hofra who says he can't hold his job down and then hearing witnesses of a murder of a Kabbashi by a Zeyadi from Darfur.

A very hot day and a warm night.

19.10.31

In the morning dealt with (1) The murder of Fadl El Mula Belula, and sent the witnesses to Kuttum to be there on 20 November 1931. (2) Slave cases—making a date for hearing at Soderi 10th November 1931. *N.B.* I asked Sh. Ali El Tom whether it wouldn't be better for the cases of slaves who run to Nahud to be heard there. He said, "No": there was more chance of their being settled with their tribes if they were brought back to Soderi for hearing. I explained to him that I didn't like slaves who refused to return to their masters squatting in Soderi, and proposed to send irreconcilables right away for settlement in another District. He agreed—he did not like seeing runaways in Soderi. (3) various summonses produced by A.T. (4) Nimr Ali Arti, who has been made to guarantee the production of Adam Murdas, the kidnapper, within 15 days from now. I thought long about it and gave him 30 days. (5) Koko Maafa, the Ferhani resident with A.T. and suspected by Abdu Omar Gash of being a rallying point in the west for discontented Farahna. A.T. made a long defence of his own conduct and of Koko's harmlessness. Koko to appear this afternoon with his brother Sheikh El Hadi Maafa. (6) The bloke who complains about a camel of his which is in Muhammad Awad es Sid's herds turned up. He said he would shut up only if Muhd. Awad es Sid would swear that the camel came to him with those returned in 1927.

There is a Kahli slave who is always worrying me about his hire and saying A.T. won't do him justice. I think I'll offer to settle the Kabbashi's case if A.T. will deal with the Kahli's. The unjust judge as usual: I find that judge an admirable example for an indirect administrator—do nothing till you are compelled to. Ali El Tom left me at 12 noon and I wrote two letters to Kuttum and one or two others for the Mamur and felt pretty tired. I had little rest, however, for Sheikh Ahmad Gismallah turned up from the Kawahla with a rifle to be registered.

Chapter V

Soon after he had gone, Koko Maafa and his brother arrived. His story was a long one going back to the days of Young and Reid and before that. An amusing old rogue—a devil I should say. Later Ali El Tom arrived again and said that relations with the Meidob had improved. Also he said (1) that he hoped, with effort, to get this year's herd tax paid, but that he hoped to goodness that, in view of the fall in animal prices, the government was going to do something about next year's. This led to talk of prices. Sheikh Belal El Mahbas, the Omdurman agent of the tribe, turned up in the middle of the conversation and it appeared that the following drops in prices had occurred:

Camels for slaughter in Omdurman:
1930 October: good camels and nagas averaged £E6 to 7.
1931 July: maximum price—£E4.

Cattle. Bulls	Oct. 1930	July 1931
Robaa	£E1.500	robaa & saddis 60 PT
Tini	£E1 to 1.200	

Sheep	Oct. 1930	July 1931
Tini	50 PT	25 PT
rubaa [sic]	60–65 PT	50 PT

(2) That he wished to re-list all animals this year. *N.B.* I must get early approval for this. I agree it should be done—cattle plague has been bad.

In the course of our conversation, but before Sheikh Belal arrived, a curious thing occurred. Two negroes came to greet me. I thought at first they must be slaves but for their dress. They could hardly talk any Arabic at all and asked permission to dance for us. I granted it. So here was the spectacle of an Arab chief (and the biggest in the Sudan) and an Englishman watching two Dinkas sing and dance in their own tongue. The two men came apparently from "Jangai" (?).[10] They have been up here for some months, singing and dancing—to Arabs for money, and propose to ask to be allowed to herd cows until the next rains permit them to return to their own country. Sheikh Ali said, "See, your honour, the peace brought by this government, that these two blacks should be able to walk free and unhindered so far." I agree and wonder whether they will be allowed to walk back again. I stopped them soon and sent them to my servant to be given drinks and money.

---

[10] Possibly *Jeng*, that is Dinka.

Sheikh Ali seemed to think that relations between himself and the Kawahla are satisfactory, but I wonder.

Belal El Mahbas took a dose of chlorodyne from me to Salim wad Belal who has malaria and is suffering much from vomiting. Went to bed at 9.30.

20.10.31

A similar day to yesterday as far as work was concerned. Sent off mail in the afternoon.

In the evening I rode with A.T., Muhammad El Tom and Ibrahim Faheil (who looks very ill) to see the herds of sick cattle, and in particular Koko Maafa's. Koko made me go and see his wife, who was bitten by a snake in the hand 18 months ago and appears to have become paralysed since then. I know of nothing I can do for it. Koko has 35 cows in the herd-tax list. I counted (surreptitiously) 60 in his herd, not including calves which were in a zeriba apart.

Ali El Tom came late in the evening to talk. Nothing particularly noteworthy—history of the Darfur campaign. I could not get him on to things I wanted to discuss: I opened on "hukms" among the Kababish apart from his own and mentioned Musa Kerfees' [*sic*] unauthorised judgement upon which I stumbled last May, but he laughed it aside.

21.10.31

I started drawing a gafala tree before breakfast. Sheikh Muhd. El Tom came with Koko Maafa. The latter swore to his animals, taking the Koran on his head. He swore to 80 cows and 10 camels (Herd Tax list 35 cows and 3 camels). Muhd. El Tom also brought the boy Said his slave to whom I gave avuncular advice. We talked for a while of Kababish economics and of slaves. He said that the drawing of water for camels had been too much for their slaves so that many had complained and fled. Hamilton's devices for drawing water by means of camels had been a great help.

I had asked for the loan of a horse to go and see the pool of Um Gozein (El-'ada) and about 4 p.m. Sheikh Ali arrived with horses, excusing himself for not having come to see me earlier in the day on the grounds that he had drunk medicine. We rode all round the west side of the pool (the east I had seen before). There is an enormous extent of water and very fine trees. He showed me the sayaal trees near which he had camped 2 years ago. We were much amused by the efforts of a man to cross the ford where I had crossed the other day. Sheikh Ali rode down to the water and cracked his whip to assist the man who was trying to drive his two camels over: it had no effect, but looked well. We watered our horses and returned. The Kababish have a very simple and effective bridle—there is a thin head stall and no nose band at all.

When we returned, the two Dinkas met me and said they wished to stay with Ali El Tom all the winter. I said I had no objection if he had not.

Ali El Tom came to talk after I had had my tea. I had been reading an article in the Arabic paper, the "Hedara",[11] on the education of women, and asked him his views, which were "Maybe in the towns but no need in the desert". After talking of the schoolmaster and my expressing pious hopes that Ali El Tom would do what he could to smooth his path among the hardships of these outlandish parts, Ali El Tom suddenly said he wanted to open his heart and then led up to the Kawahla. He swore with many oaths that he had no desire now-a-days for anything but peace. From this he passed on to saying perhaps I had heard about the alleged thefts a few days ago (as of course I had), and expressed his regret that there should apparently be this attitude of intransigence and suspicion on the part of Muhammad Fadlallah and his family. The Kawahla and the Kababish had in the last two or three years been intermingling freely and no untoward events had occurred—only the attitude of the Eaysir family remained hostile. (Personally I am not surprised, considering A.T.'s past behaviour.) I ran over the points in the peace of 1927 with him in order to lead up to Hamid Ajur and Co. I did not stress the point of Hamid. I have therefore now four Kabbashi-Kahli cases outstanding and A.T. in rather an annoyed frame of mind, and I agree with A.T. that if they won't settle themselves I had better settle them before I go. He said that Muhammad Fadlallah was coming to pay tribute of mourning for Ali El Tom's uncle, next Thursday being the day. A.T. mentioned, what I had noticed, the ill manners of Thabit Murjab yesterday, when he refused to stay to take even a cup of tea with A.T.

And so to bed a little disturbed in mind.

22.10.31

Did some more at the gafala tree. When we were riding yesterday, Ali El Tom had asked me if I had heard that troops were going up from El Fasher to Bir Natrun or Nakhila after the Guraan raiders. I said I had not. A.T. said that Berti and Zeyadia who had come to see him had said that the government had sent out 300 transport camels and had taken guides, a Zaghawi and Zeyadi. I have heard nothing of this.

This morning there came to see me Sheikh Gismallah Muhammad and two of his Kawahla, who said that 26 and 42 respectively had died, since the listing this summer, of tryps. I said they must pay on them this year and I would ask for a striking off of half their claims for 1932 . . .

The hamla moved off to go to Abu Bessama about 2 p.m. I was taking

---

[11] *Hadarat al-Sudan*, a Khartoum newspaper.

a rest when Muhammad Ahmad Effendi turned up and talked (a) about the Kahli with a hole in his head, whom Muhd. Fadlallah, with incredible stupidity, has let go away without seeing the doctor (b) at my instigation —the education of women. He said many of them had their manners, if not morals, ruined by it, and turned out no good as wives, because they would not do a hand's turn in the house and expected to be treated like European ladies. I pointed out that quite a few European ladies had to do jobs in their own houses. He said this applied not only to women, and went on to point out defects in many Gordon-College[12] products. When he was speaking of educated women, he instanced Ali Eff. Babikr Bedri's divorce of his wife, which he did openly and not in accordance with usual custom. He then turned (as he always will) to religion.

After a while Sheikh Ali turned up to set me on my way and we rode off. Sheikh El Tom, his son, is to accompany me on my trip, which I intend to be more or less a pleasure outing to give me time to think over this everlasting Nurab anti El Eyasir problem, and also to see if I can manage to hang about long enough to settle the schoolmaster back in his job.

We passed the southernmost hills of Um Botatikhat [Umm Batatikh] before dusk, when we found the hamla in camp. The countryside has dried up a lot here; also the ground is harder, and there are occasional stony patches.

After I had had supper, Sheikh El Tom came to talk to me. He said, *inter alia*, that the Awlad Tereif, the Awaida and the Atawia Kababish are now well north of Jebel Meidob, now pasturing on khareef [sic] grass. There is no news of the "jizzu" yet. The camels are not drinking now up there and men and women, when they want to drink anything but milk, go to the gelts (water-filled clefts in rocks) in Jebel Tageru.

23.10.31

Rode just before sunrise. A strong wind got up from the north and it was cool. In fact it has been cool all day. We got down on hard ground among a number of seyaal [sic] trees, of which there are many fine ones hereabout. I spent most of the morning thumbing a dictionary with little gusto. Muhammad produced some ghastly curry for lunch and I had settled down to try and draw a seyaal when Sheikh Ali El Tom turned up and we talked of Abu Tabar and Gebra and the noted case between Niama Sirkatti and Ali El Tom at Wadi El Wuzz.

Rode on about 4 p.m. and by 5 we were in camp at Abu Bessama. As we came in I had seen the mountains of the Hataan [sic] away to the north. Most of the pool bed which had been watered here two years ago is bone dry and all the grass is yellow.

---

[12] The government's secondary school in Khartoum.

Sheikh El Tom says that people who sold camels recently at Fasher realised only £E2.100 for "higg" (3 year old) camels and £E1.200 to 1.400 for "wad lebun" (2 year olds). I sat writing and reading till 10 p.m. In spite of the cold and some wind there were large numbers of mosquitoes. Slept rather badly.

24.10.31

Tingle appeared with camels before I had had time to finish shaving. We then rode with Sheikh El Tom round the pool, across the part now dry, and up a hill on the other side in order to look at the Hataan. I had a good view from the hill-top at the plateau of the Hataan which stands up well out of the plain. On the other side one could see a hill called El Lueiga [al-Nuayqa]. We descended and went round the other side of the pool which is not very large this year. At one point we saw guinea fowl and I got down to try and get a shot at them. I could not get close, however, and Sheikh El Tom's white clothes did not help.

I spent the morning rather gloomily feeling hot-eyed and weary, and a dusty wind blew. I talked to Sheikh El Tom for a while and read for a bit. As soon as the hamla began to pack up I went out to try a drawing.

We rode at about 4 and by sunset found the hamla. After supper I talked to Sheikh El Tom mainly about merissa (beer).

25.10.31

It was a cool night and I slept like a log. Rode just before dawn and by about 8.30 found the hamla in the wadi under very large trees. On the way I asked El Tom whether the Kababish, when they sold animals, sold mostly sheep or mostly camels. He said, "Sheep"—except the Awaida who have none. No other section has no sheep, he said.

. . . I find (as I was getting liver for breakfast) that Sheikh El Tom must have either misunderstood or misinterpreted what I said yesterday when he came and said he could find no animals in Abu Bessama—only one ewe. I had said, "No. Thank you—please don't slaughter that". However, he appears to have done so.

I made two attempts today to get near some guinea fowl which were calling near by. I had no success.

After lunch I tried drawing a tebeldi tree. We arrived at Sheikh Ali's ferik at about 5 p.m. He came and talked to me late in the evening: meanwhile I read a mail which had arrived yesterday. Another Kahli-Kabbashi theft case had occurred, so the police here informed me. Fortunately the owner recovered the sheep he said he had lost, but the thief fled from him.

26.10.31

This was a hot day with clouds in the sky. I sent a message to Muhd. Fadlallah to say I would call upon him on Wednesday and spend the day with him. I shall leave here for Soderi on Friday—a bad day to start a journey but I can't help that.

One of the main witnesses in the Zeyadia murder case was sent to me by the doctor as unable to go to Kuttum because he is suffering from consumption in the third stage. He looks very ill. Took his evidence on commission.

Sheikh Ali El Tom did not come to see me until late afternoon. I talked firearms licences and a case concerning cows lost in 1923. Kamil, the clerk, took from me a list of the outstanding un-renewed licences. I then talked to A.T., asking where the normal summer quarters of various sections of his tribe are.

After he had gone, I wrote letters until about 7.30. Sheikh El Tom appeared and talked for some time. He got going on the Kawahla, saying that relations between them and the Kababish were good—the Dar Bahr, Awlad Barok and Kawahla had all been up round Abu Gow and beyond with the Kababish this rains. But there was still the house of El Eyasir [*sic*] who maintained hostility.

He said that the trouble over the Kababish cows last March had not been really because of fear of disease but—and he rocked with laughter —because two or three years ago Koko Maafa had promised Fadlallah a cow if he would let him water at Um Badr and then he refused to pay up. When the talk occurred last March, because Muhd. Fadlallah made a fuss about the cow, Koko said, "Oh! well—for the general good I'll pay up". Sheikh El Tom then went on to talk of Muhd. Fadlallah's latest. El Tom has a slave, whom he sent out a few days ago to look for stray camels. The slave slept in the khalla[13] and in the morning went to the merchant in Muhd. Fadlallah's ferik to buy tobacco. Muhd. Fadlallah came into the shop while he was there and said, "What are you doing here?" The slave told him. He said, "Where did you sleep last night?" The slave told him. "Why did you not come and sleep in the ferik near me?" And then he took and sent the slave back to Sheikh Ali with a note. Now I doubt both these stories, though they told very well, and I could not help laughing. I told El Tom that he must be mistaken about Muhd. Fadlallah's reason for sending the slave back.

Query: did Muhd. Fadlallah, through fright of A.T. and A.T.'s position and fear of theft by the Nurab slaves, make a nervous ass of himself? and behaving like his double, Edward Marjoribanks, M.P.?[14] and

---

[13] Open country.
[14] See above, 22.

like the prefect in a small public school? Or is he, from a very natural grudge against the Nurab (seeing they tried to get him hung in 1926), trying to provoke them? Does Sheikh Ali really want peace? (a) between the tribes (I think there is no doubt of this); (b) between the Nurab and the Awlad El Eaysir? Feki Fadl El Mula says he thinks A.T. does want peace. Or is A.T. working a very deep and diplomatic scheme to discredit Muhd. Fadlallah in the eyes of government by making him appear ridiculous and always in the wrong?

I told El Tom that I had been talking about Um Inderaba and that I thought it needed more frequent visits from El Tom or from A.T. In particular I instanced the cow case and suggested that, if the Kajmar meeting came off, Ali El Tom might go to Um Inderaba and see about the state of the nation there.

As soon as he had gone (about 9 p.m.) I had supper and went to bed at 10. Whether it was the moonlight or a turn to warmer weather or a supper of fish and cocoa I do not know, but I woke at 1.30 all of a dither.

27.10.31

My Bishari camel has a split in the callous of the pedestal. I hope to goodness the split won't spread or turn into an ulcer. I've had that before and it is the devil to cure. Elias's camel has a swelling of the muscles at the top of the near fore. That of the policeman who came with the mail has sore feet—two lahads on the back and is in shocking condition. Williams saw it (so the bobby says) and passed it "good".

I sent off Ahmad Ali Mahmoud to Muhd. Fadlallah to produce the slave accused of stealing sheep . . . .

28.10.31

I had arranged to ride over to Muhammad Fadlallah's ferik for the day, starting about 6.30 a.m. after an early breakfast. Just as I was about to start, Ali El Tom came to my tent and gave me another quite long exhortation on the subject of Muhd. Fadlallah and the fact that, while relations between the two tribes were now good, coldness continued between "those tents over there" and his own. He urged me to advise Muhd. Fadlallah to adopt a more friendly tone. I replied that, in view of what had happened in the past, it was no wonder that Muhammad Fadlallah should find it difficult to believe that Ali El Tom really wished to have peace and to make friends. I said that the government considered no sheikh greater nowadays than Ali El Tom, no man had so great a name with the government: was it not natural that Muhd. Fadlallah should mistrust Ali El Tom and his influence a little in view of the past? Time alone could heal the breach: but I suspected the sons of El Eaysir would need a kind of sign of a miraculous kind . . . to believe Sheikh Ali's conversation.[15] But I was sure that no one wanted anything but peace and good will and that nothing but lack of mutual understanding stood in the way. Please God, in time mutual understanding would come.

Ali El Tom seemed pleased and cheered up and I took leave of him and rode off. It was a pleasant ride. I arrived, too, I am glad to say, without the usual fanfares and horsemen being sent out to meet me. Muhd. Fadlallah had moved his camp east and south from where he was to a rather pleasant place.

The slave Zaid, belonging to Abd El Gadir El Eaysir, had been arrested and was waiting for me. I had ordered Gima Teyrab Teraybih to appear with one Abdallah Hamid of the Kababish and his "Khaal" (i.e. maternal uncle) who were said to be witnesses to the theft of the 23 sheep by Zaid, and to his having fled later with a rasan[16] tied round his wrists. Eid, a Hababi slave of Muhd. Fadlallah's, I had also asked for. He was not present.

I was told by Tingle and also by Muhd. Fadlallah that Zaid confessed he had driven the sheep off with his camels, but put up the defence that he had found them astray, did not know whether they belonged to Kababish or Kawahla, and had taken them into his herd (the usual native custom as between friendly tribes). I very much doubt the honesty of Zaid's intentions, and am pretty sure that, if I had seen the case myself, as I had almost decided to do when I went out, I should have put Zaid in "chokey" for nine months.

However, after some thought, I acted on an impulse which came to me while I was in Muhammad Fadlallah's tent and decided to go on the way I had been taking so far with all this talk between the Kababish and the Kawahla—or rather the Nurab and Awlad El Eaysir, and let them settle it for themselves, and let the probable punishment of a thief by prison slide. Accordingly I told Muhd. Fadlallah to hear the case, and if he found that in his view the slave deserved punishment, to hand him over to me. Let him, I said, show the Kababish his justice.

This was an experiment and a risk, but I wanted badly to avoid doing myself anything which would give the Nurab the chance of saying, "Ha! these damned Awlad El Eaysir are thieves after all", or which would cause the Alwad El Eaysir to go to visit Ali El Tom next day in a more than ordinarily aggrieved frame of mind. The risk, in the event, was not, I think,

---

[15] *Sic pro* "conversion"?
[16] Head-rope of a riding camel.

justifiable or in accordance with the proper principles of administration in this district. Muhd. Fadlallah gave the slave the benefit of the doubt and did not bring him to me. Before I heard this result I felt I had made a mistake in not hearing the case myself and as a consequence became extremely depressed for the rest of that day and all the next.

Meanwhile I finished off that tiresome claim of one Muhammad Ahmad of the Nurab against Sheikh Muhd. Awad es Sid for a camel, by having Sheikh Muhd. swear on the Koran that he had properly acquired the camel at the time of the mutual compensation for thefts between the tribes in 1927.

Various other business was done—including a complaint against one of the Hamar Nazirs of Western Kordofan for unjust fining of Kawahla. This is the second complaint against this Nazir (Nasir Muhammad El Sheikh).

Muhammad Fadlallah gave me lunch, some of which I ate (including a pleasant drink of camels' milk). I gave Muhammad Fadlallah much advice on friendlier relations with the Nurab and in particular with El Tom Ali El Tom, and I warned him against Muhammad Awad El Sid as an adviser. It appears now that, in 1927, Muhammad Awad El Sid caused Sheikh Muhammad El Tom to be sworn about certain camels and therefore now the Nurab want him sworn (an oath being something of a dishonour). Well, he has been: let us hope that will even the account. I dunno.

I rode back about 3.30, arriving about 5 p.m. to find that another Zaid (a Kahli slave also), who has a claim for wages against one of the Nurab, and for whom I had arranged with Sh. Ali that Sh. Ali should re-open a case in which he himself had given a decision (a great concession)—had refused to stay in my camp and had disappeared for the day—to Sheikh Ali El Tom's annoyance. The police produced the lad and I cursed him fully and furiously for a quarter of an hour.

Almost immediately Ali El Tom arrived and said he had decided that he could not descend to making a near relative take an oath over so small a matter as a two-year-old camel, and he had promised Zaid a young camel (which was the wages claimed) to close the business.

Later the doctor came to see me and later still El Tom Ali, who discoursed of how to get along with herds of camels when you are in a strange country looking for grass, without getting into trouble with the local natives. He goes southwest at the beginning of the rains among the Berti.

I got to bed about 10.15 very tired and depressed.

29.10.31

This day was the day on which Ali El Tom had invited Muhammad Fadlallah and party to come over for the "Ma'azza" of Ali El Tom's uncle and sister. It appears that a "Ma'azza" is a kind of memorial feast. The nearest relative of the deceased makes a "faraash" (bier), and about a week or so after the death friends who have heard of it bring each his offering according to his wealth—a bull, a sheep, sugar. The animals are slaughtered and an enormous feed ensues.

The Kawahla arrived about 9 a.m. I, of course, was left severely alone all the morning, as everyone was busy about entertaining guests. About noon Ali El Tom turned up for a chat, however, and was recounting tales of the Dervishes[17] when Muhammad El Tom suddenly roared a greeting at me from the tent door in such a bo'sun's voice that I upset my glass of tea all over my shirt and shorts. Roars of applause. Muhammad El Tom was clearly the better for beer. We chatted for a very short while and then Ali El Tom more or less indicated to Muhammad that they should push off. I expect he said outside, "You're tight as an owl, brother. Better come away."

In the late afternoon, when the feast had broken up, the Kawahla came to take leave of me.

About 8 p.m. Ali El Tom came to talk. Amongst other things I drew him onto the subject of these courts which have been set up in the last three years. I led up to the subject through talk on Arab custom, saying that, although I had no right to an opinion, it appeared to me that prison was a thing not known to Arab custom and that therefore it was a little inconsistent to ask a sheikh to judge according to Arab custom and to award prison as a punishment.

A.T. said prison was unknown to the Arabs. As to the courts, he said, he had hearsay only. He had only once been in one, at Bara, but from hearsay he had formed the opinion that they were unsuitable to real Arabs. A mejlis is one thing, a court another. The mejlis hears all men and settles the business at once without delay and without fuss with books and records and so on. A "court" caused a sheikh to think himself a "haakim" with paraphernalia, and "Come tomorrow", and ghaffirs and "entry by names on a list'. The government had offices and courts and police and it all had worked well for 30 years, and men knew that if they went to government, they would get justice. Why did the government want to set up a second set of offices and courts and what-not beside itself? For himself, he held that it were better a man should seek settlement of a dispute by the mejlis of his own people and sheikh, and then, if he were dissatisfied, go to government. I asked him, "What about inter-tribal cases: would he not have a Kabbashi go to the sheikh of another tribe if he were aggrieved by a man of that tribe?" He said, "Yes, but if he got no satisfaction, then let

---

[17] The Mahdists.

him go to government. If the other sheikh has a court, then the case is heard and closed. It is more difficult to go to government if you have not had justice done you". From what he heard, Kababish would rather not tire their camels to go to a Native Court. *N.B.* This was what he was at at the beginning of his talk about the Zeyadi murder. He did not want a Native Court to hear it, I believe. Of course, no Native Court, in point of fact, can hear a murder case.

So a second day of depression passed, and I am still wondering if the sheep-theft case was a bad blunder on my part. This business is very like a game of football (if you play in a position from which a player rarely scores a point)—one cannot tell whether one is doing well or not. No doubt its attraction is similar to that of football, which is, in my opinion, a better game than most, because less completely disheartening to the average player.

N.B. This evening Sheikh Hasan Ahmad Nagila arrived. My delay in order to see him was not therefore wasted. I gave him more advice. . . . He has brought a servant and still complains how hard life is: that there is no white chalk—the Dept. sent coloured chalks, and as these were not what is wanted, he left them in Soderi. (Damn little fool.) I pointed out, as regards hard life, that it is just as hard for, e.g. Muhammad Ahmad Effendi, who is a man from the river—and what about me? He said, "Oh, you're different!" To which I replied, "Yes, and the difference is that there's a darn sight more difference between what I'm accustomed to in the way of eats and comfort and what I enjoy here than there is in your case". However, I promised that, if he still found it hard to get the food he wants, we would try to fix him with a better servant. The boy just *makes* difficulties, I also told him to let me know if he still wanted to complain or to get out of the job. Spoilt by Gordon College and too young, that's his trouble. A nice lad. He had the cheek to say that, as it was now not a matter of personal tuition but of a regular school, he had thought govt. would have paid his wages and not called on Sheikh Ali to make it good. I told him that was not his business. He gave me "towkeels"[18] for drawing his wages and a letter to arrange a part of his wages to be deducted and paid to his people. Poor little devil—he gets £48 a year—little enough after all.

Sheikh Ali says the school is a "calamity" though necessary, because a man who is taught otherwise than by a khalwa fiki [*sic*] is bound to change his ways and outlook. His boys have more chance than others because they are in the atmosphere of their family.

---

[18] Authorization; proxies.

30.10.31

I told the two Dinkas that Ali El Tom does not want them here and they must report to Nahud before 30 Nov. 31. I must write Nahud about them.

Ali El Tom produced an ancient lady who had sold a house in Omdurman to Eid Belila, the second Kabbashi agent there. Eid wants it registered in his name. The Muhammadan Law Courts will not register without her presence or a power of attorney. She is too old to travel all that way. I said I would see if I could help. The clerk Kamil made me out two forms of power of attorney.

This old lady, a Kabbashia, it appears, married a Turk[19] in the Mahdia who had been captured by the Dervishes, and was employed as a clerk or sort of quarter-master and attached to the Kababish in that capacity when they were brought to Omdurman by the Khalifa. Later, when famine came, the Khalifa sent the remnants of the tribe to live on the country near Karkoj in the Fung, and the Turk and his wife went with them. At the re-occupation, Hussein, the Turk, was restored to his family and lands in his native Egypt, and she and her sons went with him. When Hussein died in Egypt, she asked to return and came back to Omdurman, whence, after her sons grew up, she returned to the tribe. Her son is now with the Nurab.

Sheikh Ahmad Gismallah of the Kawahla came to take leave of me and see me off and take back any final instructions.

Ali El Tom asked me to lunch, and also Muhammad Effendi and Hasan Nagila. A very good lunch he gave me too (except that I couldn't manage the liver and the kisra—but the chicken he had cooked for me and the doughnuts were prime, as also were the sour milk and coffee). After lunch we sat in his tent and talked of aeroplanes and of Kabbashi songs. I rode away about 3.30, with the usual concourse to see me off.

I asked Tingle after we had left if the Kawahla had been pleased with their reception, and he said they had been—had had nagas slaughtered and sheep and merissa (beer) "more than necessary". Maybe my supine policy may have been of some use.

Rode to near Galaa El Tin—pleasant ride. I went to bed early and risked sleeping without a net, as there seemed to be no mosquitoes.

31.10.31

There were, however, as I woke bitten on the hands. Cool ride from 5.30 to camp at 8 a.m. The going over hardish sand, sometimes gravel on high ground, thickish bush.

---

[19] Meaning here a civil servant or white soldier of the Turco-Egyptian regime, not necessarily a Turk.

Rode again about 4 p.m. till 6 p.m. We passed by hills called Um Hatob and descended to where there is at this moment a pool below these hills, among trees. Here our camels drank and my camel knocked me off its back by turning from the water suddenly under an overhanging branch. We found the camp by a camp of Arabs who proved to be Dueih and the Omda's own people at that.

Some of them came to talk to me. They have not been very peripatetic during the rains. They moved from Khor Es Sunt to this neighbourhood and have remained about here since. The Omda was out looking for lost sheep. He returned about 8.30 and talked to me. He had recently been to Khor Es Sunt and remarked upon the wretched condition of the Kawahla slaves there. Only one Dueih slave, so he says, has ever complained and that was old snowball Kheirallah, whom I saw last March. The story of the Dueih who were arrested and fined by the Hamar was retold, with the addition that apparently the Dueih signed some paper with their seals at Khommas. The Omda apparently rose in the middle of the night to kill sheep for the police, which was very hospitable of him. I got to bed at 9.30 and slept very soundly till dawn.

1.11.31

The Omda saw us off, asking me at the same time to warn the people at Hamrat Esh Sheikh that he had lost sheep.

Rode over rolling country and past a flat-topped hill called El Mereikeh, and between it and another called Mereybia, to find camp near the latter. I spent the morning writing a note for Hamilton to read and give me advice upon. After the hamla had gone on I felt fit but unenergetic, and read a little until we rode on. Just after sunset we reached camp on the slope of a hill. The evening was cool and I did some more writing. The night was not so cool as it had promised to be, with the result that I awoke at 3.30 to hear the hamla roused and saddled. This left me little time for more sleep.

2.11.31

Rode till about 8 a.m. towards the hills of Hamrat Esh Sheikh through Wadi Um Hayaia. Finally we came into some very extensive cultivations and so to the huts of Sheikh Ali's left-behind slaves and old people. This appears a much happier and more prosperous settlement than the hovels round Um Badr. Tindil, the agent, came to greet me. A bobby called Ibrahim had arrived on Thursday with mail (a good big one too), and I had a bath. A strong wind blew all day from the north. I spent most of the day resting and reading a novel S. had sent me. About 1 p.m. I took a walk along the wadi the tent was in to the wells and passed the time of day with a couple of girls who were drawing water.

In the afternoon I interviewed the merchant or feki called El Amin about whom Ali El Tom is so hot. At 4.30 Tindil, the agent of Ali El Tom, took me for a ride through the settlement of Awlad Gereish slaves to the pool farther along the wadi. A pleasant evening scene at the pool which is not very full just now—it is over-hung by high sandstone bluffs. Tindil came and drank a little tea with me.

3.11.31

As I was getting up about 5 a.m. after a rather poor night, I saw a slave woman approaching through the half-light—pulled on my shorts and shooed her away, telling her to come a little later. It is astonishing how someone always turns up with a complaint just as one is moving off. There were two women this time—one about an assault made on her by a slave —soon dealt with.

Rode across the hills by Athat [Adat] El Gawad till about 8.30, when we found camp among sparse bush. Weather much fresher. Spent the morning and afternoon writing letters to go off tonight. Rode again 3.30 till 6 p.m., when we arrived near Abu Zaima wells. No Arabs came to me. But I could hear dogs barking.

We are now on the road made by Watt from Soderi to Abu Zaima. Mail left for Soderi.

4.11.31

Rose 4.30, rode 5 a.m.—bright moonlight. The sun was not up until 6. There was a fresh north wind and dust in the air, so that the sunrise looked yellow and hills of Um Zebad in front of us were blurred as if with mist. It was fairly chilly for the first time. Reached camp 8.15 a.m. pretty tired. The Bishari camel is not the easy ride that Zerzur [*sic*] was yesterday.

A mail has arrived. Several notes from Charles de Bunsen, who agrees to the proposed meeting at Kagmar [*sic*] about Christmastime (thereby incidentally avoiding Christmas at El Obeid). Feeling very sleepy. The day quite cool—jumper on under tunic at noon.

Rode again about 3.30, a very long ride until well after dark, when we arrived at the village of Um Khirwa (lit. Mother of Castor Oil). I was dead beat. The Sheikh had a chat about bovine pleuropneumonia, which has just broken out here (it would, as if we haven't enough cattle plague in the district already), and about the Kababish. All this he produced not in the evening, but as I was about to mount in the chill before dawn. I was rather costive and feigned very stupid.

5.11.31

A very long morning ride over sand dunes ending up among the Jebels to the west of Soderi. The way was enlivened by my fruitless attempts to get near enough to some guinea fowl to shoot them. I had one shot but it was a hasty one and I only knocked off a few tail feathers. The tent was pitched, when we reached it, in a valley between hills—one might have been in a miniature Cumberland. I tried drawing my horse, but the effort was spoiled by his being watered, after which he started grazing and spoiled the pose. I could not get him to look at me, which was the position I wanted for the head. After the hamla had moved on I drew the surrounding hills. It was pretty warm at mid-day.

The morning ride had been 4.30 till 8.45 a.m. The afternon one was short. We emerged from the hills and soon saw Soderi and found Akib Effendi and the rest waiting for me on horses and donkeys. As we rode on together, Sheikh Niama, who had the same afternoon arrived from Haraza, appeard on a camel. I was very pleased to see him. He does not look very fit. And so about 4.30 p.m. I arrived at my house again after 40 days and 40 nights in the wilderness. And thank God it was Thursday evening and the next day the weekly Sabbath.

The luxury of a warm bath, an oil lamp, and a cushioned chair made me rapidly forget the stiffness of 3 days' steady camel-riding and long rides at that.

6.11.31

I spent this day like a European Sunday: rose late, gave out groceries to the cook, and spent the day doing accounts and sorting out papers I had brought back from trek so as to take action on them next day. Another great event of this day was a hair cut, the first since I had one on "The Staffordshire" on 2 Sept. Muhammad Musa Lawlaw, who had arrived the day before with taxes from Ali El Tom, came to see me in the morning and Niama in the afternoon.

Chapter VI

A Trek in the Northern Hills

[Soderi—Jabal al-Nahud—Jabal Haraza—al-Rukab—Dar Zunqul—Hishayb—Khawr Hillat Marakha—Mazrub Wells—Ban Jadid—Soderi]

7.11.31 to 12.11.31

This week at Soderi passed with much more business to do in it than I had hoped. I was full up in the office every day and always seemed to have work to do outside in the house as well. On the 7th Feki Gumaa Sahel arrived and made for my house while I was trying to hit a golf ball in the evening. He talked for hours.

I engaged a cross-eyed lad as groom and rode out on my new horse three or four times in the mornings and evenings. Sand grouse were watering at the pool by the wells in the mornings. I didn't try to shoot any, however. Akib has dug a new well just below the hill on which the offices and prison stand. It gave sweet water at first but has now turned a little brackish.

On Monday evening Gumaa Sahal came in for a talk and stayed very long.

On Tuesday I worked all the afternoon and Niama Sirkatti came to tea just after sunset, when I had done looking at my camels.

On Wednesday afternoon, Akib the Mamur came to tea: the cook had made cakes. They might have been lighter, but weren't a failure.

I can't recall how the time in the office went—there was a homicide case and a theft, and the rest of the time seemed to be occupied with routine correspondence and with slaves. The correspondence I never managed quite to finish and had to take two or three things on trek; and yet I was idle only one whole evening when I read a farcical book left by Hector Watt.

On Thursday afternoon, after a hectic morning. I rode out of Soderi about 4 p.m., and camped in the sand-dunes to the north about 5.30 p.m. The night was cold: I took a long time to get to sleep.

N.B. Niama said that, while it is true that none of the Hufra [*sic*] Nubas ever hire themselves out as herdsmen, the lads of the Jebels Haraza, Abu Hadid and Um Durag do. Especially those of Abu Hadid.

On Thursday morning all the Sheikhs and one elder from each village in Katul turned up. Niama had previously told me he had told them to appear, but I had hoped they would arrive a day or two before my departure—or else miss me. The question is the choice of a successor to old Tamar Agha,[1] who died in September. Niama had told them to assemble and agree as to which one of his sons they would have. He had told me that Hamadallah, the younger, had been his father's agent, while the elder, Khamis, was the stronger man. I could not get Niama to say that he would strongly prefer Khamis appointed. The assembled sheikhs and elders said that the sons of Tamar Agha were alike to them, but that, as the old man had chosen Hamadallah as his representative and agent in his life time, they would not refuse him if he was appointed. Again I could not get Niama to express a strong opinion, so I accepted the popular choice. Maclaren's notes of 1926 say that Khamis is harsh and unpopular. Both Niama and the Mamur said that the people preferred Hamadallah because Khamis was a bit stern with them. Anyway I shall ask approval for Hamadallah to try his luck for 6 months on probation. He can always be kicked out if he is a notable failure.

13.11.31

Rode from 6 to 8.30 over sand-dunes and then down into a bottom among trees and 10-foot-high Adaar[2] grass, and then up on the far side to find camp among trees on hardish sand. Jebel Er Rueis to the north—the bottom we passed through is Er Rueis, where there are salt workings.

Wrote a note on Um Badr and Hamrat esh Sheikh for Hamilton. Tried to draw a camel in the afternoon.

Rode on at 3.30. Soon among dunes again. There appeared on our left the hills of Um Danun, and in front of us E.N.E. Jebel Es Serj. . . . Just before sunset we rode down off a dune to see the pool of Gamaama in front of us with the Jebel beyond. The colours were amazing, from light blue above to pink tinted with violet on the jebels, with dark green trees in front and then the blue pool and brown earth, with cows and a few Arabs and a lady wearing an orange robe.

We rode to the pool and I spoke to the Arabs (Farahna) while our camels drank. Camp was about a mile farther on towards the Jebel. We arrived at 5.45. Cold night.

14.11.31

Started at 5.45 and rode till 8.45. On the way Sheikh Hamid Ali of the Awlad Ugba came to meet me (a policeman had been sent to fetch him from beyond Jebel Um Sunta). I chatted with him during the ride.

---

[1] *'Umda* of Katul.
[2] *Sorghum arundinaceum.* Massey, 13.

After I had breakfast and a shave, I had Hamid Ali to talk and told him that I wanted to warn him not to let the young men of the Gajaja have hard words with the Nuba as a result of the homicide case last June. He retorted that the Nuba were the aggressors at the moment and continually thieving. He instanced the slaughter of three nagas the other day. Now this was a case I tried in which the accused pleaded guilty. According to Hamid Ali I have been hot-stuffed by Niama: (1) the man who owned the nagas was a Geryati only by ancestry, but born and bred with the Awlad Ugba (2) the nagas were stolen, not stray (3) the whole village was involved and not two men, the accused, only. I said, "But why did not the Uqbi come in and complain?" He said (a) Niama had promised to make good their loss from his own camels (b) Niama had told him not to (c) there was no news that I was at the merkaz. I told him to send in the complainant to see me in 23 days' time. But I'm not sure I hadn't better see him here before I go to Abu Hadid.

Hamid Ali had much more to the same effect. I felt very weary and had rather a headache all the morning. When the hamla had started, I tried drawing a tree, but the sun was in my eyes, time was short, I was seated uncomfortably on a bank, and I made a mess of it.

I told Hamid Ali that the complainant had better catch me up at Hamrat El Wuzz, and he rode on with us to try and find them.

I slept like a log this night until dawn.

15.11.31

Rode from 5.45 till 8.45 over very open country. Jebels Um Durag and Abu Hadid to the east and the two Nihid in front. There was much "dereis"[3] grass which has a thorny seed like a calthorp, which tires the camels and gives them sore feet. We found the camp beneath big trees at the place of the wells under Jebel En Nihid (at present there is still standing water). My tent was pitched by a big tree, from under which there was the most perfect view of the pools and the mountain behind. I tried a drawing of it twice over and spent all the remainder of the morning over it.

As soon as the hamla began to pack up, Sh. Hamid Ali appeared and said the complainant in the case of the three nagas and his witnesses had turned up. I took down their statements, which have the sound of truth, and, if they are true, I have been fooled by Niama. Thank Goodness I did not settle the question of the fine. I summonsed the complainant for 6th December with his witnesses. I shall ask Mayall's advice about the case. Niama would have done well according to his own and Arab lights, if only he had suceeded in settling the case and satisfying the owner of the nagas.

---

[3] *Tribulus terrestris.* BM, 86.

This he has failed to do. I think Niama will have to be reprimanded severely, and I shall suggest to Mayall putting an administrative fine on the village if I find that I consider the complainant's evidence true. Alternatively, as I proceeded before on a charge of mischief, I might re-open the case on a charge of theft this time (a dirty trick—but one bad turn deserves another).

Rode at 3.45 and continued riding until nearly 7 p.m. Tingle fell out on the way—his camel baulking at the dereis. I was left with one policeman and we seemed to ride on for ever. However, ultimately we arrived at the Locust Dump where I last was on 5th May.

The Omda Salim Ibrahim Dolib came to greet me and drank tea. He complained that the Awlad Ugba are digging wells here in a part of the wadi where they should not dig. Naturally Hamid Ali had complained earlier in the day in exactly the opposite sense. All very difficult. I am to go and see the wells tomorrow and shall probably, I expect, merely issue an order than no one shall dig except where they dug last year.

Slept early.

16.11.31

Rose about 6.30 a.m., very grateful for a good night's rest. As I was shaving, Koko reported that the hamla of the "Insect Inspector" had arrived, i.e. of Darling who is cruising around Northern Kordofan. He came in himself by breakfast time and breakfasted with me.

After breakfast the Omda turned up and he and I went to look at the wells. I found the talk a bit hot between the Kababish and the Nuba. Finally, after inspecting all the well field and finding out more or less where the various tribesmen usually dig, and having heard that Sh. Muhammad El Tom years ago made a line between Nuba and Kababish, I marked down a Sayaal tree at the south end and a Higlig[4] at the north end and took five ancients of the Kababish (by good luck including a sheikh) and told them to come to the locust huts. There we talked the matter over. It appeared that the talk all arose from the action of a certain Salim Bella, an Atawi, who went and dug to the east of where a Nuba Dolabi, Fadlallah Lain, had dug. Therefore after taking due council [sic] with the Omda Salim of the Nuba of Haraza and the five Kabbashi ancients, I issued an order saying that on account of the talk and because there would be thirst if no more wells were dug just now, and pending the arrival of Sheikh Ali El Tom and Sheikh Niama Sirkatti next month, no Nuba shall dig or drink west of a line from the Higlig to the Sayala [sic] and no Kabbashi east, except for the Kibeyshab, who shall stay on their old wells. This means

---

[4] *Balanites aegyptica*, the soapberry or desert date tree. *IT*, 84.

little upset. The wells at the spot where the trouble arose shall be closed down.

By this time it was 2.15 and Darling was rapidly summoned to lunch.

After lunch, when the hamla had gone on, the sheikh of Tilib village in Jebel Um Durag arrived to ask for leave to go back to Nihid wells. His is the village which slaughtered the nagas the other day, and I pitched into him and took a guarantee for his appearance in Soderi on 7.12.31, with one El Amin Ziyada. I also said there was not a hope now, in view of the theft, of my giving the people of Um Durag leave to return to En Nihid till the talk had died down. This jebel is the home of the man who killed the Kabbashi at Nihid last June, so the theft has made things much worse.

Darling rode with me to Gafala village under Jebel Haraza. I mounted him on Zurzur because he owned it once about a couple of years ago. I rode my horse, which went along fairly well, after a frisky start, except when some women "lulu-ed" at me on the road, which made him shy. We reached Gafala just about sunset. Darling will be in Omdurman on 30.11.31, so I shall give him letters to post. Also he has camelmen returning to Bara, whence he started, and they shall take letters to Hamilton on official matters. Darling's arrival has broken my hope of seeing what it felt like to be on my own for over ten weeks, but certainly his arrival has put me in a good humour, when Niama's wiles and the rather unfortunate and possibly serious rows between the Kababish and the Nuba had considerably depressed and worried me. I sat up writing in order to get letters to Bara about various business with which I was in arrears, and a letter to Hamilton asking him about his advice about the Nuba-Kababish situation and Niama's hot-stuffing me. I didn't finish until after 10, when I was dead tired and went to bed. But—as they say in novels—not to sleep. The villagers had organised a dance (I discovered afterwards it was supposed to be in my honour), which went on till midnight and later. The noise is much too exciting for me to hope to get to sleep in it.

17.11.31

Consequently I rose at 5.30 very bleary-eyed and weary, took leave of Darling, who is returning to Hamrat El Wuzz, and rode into the jebel.

MacMichael has written a well-known account of Jebel Haraza[5] from the archaeological and historical point of view, but I've never seen any description of it. As one approaches it, one goes up a defile filled with red sand between granite hills of the usual boulder-strewn type. In front are range after range of red granite hills rising to greater heights further off. We passed the village of Hasan Doleib, the old man who went to Abu

---

[5] "Notes on Gebel Haraza", *SNR*, X, 1927.

Uruq with me in May. It lies under a jebel called Tendelti (one of the ranges of Haraza). By about 8 we reached the top of a dune which made a kind of pass, and down on the other side appeared away to the east tucked in the hills the village of Khor Jaadein, which is the home of the Dolib family and Niama Sirkatti. The whole valley is called Khor Jaadein. As one enters it from the west, Jebel Tendelti is on one's right and behind, while a long way in front, are the heights of Jebel Keilum (a flattish-topped jebel). I have a very bad sketch of its shape as seen from my tent in Khor Jaadein.

We descended into the valley to a well which is there. Actually there are two wells: one now being worked which is 17 $\frac{1}{2}$ ragils (ragil = about 5' 9") and the other a most extraordinary "sania"[6] about 30 yards to the N.W. of it. The sania consists of an enormous hole in the ground about 15 yards across and going down deep into the rock below. Underneath a cavern runs back eastwards and the water is some 10 yards away from the side of the well-opening. Thus a number of men may be required to bring water to the surface. The water is at a depth of 16 ragils. There were no people drawing water at present, so I could not go down. The Omda suggests that, if the ground below the wide opening to the surface were dug out, probably water would be found directly below. They say this well is Anaj work (the Anaj being the fabulous race of giant size who preceded the Nuba and the Arabs).

I was so tired and the day was so hot that I did practically nothing all the time we gailed. I fell asleep for about half an hour at 1 p.m.

At about 4 p.m. we rode again, I on the Bishari. The Omda had sent for young men who had watered our camels. They were originally two: but, after I had said I would give them a reward as they came specially, they became four and watered all the camels, instead of only the riding camels. So they took a sugar loaf and departed. We rode round the corner of a jebel called Azib and over another sort of pass made by a sandhill. Here, lying back of a valley full of trees, ruins of a village of stone are to be seen high upon the hillside, with a stone wall (for protection) in front. This is the village of Abdel Hadi, ancestor of the Dolib, the ruling house (of Dongola Arab stock) of Jebel Haraza. I had already passed one of these ruined villages, and a similar wall called a tirji' . . . (i.e. presumably "You get back"). Here in the valley there is much cultivation, and feterita[7] is grown.

We got down for the night at a small village on the top of a sand hill, called Izeib. To the east rose the cliffs of a jebel called Shingul.

The colours, especially at evening, in this countryside are remarkable.

---

[6] Deep well.
[7] *Sorghum vulgare*, the most common variety of *dhura*.

The blue of the sky goes down into the blue shadows over the dark red hills, and between the hills and around the range are sand dunes of light terracotta colour covered with tufts of grass and merkh bush. In the low valleys are trees.

I went to bed at 8 and made sure of sleep. The night was fairly warm but the morning cool.

18.11.31

At about 5.45 we started from Izeib down the sand hill towards Shangol [*sic*]. When we got near the foot of the jebel we dismounted and the Omda pointed the way up a very stony and narrow track to wells which are above in the rock. We walked up and found some difficulty in letting strings of donkeys, laden with water and driven by girls, pass downwards. After a fairly long climb we came to the wells. There are two, one below the other. The lower one is a hole in the rock with a platform of rock in front, which makes drawing the water a fairly simple matter. The upper one is reached by a scramble, and the curious may then descend, also by a scramble, into a cave and so into the dark hole where the water is. When, e.g. in the summer time, the well is much used and the water little, it can be heard dripping from the rock into the pool in the heart of the rock. Niama wants the crack out of which it trickles widened. I couldn't see it, of course, at present, because the water level is above it. I went also into another fairly long cave running back into the mountain. The Omda said there had been a well in front of that and it had fallen in. He told me also that a great snake inhabits this well—Bir Shangul—but appears in the open air only at the beginning of the rains. It does no harm and is given offerings of milk! They told me I was the first Inspector who had ever been right up to and into these wells. Surely MacMichael must have been, if not others, but they say not.

When I came out of the dry cave and turned towards the northwest, there was a magnificent view down the gorge which was still in shadow, out onto the plain far away and below. So we descended into the sunlight. Tingle drew comparisons with rock wells in Jebel Meidob.

Then we rode on and climbed another sand-dune pass, turned a corner eastwards, and found a village called Er Rokab tucked away in a horseshoe of hills. The village has trees and there is actually a dom palm. Here was camp pitched.

The plateau on which this village stands must be 300 to 400 feet at least above the plain. In front to the north is a jebel called Um Karoos, in which there are, they say, gelts (water-filled fissures) and wells. Beyond to the N.N.E. is a tremendous long view away to a ridge called Dahr el Humar (the donkey's back), and far beyond it to Dubeisat el Tuwal and Kol Ez

Zerga and Kol El Hamra—over 30 miles away. These last two jebels I passed to the east of on my way from Abu Urug to Omdurman in May. The air up here is magnificent.

I omitted . . . to note that as we passed round Jebel El Azib the Omda took me right up under the foot of the jebel to show me the ruins of the Doalib village of the last generation but one. Niama has had bits of it rebuilt, and he and the Omda Salim and their families live there now at the beginning of the rains. A little further on in the valley we passed the Omda's present huts among the trees and I greeted various brothers and nephews.

N.B. The huts here are usually built of stone and mud below in a circle and a conical roof is out on the stone walls. The Nubas also build conical bee-hive-shaped mud and stone grain stores called "sueyba".[8] These are a conspicuous feature of the villages.

At Er Rokab after breakfast the Omda, Sheikh Ajabna Hamid of the village and a number of elders came and chatted over tea. They told me the names of the surrounding hills—from west to east: Sago, Kuweili, Kaiser, Dunkus, Tugunju. Sh. Ajabna told me the following legend of the origin of his house and of the people of this part of the jebel. In days long past when the Anaj were still in the land, Zeyadia Arabs were masters of the plains round Haraza and at war with the Anaj, who lived in these hills. The Zeyadia used to "nishugh", i.e. move west in the rains as the Arabs still do. One year at the beginning of the rains they sent a slave girl saying, "Go to the Anaj and find out what manner of people they are we war with and how many". So this spy went off to the Anaj and said she had run away from her masters. She stayed for the rains with the Anaj and then later returned to the Zeyadia, when they had returned from the nishugh. She reported to them that the Anaj were seven brothers only and a woman their cousin. The Zeyadia therefore attacked the Anaj and slew the brethren and took the girl cousin prisoner and carried her to Hamrat El Wuzz and named her Hamrat. Later a Rikabi (Arab) merchant named Hamid Muhammad came and stole Hamrat from the Zeyadia and brought her back to her mother to Um Ka' in Haraza. (Her mother apparently was Melika—queen—of the east of the jebel.) Hamid then paid dowry and married Hamrat and had her son named Mahmoud.

Now Hamrat, before she married Hamid, had had Anaj daughters by an Anaj husband. These daughters were three, named 'Asa, the eldest, Kaka and Bol. Bol was barren; but 'Asa was the mother of the Nogara family (khashm el Beit)[9] from which sheikhs of Er Rokab are still chosen.

---

[8] Arabic pl.: *suwaib*.
[9] The extended family (of the ruling house).

Kaka was mother of the following khushm buyut: Jaalia, Ajuz, Gimeila, Zeinab, Zerga (all called "Bagara"). When Hamrat came to die and divide her possessions among her daughters (she was melika of all the countryside and had great wealth), she collected her possessions and her daughters round her. She told the eldest to choose what she wanted as her portion and 'Asa laid hold of the nogara (the chieftain's drum) and its stick and beat it saying, "Let me have the chieftainship and the others can have the rest".

Mahmoud, son of Hamrat, daughter of Hineia, daughter of Hanaana begat the following khushm buyut: Matara, Dugaaga, Baggara, Derham, Ahl Koubi. The ruins of Hamrat's villages are still to be seen on the slopes of Jebel Kersei.

This is the genealogy of Sh. Saalim Ibrahim Dolib:

El Feki
Muhammad El Feki = Bakhita bt. Joda
Abdel Hadi
Dolib
Ibrahim
Saalim

N.B. The old man of the Um Durag whom I met at Hamrat and who said he had been with Amir Arabi Dafaallah at Rejaf during the Mahdia is Jaad er Rab El Nur, ex-omda of Um Durag. The family of Nogara now make their camel brand thus: I O representing the drum O and stick I of their ancestors.

Later Ajabna came to complain about 8 men who had been removed from his sheikhship and added to that of El Haj Khidr Ed Dokri when El Haj Khidr was moved from Abu Tabr this summer to Haraza. Later still he came again with a year-old order from Niama to the effect that herds should not drink at Shungul. I referred him to the Omda. After the hamla had moved I tried to draw a part of the village and surrounding hills.

We rode at 3.30 down off the plateau past two Bagara villages and two Matara villages and round a corner into a very pleasant valley with a watercourse to the east and beyond that a high dune and hills. Here the camp had been pitched and we were down by 5 p.m. If there is rain there ought to be plenty of corn in this valley.

El Haj Khidr Ed Dokri turned up. His new village is in the same valley just round the corner of some rocks standing out in the plain.

After I had had tea, Salim Ibrahim and El Haj Khidr came to talk. I asked the Omda about the men transferred from Ajabna. It appears they were all transferred at their own request. One Adam Daoud had later recanted, but it appears he had agreed before me to follow El Haj Khidr. (I don't remember this.)

The two then went on to talk of this and that and I drew with great ease from El Haj Khidr a repetition of his story of Slatin's escape from the Khalifa in Omdurman. They went on talking about the Mahdia for some time and then turned to talk of their relations with the Kababish today. It appeared to me from their talk (1) That the Nuba will reckon it a great misfortune if any boundaries are drawn between them and the Kababish as a result of the meeting between Ali El Tom and Niama. (2) That the sections of the Kababish they really object to are the Awlad Ugba and the Atawia. They dealt at length with the story of the row between the Awlad Ugba and the Kibeyshab at Hamrat 4 years ago, which led, so Saalim said, to Sheikh Muhammad El Tom's fining the Awlad Ugba £E50 for wounding a Kibeyshabi with a spear in the thigh, and dividing them on the wells. After that event, so I understood them to say, Hamid Ali removed all the Awlad Ugba to Nihid.

They went on to talk on Niama's row with Ali El Tom last February, when Niama called A.T. a liar.

Then Saalim was roused by El Haj Khidr's telling him that Rahma had been going round Haraza "hukming" people with fines on alleged authority of Niama. Also Dolib. N.B. Medowi wad ? [*sic*] knows the Dolib genealogy.

About 8.30 I was nearly asleep and sent them away. It blew hard in the night and woke me up so that I did not sleep very well.

19.11.31

Rose about 5.30 and rode up into the hills behind to see the wells of Guzz. I walked much of the distance, and saw three wells in the gorge. We were back at the village by 7 a.m. and the sun was warm, but we met the wind again, which the jebel had kept off before.

I said good-bye to El Haj Khidr and we crossed the valley and watercourse and climbed the sand dune going due east. Later we turned southwards round a corner of the jebels and the Omda said these were the Kobi Hills. Further on he pointed out the curious rock up aloft which is called Bint Kobi (Kobi's daughter). He said it would look better when we had turned the corner westwards again and come to our camping ground. He also showed me some rock drawings under a large boulder.

When we had turned the corner and entered a very pretty narrow valley between very rocky hills, filled with trees most of which are in flower and smelling fine. He was right—for Bint Kobi in the morning light appears from this angle a very excellent example of Epstein's art representing a lady, probably pregnant, kneeling high up on the rocks with her hands behind her back.

My tent had been pitched right under a tree on the bank of the watercourse in the bottom of the valley. Cool and delightful view of the very high rock hills round about, which look like architectural designs.

We took 2 hours and 20 minutes from Abu Gereyid, the last village we stopped in. Sheikhs whose villages we passed are: Bagara—Sumain Ghabosh; Matara—Muhammad Mahmoud and Muhammad Ahmad Hasanein; Dugaga—Muhammad Ali Abu Kis and Hamid Mustafa; Abu Gereyid—Ziyada Hadi, El Haj Khidr.

By the time I had had breakfast it was 10.30 and then I shaved and washed and felt pretty weary and read files about Abu Hadid and Um Durag.

About 1 p.m. a Howari, resident with the Nuba here, turned up about a case concerning a cow, which he had bought at Ridba off a Hassani of Dueim four years ago, and which is now claimed by a Nuba here as his. As we went on talking, more and more people turned up, including the Omda and the talk continued till 2.30. Incidentally, the custom of making a stranger have a neighbour (jaar) of the tribe he resides with, who is his surety, apparently exists in Haraza, as well as among the nomads.

I had lunch and had just begun attempting to draw a jebel top, when the Omda came and asked me to go and see the wells. We went up the defile and came to a wide space among the rocks. There is only one well working: a fairly shallow one. This well Niama is supposed to be building with government money to assist him. Very little seems to have been done. Salim said the builder who had been employed was useless and had run to Hamrat and been sacked. A newly engaged one should have arrived, but has not yet appeared.

They are attempting to build with badly burnt brick made at Hamra. This seems to me stupid, as stone is galore here. Also they will need a very strong wall, especially at the well-mouth, for the water-course, if it comes down in spate here, would break anything except the strongest that can be built. I explained this. I also suggested they might pull the bucket with a camel attached to the rope.

I shall be sorry to leave this jebel tomorrow. I have thoroughly enjoyed its very dramatic scenery and colours in all lights and at all times of the day—were they painted as they are none would believe the colours. And the air up here had done me good. I sat and watched the light change and fade on the mountaintop I had been trying to draw, until dusk came.

About 7.15 I sent for Sheikh Salim to ask him about: (1) The question of what exactly happened when Muhammad El Tom is alleged to have come to Hamra and when that was. (2) The cause of the disputes this year.

(1) It appears, so far as I can make out, that Sheikh Muhammad El Tom appeared only once at Hamra and that was 4 years ago, to settle the

dispute between the Awlad Ugba and the Kibeyshab. On that occasion, these two sections of the Kababish had an affray on the wells which ended in the wounding of several and in especial one with a lance in the thigh. According to Salim, he fined the Awlad Ugba £E50 and put them on the west of the 'idd and the Kibeyshab he left on the east. Salim also says that in "Davies's time" (it can't have been if the next bit is true), before Hamra wells were opened, there was a dispute at Masarin between Nuba and Kababish and Muhammad El Tom divided them. In Turkish times, so he says, El Tom, father of Ali El Tom, gave half Safia and half Masarin to the Nuba.

(2) He says that the cause of the trouble in the cultivation was one Wad Esh Shaib, a Ghileyani sheikh, who was given cultivation by Nubas, and refused to pay "sharia"[10] and complained to Ali El Tom. The trouble on the wells was all due to the Atawi Salim Bella. N.B. Salim also says that Hamid Ali withdrew the Awlad Ugba about 2 years ago from Hamra to Nihid.

Salim then went on to expatiate on former Doalib claims, e.g. that the Kababish would not pursue slayers nearer to the jebel than Abu Hashim, and so on. He then said that much could be done if only Ali El Tom would settle one of the Nurab in the vicinity of Hamra to be a responsible wakil.

He then complained of Maarufin that he takes a sheep a flock from Haraza herds watering in the rain pools at Gabra and then a rial from anyone who later wishes to dig a well there. Salim said he complained of this to A.T. when the latter was at Gabra last year on his way from Khartoum, and A.T. gave him an order in writing that Maarufin was not to take from Doalib.

A wind sprang up in the night and woke me at 2.15. I slept again but with rheumatics.

20.11.31

Started at 6 a.m., rode out of the gorge and turned south. "The girl Kobi" looked well from further away. The ground during most of the morning ride was stony and there were several khors. Passed old iron-working under Jebel Arangol, crossed Khor Shekhakha, which comes from a cleft in the hills of the same name, and Jebel Shebb. Behind these is Shagmal. Rode for 3 hours and 35 minutes and arrived up a hill, well to the south of the Haraza ranges, to the village of Dar Zunqol.

N.B. Yesterday evening Salim Ibrahim told me that cattle plague had broken out again in his brethren's herds, and this morning we passed

---

[10] Monthly pay, salary.

them—9 dead. They are quarantining. Apparently the Nuba understand quarantining and washing thoroughly.

From the place where my tent was pitched, I had a very pleasant view over towards Haraza, across a valley with patches of red sand up against the jebel beyond.

I felt pretty weary—wrote a little. The ladies of the village, unasked, made a song and dance and serenaded me, which cost me 6/-, and then, thank God, removed their noise further off. When the hamla moved on, I was shifted into what was evidently the sheikh's hut, and there I sat and talked to the Omda and Sheikh Musa and the Omda's cousin Ahmad Yasin Dolib. Meanwhile, two very old men with Puck-like faces came in and squatted, and another man repaired a girth of the Omda's saddle in the background. I got them talking about relations with the Kababish, and the wells at Hamra in particular. The Omda showed me the ragged remnants of his father's Powers under the Powers of Nomad Sheikhs Ordinance 1922, which he inherited. The old men soon almost forgot my presence and went on talking about the wells and cows and corn. Meanwhile I sat and reflected how impossible it is to enter into another man's life unless one actually lives it with him. In the case of blokes like these, it is very difficult and needs the greatest concentration to follow their more private conversation. Naturally so: even when one is of the same race as another man how little significance much of his internal family shop and jokes has for an outsider listening in.

I have recorded their remarks about Hamra and about the cultivation disputes with the Kababish elsewhere. The main point was put by one of the very old men. 'Sheikh Ali wants boundaries, they say his son doesn't. We certainly don't. We want things to go by 'muhanna' as they have done in the past."

I rode off on my horse about 3.30 and the Omda saw me part of the way. We passed through cultivations going south towards Um Durag Jebel and got down just before sunset on the side of a sand-hill.

I had just got my boots off, when I saw a policeman, whom I recognised by his white camel and his stocky figure as Ibrahim, coming down the opposite slope from the direction I had come. He carried mail and had been passed by us near the cultivations. Spent the evening reading mail, writing, and writing a note on the Nuba view of their dispute with the Kababish.

A cold night—cramp in the knee in bed.

21.11.31

Started on horseback just before dawn. A long and slow ride over sandhills southwards—general slope steeply uphill. I walked much of the way, but it was pleasanter than camel. Arrived up the last hill, we turned a corner of Jebel Um Durag and arrived at Hisheib village (on a sand hill), where the omda Ahmad Gumaa Abu Gideiri met me with the sheikh of the village, one Adam. Arrived 8.45. There is the rest-house of grass huts here, so I have a hut instead of a tent. Moreover I was given my first bath since the morning of the 16th. Just after I had done shaving, another policeman arrived with a mail—Camel Corps query about grain for a training march, urgent from Bara; and a private note from Dicky Mitchell who commands the company. At the same moment the noise of aeroplanes far to the south was heard. Tingle said he saw them, but I mistook a distant hawk for one and by the time I'd brought glasses to bear, the aeroplanes had disappeared behind a bit of the jebel. I wonder if it was Dicky going to try to see me at Soderi. He said in his note he had hoped to make an aeroplane trip to do so.

The Omda Ahmad Gumaa then came and talked. He badly wants leave for his people to go back to their wells at Nihid, from which they have been excluded since the homicide in June. They have been watering during and since the rains at a pool called Mufannikh to the east of here. That has now dried up and they are digging temporary wells in a khor between this and Abu Hadid. He says it will do them no good to go to water at Hamrat El Wuzz because there is not enough grass there for cows. If I will not give them leave for them to return to Nihid, they will all be going south and there is yet the blood-money to collect.

I pointed out that, as men from Telib village here had now committed theft of 3 nagas from the Awlad Ugba, there was no hope of my giving such permission, until that case had been settled and the talk had died, and until the two Nazirs had met and made an agreement and peace. He went on at some length to try and persuade me. I said that, 3 years ago, when he was appointed, he and all his sheikhs and elders had sworn they would not countenance theft and would hand over all thieves to government. I explained the point of view that the owner of the 3 nagas and the Awlad Ugba and all the Kababish were certain that there were more people in the theft than the two lads I have put in prison. He said it had happened in his absence and neither he nor the Nazir had been able to produce more thieves than the 3 brought forward. Had I done anything about a fine? I said. "No, what was the use? Had those two boys enough wealth to pay a fine?" He admitted they hadn't. I said I held open the question of a fine till the owner of the animals arrived. I urged him that there was no use of his talking about returning to Nihid until he had done something about satisfying the owner of the slaughtered nagas who now demands more guilty persons and compensation for his animals. In the end I gathered that the Omda proposes to be in Soderi when I return to meet the Awlad Ugba and also to waylay Niama and if possible Ali El Tom (who may get to Soderi about 15th or 16th December). I think I shall get either Niama or Ahmad Gumaa to offer to make the village pay the fine, which would be good.

He and Adam told me the full story of the Nihid row. I knew the June row but did not know what had preceded it, viz.: Last "derat" (i.e. about November 1930) Nuba went as usual to dig at Nihid for their wells, and Ali El Tom's slave Ali Dafaallah and four Awlad Ugba—Bella Zaid, Hamid El Boseer, and two others—tried to prevent them. The Nuba complained to Watt who said the Awlad Ugba had no right to stop them and they should continue in peace. The Awlad Ugba then said the Nuba cows had plague, and Watt sent a policeman who quarantined the cows.

I spent the rest of the morning and the afternoon till 4 p.m. dealing with a request from the Camel Corps to arrange grain and water for a march of theirs through the south of the district in January and February. This had arrived this morning urgent by a special policeman. I also wrote a note to Hamilton and a summons to El Dokri El Haj Khidr [sic] through the Omda Salim and sent the policeman off. He should get to Bara on Friday morning. After this I felt fearfully tired for some reason. But old men including Sabil Zaghawi and Timsah, both of whom are about 90, had turned up to talk. So they drank tea and talked (about 8 turned up altogether), but I was in poor form. They talked a little of the old Nuba language (now not known to the younger men and children) for my benefit. They say this language is akin to that of the Danagla in Dongola and that their genealogy comes from Metemma (Hobaji). They say also that the language of Abu Hadid was different: Obeidallah, father of Holi the thief, could speak Hadadawi but could not understand Daragawi (Obeidallah died this year. All the sons of Obeidallah are thieves).

They left at dusk and I felt dead beat and went to bed at 8 p.m. and slept till 4.30, when cold and cramp woke me to a magnificent starlit night, after which I half slept and dreamt ridiculous dreams of the "hopeless search" variety . . . .

22.11.31

After I had done stoutness exercises and had a bath, I felt much better and made a drawing of sorts of the head of Eleasir, my horse.

After breakfast the ex-Omda Jad El Rab El Nur turned up and then the Omda and Jud Sabril (another ex-Omda—all sacked for thieving or being mixed up in it), and three sheikhs. The fourth is burying his wife. Much talk. Chaps here are short of grain owing to flying locusts.

(1) History of the wells at Nihid. After the taking of Fasher by the British (and probably in 1918 or 1919), Atawia Kababish first dug and

found water at El Nihid. Previous to that, the bed of the pool there (after it had dried in the autumn) had been all cultivated by Nuba. Nuba dug with the Atawia. By the next summer the wells all dried and the people left. The Atawia then had a row with the Ferahna as a consequence of which the government removed them all from this neighbourhood. Three years later, i.e. about 1920, the Awlad Ugba Dar Omar came to the Nihid-Hamrat El Wuzz neighbourhood. That year the Nuba dug again at El Nihid and the Awlad Ugba with them and found water. Either that year or the next, i.e. 1921, El Tom Ali El Tom came and, apparently as a precautionary measure, did not divide the well-field but told the Awlad Ugba to keep their digging to the west and leave the Nuba to the east. Since then there has been no trouble till this year.

The Nuba said that they had never had trouble with Awlad Nawai, nor Atawia nor Seregab nor Awaida, who used to be here—only with the Awlad Ugba. . . . Gad [sic] El Rab said, "There'll never be peace unless the Awlad Ugba go away". Others complained of the slave Ali Dafaallah, Ali El Tom's agent at Nihid (and rightly complained, I think).

(2) The recent slaughtering of the Uqbi's nagas. The sheikh of Telib said the following Nuba went with the Uqbi to see the bodies of the nagas:

Faadil Gabir*
Beshir Shereyb*
Mohammad [sic] Shateita
Awad Es Sid Ismail
Fadlallah Ismail*

* Swore in 1928 February before Watt to reveal all thieves.

I urged again that compensation must be paid. Sheikh Ahmad Gadeil of Telib said that the two boys now in prison could not pay a fine. The Omda said that whatever government imposed or whatever Sheikhs Ali and Niama agreed to, the people of Um Durag would assent to, because they want restoration of good relations and water at Nihid.

Um Durag customs:

(a) As to cultivation. N.B. What the govt. calls Omda was formerly the Mek of the Jebel (King of the Mountain) and what we call sheikh was called Jindi.[11]

In times of drought at the end of the summer, the Mek takes a ram to the top of the mountain, and there it is slaughtered, roasted and eaten. Clothes are put on the top of the mountain. This magic brings rain at once. This custom is still followed. In the early rains no one may hoe till

---

[11] Under the Funj sultanate of Sinner, the *jundi* was a high official at court. See R. S. O'Fahey and J. S. Spaulding, *Kingdoms of the Sudan*, London 1974, 44–6.

the Mek has first hoed. When men sow, the Mek carries milk before them and sprinkles it upon the earth to make it fertile. In the autumn, when the corn is ripe, no man may cut and thresh before the Mek has been enthroned on an angareeb[12] and the tribal drum has been beaten and he has ceremoniously cut and threshed the first ears. These customs are still observed. Moreover, if government would let them, the Nuba would change their Mek when seasons are bad—to change the luck.

(b) As to blood-money. I asked what happened about blood-money in Turkish times and before, i.e. before Niama's nizara united all the Northern Nuba. They said: (1) Since the Doalib of Haraza had possessed all the land, Abu Hadid and Um Durag had been under the Doalib family of Haraza (Abdel Hadi and sons), and the 3 jebels had met blood-money charges together. (2) Apart from that, and before the Doalib, they paid by tribes, i.e. Bugara [sic] would all pay if one of them slew a man, Motara [sic] if one of them, and so on. Sabil Zaghawi was then called to say what a man's price would be. He said 20 cows large and small. A woman's price was half a man's.

They also have a custom that, if a man puts a woman in child and she die in childbirth, then the man pays 7 cows. Three of these are slaughtered at the woman's funeral feast and 4 go to her father. The same applies to a man losing another man's horse. The custom is called dobaih.

When they had gone I wrote down all the above and had lunch and then my hamla started off. I wrote a letter until it was time for me to start also, when all the old men lined up—thieves and retired thieves—to say farewell.

I rode out of the village southwards into a gorge between two hills where even police did not think of riding—so we all dismounted and led the camels down. Had there been a little less red sand and a little more vegetation, one might easily have been in Sicily, or one of those rocky valleys by the sea in Italy, seen in the summer dry and bare when one passes in a steamer. The place is called Khor Kudla and here are the temporary wells in the sand a few feet deep from which the people of Um Durag are drinking at present. Another month, and the khor bed will be dry. At the end of the khor we took leave of the Omda and rode out into the plain. It took us a good 2½ hours' riding, mostly at a fairly smart trot, to get to the west village of Jebel Abu Hadid. We arrived in the last of the daylight after sunset and the Omda met us.

He has built and keeps up a very spacious rest-house compound. There are a large rakooba and two huts for the visiting official and there

---

[12] Bedstead.

[are] more rakoobas (for servants and police) besides "usual offices" (which are better here than at Um Durag, where they were embarrassingly inadequate).

He had his nogara beaten and most of the elders lined up to meet me. I found that a government messenger from Bara had come from Hamilton with notes from him and Charles and (which was perfectly charming of him) a present of a bottle of Graves and a loan of three books. I was quite moderately tired, but, as I wished to send off mail next day, I sat writing till fairly late, and then found that the villagers were dancing some little way off so I continued till 11 writing, when I went to bed. The noise was too much even for a sleeping dose. But at last about 1 a.m. I fell asleep—the dance was still going in full swing.

23.11.31

The Omda did not seem to have any business (except that I wanted from him a man for trading an unlicenced gun), and I spent all the morning and afternoon till 3.40 writing notes on various points for Hamilton and my private mail. I then sent off the ghaffir to Bara and the mail policeman to Soderi and went for a ride by myself on my horse for exercise.

The Omda came in the evening to drink tea and I went to bed very weary about 8 p.m. The night was warm.

24.11.31

I had agreed with the Omda to go this morning to see a well not far from here (at a place where there used to be salt workings), which has fallen in. The place lies towards Um Durag and he said it would be about $1\frac{1}{4}$ hours' ride. He proved accurate—wonderful to relate. He also wanted me to see the local khalwa (very elementary school) of Sheikh Medowi (his private chaplain, so to speak) which is at present in the same direction. So at 6.45 we rode off and saw the well and then to the khalwa, where I sat under a tree on an angareeb, and small boys recited the Koran and wrote and did sums for me. I also asked them simple local geographical questions. When we'd had enough of this I made some of the smallest run races for sweets and, of course, ultimately gave a few sweets to each child and made them scramble for more (which delighted them). We got back to the village about 9.45 and I had breakfast.

The Omda El Ajab strikes me as a very sound chieftain and a very pleasant man; among other things he has a most infectious laugh. He has the reputation of having a strong control over his thievishly disposed people. He looks about 45—no grey hairs. The father of the worst family of thieves died this summer. N.B. Niama Sirkatti has a small son in the khalwa here.

Mosquitoes are very bad here by day inside the huts; by night there are none. I suppose it has got too cold for them outside by night, but they lurk all day in the huts.

I felt rather lazy after the morning's ride and spent most of the day reading a book Hamilton had sent me, *Nigerian Days*;[13] with a few details and names changed, parts of it might easily be a description of life and work in the Sudan.

El Ajab brought me a fellow who has been wanted for over a year for selling an unlicenced gun.

And so a rather hot day drew to a close, and at sunset a heated altercation between a lady and a man went on for half an hour. I thought it was a case of a hen-pecked husband, but El Ajab told me later in the evening when he came to drink coffee that she was a bachelor girl. This freedom!

I had had to turn medical adviser today and could do nothing for either case. One, a young man, nephew and son-in-law of Sheikh El Nur Obeidallah (of the thieving clan) I diagnosed as appendicitis, I think correctly. The other, a remarkably swollen little girl, whose belly was like a football, I could make nothing of. Advised both to be taken to hospital. Slept well till about 4.30 a.m.

25.11.31

Started at 6 a.m. for cultivations in wadi called Rahad Ed Dabib (the Snake Pool) en route for Katoul. A pleasant morning ride W.S.W over ground almost all "sees", i.e. hard or stony. I rode Zurzur and he went well.

About 8.45 I saw two figures approaching at great pace, a taller and a shorter. They soon appeared to be a knight on a richly caparisoned horse, followed by his squire on a camel. The knight came at me full tilt (as is the custom) with an enormous Remington rifle clattering against his saddle. Zurzur hates this performance, being a thoroughbred Red-Sea-Hills camel and unaccustomed to horses. The knight pulled up short with a flourish of his whip about ten yards away and proved to be Adam Son of Light son of the Little Slave of God; and the squire—Holy the Thief son of the Little Slave of God, i.e. Adam El Nur son of the Sheikh Nur Obeidallah and his uncle Holy Obeidallah (twice in jug for cattle lifting and strongly suspected of murder). The horse, of which he was intensely proud, as it is the only one in the Omodia (and probably stolen I expect),

---

[13] By A. C. G. Hastings, London 1925.

was of a curious pink and white colour. So we rode into the wadi of Rahad Ed Dabib together and they presented me with two (unripe) melons, which was very kind of them, and later drank my tea and tried to persuade me to issue orders giving them rights to trees and things, which hereabouts belong to Allah, the government, and the first comer.

I addressed Christmas cards and wrote a letter and after lunch tried to draw a very nice Meikah tree. Alas, I needed ½ hour more to do it.

Rode on at 3 p.m. and on and on with the sun bang in one's eyes, until the sun went down, the moon came up, and the afterglow died. And found camp under a hill called Murabba![14] Rode 6 to 9 a.m. and 3 p.m. to 6.10 p.m.

26.11.31

The night was fairly cold. Rode at about 5.30. We continued westwards over hard ground till about 8.30, when we entered cultivation on sand and climbed a dune. Then suddenly I found that we had arrived at Hillat Mereikha, the village of the Omda of Katoul. I hadn't expected to arrive till the afternoon. Since I was here last in 1930, a rest house of grass huts has been built by the Omda on the lines of those at Abu Hadid and Um Durag.

After breakfast, bath and shave, I had a long chat with Khamis Tamar Agha, and an old man called Marien Balila, an ancient warrior, who was a "Rasmia" [*ra's mi'a*] (centurion) of dervishes, and later on a colour sergeant in the XIth Sudanese. He had been all over the place—to Wau amongst other stations. The new Omda Hamadtallah [*sic*] was away. The rest of the day till evening I spent writing mail and reading a large mail which I received from a policeman this morning.

The aeroplanes we sighted the other day contained, amongst others, Hector Watt, and they had landed at Soderi and slept in my house. A note from Hector all about it. Also his note gave me much Khartoum gossip and the news, amongst others, that Tom Maclagen[15] is transferred to Khartoum as Police Magistrate. The planes were doing a reconnaissance to try and find a new "North West Passage" for a motor road to Fasher more direct than that via Nahud.

In the late afternoon, people came to talk again. It was very cold in the evening and the night was bitter.

27.11.31

A cold morning. Nothing to do. Khamis came to talk and we talked of this and that and customs, Maal—bride price—in particular. The Nubas

---

[14] Jam; preserved fruit. Lea may have misunderstood Jabal Murabba (Jam Hill) for Jabal Umm Ruaba, which indeed he passed on 25 November. Sudan Government map, "Sodiri", Survey Office, Khartoum 1934.

[15] T. A. Maclagen, SPS 1926–50; later chief justice of the Sudan (1947–50). *SPS*, 50.

limited the price of wives to £E4 a few years ago because, at the former high prices, young men could not afford to marry and so contented themselves with making cuckolds of the richer men who had got themselves wives. This created annoyance. He said Katoul had not the 7-cows custom the Um Durag elders told me about. We arranged to go and see Taffalung well in the afternoon. I spent the morning reading a great deal of Arabic. At 1 p.m. Tingle came and told me that the mail policeman had come in on his way to Bara. So I hastily finished my mail and sent it off.

At 2.15 Khamis on a donkey and I on my horse rode off to see the well, which is about 4 miles away. A pleasant ride, the day being cold. On the way back I tried cantering my pony about for exercise and gave him a gallop. He then took the bit between his teeth. I gave him his head. But, when I tried to pull him up, one of the curb chain hooks broke and he got away with me. The result was a grand scamper and some very Arabian cat-jumps. His excitement was further augmented by an old lady we met who thought it was a race and "lu-lu"ed at me. However, he slowed down after about ¾ mile and I managed to stop him and return to find Khamis like Sancho Panza galloping along on his moke. We laughed long and heartily and so home. I had a pleasant afternoon's exercise and have had two peaceful and slack days, both marvellously cool and bracing.

I started my long-postponed letter to the Australian Uncle. I must get it finished and get down to Arabic. No drawing yesterday or today.

28.11.31

The night was again very cold and the morning extremely so. I rode off soon after sunrise to get to Gannetu village a short way S.W. along the jebel. I did not get warm at all in spite of two jerseys and a muffler, until I had given the pony a canter or two. Reached Gannetu at 7.30—about an hour's slow ride. A biting cold wind was blowing and the Nuba were chilled to the bone.

There are two sheikhs here—Zaid and Torfigga. When I sent for them to drink tea, both said their people objected to paying the blood-money for the Kabbashi. Ban Jadid village had complained to me in the same strain on my way off leave. Later a large assembly of men arrived and one Ahmad Niama acted as spokesman and voiced this grievance. I said that all the sheikhs of Katoul had recently been in the merkaz and had met me and not one of them had raised this complaint. I told them they must consult their Omda before they did anything else and, if he did not settle the business, then the Nazir also. I had already told the sheikhs I thought they were mean skunks. I also pointed out that Tamar Agha had agreed to the jebel's sharing in the blood-money. To the sheikhs, but not to the people, I said that I would make sure, if Katoul oozed out of this blood-money, that if in future a Katulawi killed anyone, no other jebel should help Katoul.

The position is that all jebels never joined in paying blood-money until 1928. Katoul on a previous occasion paid £E300 by itself. In 1928 Tamar Agha voluntarily made the jebel join in the payment. His sons are not as strong as he was.

Queries: (1) How many taxpayers in Katoul? Niama has put £E50 on the jebel. I don't think the division would come to more than 10 PT a head. (2) What benefits does Katoul get out of the Nizara, if any?

Very sleepy with wind and cold. Spent the rest of the morning rather sleepily and with slight headache. When the hamla had moved, I sat in a hut, the roof of which only had been built, and tried a drawing.

At about 3.30 rode on by horse to Gumburra. Khamis and Marien went with me. Arrived about 4.30.

As soon as the sun had set it became so cold that I moved into a hut in the rest house instead of sitting in the open. There I had a chat with Khamis and Sheikhs Beshir, Muhammad Harig and Musa Adam. They complained of the badness of the crops, said that much damage had been done by locusts, which there had not been enough bran to destroy, and that there would be shortage of grass before next rains. I don't doubt that there was damage by locusts, but I doubt the extreme badness of the crops, especially as we bought grain at Markh at 1 PT the midd,[16] i.e. cheaper than Soderi. Tingle says there's shortage in Katoul.

I remembered to tell Khamis to bring his father's robe of honour[17] into the merkaz. The mail policeman arrived and I opened the bag and took my mail out.

A very cold night. Also dogs barked and I felt nervy and could not get to sleep. At 3.30 the hamla moving on woke me afresh. A wind blew dust into my eyes and into the bed. Altogether a rotten night. Woke chilled, and rode on about 6.

29.11.31

We rode to Bir Tinni where I saw an ancient haraz tree under which Tamar Agha[18] had been made sheikh about 100 years ago. Here Khamis and Sh. Beshir who was with him left us. Rode on for another hour to Faja El Hala (arrived 7.30). Headache and chill and very cold. Took quinine.

The young sheikh here complained that he doesn't make enough out of

---

[16] In Kordofan, 1 *midd* = 8.25 litres.
[17] Awarded by the government, and surrendered upon the recipient's death.
[18] *'Umda* of Katul from 1841 until his death in 1911. *BD*, 355.

being sheikh. As his sheikhship consists of 4 men this is not surprising. The rest of the village belonged to sheikhs back in Gumburra when the place was colonised some years ago. He says he had asked Tamar Agha to give him a gum garden and nothing had come of it. I promised to enquire. It is ridiculous to allow these tiny sheikhships. I must tell Niama about it.

Rode on, still feeling pretty muzzy in the head, at 3.30. Passed Girgil wells, and got down in fairly thick bush at 5 p.m. Felt better after tea and ordered myself a large fire by where I was sitting. This made things warmer and more cheerful; all night moreover no wind. Slept like a log from 8.30 to 5.30 and awoke feeling fit.

30.11.31

St. Andrew's Day. Rode 6 a.m. to 7.30, when, having been met by Gumaa Sahal and a troop of friends and relations, I reached the rest house at Mazrub Wells. Gumaa S. has built new huts and the place is much more inhabitable than when I passed in September (it was then mud and water and with ducks on it and tall rank grass and mosquitoes and locusts).

I had had breakfast and was just going to get into a bath when Feki Gumaa Sahal bobbed up again. So I postponed the bath hurriedly and prepared to chat. He produced one Sheikh Salim Medowi of the Beni Gerar, who told me the whole story of the second of the brigandage cases at Abu Asal, in which his nephew Salim was killed about 3 weeks ago.

The Beni Gerar and the police appear to have taken 4 days to track the brigands from Abu Asal to Idd El Merkh, which a man can ride in a day. Salim says the ground was difficult for tracking (Ali, his son, was the tracker), and they had to cross three watering places: Er Rueis, Um Dam and Merkh, at each of which there were innumerable animal tracks of course. They took the tracks to a tent in a camp of Howawir, where they found no men, only women; but they found one of the camels. The police arrested 3 women and of these one confessed that the men were Muhammad Ali Daaj, Wad Kabjan, 2 sons of Yusuf Wagiallah and Wad Ali wad Shueid. She also said that Muhammad Ali Daaj had gone to the camp of Nas Kabjan near by. (Sheikh of all these men is Gabir Tagga of the Khomasin.) Now the police did not go off to the camp of Nas Kabjan and try to catch Muhammad Ali. Why? They did not go on to Abu Urug— only a day away—and warn Sheikh Nimr Hasan Khalifa. Why not? Nor did they speak to Gabir Tagga, who can't move from near Merkh because of his half-broken leg. *Why not?*

I wrote to Hamilton and to Akib Effendi and then at 1.30 I had my postponed bath. I was just going to have lunch about 2.15 when Gumaa Sahal turned up again (he does choose the most awkward moments) with his son and a sheikh whom he dislikes and they asked footling questions about Herd Tax and rifles and ammunition. Finally they faded out about 3 p.m. full of my coffee, and I had my lunch.

I had read about ten pages of *Blackwood* after lunch when Gumaa Sahal summoned me to see two wells he is having dug—of course as works of expensive charity, if you would believe him! After we had returned he sat and talked with me while giving me one or two traditions of tribal origin and pedigree.

I then sat up till 10.15 writing letters for the mail which I wished to send off the next day. Slept not too well.

1.12.31

Rose about 6 a.m. and had breakfast. By 7.15 Gumaa Sahal and I with an Arab and a policeman rose westwards out of the well-field along a fairly wide track. We soon came to sand-dunes. After an hour and 20 minutes fairly fast trotting, we reached the village of Sh. Ali Ajabna of the Awlad Madi, a big sheikh in the tribe. He is a dark, stout old man with a white beard, quiet in manner, but with a merry eye. With him was Feki Muhammad Kaddad who keeps a school here, made the pilgrimage with Gumaa Sahal 2 years ago, and has a great local reputation for learning and piety. These two and one Sh. Shigeyla from El Gleit direction, who is suffering from a carbuncle in the behind, kept us company in an Arab tent all the morning. They were quite amusing. We all had lunch together and drank large quantities of tea. About 1.15 we started to ride back. As it was hot I rode at a walk and also had to stop for a while as I was seized with pangs and had to wait till I felt better. We reached Mazrub at 3.45. Gumaa Sahal turned up for a talk after I'd had about an hour's rest and we discussed the tribal resources, his proposal to reduce the number of powers of fine among his sheikhs and the sheikhs he wanted sacked. Then the sunset and he went to pray.

I started writing some notes on our conversations and had not finished before his son Gabir arrived and talked about the Hamar, Kawahla and Howawir. He said, among other things, that the Ababda did not want Muhammad Fadlallah. He left at 8.45! I was pretty well dead beat and had a hasty supper and turned in. Woke at 4.30.

2.12.31

At 7 a.m. we started to go to the village of Ibrahim Musa. Rode south from Mazrub. Hard going through thickish bush nearly all the way. Arrived about 8.45.

Here we found Muhammad Nasir, the biggest sheikh of Nas Tibo— also the local holy man, a charming and amusing old boy called Abd El

Gadir. They all left me after much tea drinking about 11 and Feki Gumaa had a large and long mejlis in a hut near the tent which had been erected for me. I dosed and tried to read some Arabic newspapers. We started back about 1 p.m. and got in at 3.45. A thoroughly pleasant day. I wondered on the way back through the thick wood of "maarab" trees which surrounds Mazrub, whether the magnificent air of these parts owes anything more than scent to these balsam-smelling trees, as, for instance, in former times (when these were many) pine woods were said to make Bournemouth a health resort. When I got in I felt extremely sleepy. Feki Gumaa brought the Ayadia sheikhs, who had come in, to see me. They all live in villages near the Nahud border, S.W. of here. After they had gone, I really could face no more. Had supper at 7.45 and went to bed . . . .

3.12.31

Much stronger this morning although the cold and the moon had wakened me at 2.30 a.m. after which I lay awake for some time and slept uneasily with cramp in the knees and dreams in the head. However, a good night.

Rode at 6.45 to Baanat village—sheikh Gibril Ibrahim who holds powers of fine, of the Hamidia. With him was Sh. Muhd. Abu Kabar, an older man who is very ill, looks it, and has a badly enlarged spleen from malaria. I offered to take him to El Obeid on 14th December by car, if he would turn up at Mazrub, and put him into hospital. He is afraid of expense and I promised to tackle Anderson to get him cheap if not free treatment. Muhd. Naris turned up, also Ibrahim Mustafa of Nas Tibo and Adam El Tom of the Hamidia. We drank milk and tea in the tent erected for me.

In the course of conversation Feki Guma [*sic*] delivered himself of the following recipe for curing trypanosomiasis (Jufaar) in camels:-

Take 1 midd (of 7 rotls) dabaagh (garad) (tan)
     1   *"*   *"* *"*   *"*   atroun (i.e. saltpetre)
     1   jirr   gutraan[19] (vegetable tea)

Powder the dabaagh and the atroun and mix to a paste with the gutraan. Give the camel 5 lugmas (i.e. balls about the size of the meat of a drumstick) every morning with water to wash it down, till all the medicine is finished. The camel should also be given 2 ras (loaves) sugar, half a loaf in water every fifth day. He admitted that the Vet. had also somehow managed to cure a camel of his with one injection of naganol: a much easier but not more expensive method.

---

[19] One *rutl* = 449.28 grammes; *dabbagh* (tan) here means tannin; *gatran* is literally tar; 1 *jirr* = .064 litres.

Talking of Arabs selling water (which nearly all of them do and I expect Feki G. himself), he said that water used to be sold by "kashkash" (i.e. by midds of corn which, carried in a leather bag, make a noise "kash kash" as you ride along) at Mazroub and he abolished sale of it after taking Ali Ajabna's advice. Hamar still sell water. But selling water is "Haraam" (i.e. taboo) . . . . We got back to the rest house at 11 a.m. Many camels on the wells. Feki G. said his son Muhd. had lost 4 and that near Abu Asal had tracked them to a place where thieves had rested their guns against tripods.

I summoned Sheikhs Musa and Muhd. Idris of the Ayadia and warned them that, if I heard any more complaints against them they would be for the sack.

Tingle, to whom I talked about our moving on tomorrow and about quietly finding out any news of Ban Jadid village's giving help to brigands, said (a) he had heard that the Khalaifa had made another row with Awlad Barok: (b) that Muhd. Fadlallah had fined the Barok 8 camels in addition to the fine levied by me and that the Khalaifa insisted on payment by money of the £E250. Damn Muhd. Fadlallah, has he no common sense?

It appears that the grey french blue hawk with an orange bill is lucky, at any rate if seen on the righthand side of the road.

Did little for the rest of the day. Feki G. appeared just before sunset. He told me among other things that there had been a theft from a passing Hamari at Ban Jadid and the police had arrested the son of Ali El Basha, himself a sheikh.

Inspected camels. Early to bed.

4.12.31

Rose late. Ought to have felt refreshed considering the length of time I slept but did not. Was in fact in a poor temper.

Feki G. appeared with a swollen big toe. I think it is either a bunion or a chill blain. He had it covered with a mixture of saltpetre, tar and egg, so I couldn't tell. With him came Muhd. Gedid of the Awlad Rumia, who wants medicine for malaria and enlarged spleen. I allowed his son Zeriba to be appointed his wakil as he is ill.

They talked about Abderrahman El Mahdi.[20]

Hamla started about 2 p.m. I at 3.30. Just before I rode Feki G. produced secret news regarding a murder case at present under investigation in Bara. Got down by the new cultivation at the side of the Soderi road just before sunset. Soon after dark a wild figure appeared which proved to be Sh. Na'im Fereih of Um Khirwa, who said Niama Sirkatti

---

[20] 1885–1959; son of the Mahdi and leader of the Mahdist sect.

had seriously done him down. If his story is true Niama must be a bit off his rocker. Later appeared one Sh. Ghubush Awad El Kerim, a Magnuni Fadaala, who has a village just by here. He reported theft of a camel of a passing Rahli, and that he had tracked the thieves towards Katoul. He also produced a number of certificates (in the course of conversation) to his prowess as a tracker and a shikari.[21] One was from Col. Savile[22] dated 1914 and two others from Count Hunyadi.[23] It appears Ghubush had been as far south with English tourists as Wau. Slept very well.

5.12.31

Rode 6 a.m. Reached Hillat Ban Jadid by 7.45. There are four sheikhs of the villages included in Ban Jadid, and all have gone to the merkaz except one. The reason for this was that one of them, Nawashi Ali El Basha, had been arrested for robbing a passing Hamari tribesman of £E40 in cash and goods of other kinds (the Hamari's skull cap had been found on his, Nawashi's head!) Consequently the rest had gone to pay in taxes and see the fun and Ali El Basha had taken in his other sons to confess to the theft and so get their elder brother off. I was privately informed by Tingle that without a doubt Nawashi was the actual robber. I had a talk with the one remaining sheikh.

After the hamla had gone I did a little drawing, and when it came to be time for saddling up, I found quite a crowd collected and had some badinage with an ancient called Haamid, whose son, I'm told, is doing time for kidnapping. They had all rolled up (though they did not say so to me) to discuss with the police another theft case. We had heard shouts in the distance on our way this morning. This was chaps searching for thieves, also of Katoul, who had taken and slaughtered a ewe.

Rode on about 2.30 and at 6 p.m. reached hamla in camp on the W. slope of the big sandhill running N. and S. from Katoul to Jebel Abu Asal. It is remarkable how long light remains in the star-lit sky after the sun has set above the place of its setting—sunset 5.17 and at 7 there was still a lightness in the N.W. Elias and another constable turned up on their way back to Ban Jadid with a search warrant to try and find the remaining goods and money. As I expected, the other sons of Ali El Basha have confessed to try and clear their eldest brother. Well—it looks as if I'm going to have a busy week in court in Soderi.

---

[21] Guide.
[22] R. V. Savile, SPS 1902–23; governor of Kordofan, 1909–17, and of Darfur, 1917–23, *SPS*, 12.
[23] See Daly, *Empire*, 101.

6.12.31

Slept well and was on the way by 6 a.m. Akib and the others met me and I reached my house at 8 a.m. By 11 I was in the office and stayed there till 2.30 and returned at 4 and stayed till 6 p.m. There remained innumerable papers to read and police investigations of cases to go through. I hoped that Mayall would turn up to help me make decisions on certain points which needed experience. Went to bed pretty weary.

7.12.31

Rose late. Mail came in. No news from Mayall. Office till 2.45 p.m. and again in the afternoon.

After dark Niama Sirkatti came in and we talked and discussed Kababish relations and the Um Durag case.

8.12.31

Office as usual, but did not go in the afternoon—sat reading papers and writing in the house.

9.12.31

Made my decision about the Um Durag case and arranged that the village pays either 3 nagas of like age to the Awlad Ugba, plus £E6 fine to Government, or £E16 to Govt. out of which I will pay compensation. This is to be produced to me at Hamrat el Wuzz. I took statements in one or two other cases.

About 11 a.m. Mayall's car arrived. I went up to the house to meet him. His arrival was unexpected but none the less welcome. But his announcement that Gillan wanted him back in El Obeid by Friday night in order to deal with the mail on Saturday morning, was something of a shock entailing as it did doing 4 days' work in 2 and also arranging all the details of my trip to Dongola at the same time. I gave him a drink and returned to the office till 2.15 when we had lunch.

I went back to the office just after 3 until dusk. Then, after dark, Niama Sirkatti and Ali Kheirallah came in at my request to drink coffee. Ali Kheirallah was on his way back to Um Inderaba, his home, after paying in his tribe's herd tax to Ali El Tom. He was much agitated about the kidnapping case, and, two days before, had said he wanted to stay in Soderi until I had given judgment in the case. I told him Mayall was coming but that I could give him no guarantee of when the case would be finished: the Hamar accused of the actual kidnapping were in Nahud and I did not know what action had been taken or what the Governor wanted done. He said he would wait for Mayall.

Mayall and the two sheikhs talked about old times in Nahud and so on.

After they had gone Mayall and I talked a bit of this and that and the difficulties of Government (he had brought with him news of bombshell character concerning further drastic retrenchment) and our families. He showed me photographs of his daughter at the age of 5 days and dilated at length. We retired fairly early. I was very glad to have him and he is such a cheery and amusing company. He has, I think, one of the greater senses of humour.

10.12.31

While we were getting up about 6.30 a.m. and preparing to go for a walk to the wells and village, there was a noise of the alarm in the merkaz. I looked out to see Tingle and others running who called to me that there was a fire. I finished shaving hurriedly, dressed and went to find that the Mamur's kitchen hut in his compound had caught fire, and, being a grass-roofed mud-walled affair, had gone up in one puff of smoke. When I got there I found all that could be done had been—police were sitting like crows on the grass roof of the Mamur's house and there was no danger of the fire's spreading. I therefore commiserated with Akib Eff. on his misfortune, said good morning to Niama and various other notables who had arrived on the scene, and waited for Mayall to come over from my house. When he had arrived we went down to the wells and returned via the village, the market and the dispensary to breakfast.

After breakfast I dealt out stores and divided them into two lots—required till I reach Hamrat El Wuzz and required for the trip to Dongola. The latter with corn and extra camels and police will go direct to Hamrat El Wuzz and meet me there about 31st. December.

Mayall had come down to the office and sat with me (after he had inspected the prison, stores and offices) for a while, giving me advice on various cases and points.

I left to give him lunch just after 2 p.m. and returned again later to finish up with one or two ex-slaves who had complaints, and pull out the files I needed for trek, and the maps to take me to Dongola.

I got back to the house by 4.30 p.m. and the Effendia came to tea in my "garden" to meet Mayall. He knew Akib years ago in the White Nile and the party was quite a success. Yasin Effendi stayed behind afterwards for me to sign some papers and to write one or two Arabic notes—particularly one to Muhammad Fadlallah to keep the Kawahla out of the Hamar country because Vicars-Miles had reported from Nahud that various bodies of dead men had been found in Kawahla camping grounds in Dar Hamar.

Then I had to pack—not only trek kit, but all the civilised stuff I should have to wear in El Obeid and later in Dongola and Khartoum.

We dined about 8.45 and I went to bed dead tired and hoping vaguely but fearfully that I hadn't left anything vitally important undone.

Chapter VII

A District Commissioners' Meeting

[El Obeid]

11.12.31

We were ready to start by 6.15 a.m. Niama the evening before had come up to tell me that the freed slaves in Soderi had complained to him against the policy being put in force of removing them for settlement elsewhere—farther from their late masters and in the country of more certain rainfall. They wanted to form a village in Soderi. They turned up (six of them only) this morning and said they hadn't yet threshed their corn and might they remain. This was, obviously, lies, but I allowed them 15 days' grace.

Then we went off, and reached Mazroub by about 8.45. As we had arrived on the wrong day, of course Feki Guma Sahal was not there nor the old sheikh to whom I had promised a lift to El Obeid. I wrote them letters of apology. Guma Sahal's brother turned up. I handed over medicines for Jabir Guma Sahal and a pick for well-digging.

Mayall, over breakfast, talked about playing with children as a means of winning the confidence of natives. I said I rarely saw children here and didn't know how to cope with them if I did. He said Bence-Pembroke[1] had made this his method in Western Kordofan, and he, Mayall, had followed it. We also discussed the question of giving money for dances. Mayall said MacMichael had condemned the practice. We looked at the wells which are being dug and went on again at about 9.45. The road is monotonous and sandy. We argued about Khartoum (for which Mayall is destined as Asst. Civil Secretary for Personnel in a month's time) and marriage and women and children and so forth for the whole day. We stuck once on a sand hill at Um Shidera, and we stopped for lunch under a small tree about 2.30 p.m. At 4.30 we reached El Obeid and went to Mayall's house. Gillan, who had been playing tennis on the courts near by, came over and passed the time of day and told us to come round for a drink. Mayall found bottles of beer which were most welcome. We then sent the lorry to unload my stuff at Macphail's[2] house where I was to stay and walked in that direction

---

[1] R. A. Bence-Pembroke, SPS 1907–27, served in Kordofan from 1908 to 1915. *SPS*, 18.
[2] J. G. S. Macphail, SPS 1922–47. *SPS*, 39.

ourselves. We met Macphail returning from exercising his pony, with Salmon[3] (Asst. D.C. of El Obeid).

After a bath, I went over to the Governor's house to call on Gillan and found it in semi-darkness—so I lurked in the drive until Gillan had come out into the garden and lit a lamp. Mayall turned up shortly afterwards and also de Bunsen (who was staying in El Obeid to read Arabic), Elliott[4] (a young and new Tutor of the Gordon College), and Macphail. After a while we made our excuses and drifted off to the Club, where I got Elliott to tell me all about the recent strike of the boys at the Gordon College. The Government had published new and lower starting rates of pay for government officials and the Gordon College boys had struck. Efforts to get them to go back had proved unavailing and so the College had been closed till January when the first three years may go back if they want to. The fourth and senior year is sacked and none of them will be taken for government jobs. It all seems rather a bad show.

Then we returned to dine with Macphail. Aglen[5] and Salmon were there and a lad from the British Trades Expedition which is held up here.

The party broke up after gramophone records about 11 p.m. and I retired on Macphail's verandah done in.

12.12.31

Awoke somewhat weary. Macphail was due to go to Bara to see Hamilton, so it was arranged that he and I should breakfast with Mayall and that I should stay the next two nights with Mayall.

I had protested in Soderi that I would rather stay in a Rest House in El Obeid than be a burden and a guest to anyone. (The real reason is that one is less under restraint and more able to spread one's things out and be at peace in a Rest House). But I was not allowed to have my way and again now Mayall waved my protests aside.

In the office, after I had done some small business with Anderson, the doctor, at the hospital, I tried to help Charles de Bunsen with some Arabic. I think I was little help, and it proved later I had told him one or two things wrong.

(*N.B.* The diary of 11th. to 21st. December was written on 21st December and is probably a bit muddled.)

After lunch and a rest, Mayall took me to play tennis. It was a polo day and no one else turned up. I gave Mayall little exercise and it must have been rather boring for him. After two so-called sets we sat out and

---

[3] R. Salmon, SPS 1930–41. *SPS*, 59.
[4] A. V. P. Elliott, SPS 1930–33. *SPS*, 58.
[5] E. F. Aglen, SPS 1930–55. *SPS*, 58.

PLATE 5

S.A.D. 587/2/212

Kababish slave women

PLATE 6

(l.–r.) Angus Gillan, J. A. de C. Hamilton, and Harold MacMichael at Soderi, 1929

S.A.D. 588/2/54

PLATE 7

Kordofan Province Police   S.A.D. 2/14/27

PLATE 8

Kordofan shaykhs at Bara. Far left, 'Ali al-Tum; to his left, his brother Muhammad and Muhammad Fadlallah, *nazir* of the Kawahla

S.A.D. 587/1/118

discussed our murky pasts, to my great amusement. We went later and took tea with the Williamses (Province Vet.), where we found the Waughs (Water Engineer) and their small son, whose conversation I found more amusing than that of the grown-ups, who mostly discussed the shortcomings of their cooks.

Mayall had one or two of the younger lads to dine and they left early.

13.12.31

A similar day to yesterday but I felt more rested. Had some rather comic tennis with the Williamses. 6 p.m. to church in Gillan's house. Mayall went to the Club in the evening and wrote letters till dinner and we went to bed arguing at 9.30. Mayall, who is a most sentimental bloke, decided that I lacked sentiment and that I was "a contradiction in terms" —turned over and went somewhat noisily to sleep. I slept like a log. A cool night.

14.12.31

This was the official day for D.C.s to arrive for the meeting. In the morning before breakfast the Skeets[6] and Jock Young (of the Agriculture) arrived and had breakfast with Mayall. After breakfast Macphail and Hamilton came in from Bara. Hamilton was in very good form but had a wretched cold. He brought my mail with him. Hamilton and the Skeets were to stay with Mayall. I moved back to Macphail's house.

In the afternoon I went out early, about 4 p.m., and played singles with Aglen. He, who normally is a goodish player, was in poor form, and I, after one set, began to give him something of a game in a second set. Then two more men—Gough of the R.A.S.C.[7] and a sergeant—turned up and so, according to local rules, we had to make up a four. It was pleasant exercise but poor pat-ball. Later I played another set with Gough against Gillan and Bethell[8] (D.C. of Rashad).

Dined that evening with Macphail. Aglen and Guy Moore (D.C. Fasher), who had arrived by the evening's train on his way back from leave, were there. After dinner, "table bowls" on the mastaba.[9] It was most amusing. To bed at 11 p.m.

---

[6] C. H. L. Skeet, SPS 1920–45; later governor of Khartoum, 1939–42, and of Equatoria, 1942–45. *SPS*, 34.
[7] Royal Army Service Corps.
[8] D. J. Bethell, SPS 1919–38. *SPS*, 27.
[9] Outdoor platform.

15.12.31

This was the opening day of the District Commissioners' Meeting, and at this morning's session all D.C.s and Asst. D.C.s present were to be in the meeting. The next days were to be devoted to discussion between the Governor and Senior District Commissioners of the appalling problem of how to reduce the Province Budget by 20%. Before the meeting, Vicars-Miles collared me and said he wanted my blood about the supposed murders of Hamar by Kawahla, and about the sale of kidnapped children to Kababish. I had ordered the kidnappers to be marched in to El Obeid under escort from Soderi, and they were by now on their way: so I pulled his leg by saying they had all escaped, and that the police had fired on them as they ran but had missed.

The meeting was fairly dull and lasted till about 1.30.

Tennis again in afternoon—a moderate set of pat-ball with Mayall, Skeet and another, and later a single with Bolton[10] (after a doubles affair in which I played with Mrs. Bolton against Mrs. Skeet and Bolton, and lost Mrs. B. the set by serving nothing but double faults in the 11th. game). Mrs. Bolton almost never stops talking, but there's no doubt she has changed Rollo from pessimist to optimist (if indeed that is a good thing, which I doubt—but he was terribly hypochondriacal before).

Called on Oakley[11] (D.C. El Obeid) and his wife in company with Hamilton, this evening. I like his wife—pleasant, quiet lady: two small daughters. She seems to have trekked a lot in the Nuba Mountains and likes it. Doesn't like El Obeid much.

To dinner with the Williamses: present Hamilton, Wardlaw, a Col. somebody who is in charge of the British Trades Expedition, Stobo, the Asst. Vet., and Mrs. Rylands wife of the District Engineer (who is on trek with the Forwoods—Assistant Director Public Works Dept. and his wife). Mrs. Rylands is a caution: she, left behind in El Obeid, rejected all kindly offers from other women of hospitality in her husband's absence, and lives by herself. . . . She didn't think much of my friend John Winder[12] (who lived with Rylands in Port Sudan)—I reckon he put her in her place. After dinner, I for one and Hamilton for another would much rather have gone to bed. However, one had to stay and play vingt et un. It was chilly. The Boltons having left their dinner party with Mayall, came and joined in. The wretched card game went on till midnight.

---

[10] A. R. C. Bolton, SPS 1922–47. *SPS*. 37.
[11] A. S. Oakley, SPS 1923–48. *SPS*, 42.
[12] SPS 1927–55; later assistant civil secretary, 1951–53, and governor of the Upper Nile, 1953–55. *SPS*, 52.

16.12.31

Very tired. It is ridiculous that, at a time when all of us ought to be doing our best to face a crisis and in the best possible form to think out ways and means, these dinner parties should be allowed, and be allowed to go on late.

The D.C.s continued to confer on economy and the Asst. D.C.s sat outside in uncomfortably crowded offices with nothing to do and not allowed to go away.

This afternoon there was a football match of a team of D.C.s against the local Effendia Club. Macphail was billed to play right back and I at centre half—a place I have never played in before and for which I'm not nearly fast enough. Thank God, we played only fifteen minutes each way. One started tired. At half time I felt very sea-sick, but avoided being ill, and felt better the second half. Macphail did a very fine run down the field and tripped over a man and fell. At the end of the game he found he had hurt his backside badly . . . .

This evening there was to be the so-called D.C.s' dinner with the Governor, which is always apparently a late show. Mrs. Oakley had said at tea that she and Mrs. Skeet had been making attempts to get Mrs. Vicars-Miles (who was staying with Gillan) to sound him as to whether there was to be a late supper, as in former years, or whether there was a possibility of getting to bed.

The dinner proved to be a most terrible show. Macphail and I turned up about 8.25 and found almost everybody assembled. Hamilton, as a result of last night's entertainment, had lost his voice entirely. Proceedings started with champagne as a cocktail. We sat down to dinner 19 strong and course followed course. I failed to compete with one or two courses. I was set between Oakley (who hardly spoke to me) and Salmon, beyond whom was Mrs. Oakley, and on her right (Salmon and she shared the end of the table) was Mayall facing me.

After dinner, Mrs. Bolton and Mrs. Vicars-Miles made an attempt to start charades. This proved a frost and the party went dead. Mayall and Skeet tried to get things going again by having Mrs. Bolton play the piano while folk sang. Everyone would have liked to be in bed. Then they played "sardines" all over the house. Then they played "nuts and may" in the garden—at which I struck and remained indoors talking to Scott[13] (who had arrived from dining with the Army). Then we all went to supper—sausages and beer—and then oozed away. It was nearly 1 a.m. No sooner

---

[13] G. C. Scott, SPS 1921–46: in 1931 he was chief inspector in the education department; he was later warden of Gordon College, 1937–43, and vice-principal of University College, Khartoum, 1944–46. *SPS*, 36.

had I got into bed than I was taken violently ill. Since I had not been conscious of drinking a lot, and had not felt at all tight, I made careful enquiries next morning and was assured by Mayall that I had not been drunk (to my relief). I suppose it was merely desperate tiredness which made the sausages the last load which upset the balance.

17.12.31

The natural result of such a night was general weariness and bleariness next day. I've no idea how the D.C.s managed to be efficient. I felt like death. After lunch Macphail and I fell asleep in our chairs. At 4.45 I went to Mayall's house for a consultation with Hamilton and Vicars-Miles (the latter was very late because he had been asleep). It was more or less agreed that Muhammad Fadlallah should be sent to Nahud to meet Munim Mansur[14] after my return from Dongola and that I should go with him.

I was due to dine with Mayall and he asked me to rise and say goodnight ¼ hour after dinner. The other guests were to be young men and it was hoped they would rise too. I ought to have warned them also, but hadn't a chance. I rose ¼ hour after dinner and took my leave. Nobody else followed suit and Mayall told me next day that they stayed till 11 p.m. . . .

---

[14] See M. W. Daly, *Imperial Sudan: the Anglo-Egyptian Condominium, 1934–56*, Cambridge 1990, 31, 149.

Chapter VIII

A Tribal Peace Conference; A Trek to the Nile

[El Obeid—Bara—Kajmar—Hamrat al-Wazz—Safiya—Abu 'Uruq—Alay Wells—Umm Rumaylah Wells—Umm Qawayz—Kurti—Merowe]

18.12.31

A Friday. Wrote mail before breakfast. Went to the market and bought various stores. Then to office to take leave of Gillan. Leicester of the Camel Corps came to lunch with Macphail. Hamilton and I were due to start at 3 p.m.

Leicester, after lunch, took me along to Camel Corps headquarters to give me a Route Report of Hector Watt's on the Dongola trek I am about to do. He could not find it. I then went to Mayall's house and said goodbye to him and to the Skeets. Macphail very kindly promised to post my mail and to see that a new valise I had ordered from Khartoum was forwarded to me.

So we set out in two lorries (one belonging to Jock Young, Agricultural Inspector, who had gone ahead with the Williamses). Wardlaw was also bound for Bara ahead of us: and the Williamses to inspect Camel Corps camels. We left at 3.30 and reached Bara about 5.30.

On the way Hamilton and I discussed the futility of these El Obeid entertainments and their wrongfulness at a time like this. We also talked of the financial crisis.

Young was staying with Hamilton in order to enquire into the state of the local vegetable trade. He and Hamilton talked much of the War after dinner and I fell asleep as they talked. To bed before 10 p.m. and a pretty good night on the roof. I felt desperately depressed all the time I was in El Obeid and still remained so in Bara. Partly this was due to the ill news of more financial cuts and partly to the fact that I had come in from long treks needing rest and found none.

19.12.31

Young and Hamilton rode off to go round the market. After breakfast, H. went to the office and Young and I followed at leisure via the market to enquire the cost of vegetables etc. There followed a hectic morning in the office. After lunch, Young and the Williamses left for El Obeid.

At 4.30 Hamilton took me for a ride to see into the question of building a tennis court for the Effendia. On the way back, we rode round and up the hill to see Keays (Commander of No. 3 Company) inspecting his camels in the evening.

About 6 p.m. we went up the hill again, and took drinks with Dicky Mitchell, the Bimbashi in Command of No. 4 Coy. The conversation became remarkably good—usually Dicky has not one idea to rub against another. Keays came in later. The theme was that Western training tends to destroy the natural intelligence and initiative and *oriental* honesty of natives.

While we were at dinner later, there came a note from Dicky asking me to go and see the "type of man recruited for the Camel Corps" at a mounted parade next morning.

20.12.31

I willingly borrowed a horse and went to see Dicky's Mounted Parade. And I saw everything—forming square from mounted column of platoons and action front—and then the stores and all the rest of it.

Another hectic morning in the office. After lunch I managed to scribble some letters for posting in Bara.

The hamla went off at about 3.30 and we at 4.30. Dicky, the Mamur and the Omda came to see us off. I rode the Feki for the first time since March—he has been ailing ever since. We got down in the road just after dusk. Slept well.

21.12.31

Shidd 2½ hours from 6.15 a.m. El Feki knocked out before I had ridden 1½ hours: so that is a good camel done for for another 2 months. I can't think what to do about it: no disease apparent. We spent the heat of the day in a village of the Meramra where the sheikh complained greatly of his Omda and of this and that. In spite of the misfortune regarding Feki I began to feel better.

Shidd again at 3 p.m., 2½ hours, and got down after sunset in the road. We intended writing letters before moving on (for we had decided to do a "makluta", i.e. a third march in one day after dinner by moonlight). But Hamilton got talking about Mesopotamia, and the action at the crossing of the Euphrates, in which he won the M.C., and the taking of Baghdad, and war in general, and how tired one feels all the time on active service. Then, after dinner, as we were about to mount, he began to talk of the financial crisis in the Sudan again as it affects Kordofan and Northern Kordofan in particular, and asked me certain direct questions about myself.

Rode from 8 till 9.30 p.m.: cool, bright moonlight. Usual sand-hill country. Slept only moderately well. I think our heads were down hill.

22.12.31

Rode at 6.15 a.m. I had arranged to mount Hamilton on my last remaining camel, Zurzur, with my saddle and his brightly-coloured Damascus saddle bags—so that he should be mounted with adequate dignity, as there was a prospect of meeting Ali El Tom. Meanwhile his heavy saddle was put on my big Bishari, "Ahdim", for me to ride. I rode the first hour and a quarter, however, on H.'s horse and had a pleasant canter for ¼ mile at one point. We passed Jebel Filya, where I had spent the night in July 1930.

When we were getting near Kagmar, I saw a flash of white robe on the road, and soon Sheikh Ali and Sheikh El Tom came into view. We all dismounted and greeted each other heartily.

As we all rode into Kagmar, there appeared a party of Arabs riding who proved to be the son of the Nazir of Dar Haamid and his sheikhs: also Abdu Omar Gash of the Ferahna appeared and we all greeted each other warmly. H. and I went on to the rest house to bathe, shave and have breakfast.

Sheikh El Tom came to talk to me and later Sheikh Ali also. I kept the conversation to unimportant topics hoping he would open his heart to Hamilton later: which he did apart under a tree, while I discussed minor affairs in my tent with certain Kawahla and with Ferahna and with Sheikh El Tom.

At 2.30 we had lunch. H. said A.T. had opened up that he feared greatly the influence of the Mahdi's son[1] with the government especially as the latter was near at hand in Khartoum while Ali El Tom is always distant in the steppes of Northern Kordofan. Also A.T. said he dreaded the effects of these new Native Courts which are now established upon all sides of his tribe, upon inter-tribal cases and inter-tribal relations. H. had been holding forth to me upon the theme that these new Native Administration schemes were tending to exacerbate relations between tribes, and A.T.'s remarks bore out his thesis.

After lunch I brought my diary up to date till tea-time. Hamilton then went off on his horse to inspect the aerodrome on which Ritchie will land, we hope, tomorrow.

23.12.31.

The weather is remarkably cold—sleep is light and unsatisfying after about 3 a.m. and a bath in the morning is too Spartan a rite to be pleasant.

---

[1] Sayyid 'Abd al-Rahman al-Mahdi.

Chapter VIII

We had just got up when the aeroplanes were heard about 7.30. Hamilton galloped off on his horse. I was persuaded to mount one of the Nazir of Dar Haamid's nags, but the saddle was so uncomfortable that I preferred to walk up to the landing ground. By the time I arrived both planes (there were two) had landed and a large crowd of Sheikhs and Arabs had arrived on the scene to greet the aviators.

Ritchie had piloted one machine himself, and a young Flying Officer called, I think, Middleton, the other. They had 3 mechanics with them. This was a much larger party than we had expected but our servants put up quite a good show extempore and provided the "other ranks" with breakfast in my tent while the officers ate with us in Hamilton's grass hut. Middleton I could by no means get to talk: he seemed to have nothing to say for himself. Ritchie as usual talked 15 to the dozen. He told us about ruinous cuts in pay—the British forces have already of course been cut. But he had rumours as to axing, i.e. who is being axed. He said that financial crisis had not yet persuaded Khartoum people[2] to cut down their extravagant entertaining and late hours.

After breakfast, we walked down to the wells and then sheikhs turned up. Hamilton had some cases to deal with which concerned the Dar Haamid people, and deputed me to take Ritchie and Ali El Tom off and act as interpreter between them. We sat under a tree and Ritchie explained to Ali El Tom through me about the raid made by Senussi refugees[3] aided by Goraan from Ennedi, who acted as guides, upon Bir Natrun in August. These people, about 50 to 75 strong, had spent the summer (April to July) in Nakheila oasis west of Natrun, and in August raided a caravan of Dongola Arabs who had gone to Bir Natrun for salt. I had been ordered in September to try and gather information about the raid but had found none of value that the Government had not already to hand.

In October and November aeroplanes and the motor machine gun battery from El Fasher, with young Sandison[4] as Political Officer and mapper, had gone north from Malha in Jebel Meidob (Darfur) with one Badi (a Berti) as guide, to Wadi Shau and Bir Natrun and Nakheila on reconnaissance with extremely interesting results, which proved that the best way to deal with Western Desert raids is from Darfur and not from Dongola (the route from Dongola is too sandy and difficult).

The Kababish herds of camels are now all up in the Wadi Shau and (before Ritchie was there) were north of it grazing upon "jizzu" grass (i.e. green grass caused by late rains in the desert there). This is their habit

---

[2] That is, British officials.
[3] That is, refugees from the second Italo-Sanusi war, which ended in Italian victory in 1931.
[4] P. J. Sandison (SPS 1928–54) was stationed in Darfur, 1930–35, *SPS*, 55–6.

whenever such grass appears. It has not done so for five years. Ali El Tom is therefore interested in possible raids and means taken by the government to protect the Arabs against them.

The conversation was confined to showing what government has done and hopes to do, and to reassuring him concerning this last band of raiders. Ritchie opined that, as these Senussi are not normally brigands but men of substance who have been ousted from Kufra by the Italians, and since the Italians have now proclaimed an amnesty, they would return to Kufra, or at any rate to French territory and not worry us again. Ali El Tom pointed out that a large force of brigands descending on herds would frighten the animals and cause loss by straying out of all proportion to the loss by robbery they could effect. The stray Goraan thief is no serious problem and with him the Arabs can deal by themselves. We urged Ali El Tom to ensure that the Government has early news of any threatend raid in future. News would have to come from the "jizzu" area 10 days from the north to Tageroo (because a camel cannot trot there—too little grazing and no water for man or beast), three days from Tageroo to Ali El Tom, three days from him to Soderi and four days to El Obeid or Bara. Total 20 days. Ritchie said it would still not be too late for aeroplanes to start and, based on Wadi Shau, catch a raiding party, who, laden with booty, would not be able to make more than 25 to 30 miles a day.

After lunch the airmen started to return to Khartoum. The mechanics were much thrilled by being given camels to ride from the rest huts to the landing ground. They took our mail with them for posting in Khartoum on the mail train for the north the same evening.

We returned to listen to talk and cases until dusk.

24.12.31

This was a very busy day and, owing to the cold, or some other reason, I felt none too bright.

A number of Zaghawa had complained of the assessment of their crops of dukhn (bulrush millet) of Government Tithe.[5] Hamilton agreed to go and see certain of the cultivations near Jebel Gahaniya east of here. So we rode out there on camels in the afternoon.

Much shouting and protesting and demonstration of boundaries of cultivation plots (most about 3 or 4 acres or more). We re-assessed by eye and asked the assessment board their former assessment. The board is completely in the hands of a Soderi merchant who is acting as its clerk—a thing I don't like. Hamilton decided that the assessment was on the harsh side, but that, if he reduced the assessment, there would be such a crop

---

[5] '*ushr*.

of complaints as would not be warranted by the slight over-assessment of certain individuals. He promised the cultivators (and later Sh. Ali El Tom) that next year the Bara system of each village assessing its own crop and the Omda checking should be introduced. Sheikh Ali El Tom in the evening said he thought the present unsatisfactory board had better complete its work this year. The most amusing thing in the afternoon was the total indifference of Ali El Tom's representative, my friend Muhd. Musa Lawlaw, to anything in the way of cultivation: beneath his notice—a typical Bedouin attitude.

Talked to Ali El Tom after dark.

25.12.31

Cold night and morning—the only thing which recalls Christmas at all. After breakfast we both had a busy morning, although the Dar Haamid Nazir had come to take leave of Hamilton before he was properly dressed, and had gone away.

Hamilton determined to go off in the afternoon to see some more Zaghawa cultivation to the West and leave me to bring on Ali El Tom to join him at Hamrat El Wuzz. It was cold all day. I wrote letters to send by a policeman who was to take mail to Bara.

Ali El Tom is insistent that the wretched trader El Amin Ali Kheirallah at Hamrat esh Sheikh, who married a girl against Ali El Tom's will, shall be turned out. Arranged accordingly with Hamilton and wrote to Mamur Soderi.

After Hamilton had gone I walked up to the landing ground and hit a golf ball about. There was a very strong wind.

No one came to talk to me after sunset, and, as it was perishing cold, I read *Africa View*[6] till 7.30 and then had supper and went to bed.

26.12.31

An arctic night. Woke at 2 a.m. and never got warm enough again to sleep soundly in spite of putting on a tweed coat over the sweater I was already wearing and wrapping a fleece lining from a trench coat round my legs under four blankets. Spent nearly 12 hours in bed and felt too cold to get up till 7.30 a.m. In spite of stoutness exercises and breakfast (which was vile) and sitting in the sun and hitting a golf ball I could not get circulation going in my hands and feet until 11 a.m. No one came to talk so I wrote the above.

Hamilton, when he left, had been roused to an adequate state of anxiety about the meeting between Niama and Ali El Tom at Hamrat, and

---

[6] By Julian Huxley, London 1931.

so proposes to get to Niama before I do and tell him he must make friendly overtures. The Nazir of Dar Haamid, old Timsah,[7] had asked him for goodness' sake to stop this quarrel between old friends.

I have forgotten to mention that Ritchie told us that the north of Soderi District is now littered at intervals with abandoned cars of the Khartoum Motor Machine Gun Battery, which went to try and find a North West Passage to Fasher. The central government might, in courtesy at least, have told us that they were going. And this is economy, I suppose, in times of financial crisis.

Rode at 3.50 p.m. till 5.50. The going good over a big goz by Jebel Rowyan (10 miles). My intention was to reach Um Debba [sic] village if possible but the hamla stopped short of it. On the way I tried to discuss with Ali El Tom, at his request, the causes of the present financial crisis.

All possible clothes—underfugs, pyjamas, grey flannel trousers, vest, shirt, sweater, shooting jacket, trench coat and a fire failed to keep out the arctic wind. Slightly warmed by whisky, went to bed but woke at 12 and again at 2. The wind came in through everything although I was lying in bed in all my clothes.

27.12.31

Started just before sunrise at 6 a.m. Bitterly cold—the Arabs were not yet more than just stirring. Passed Um Debbi Village at sunrise. Hamilton had gone on yesterday afternoon. Left Jebel Atshan behind. Fairly good going for 2 hours till we came to Breiga, a low hill of sandstone. Here ground became stony and then we entered sand-dune country. The wind was bitter and gave me a headache. Just after 9 a.m. (I had several times asked the police if they were following the tracks of the hamla), I found the police had lost the track and were riding on what probably was the track of Hamilton's hamla. . . . As we were casting about, Sheikh Ali and his Arabs arrived—about 25 strong, looking very comic opera. He himself had on a sort of trench coat with a hood and his turban wound round the hood. They had seen my tent in the distance further back. Sheikh Ali took command and made me alight under some bushes near by, sent lads to fetch my hamla, and later fed me with dates and kisra (the latter I couldn't cope with). I got down at 10; the hamla did not arrive until 12.

This is the coldest day I have ever experienced in the Sudan. It was never warm, and I continued wearing all the clothes I had put on last night and slept in. Read *Africa View* and felt very tired and full of ache behind the eyes. Ali El Tom talked for a short while about gun licences. About 3 p.m. El Tom came and talked. It appears there are two wadis west of

---

[7] Timsah Simawi Jarajir (d. 1932). *BD*, 359.

Wadi Shau in the Bir Natrun area—Wadi Howar and Wadi Khasi. Rode 4 p.m. to 6 p.m. over sand dunes to near Jebel Um Durag. Wrote notes to Hamilton and Niama. Ali El Tom says the Zaghawa round Kagmar were mere thieves in the time of his grandfather Fadlallah, and settled as cultivators later.

Sat over a roaring fire and was fairly warm, and continued reading *African View*. By dint of pulling my flea bag well over the blankets and then drawing a ground sheet over the whole bed from the windward side, kept warm fairly well.

28.12.31

Did not start till just on 7 a.m. Damnably cold. Rode down hill over sand dunes all the way in the teeth of the wind. Conversation was difficult as Ali El Tom was wrapped in his comic opera hood and coat and couldn't hear what I said in my broken Arabic. A truly horrid ride and bumpy. In addition, as I had not had my clothes off now for 36 hours I felt very dirty and lousy; also I hadn't shaved for two days. By 8.30 we had descended into the first trees of Wadi Hamra with the peaks of Jebel Um Durag behind us to the south and Jebel Nihid to the west. Camp in the first trees of the wadi. We are now only about an hour from Hamrat El Wuzz.

The tent gave me sufficient shelter for a wash more or less all over and a shave. Ali El Tom sent me some liver for breakfast and I felt much better —no headache today, thank God. We are out of water now entirely.

He came to talk later and raised the question of Abu Hadid Nuba cultivating at Sifeyia . . . .

We rode on at about 3.45 p.m. after I had spent about three quarters of an hour trying to make a drawing of Jebel Um Durag in the afternoon light. We had not gone more than ½ mile through the wadi trees when Sheikh Niama met us with an enormous turn out of people on camels.

I left the two Nazirs to chat with each other as much as possible and we rode on to arrive at Hamrat El Wuzz within ½ hour, where we found the drums of the Dolib family "nahass"[8] being beaten furiously and Hamilton waiting in the rest huts.

Hamilton gave me tea. Meanwhile several, quite elderly, men were doing the deuce of a sword-and-spear dance in front of the drums and a large crowd sat their camels all round them—a forest of long legs— watching. The noise was terrific. Hamilton told me that Niama Sirkatti had prepared gargantuan feasts for Ali El Tom and his party: and that Niama proposed to entertain them to the best of his ability that evening and not talk business until the morrow, which is good Arabian manners—and

---

[8] War drum of a chief.

indeed I thought it was for this reason that Ali El Tom had been so particular in his desire to arrive in the evening.

The reason for the summoning of this meeting was that a personal quarrel between Ali El Tom and Niama (who until then had been old and firm friends) which took place at Soderi in the Ramadan Bairam in February 1931, had led to strained relations between the Kababish and the Nuba.

Since before 1926 a friendly dispute had been going on between those two sheikhs as to the collection of an a-legal tithe on the crops of the Nuba and Kababish who cultivate in lands by the Wadi Hamrat [sic] north of El Wuzz. The Wadi Hamra runs from Showil, south of here and W. of Jebel Um Durag to El Wuzz (a pool in the rains), north of Hamrat El Wuzz. There the watercourse becomes two—or rather another runs from the N.W.—the Wadi Abu Soneit—and the other branch bends east and then N.E. of Wuzz in the "bifur", Ali El Tom claiming up to the E. branch.

In 1926, Maclaren and Kennedy-Cooke[9] between them had made a temporary arrangement, until one of them could go and see the land. Kennedy-Cooke issued a written order to Niama Sirkatti and Ali El Tom that there should be a boundary between the Nuba and the Kababish from Showil to Wuzz—east of the wadi to the Nuba and west to the Kababish (this boundary Mac had made), while north of Wuzz there should be no boundary and Nuba should go on cultivating their old patches in the "bifur" until a D.C came to settle the matter. This order Niama concealed from his people the Nubas.

Last winter Niama took a reika of dukhn grain as tithe (he says it was a free gift, but that is clearly nonsense) from a Kabbashi and Sh. Salih wad esh Shaib the Ghiliani, who was a local cultivating Kabbashi, complained to Ali El Tom. Ali El Tom taxed Niama with this at Soderi in February and hot dispute followed which ended with Niama's saying to Ali El Tom, "You are a liar", an insult which caused Ali El Tom to leave Soderi in great wrath, and had dire results.

News of this quarrel between the old friends immediately spread through the land and beyond the boundaries of Soderi merkaz. The Kababish began to adopt an insolent attitude towards the Nuba, out of loyalty to their insulted sheikh, and the Nuba heard for the first time to their chagrin and alarm that Ali El Tom and Niama had a boundary between Nuba and Kababish, whereas formerly there had been no boundaries anywhere between the two peoples who had lived in amity from Turkish times, Nuba grazing in Dar Kababish and watering at Kababish wells by virtue of "muhamma", that curious Arab notion of

---

[9] B. Kennedy-Cooke, SPS 1920–43; later governor of Kassala, 1935–40. *SPS*, 30.

mutual understanding and assistance between neighbouring tribes which cannot be translated into English. ("Muhanna" [sic] means more or less a "gentleman's agreement" whereby he who asks politely is never refused his request, if that can be helped.)

Niama had betrayed them, they felt, and their confidence in him as their chief was shaken. They therefore presented to me at Hamrat El Wuzz last May a long petition very carefully drawn up, which said they had only just heard that Ali El Tom and Niama had a boundary between them (as per Kennedy-Cooke's order), and that they had always thought that Nuba and Kababish had been on terms of amity and "muhamma". They would prefer the "muhamma" and amity to continue as of old: but, if there were to be boundaries between Dar Nuba and Dar Kababish, then they wanted those boundaries made by "the just officers of government". If these officers made boundaries to their detriment and oppression they must submit, but if the officers of the government proposed to make boundaries, then they, the elders of the Nuba, wished to point out that it was rot to talk about "east of Wadi Hamrat" and "west of Wadi Hamrat", because the two Gebels Nihid were Dar Nuba. They proceeded to prove this by reference to blood-moneys [sic] they had paid in the past for men slain near Nihid. If Nihid was to be cut off from "Dar Nuba", then would government please return them this money? I deferred my answer to this petition at that time. . . .

The next month, Ali El Tom's slave agent at Nihid wells, where Nuba and Kababish had always watered together by "muhanna", most unreasonably prevented a Nuba from having his water-skin filled by a Kabbashi friend from a Kabbashi well. A dispute followed. Sticks descended on opposing heads; a young Nuba of Um Durag, who was apart from the affray, saw his father being beaten about by a Kabbashi, rushed up, drew a knife, stabbed at the first man he met and slew him.

He was sentenced by Hamilton to 10 years. But, on my return, a blood-money settlement was arranged between Sheikh Ali El Tom and Sheikh Niama (and in this case probably the Governor-General will release the lad when the blood-money is paid).

But feeling between the tribes now ran high and was heightened by the slaughter of three stray nagas of the Awlad Ugba Kababish (the section of the slain man) by men of Jebel Um Durag in November. And, when I arrived at Hamrat El Wuzz wells on 15th November, I found an angry buzz of hornets between the two peoples (as already described in this journal). [See above pp. 135–6]

The meeting between Sheikhs Ali El Tom and Niama Sirkatti had therefore been called to settle the cultivation disputes between them. But far more than that was involved. And, above all, though they had exchanged notes and Niama had apologised for his insulting language, they had avoided each other ever since February.

Hamilton and I talked a while, then I went to my hut to change. To my surprise, Ali El Tom came to talk and opened up immediately about the cultivation dispute. This was ominous. He ought to have played the guest and thought nothing of business that night. He must have been talking business with Niama already—very bad manners in a guest according to the Arabian code: "First day greetings—next day talk—third day business". However, he said that he and Niama were going the next morning to see the cultivations.

Hamilton and I dined at 8.30 and discussed African politics and the general futility of things.

29.12.31

While I was having my morning bath after a bitterly cold night (I had to go out and play golf in 3 sweaters and underfugs and grey bags to get warm enough to shave and bathe) I heard a dispute arise outside and Sheikh Ali and Sheikh Niama go to Hamilton. Ali El Tom talked loud, excitedly and angrily to Hamilton who calmed him down. In fact Niama and Ali El Tom had been more or less publicly quarreling before the crowd —a most unfortunate affair.

When I emerged, I found that the reason was that the Nuba elders, who knew the cultivation and the boundaries of each man's patch, had refused to go out with the two shaykhs to see the place. (They feared that the two Nazirs were going to make an agreement to the detriment of the Nuba tribesmen.)

However, the two Nazirs eventually started without these elders. Hamilton and I played golf meanwhile, mashie shots in and out of the resthouse zeriba, at which he is very good and I am hopeless. When Ali El Tom started with a good following on camels, we noticed Ibrahim Faheil, that noted firebrand, his uncle, going too. We sent and brought him back on the pretext of urgently needing his advice—he would have wrecked everything. The Nazirs took two police N.C.O.s from us to watch—a curious phenomenon.

Hamilton and I had breakfast, chatted with Ibrahim Faheil to bluff out our pretext and played more golf till 10 a.m. It was another very cold day.

When we got up from talking to Ibrahim Faheil (and Muhammad Musa Law Law [*sic*], who had come in with him) we saw a long line of Nubas all squatting about 20 yards from the zeriba, with the two Omdas of Abu Hadid and Um Durag in front of them. Hamilton told them to go away, as the Nazirs had gone to settle the business and there could be no talk till their return. However we invited the Omda of Abu Hadid to come and play golf with us (he hit a very good ball several times with a niblick) and so learned that the trouble was the Nubas were not going to consent to the Nazirs' making boundaries over their heads. They did not trust Niama to act for them, it seemed.

We saw various people who came to us, but spent most of the time waiting for the two Nazirs to return. They didn't get back till about 3 in the afternoon, when they promptly came to my hut. They said they had agreed and all was well. They had delimited a boundary between themselves with the help of such "agawid"[10] (counsellors, roughly speaking) as they could find, and were in agreement and all would be love and kisses. Sheikh Ali El Tom rose saying, "Now we will go and write it all down and bring you a copy of the agreement".

Hamilton and I therefore left them to rest and went off at 4 p.m. to call on Omda Salim Ibrahim of Haraza who is ill, further north up the wadi. We returned at sunset. Hamilton had briefly discussed the district and my future on the way.

Noise arose again after dark and the Nazirs came to see me saying that the agreement was upset because the Nuba had raised the question of cultivation in the Adhat (rain pool) of Wuzz. It proved that this place, which is miles away from the land hitherto in dispute, had not been watered for years. The Nuba therefore had clearly raised this academic red-herring in order to torpedo the agreement the Nazirs had made this afternoon.

Hamilton and I therefore sent for the Nuba elders (most of those concerned apparently came from the Derham clan or from the Doalib) and waited in the cold for them to come, fortifying ourselves with whisky and hot water. I was firmly convinced that the reason for this torpedoing tactic was the boundary made by Cooke and the order concerning it which Niama held. I therefore asked Hamilton if I might put this to the Nuba and, if they said this was what was upsetting them, tear up that order. He agreed.

When the Nuba elders arrived I made a long speech recapitulating the causes of the dispute between them and the Kababish and the events leading up to the making of the order, and recalling to their minds their petition to me of last May, wherein they had said that they wanted the ancient "muhamma" between the two peoples and no boundaries. They admitted that this was what was at the back of their minds and what had caused them to drag in the Wuzz red-herring to cook the goose of the Nazirs' arrangement. I then tore up the order and Hamilton explained that that order had been intended to be of a temporary nature and that henceforth, so far as government was concerned, there are no boundaries.

---

[10] Sing.: *jawad*.

But naturally, in the matter of cultivation each man must know where his plot ends, and therefore whatever arrangements the two Nazirs might make for good order should stand. But that would not prevent Nuba from cultivating by "muhanna" in the Kabbashi part of the wadi and vice versa.

The elders appeared thoroughly satisfied and left. But Niama said that they would now think that the Nazirs' arrangement of that afternoon should go by the board. The elders were therefore sent for again and I repeated the sense of the last sentence of the preceding paragraph. They departed apparently content. Niama said as he left, "Well, now we need not write anything down", and we said, "Please God not".

Hamilton and I were then free to have our dinner—it was well after 8 p.m.—and settle down for the night after a short chat on general topics. I slept inside my hut.

30.12.31

The morning was not quite so cold. Hamilton was most anxious to leave this afternoon.

First thing in the morning, while we were trying to get warm by hitting golf balls, Ali El Tom came rushing to me and opened up about his damned government rifles. He now makes out that certain licenced rifles I have never seen have been seen by me as government issue. This is all lies but I can't tell him so bluntly. I said that his discovery that the rifles shown against the licences are not in the tribe was an entirely new thing and would make my work of a year appear inaccurate and useless in the government's eyes. The matter was out of my hands. I would speak to the governor through Hamilton and he could decide whether he would cancel the licences in question.

Ali El Tom said he and Niama were now going off to see into the question of the wells here at Hamrat El Wuzz.

Meanwhile a new hitch arose. Ali El Tom had insisted, it appeared, that his and Niama's arrangement of yesterday must be written down. The Nuba objected. Hamilton, by the grace of God, managed to get all parties to agree that nothing should be written—only a note of the boundary the Nazirs had made, [to be] kept in Soderi files. Two men stayed and described the boundary to me, and the Nazirs went off to the wells.

They returned about $1\frac{1}{2}$ hours later, descended upon me and said they had agreed, "Praise be to God" and, as they were thirsty, would go and rest. Before they could get up, Nuba, headed by Omda Ahmad Gumaa of Um Durag, came in, sat down, and said the Nazirs' arrangement at the wells was oppressive to them. The fat was in the fire again. Hamilton came in. I sent them away to cool off, while we considered what to do.

As a last resort, Hamilton decided to send for Sheikh El Tom Ali (son of Ali El Tom) and put the case fully before him and ask him to urge his father to make concessions to conciliate the Nuba (since it was clear they would not trust Niama or accept any arrangements made by the Nazirs). El Tom came and H. said to him, "Tell me frankly what is the real root of the trouble". El Tom said, "Niama's rude words to my father last February and his behaviour about the cultivation then". H. said we knew that Niama was to blame, but Niama himself had apologised to Ali El Tom and admitted his fault. He explained that boundaries were one thing and "muhanna" another. If you go making boundaries, there cannot be muhanna: further it was clear that the Nuba at the moment had lost confidence in Niama. El Tom of his own accord suggested that his father and he should go to the Nuba and propose that things in the future should be worked on the old lines of "muhanna". He went out and reappeared with Ali El Tom, who said he was going to try this expedient.

Shortly after, the Kababish went to Niama's house (about ¼ mile north along the wadi). We waited anxiously—H. all packed up, his camels to hand, but afraid he would not be able to get away. About 3.45 the crowd came back from Niama's house and all parties said they had agreed to no boundaries and "muhanna" and that they had all pardoned each other and sworn friendship. I said before all the crowd that I would credit the fine due from Um Durag to the blood-money so soon as it was paid.

At that very moment, Omda Ajab Ahmad, who up to date had come so well out of the show, said, "What about the Abu Hadid Nubas' cultivation at Sifeya?" This new cultivation had been a point which Ali El Tom had told me he was going to take up with Niama on the grounds that the place was grazing for Kababish and Nuba alike and ought not to be cleared for cultivation for fear of theft if Nuba settled there. I quickly shut El Ajab up and Hamilton took him into a corner and told him off severely in private.

Hamilton then had tea with me and rode off about 4.30. Niama, Ali El Tom, and I and El Tom rode to put him on his way and took leave of him.

On my return I moved into his hut, which was further from my servants and the Arabs than mine. El Tom came back later and tried to open the question of Sifeya. I fobbed him off, and no one else came to me that evening.

Read and wrote till 8.30. Slept well. Night was a little warmer.

31.12.31

My hamla and the doctor arrived from Soderi while I was in my bath. As soon as I was up I sent for Ali El Tom. He held forth about Sifeya and I fobbed him off saying that this was not the cultivation season and we would make a plan later. He talked about arms. I drew him off dangerous subjects by asking what he would think of a proposal to put the Zaghawa on poll tax instead of tithe. He did not like it, saying that they were under an Arab nazirate and were not people who could always be found; also many of them do not cultivate. He did not want a sedentary type of tax introduced. He never mentioned the religious prejudice against poll tax,[11] so I asked him if that was a reason. It probably was. He also spoke about his teacher's salary.

Then I said, "I know you want to get away—don't wait for me to go. I have to wait for the camels from Soderi to be rested". To my surprise and delight he bit and said he would like to get away that afternoon. I was afraid that, if he stayed on, all would be put in the cart again, as he has been difficult all through the meeting. Various odd jobs cropped up.

At 3 p.m. Niama, the doctor and I and others rode to see Ali El Tom and his enormous posse off. The drums beat and off we went—but he did not let us get far.

After I had returned I went out and hit a golf ball—my blister on my left hand put me off my stroke. Little Feki Medowi Mustafa of Abu Hadid came from the direction of the doctor's tent and asked to play; he became quite enthusiastic and we went on playing till dusk when he departed to pray.

This meeting appears to me to have brought out the following points:
(1) The folly of ever making boundaries if you can possibly help it when you are a D.C.
(2) It all began about 1 reika of grain (210 lbs) and an insult.
(3) It showed clearly that Niama is by no means absolute master of the Nuba. He is the adventurer who has risen by the help of the government and his own force of character and unscrupulousness. He is not the type of the hereditary chieftain that Ali El Tom is and he cannot get his Nubas to follow him unquestioning.
(4) Niama had betrayed the Nuba and they had lost their trust in him.
(5) As a corollary: clearly (a) that proposed Nuba Court at Soderi would have been a farce (b) in case of Niama's death there's no need to look for a successor: the clan feeling of jebels would let them carry on as units.
(6) Ali El Tom showed up at his worst and as a hopelessly bad diplomatist —and even ill-mannered. But remember he did well and was in quite a different frame of mind at Kagmar; and precision and writing down worked wonders last year at Um Inderaba with the Gumuwiya.

N.B. Hamilton and I all through stuck to the line that we wanted no

---

[11] Under Islamic law, poll tax (*jizya*) is not levied on Muslims.

boundaries—only the ancient state of amity and "muhanna" between the two people.

Read and then wrote until 10.30. Very interested by *The Sculptor Speaks*.

1.1.32

Did not realise it was New Year's Day for some hours, until Muhammad Sadig and Tingle wanted money. Got up late. Friday—and market day here. After breakfast Niama brought a well-builder to see me who is going to build Khashm el Laban well at Kobi. Discussed details of cement needed and prices.

Omda Ahmad Gumaa of Um Durag came and I told him I was going to put police on his hill until the £E6 fine is paid.

Omda Ajab of Abu Hadid, whom I told to shut up about Sifeya till I can see the place, [also came]. He admitted the place is newly-opened cultivation and says Abu Hadid needs new grounds for tillage and that Ali El Tom is very unreasonable to adopt his present attitude in view of his agreement of peace and friendship. All no doubt true, but he must shut up now and not let anyone cut more trees. He has fever again.

Various odd petty cases—several slaves occupied the time until 4 p.m.

Golf: Feki Medowi joined me later and then he and the doctor came to drink tea at sunset. All is very quiet here now. Tomorrow we start for the Howawir.

In view of the financial situation I expect I shall emerge a Rip Van Winkle to a changed world in Dongola—possibly to find myself economised: but my expectations of that are small, for it has taken me a year to get round this district and become acquainted with the chief men and, as Hamilton says, they won't want to bring in a new man to Soderi if they can help it at the moment. At any rate, when I get to Dongola it will be February and I may then know when I may escape to get leave.

Warmer this evening.

2.1.32

Rose late. After breakfast Niama brought the Omdas of Abu Hadid and Um Durag to take leave of me. The latter has collected his six-pounds fine mainly by loans from merchants, I gather.

Case of a lad, girl and baby—slaves of a Magnuni—dealt with temporarily. They stay with Niama till I get back from trek.

Niama produced the well expert again. He has agreed to £E40 wages for Khashm el Laban—all materials and labour on Niama. Niama wants to finish Nizeyha also.

El Tom came back. Finished mail.

Left Hamrat El Wuzz 3.45 p.m. El Tom started for Omdurman at same time. As we were parting Niama said, "Please don't summon me for anything in 2nd Fatar (i.e. March). I want to circumcise my sons". This is a little ridiculous, as we had just been discussing about 3 hours before my wanting Niama for the gum-garden dispute at Geili in March.

Rode till 5.35 p.m. Country soon became bare upland with small bushes—this is the same way as I rode to Safia in May. 110 minutes trotting, 170 minutes walking.

Warm night but slept ill. Some woman with a baby travelling had come and bugged [sic] down near us and the baby squawked till rather late. Name of place—Bisheyrat.

3.1.32

Rode 6.17 to 9.06 when we reached Wadi El Masarin. 169 minutes trotting, 275 minutes walking. Felt tired and slack and headachey. Read Howawir files. After lunch tried drawing—a failure.

Rode again 3.50 p.m., easy going over sand, at first uphill—then stones and then sand again. Arrived by Merafiibaat [Marfa'ibat] hills 5.30. Fairly warm evening. 100 minutes trotting, 159 walking.

Had the doctor to drink coffee and talked to him about financial crises and odd things and Dongola and the Muslim conference at Jerusalem.[12]

4.1.32

Rode 6.40 because Safia was near. Had stayed last night short of the wells in order to get grazing for camels—no grass in Safia. Passed Jebel Shuaaf [Shuwaf] and reached Safia, ruins of old merkaz, at 8 a.m. Going easy, downhill over sand. Trotting 80 minutes, walking 125.

Went down to wells (tent had been pitched by old D.C.'s house) and tried to put up and shoot sand grouse—stayed there an hour but no luck: fired six shots and missed badly. Haj Hamza and two others (Yasin and his father) of the merchants came to see me, and a Dongola Kabbashi who has been looking for six months for a man who has a camel and naga of his. Ali, Son of Sheikh Muhammed El Tom, appeared and with him two others of the Nurab—he is tax-collecting. Later Sheikh Muhammad Hasan Khalifa arrived. He had been to Soderi to hand over 4 out of 5 men wanted for brigandage with murder. As he and his camels were tired, I agreed to stay the night at Safia (which I don't like doing much). Naturally, the man

---

[12] In 1931 a meeting of Muslim religious and political leaders was held at Jerusalem, reaffirming the unity of Muslim peoples despite the abolition of the Ottoman caliphate. This conference led to another, in 1937, and ultimately to the founding of the Arab League in 1944.

of the party of 5 brigands, who was said to have been badly wounded in the fight by the Beni Gerar, and whose wife and mother we have in jug in the hopes of making him surrender, has not been brought in. His name is Muhammad Ali Da'ai. Muhammad Hasan says that Muhd. Ali Da'ai was in prison in Bara and, since his release, nothing has been heard of him. I sent off letters by a Howari who is carrying a note from Nimr Hasan Khalifa to Hamilton.

There is no ostensible reason why Safia should be depressing unless it is much sand and no grass and only low black-rocked hills in the neighbourhood. I have now been twice to Safia and have felt miserable both times. However, I find that the doctor is similarly affected by the place: it cannot be mere morbidity on my part.

Went out and played round with a mashie. Hit several quite good shots. In particular three each between 120 and 130 yards in succession, straight into the sun. The doctor then joined me and said he wanted to learn. After a short while he hit quite a good ball.

Took him back to tea at sunset and sat discussing Khashm el Girba, and religion and Effendia [and] the discontent of Army officers until 7.15. The doctor lent me a book for which I am grateful. I wonder if I shall get through it by the end of the trip. Read the said book until 8. Warmish evening.

5.1.32

Rode 6.12 till 8.30—arrived wadi near Jebel Sunugh [Sumugh]. 138 minutes trotting, 240 minutes walking. Shaved for the first time for three days.

Talk with Muhammad Hasan about Nakheila and the raid on the Dongola Arabs, and the Robab and Herd Tax and the wanted Muhd. Ali Da'ai. The doctor told me on the way that he had heard this morning at Safia that the said Muhd. Ali is at Merkh. How I can use this information, even if it is true, I am not sure. To send a policeman there would be useless —the wanted man would be quietly removed into the bush until the police had gone.

Felt more bored than usual. Tried a drawing of coffee pot (gebana) and cups till lunch. After lunch and the departure of my hamla, tried drawing a camel which would not stay still. Ali Muhammad El Tom arrived just as the camels were being driven in to be saddled.

This countryside up here consists of alternate long stretches of hardish sand-hills reddish-yellow in colour and covered with tufted grass and dried herbs and short stretches of outcrops of blackened stone. Trees, or rather bushes, are scanty. Even in the wadis (watercourses) they reach no great height. In fact, the wadis tend to be more like what we called wadis in the northern Butana—viz. depressions between the undulations of the country filled with scattered bush 10 feet to 15 feet high.

Rode 2.55. Just before we started I was sitting in my chair resting half asleep and the noise of the wind through the dried tufts of grass made me think of the Cornish coast—something of a contrast!

Country on march as before. We kept along a ridge with Wadi Abu Urug on the west (left hand). On the far side of the wadi are ridges of black rock and stone. In front and slightly to the right was the pyramid-shaped hill of Nasb el Husaan [sic]. At 5 p.m. we came up with the hamla, passed them, and rode on till 5.55 when we got down in the dusk among bushes and some grass. I felt very tired. Hamla arrived in the last of the light and unloaded by the light of fires. Read the book the doctor lent me. It is amusing and not too difficult. Slept well 9 p.m. till 2 a.m. and after that only lightly.

6.1.32

Rode 6.15 to 8.05 a.m. Were met about half an hour from Nimr Hasan's tents by his son Hasan. Their camp is in a better place than that of last summer and south instead of north of the wells at Abu Urug. Nimr and Adam Hasan Khalifa greeted me and others with them. Goodish breakfast, cool but not cold morning, bath in the Arab tent they had put up for me.

Nimr arrived about 10.30 and we drank coffee and chatted. I kept to condolences, compliments and general conversation for about an hour and then sparred for an opening and talked:

(1) Of Nimr's succession to his father as Nazir. The appointment of course is made by the Governor-General but, having explained that, I told him to carry on in his father's place, and, please God, he would be as good as his father and better. I said government is behind him and I wanted him to travel with me so that the tribe might know that fact.

(2) Of Powers. I told him to use his father's powers under the Nomad Sheikh' Ordinance . . . and (a) tried to impress upon him that his judgements must be customary, just, and given in open meglis [sic], in the presence of elders and well-known proper assessors, in order that he should not fine people arbitrarily. But I told him another reason, viz: in order that his judgements might have authority and weight and that his reputation for justice might be enhanced. (b) I told him also that only he and his brother Adam might use powers. If his other brothers did so they would be punished. He said Mr Watt had already told him that. I said I knew: but people forget, and I proposed, at a convenient opportunity, to repeat Watt's remarks to the brothers. (c) I put in a word as an afterthought that, as at present times are so hard, as far as ready money is

concerned, I advised that *money* fines should be as light as possible — animals and other fines in kind are a different matter.

He asked me, was he to hear cases of foreigners, e.g. Kababish, Nuba, Geryat etc. against Howawir and settle them. I said, "Certainly, according to custom as your father did". (Ali Ibrahim Dolib has turned up to complain against a Howari.) Cases too hard for him or cases against known malefactors who deserve prison, or cases of an importance or kind outside his powers (e.g. man-slaying, brigandage), he must refer to government. All others by custom and meglis. We then talked generalities again, I reserving other things for later. *N.B.* To repeat all this advice to him again later to make sure it sinks in.

He said most of the Arabs are to be found further north now, near Um Rumeila and Um Ratot for the "gizzu" grass and for the cultivation at Um Gawasir.

Muhammad Adam Abdallah is appointed sheikh of the Robab in place of his late father. This, apparently, at the request of the section itself, and Nimr agrees. *N.B.* Nimr said that large numbers of Robab came to mourn for Sheikh Hasan Khalifa, and that the appointment was made then. . . .

From about noon onwards I felt very weary. Spent most of the afternoon reading tribal files. About 4.30 Ali Ibrahim Dolib and another Nuba of Haraza turned up (for the second time today), Ali Ibrahim about the nagas he lost 3 years ago and of which he says all three were taken into Wad El Digeir's herds (a Howari) and one sold to the Awlad Ugba. The Nuba had recently watered his flock of sheep at Bir Shungul with Omda Salim Ibrahim's written leave. He is now afraid that Niama Sirkatti will fine him. The question of the watering arrangements at this well came up when I was at Rokab in Haraza in November, and Sh. Ajabna Ali tried to drag me into it then. There is a difference of opinion in the matter between Salim Ibrahim and Niama. I won't interfere if I can help it.

While they were still talking, Nimr arrived for his evening session and as soon as the other two had retired I went through various papers with Nimr. He said he wanted me to wait here five days, because his camels are away. I shall have to do so if he can't be ready before then.

7.1.32

About 2 a.m. the wind began to blow and I awoke. From that time till dawn rheumatism in my shoulder and the breeze kept me more or less awake. After dawn a real high wind began to blow and the world to a height of 20 feet above the ground became a cloud of sand and dust. I think it is with the Hasan Khalifa family as with consuls: "nobody but a fool would be a consul, therefore all consuls are fools"; "nobody but a fool would live at a place like Abu Urug, therefore everybody who lives there is a fool". I sat and endured it, reading until about 1.30 p.m. in the Arab tent. Nimr came and talked to me for a short time. There was too much wind for it to be possible to go and visit him. At 1.30 I had lunch— too much wind for the lunch to have been cooked so I ate tinned fruit.

Soon afterwards the wind dropped a good deal and Hasan Nimr came from his father to ask me to go over to his house. Talked and drank tea and ate (as little as possible) kisra. Feki Abderrahman, Sheikh Ali Adam, Hasan Khalifa, the other brothers, Sh. Abd El Kerim Muhammad of the Robab were there, also the doctor. Nimr and the doctor walked back with me to my tent and sat and talked till after 4.30 p.m. By that time the wind had dropped. I felt dead tired, as so often one does after [a] prolonged spell of sand blown into the eyes and ears and nose. Hit a golf ball till it was dark.

Slept till 2 a.m. and after that but little. Hope to goodness all this trek is not going to be like this.

8.1.32

Friday. Rose late, feeling rheumatic and depressed. However, thank God, the wind did not become very strong. After breakfast I got out maps and pinned them on the walls of my tent to see my proposed route. Shortly Tingle brought Feki Magdoub, the schoolmaster of the "khalwa" to see me. He cheered me up considerably with talk of astronomy and of his people in Damer and on the Atbara (he is related to the Awlad Sheikh El Magdoub near Goz Regeb). Later Nimr came.

(1) I gave him a list of the Howawir wanted for renewal of rifle licences and said I would punish no one who turned up now. But if they failed to appear during my trek the licences would be cancelled and the guns confiscated if found. Not a strong policy, but probably none will ever come in if they think they are going to be fined.

(2) *Herd Tax*. I told Nimr that government considered that failure to pay off arrears of 1930 and failure to pay even one quarter of the tax of 1931 before the end of the year showed slackness on the part of the sheikhs which could not be excused by the fall in prices of animals. The whole of the tax for 1931 had got to be collected. For his private information I told him I hoped that government would lighten the tax in 1932 and keep it lighter temporarily until prices of animals improved. He said did I approve of the sending out of "manadiib" (i.e. legates or deputies) to help the sheikh collect, or must he work through the sheikhs only? This leading question brought me on to the question of customary dues to the sheikh and the exactions of his brothers and followers in the past. It was not a question easy to answer, for, of course, if one says, "Use manadiib", the way is open for the descent of a greedy horde of brothers and dependents

and exactions unlawful and unlimited; and if one says, 'No manadiib", his answer is, "well, don't blame me if taxes get in arrears and summonses are not obeyed". I therefore hedged and said, "Do what was done in your father's time—make your own plans for running the tribe as you are now its head", and went on

(3) To lecture upon the customary dues of the Sheikh and over-eating of the people.[13] I said Hasan Khalifa had told me that the customary dues in the Howawir were three only—tithe of crops (when there are any, which is rare), a sheep a flock a year, and the "rial ed dho" (I don't know yet what this last is). Nimr said that was well known and that he took no more than that. I said that, from Mr. Reid to Mr. Watt, D.C.s had warned him and his father to check "over-eating" by his brothers and that I was now repeating that advice. I said that I feared that, if he sent out "manadiib", there would immediately be complaints from the Howawir of eating. I had no objection to manadiib, provided they confined themselves to assisting in tax collection only; but they must not "eat". The Howawir were an independent-minded crowd and not silly sheep—men who will not brook oppression. He said he quite well knew that and that he had done his best to carry out Mr. Watt's instructions. I said that Arabs will stand for the lion eating his due but not being eaten by lesser animals in his train.

Then we talked of minor matters and our trek. He says that most Arabs are on the Wadi Mugaddam from Gumar northwards. There are numbers of Arabs round Bayuda.

He said also amongst other things that Omar Yasin Dolib has been charging "mabrak" of 5 PT a camel in the market at Hamrat El Wuzz and that this is a bit hard. I agree. I had not of course heard of these unlawful dues (if the tale is indeed true). He left and I proceeded to write for a mail, as Atallah the ghaffir may be leaving here for Soderi in a day or two.

I spent my afternoon trying to make a sketch of the hill east of this camp. Failed dismally to get a sky washed in. The paper dried so quickly, the afternoon being pretty warm. After that a little golf.

Just at sunset, Nimr, Adam and Feki Abderrahman came, bringing one Sheikh Muhi ed Din Mahmoud, a Dongola landowner whose mother was Hasan Khalifa's sister. He proved a most chatty little man and we sat bucking till 7 p.m. He made me try to explain the cause of the lack of money.

Sat up till after 10 drawing and writing.

9.1.32

Felt fresher this morning. After breakfast went to see the khalwa (Quran school) and sat for a while chatting to the Feki and making the

---

[13] That is, over-taxation, with proceeds to the collector rather than to the government.

small boys write. Then we had running races outside for acid drops. (Hope they aren't ill.)

A high wind got up by 10.30 and I spent the rest of [the] time till 3.30 sitting reading Arabic while everything became steadily grittier. Found a very good article in the "Hedara" on the gold standard, bank rate, rates of exchange and foreign trade—simple and made me understand what I had never understood before.

About 3.30 Nimr turned up to talk and shortly after him Muhammad Effendi. Nimr produced 8 guns of government issue for registering. By sunset it was fairly cold. New moon of Ramadan appeared.

I find from Tingle that we shall get away from here the day after tomorrow. Nimr's camels have come, but tomorrow is Sunday and unlucky for making a start. Thank God. I want to change my dust heap. I am tired of this variety of sand and of sitting idle.

10.1.32

Nothing of any account happened today. I played a little golf in the morning, read Arabic papers (but was too idle to look up words I did not know), [and] did some attempts at sketching in the afternoon.

It blew fairly hard most of the day. Nimr says he does not now want anything in the way of strong measures taken with the Robab of whom he complained in the summer. Slept well.

11.1.32

A mail turned up from Soderi brought by the tribal ghaffir. Yasin Effendi the translator is transferred to Finance Department and Mustafa Omar El Tinai, son of the merchant in El Obeid, comes in his place. Got warm by hitting a golf ball.

Muhammad Effendi came and chatted for a short while—the chat was interrupted by the arrival of Sheikh Nimr and his brothers, for whom I had previously sent. As they were fasting and he was not, I had a good excuse to leave him to drink his coffee while I saw them in the other tent.

I said that the government greatly regretted the death of their renowned and noble father. But, praise be, his sons remained. The appointment of Nazir was not in my hands but in those of the Governor-General. Meanwhile until His Excellency's approval and confirmation arrived, Sheikh Nimr would continue to act as head of the tribe, and, please God, with good results and good luck to him. I knew that Sheikh Hasan before he died had given them all the good advice possible and I did not wish to say more, but only to give them counsel on behalf of the government and to remind them of what Watt had said last year at the time of the trouble with the Robab. Everyone knew that it is the custom of the Arabs for the

Sheikh of the tribe to settle his people's disputes according to their ways. But 10 years ago government had given powers to Sheikh Hasan; now no one must use these powers except Sheikh Nimr or Sheikh Adam his eldest brother.

Sheikh Nimr said that was understood. But he then returned to talk of "manadiib", saying he had asked me about using them and proposed to send out his brothers to assist in tax collection. As for tribal dues, he proposed to take only the "ushr", the sheep a flock, and the "rial ed dho". I said nothing good or bad to that (it was an awkward moment).

Sheikh Adam said that I was now as their father to tell them good from bad. I replied that there is a great difference between the position of a father and that of an Inspector, but, if it pleased God, there should be real friendship between us and we should agree together and all would work together for good. I then sent them away.

N.B. To point out again to Nimr at a suitable opportunity that these tribal dues are a-legal: government cannot back him up if people refuse to pay them.

Spent the rest of the morning writing mail. Rode 3.15. Arrived Wadi El Gelta 4.55, half way to Hobaji. Chilly evening. Had a large fire and talked to Nimr by it.

"Shidd"—native boys' game. Two sides pick up and a goal is made (tree or mound or rock). The attacking side appoints one of its members the 'aroos (bride). All have to hop on one foot holding the other in the hand. The bride's object is to reach the goal and her side's to help her to do so. The other side try to catch the bride and "kill" her. If she is killed she joins the killers and so on, as for prisoners' base, until no one is left on one of the two sides.

100 minutes trotting, 157 minutes walking. Very finely coloured late sunset sky with new moon and star below it. Scarlet-to-orange rays fading into light green, blue running above into ultramarine and almost black. Cold night, no wind.

12.1.32

Woke at 5, rode 6.15 to 7.45. Arrived Um Inderaba wells, Hobaji. The way from Wadi El Gelta is over a level plain of sand with very scant grass towards a line of rocky hills about 200 ft high and I should say 15 to 20 miles from west to east.

Went to look at the wells after breakfast and found Jaaliin of the Kababish there; was given sheep's milk and chatted to an old man called Sadig wad Koko. One or two not bad-looking girls there. 90 minutes trotting, 125 minutes walking.

It struck me while I was talking to the Jaalin [sic] that Marmaduke

Pickthall's[14] remark applies here: these people are really happy; they have no irking worries; occasionally they have the excitement and enjoyment of a big calamity—drought or death; occasionally they become "Za'alaaniin" (a state indicating rage and despair) or "madhluumiin"[15] (the world blackened in their sight on account of wrong, real or imaginary, done them). But normally they are as children of the sun, good-tempered, easily laughing, polite and chatty. Above all they have no self-consciousness and no class-consciousness. My white face and queer clothes embarrassed them not at all: all men are equal.

A small boy to whom I gave sweets didn't know what to do with them and was afraid the one I put in his mouth wouldn't melt.

Tried drawing an ushur bush and found it incredibly difficult.

Rode 2.55. Climbed over the hills north of the wells. Beyond them is a circular plain enclosed by hills: at the end of it to the north are three hills—flat-topped and crumbling—Ummat, Uqoub and another whose name I could not catch. The hills at Hobaji are really an escarpment—this plain or plateau seems to slope very gently northwards. The going very good—hard sand with tufts of grass of various kinds. Set down 5.30 near Dirrat El Bayaad. 145 minutes trotting, 227 minutes walking. Jebel Mitni to front. . . .

Customs regarding strays:

The honest man will put stray animals which he may find in his own herds and spread the news abroad that these strays have come to him— telling his sheikh and his neighbours and people on the wells, and giving description of the stray animals. Such animals may have to stay in his herds for 2 years or more until their owner claims them. The man in whose herd they are takes the milk and hair. The owner, when he claims the animals, has the right also to any offspring they may have had meanwhile. If any of the animals have meanwhile been sick and the owner of the herd in which they have been has incurred expense on their behalf, then, if the owner is wealthy and generous, he will waive his claim to them and let the finder keep them. But if the owner wants his animals, then he will have to make a meglis and pay the finder what is owed and take his animals back.

The dishonest man is he who, finding strays, does not reveal and publish the fact that he has found them; or he who, having found strays, sells them instead of keeping them for the owner. . . .

Nimr says the Howawir originally came from Howar in the Western

---

[14] 1875–1936: prolific writer about the East. A biography is Peter Clark, *Marmaduke Pickthall*, London 1987.
[15] *za'lan*: annoyed, angry; *mazlum*: oppressed.

Desert of Egypt.[16] He spoke of El Haj Khidr's fight as a dervish against the Howawir at Gambir when Ali Khalifa was killed but the dervishes were defeated.

Slept well till 3 a.m.—after that, lightly.

13.1.32

Rode 6.26 to 8.30 a.m. Cold but not very cold. The going was over sand. After about 1½ hours we came to Jebel Mitni and crossed over its W. flank, where we had to dismount at one place to get the camels up onto a ledge of rock. From there we descended into Wadi Rikaab, where there were a few Arabs with cows. The cows were not drinking but feeding on green grass—the Arabs (Barah Kababish and Howawir) drink at Um Inderaba. 116 minutes trotting, 190 minutes walking. Pleasant wadi but the sand very heavy. Nimr wants to stay the night here because he thinks some Howawir from further out may come in from the gizzu. He has sent to tell them the doctor and I are here.

No one came to see me; the doctor, I believe, had a few patients. I felt tired and spent most of the day trying to draw. In the evening light the place looked most attractive. Nimr says this is the first time any Englishman has put up his tent in Wadi Rikab.

14.1.32

Rode 6.25 to 9.30, the going over sand good. The beginnings of gizzu are visible here: some of the grass is still green.

A line of low rocky hills appeared on the horizon which they say are called Keribat El Muarras—not shown on the map at all. There is a well behind the two tallest hills in the range. It runs W. to E. to join the Elai hills. Crossed a ridge of slag hills. The colours were remarkable. The stony hills themselves appear almost black against the light and a deep, very dark plum colour in it. There was one point where the sand had blown over the ridge to make a small dune at the top. As the sand dune was brilliant orange the effect was most striking. 175 minutes trotting, 295 minutes walking.

Got down in Wadi El Geleita. From here it is said to be about 4 hours' ride to Elai. These last three days have given us perfect weather: neither hot nor cold and mostly calm. For the last two or three nights the police and servants have been very cheery over a game called "warrad el gamal"[17] which appears to be a sort of "Cardinal Puff" without drinks. It depends on the complications of taking a camel, a naga, and a young camel

---

[16] For the Egyptian and remoter origins of the Hawawir see P. M. Holt, "Hawwara", *Encyclopaedia of Islam*, 2nd ed., III, 299–300.

to drink successively at each of three "rivers". No two animals must drink at the same time as another at the same "river". It is very simple, but easy to trip if you fail to think carefully all the time.

Tried to draw a meikah tree, but was much troubled by large buzz flies which made for my face or ears every time I put a pencil to paper.

Rode 3.15 to 5.15, when we arrived [at] Shuwaaf hill not far from the wells at Elai (about one hour's ride). The going was moderate only, much of it being stony ground where camels had to walk. We climbed out of the Wadi El Geleita over the Kerabat [sic] El Geleit hills. The scenery here in the afternoon sun was very attractive—the dark puce colour of the stones against red ochre sand, many of the hills being half sand also. Moreover the grass now becomes quite green. 155 minutes trotting, 135 minutes walking.

There is a large quantity of each of two melon-type plants about— hanzal and habash.[18] Hanzal makes vegetable tar; habash is merely good grazing for animals. . . .

The weather and air are marvellous and it is a treat to see new country —moreover this country side is most unexpectedly attractive. I feel ten times the man I did in El Obeid—or Hamrat El Wuzz.

Had Muhammad Effendi to drink coffee and talk after sundown.

15.1.32

After an hour's riding, 6.40 to 7.40 a.m. among hills and over stony ground, arrived at the wadi in which Alay wells are. The place is extrmely pretty: the watercourse coming down out of the rocky hills is nearly two hundred yards across a level stretch of sand, and has large trees on either bank. My tent had been set up under these trees. 60 mins. trotting, 90 mins walking.

There are only about 4 or 5 houses of Arabs here at present, the main person being a Fezzani named Goda. The well is covered. The few animals here are feeding on the melon-like plants, handal and habash, with which the countryside is filled, and the green trees, and so are not drinking. The men are drinking from water holes in the sand of the wadi-bed. High hills all round. Last year Watt and Tingle set up a mound on the top of one, so this time some of the police climbed up it and made another. Last year there had been no rain and there was none of this green at all.

Had a shave and bath, first since Abu Uruq—water smelt very bad. Went to see camels being watered. Condition fair only.

Very tired and restless although the day was exceedingly pleasant. At

---

[17] "Take the camel to water".
[18] *Hanzal* (Sudanese colloquial: *handal*): *Citrullus colocynthis*, the colocynth.

2 p.m. Nimr turned up with one Muhammad Haamid, wakil of Sheikh Gabir Tugga, to have his gun licence renewed. Talked to Nimr and Adam mainly about our next move, and about superstitions. As to the first: there are only women at Gambir and no people at Bohat, so it looks like going direct to Gumur from here. As to the second: two crows cawing means a friend's return; it is unlucky to see a poor man or an ugly one starting for a journey—you want to see a pretty woman or a rich man; last Wednesday in the month is very unlucky, like Friday and Sunday; 2, 3, 7, 12, 17, 22, 27 are lucky numbers: 13 is very unlucky; the white hawk is lucky; a small bird called "bilbiliya" is lucky to some but unlucky to others.

Played golf 4.15 but could not hit a thing. Then Nimr, as he crossed the wadi, asked me to drink tea, so I went and sat on a saddle in their camp and we talked mostly of betting on horse races in Omdurman and Khartoum.

16.1.32

Slept extremely badly (perhaps owing to having had for dinner what had been cooked for lunch). Best sleep was from 10 p.m. till 11.15 and then from 2. till 5.30. Wind blew from 1.30 a.m. Must admit the wadi looked pleasant by starlight.

Lost golf ball. Decided to go to Gumur, missing out Gambir and Wadi Bohat.

The Nazir's herds are at Jebel Tawagia, north of here. Had I known before I would have gone there. Nimr is sending a man to Omdurman tomorrow.

Rode 3.15 to 5.15, direction northeast. The going at first among hills of Elai and over stones—had to walk most of it. After that, going was better. Arrived in Wadi El Hassanawi near Jebel of that name. Cold evening. Good night's sleep. 120 minutes trotting, 195 walking.

17.1.32

Soon after dawn the wind, which had been blowing cold all night, became even bitterer. Rode 7 a.m. along the wadi—arrived Bir El Hassanawi. 30 mins. trotting, 65 mins. walking.

The countryside round about since leaving Elai is extremely desolate: a great contrast to Elai wadi among the hills, where there were such large trees and birds and green vegetation just now. Here, except for a few large trees on the wadi banks, the scene is howling wilderness, mostly black stone. We are staying here today mainly because Nimr wishes to send off his messenger to Omdurman and kindly gives me an opportunity of writing mail. It looks as if we are in for a cold snap similar to that at the end of December.

Should arrive at the head of Wadi Gumur this evening and go down it to its junction with the Wadi Mugaddam tomorrow. From there, so I'm told, it is only half an hour to the place where the Howawir have their largest cultivation, and where, so Nimr says, there will be plenty of Arabs and he has told his sheikhs to meet me. It remained cold all day. There appeared to be plenty of water in Bir El Hassanawi.

Rode 3.15 parallel to wadi, going good over sand dunes and dune country. Here one can see dunes actually in formation, especially when there is a high wind blowing as today, which whipped the sand round the edges of the hillocks. Very bare country. At one point in a hollow Nimr pointed out to me a small green plant with a red pimpernel-like flower called "derma",[19] which he says is "gizzu" grass. Jebels called "Humur" appeared to the south, and away to the front a long ridge running east which he said is "Galaat El Gumur". This country is like what one expects a desert to be: rolling dunes of various colours of orange and yellow tufted with dry clumps of wiry grass and black stony hills in the background. . . . Every now and then the dunes are streaked with outcrops of stones.

Set down nowhere in particular at 4.50—some grass here for the camels. Cold evening. Read Bengt Berg's book on cranes and other Nile birds[20] over a big fire. The dahabiya[21] Berg hired for his photography— the Amina—was the one I spent the night on with Penn a year ago.

95 mins. trotting, 160 mins. walking. Slept well.

18.1.32

Rode 6.30 to 8.55. Cold morning. The going similar to yesterday's until we got near to the ridge "Galaat Gumur" previously described, when the ground became stony and broken into "kerib" by action of water. This is the head of Wadi Gumur. We descended and arrived opposite the end of Galaat Gumur where the wadi runs between these hills and the hill Fag Gumur to the south. These are high hills of black stone, very imposing and barren—the yellow sand and green trees of the wadi-bed between them show up bright.

Here at Fag Gumur are many ruins of ancient houses. There is also a deep well (11 rajils) in the rock above the south bank of the wadi under Fag Gumur. Nimr says this well is very ancient and that his forefathers found it already built of stone. Stone reservoirs (hods) are built beside the well. Nimr said his grandfather told him that he, when young, had seen a strange folk from the west in great numbers here—before the Kunjara[22]

---

[19] *Indigofera arenaria.* Tothill, 946.
[20] *Mit den Zugvogeln nach Afrika*, Berlin 1926.
[21] Boat.

came. There are shallow wells in the wadi-bed. Walked round to look at the ruins and the rock well. 155 trotting, 215 minutes walking.

Tried a drawing of the mountains after lunch. Very attractive spot for anyone who likes very wild and rocky scenery, but little for the camels to eat except a small quantity of sifeyra[23] (yellow-flowered grass) and nabak tree. No Arabs bar about 4 or 5 tents some way off. Nimr decided to push on to Botha further down the wadi.

Rode 3.20. The going moderate only—heavy sand in the wadi bed which soon became 200 to 300 yards wide, and bad stones if one ascended out of the wadi. This must be a tremendous stream when it comes down in flood. The banks are much eaten away. Cold ride and high wind. Passed wells under a cliff called Gata (sand grouse), and finally reached Botha (another place where there are wells in the wadi-bed) at 5 p.m. Here there is an island in the wadi-bed. To the south is Jebel Miaygil, where the afore-mentioned battle between Howawir and dervishes under Haj Khidr Ed Dokri took place. This is on the direct route from Omdurman to Debba, and we found a merchant resting his caravan in the wadi.

Talked to Nimr after dark. Deaf since evening of 17th, couldn't hear very well. Slept in tent. Wind blew deck chair over into fire in the night and burnt it. 100 minutes trotting, 127 walking.

19.1.32

It is quite clear that, in the circumstances, I made a big mistake not to insist on going north to Fogi and so towards Debba and then down to Um Rumeila. This journey is getting exceedingly boring except that it is amusing to see new scenery. Watered camels and stayed all day to rest camels after watering. Cold day.

Nimr and later the doctor and Adam turned up after lunch and talked till about 4.30. A vile night. Bitter wind started early in the morning, about 2 a.m., and blew dust. Slept little after 3 a.m., but lack of sleep does not seem to tell on one in this rare atmosphere.

20.1.32

Bitterly cold morning, arctic wind blowing right in our faces as we rode. Just about as cold as it was Decr. 26th and 27th.

The going pretty good—a certain amount of stones. Camels went fast in spite of the wind. Found camp 8.45 after riding since 6.35. Country from here onwards was sand and sand-drifts with patches of stony ground and gravel, and many sumara, tundub and sellum[24] trees. Resembled country

---

[22] A section of the Fur.
[23] *Dipterygium glaucum*. Tothill, 952.

on Atbara near Goz Regeb. Did not get warm till I had done stoutness exercises.

Had Nimr to talk, as he had no protection against the wind. He said he had lost part of his hamla—so not only district commissioners suffer from this. Chatted about the origin of the "Gallaba Howara". Then about Um Metto cases and disputes and so to the meeting in 1930 at Hamrat El Wuzz, where a peace was made with the Um Metto, and so to the Rubab [sic] Howawir complaints against Sh. Hasan Khalifa and his sons. I said I supposed no aeroplane had ever been at Abu Urug until Hamilton landed there and told Hasan Khalifa to stop his sons eating the tribe. He said, "No." And I said, "Please God there won't be many complaints in the future." He said, "We shan't take from them more than the customary dues". This gave me the cue for which I was angling, to say what I have been wondering whether to say for some days. I said of course these dues were a tribal matter with which, as with all customs of the tribe, the government had no wish to interfere. But these dues have no authorisation from government for their collection and there is a wide difference between them and an official and legal tax. Government would not stop him from collecting what was customary, but if the collection appeared oppressive in future, government might tell him to hold his hand. I was saying this for his private ear, because he is a man of understanding and importance. The position is somewhat of the nature of the government's knowing that these dues are paid but neither sanctioning them nor forbidding them, but winking at them so long as they are light.

We then talked of camelbreeding. He said that herds run up to 100 heads but not more. Howawir do not have more than one stallion in a herd —two would fight. (He said the Kawahla find they can leave two or more in a herd.) The number of times that the stallion has to cover the naga before she takes varies: stallion is always aware when she has taken and leaves her. If one stallion becomes tired before all nagas have taken that should, another is produced.

From this we turned to sheep and I remarked that the English, being a sheep-owning and breeding race from ancient times, are always urging the Arabs to take sheep instead of camels, but of course the Arabs will not leave herding camels. He and I agreed that a man with camels and no sheep is in a poor way nowadays. He enquired regarding English sheep herding and I described Southdown shepherding. He then turned to cattle. He wants a bull from the half-breed stock at the govt. Belgravia Dairy,

---

[24] *Samara: Acacia raddiana.* Tothill 684; *salam: Acacia flava.* Tothill, 952; *tundub: Capparis decidua.* BM, 60.

Khartoum North, and I promised to arrange. He will pay. Bull should be red. Bull to be delivered next rains.

Rode 2.50 till 4.30. Arrived Um Rumeila wells in the Wadi Mugaddam. Country as described above. Passed several tents and first herd of camels. But they were of the Dongola Ahamda, not Howawir. 100 mins. trotting 175 walking.

21.1.32

Cold night with brilliant moonlight (the moon being full in three days' time), but thank goodness practically no wind. Read till 9.30 and slept well and did not get up till 7 a.m., after which I played golf till breakfast to get warm. . . .

Tingle said there were Ahamda camels on the wells and with them Salih Gelli, son of Gelli Adam their sheikh. These people live at Gambir and here and generally in Dar Howawir, but pay taxes to Dongola Province. Went to see the camels and on the way said good day to Beshir Ali (cousin of Nimr and son of Ali Khalifa killed at Miaygil by dervishes). Camels up here go to pasture (Howawir and Ahamda and others all alike) without herdsmen because theft is very rare. Only the Geriat do any thieving. Each herd knows its usual well and appears there when thirsty. At the end of the summer, when rains are expected, the owner goes down to the well with his halters and waits for his camels, which he halters as they come in, and then hands them over to his hersdmen for the rains until water standing in rain pools has dried in the winter.

Well here is 17 rajils (i.e. about 93.5 feet); the other one here is 15 rajils.

There was the usual cheerful scene on the wells: sheep and camels and goats all mixed up and men and slaves and boys and girls drawing water and thwacking the animals to make them drink in their appointed turns. Salih Gelli appeared a pleasant bloke, and had a charming small son of about 5, entirely naked and not so shy as most, to whom I gave sweets, which he shared with another small boy. One or two little girls looked as if they'd like sweets but were far too shy to approach, and I did not think fit to make bold advances on my first appearance in this country, where Englishmen are very rare birds.

Sheikh Ahmad Sherif of the Habasab Howawir and Othman Adam Abdallah (a one-eyed man—lost the other through the usual accident with a Remington), son of the late sheikh of the Robab, came up and greeted me.

As usual, news came too late or I was idle in collecting it. It appears that most of the tribe are grazing gizzu around Jebal [*sic*] Audun near the Wadi El Melik (Lat. 16° 36' Long. 30° 6') to which I could have got easily from Abu Urug and so to Fogi north of it and then across to here, missing all this empty stretch and seeing untouched country. *Experientia docet.*

Others of the tribe in some numbers are right away near and south of Jakdul (Abu Tleh way) in Berber Province; others near Bayuda. To cope with the Howawir and get a slight knowledge of them one wants to devote not a month but 3 or 4 to them.

Many Arabs, nearly all Robab, came to see Nimr. Sh. Sueytir Muhammad of the Maulka is here too.

I have been reading MacMichael on the tribes and history of Kordofan[25] with renewed interest. He did write in a different style in those days: it's like a book by a German scholar.

At about 3.30 rode for half an hour to the cultivations at Um Gawasir, where I propose to stay several days. Arabs at last are thick on the ground. The cultivations are like none I have seen in Kordofan, great expansive stretches of wadi cultivation with heavy "sofra" millet (entirely different from dukhn), which has thick tall stalks and leaves which dry a reddish colour. The cultivation here is more like that in the Abu Deleig wadis. Nimr says the year before last it was much heavier than this year. *N.B.* Water from the wells here very pure and sweet.

Read. Started reading *Du Congo au Nil*,[26] which I find exceedingly interesting.

N.B. Nimr said, talking of the light colour of the Howawir, that they are very careful [and] always have been to keep their blood uncontaminated by negro blood. They breed very little from slave women. Very few have any concubines: instead they marry as many free women as possible according to their means. Nimr has the legal limit of four. His father in his time married more than 12 women (divorcing many). The thought of Nimr's four wives fills me with solicitation on their behalf: there must be considerable risk of suffocation involved in being married to him. No doubt he is wealthy enough and the social prestige is sufficient advantage to make it worth while. I wonder what he weighs.

22.1.32 to 25.1.32

Nothing to report. Sat and sat, played golf, read (especially *Du Congo au Nil*, which I find most entertaining). I talked daily with Nimr. One woman complained that she wanted a divorce from her husband on grounds of desertion. One man said another had done him out of his share in a well. No other Howawir complaints. Occasionally Nimr brought guns for me to register. A rather jolly old man of the Ahamda called Gelli Ali

---

[25] *The tribes of northern and central Kordofan*, Cambridge 1912.
[26] By J. Hilaire, Marseille 1930.

who lives at Gambir came at one time to see me, involved in one or two complaints by Ahamda and Geriat (tribes not of Kordofan Province). On 24.1.32. I went to see camels watered. Otherwise nothing at all happened. Nimr is evidently very busy. Weather remained cold. I have omitted that police from Dongola (Debba merkaz) arrived on 22nd. . . .

The sketch map . . . shows at a glance the difficulties of administering the Howawir. By administering I mean no more than arranging so their taxes shall be paid by them regularly year by year, and any criminals wanted from the tribe, produced. Administration is necessarily indirect through the Nazir of the tribe, who is responsible for paying in the tax collected by the sheikhs of sections of the tribe and producing any men accused of crime at the demand of government.

His task is no easy one. The tribesmen are on the whole more sophisticated (especially the Robab section, which is one of the richest) than other Kordofan nomads, and they are of the most upstanding and independent character, impatient of authority, very-pure bred and proud. They are naturally unwilling taxpayers. They appear to have very few household slaves and therefore to have to work as other nomads of these parts do not. On this trek I have continually seen free men, women, and children all pulling at the well ropes. This all makes for hardness of living and individualism of character.

In addition, the country in which they choose to live is such as both to accentuate these intractable undocile characteristics and to cause them to live in more scattered fashion and to be more nomadic even than ordinary nomads. The rainfall in Dar El Howawir is considerably more precarious than it is in "Kordofan" (I use the word as the natives do, i.e. country south of the line Haraza–Merkh etc.). Sh. Nimr tells me that the cultivation at Um Gawasir (of sofra and feterit millet) has now been watered 4 times only since 1899. This is their only rich cultivation, the other being poor stuff near Hobaji. The "gizzu" grass on which they are all grazing their herds—at Um Gawasir and north of Fogi and at Abu Ban, Abu Gia, Bayuda and south of Jakdul—rises only occasionally, say every fourth year. When it does not rise they are forced to graze further south, e.g. last year the Fezzanab (who own sheep more than any other section) were all round Elai, and there were Arabs all up the Wadi Mugaddam at Gambir, Bohat etc. where now there are none; and, in a bad year, they are forced into Dar El Kababish in the Wadi El Melik near Baggaria and to Safia and El Merkh. Last year, so Tingle tells me, there was next to no grass where Arabs were to be found.

All this increases the difficulty of the Nazir's task. The difficulties of that of the D.C. who has to inspect him and his tribe are further enhanced by the fact that, the better the grazing (as for instance in this year, which is an exceptionally good one), the more inaccessible do the Howawir become, for they roam farther north and scatter even more widely. At the moment only very few of them are in Kordofan Province at all (roughly Audun—Showaf—Gambir is the northern boundary of the province). Those at Jakdul are in Berber Province and the rest in Dongola. This year Um Gawasir is clearly the most central point from the tribe's point of view. But I did not get news of the position of the people at Fogi in time to take my tour that way. It would now take 5 days to get to those people from here and then they will be grazing on gizzu, with light tents only, and two days or so from water. I have spent nearly a month on this trek and seen next to nothing of the tribe. Watt said he was pretty certain the Robab would try to break away from the rest of the tribe on the old Nazir's death. I therefore had to come, and come expecting trouble. There is no sign of trouble. But had I not come we could not have known what is happening and moreover Nimr would never have moved from his tent at Abu Urug, and no one would have lifted a finger to try to collect taxes already a year in arrears. I sit here doing nothing: but he—so far as I can tell—is doing a job. Such is the administration of nomads, and most of it consists in drinking coffee and making polite talk.

26.1.32
Having survived all the cold and been feeling unusually fit (hit several very fine balls, for me, yesterday at golf) I rose this morning with a chill on the liver and spent the day nursing it.

27.1.32
Well again this morning but not too full of life. Reading old files yesterday, I discovered that Newbold had had sheikhs of the Howawir complain to him in 1922 that Nimr and his brothers did all the work in the tribe, riding everywhere and leaving them no chance to do their job.

Nimr this morning was talking about tax collection (of which he says he is doing a good deal). I said that, if there were any disobedient blokes about refusing to pay, he had better, in the circumstances of the moment (lack of money and bad prices for animals), bring them to me to punish. (If he fines them it will only aggravate the situation.) I hope there would be none: but if there were it would be better that I should make an example of a few now so that the rest of the tribe should hear of it.

I then made use of the opening to discuss the question of "manadib" i.e. his brothers etc. riding around collecting taxes (and other things too it has usually been. . . .) I recapitulated what I had said then and said that I was not quite clear how he proposed to use manadib. He said he proposed to send them to go round *with* the sheikhs. I said I saw no harm in that provided there was no "eating". He said the sheikhs themselves asked for "manadib" so that the people should be slightly more afraid of them when they appear to demand taxes (if a man refused to pay, the mandub is a witness and will tell Nimr of the refusal). I explained that sheikhs of Howawir were men each with his position and honour as head of his section. What I feared was that, if Nimr worked more through manadib than through the sheikhs, the sheikhs would become disgruntled. He must preserve the sheikhs' responsibility. Moreover if he sent out manadib to others than the sheikhs, i.e. direct to Arabs, there would be confusion and he would injure his own reputation and his family's. He said of course if I wanted him not to use manadib he would not, but after all Sheikh Ali is always up-to-date with taxes and he uses manadib exclusively. I pointed out that there is no resemblance between the Kababish and the Howawir. I tried to make it clear to him how he should run his tribe (I have avoided throughout definitely approving or otherwise of manadib): he must make his own arrangements, and I will point out to him any things therein which appear to me wrong. At present I propose to give him advice and hope all will be well. BUT (1) No one must "hukm" (i.e. fine) in the tribe except himself or Adam. (2) There must be no excessive "eating" of the Arabs under the colour of tribal dues to the sheikh. Above all let him not be a Hakim (Ruler) but a Sheikh of Arabs, for that word Hakim they do not love. Government needs tact.

Wrote a longish note recording my various admonitions to Nimr and what little I have been able to learn about the tribe and its position, geographical, fiscal, economic, administrative. Played golf in the afternoon and, my godfathers, there was a cold wind blowing. Evidently we are in for another arctic "snap".

The night was bitter. The cold woke me about 3 a.m.

28.1.32

Bitter wind all day: dust and sand flying. Wrote letter to Ferid and other mail. Sent off Dongola police (as there's no work for them) and mail at 4 p.m. to catch the post boat Sunday at Debba or Monday at Korti. A spot of golf and then a freezing night closed in. No signs of Mulah. Nimr and Adam came (mainly for shelter) to talk to me and drank much coffee. I kept a vast fire going just to lee of the tent. The talk was quite interesting. It gravitated from Newbold and archaeological remains to the Hajj and Mecca. They asked me about Ibn Saoud, and I had to describe as much as I knew of the history of the Arab countries, Iraq, Syria, Nejd, Hejaz, Palestine, Transjordan, from the beginning of the war, and as much as I knew of the history of the Wahhabis to explain Ibn Saoud's rise and politics. They seemed interested. As everybody seems so keen about Ibn

Saoud (his fame spreads with every returning pilgrim from Mecca), I must re-read Arnold Toynbee and get hold of Ameen's book on Ibn Saoud again.[27]

Then we turned to the Senussi[28] (about whom they know as much as I), and Nimr got onto his campaign to Jebel El Akhdar. I have never been able to identify this "Green Mountain" yet, and cross-questioned him. It is far north of Wadi Howa. Now General Hilaire[29] marks Wadi Howa on his map of Ennedi. So I read names of wells and mountains, and Nimr mentioned names he knew and places he had been to. He says there is a well called . . . Ardei in the mouth of a big cave. Hilaire mentions "Archei" and shows a picture of it with a cave behind. Nimr saw the picture and said that must be it. I wonder: Hilaire's guides were Guraan, who speak a lingo of their own and would have their own names for places, wells, etc., while Nimr would hear only the Arabs' names and would arabicise any others.

Very cold night, coldest yet. Slept well once I got warm.

29.1.32

. . . . It continued cold all day. Long talk in the afternoon with the hakiim [sic], largely on Education of the Sudanese as almost invariably and, so far as I can see, inevitably upsetting their manners and morals. He says he thinks the remedy would be to teach them religion in large fids at the same time as other things, such as the new European scientific knowledge and the modern history (alas!) which they now are taught. I discoursed on the conflict between science and religion, which is not confined to Muslim countries.

Poor Nimr has a stomach ache as a result of the intense cold (*cf.* a giraffe with a sore throat), but I had to be firm and say we must start tomorrow. I could not bear another three days here (can't start on a Sunday).

I have omitted that at 2 p.m. (when it was just warm enough for Arabs to bear to move) I went with Nimr and a large crowd to see where they propose to make a dam to stop wastage of wadi water. The wadi when it flowed in 1930 and 1931 broke out of its old bed about 300 yards from my tent and so, much water was lost which otherwise would have increased the extent of cultivation. Their ideas seemed good—baulks in front and earth behind—but of course they'll never finish it (it's about 100 yards

---

[27] Arnold J. Toynbee, *The Islamic world since the peace settlement, Survey of international affairs, 1925*, vol. 1, Oxford 1927; Ameen Rihani, *Ibn Sa'oud of Arabia*, London 1928.
[28] Muhammad Idris al-Sanusi (1889–1983), later King Idris I of Libya.
[29] In *Au Congo du Nil*.

long if it is to be any good), and even if they did, then the wadi would not flow for another 7 years—what a country!

The evening closed in very bitter again.

Mulah, the messenger from Omdurman, at last arrived about 6.15 p.m. He brought me a note from Fleming[30] at Khartoum North, which said Eric Penn[31] was on trek (to Um Inderaba, I heard afterwards) and had left no instructions about any mail for me. He very kindly sent me a tin of sardines and another of peas. He had rung up Tom Maclagen and also George Bredin to ask if they had any news for me, which they had not. Very good of him. The comrade has his points—especially as far as humanity is concerned—although he is queer. I wonder what happened to my former note to Eric. Read *Hadith Isa* till about 9.30.

Perishing cold night. Last night and this slept with long pants and trousers and socks over my pyjamas and vest and two sweaters and all blankets and great coat and jacket on bed. And that inside a tent.

30.1.32

Played astonishingly good shots with iron before breakfast. N.B. Um Gawasir best golf course I have found in my journeys yet. Day slightly warmer and became not too bad later.

Mulah came to see me (his real name is Muhammad Khalifa of the Khamasin Howawir) because I had given him a loaf of sugar and he would rather have money instead. Had a long talk with him. El Tom was still in Omdurman when he was there because Muhammad, another son of Sh. Ali El Tom, had been ill and he had taken him to hospital there. Muhammad was well at Hamrat El Wuzz. I wonder what, if anything, El Tom did with all my letters. He said Sayed Ali[32] had returned from Egypt in very good health and spirits. Also he said that Fleming told him to turn up on 10 Fatar (i.e. 18 February) to take P. Clarke[33] (governor of Berber, formerly Director of Posts) and Major Maurice (the doctor) by car to El Fasher via Gabrat and Hobaji and Abu Urug, i.e. the northwest route. He proposed to cross the Darfur boundary between the Heitaan and Abu Bessama, i.e. north of where I stood and looked at the Heitaan. Nimr says, "They'll all break down again!" I must say I view the finding of this N.W. Passage with alarm and despondency. How is one to be responsible for policing a route of that kind from Soderi, with 38 police for an area as big

---

[30] M. H. V. Fleming, SPS 1926–32. *SPS*, 49.
[31] A. E. D. Penn, SPS 1925–51. *SPS*, 47.
[32] Sayyid 'Ali al-Mirghani (1879–1968), leader of the Khatmiyya order.
[33] W. P. D. Clarke, SPS 1912–34; governor of Berber, 1931–32, and of Blue Nile, 1932–34. *SPS*, 24.

as Ireland if not bigger? I suppose it won't want policing—until something happens and one is in the cart.

Mulah is a famous guide and scout and a man to know as a finder of secrets and of outlaws and of wanted men. He is an amusing card too.

We are reversing the usual order of things and propose marching in *the heat* of the day in order not to be frozen. Hamla started 1 p.m. approx. Rode 2.40 p.m., arrived Wadi Haamid 4.30 p.m. 110 mins. trotting, 170 mins. walking. Just before I started, El Tom and Ali Hasan Khalifa arrived, having been round by Abu Tawagia and the gizzu (where I should have gone). Ali has evidently taken my hint and is making for Korti.

Going in the afternoon was good—some stone. Wadi Haamid is evidently a tributary of the Mugaddam. Low hills of the usual black stony type. *But* all the ground for a mile and more round us was green with "derma", the gizzu grass. The place was green as old Ireland, as if with heather. A number of Arabs turned up to see Nimr, and the night closed in very cold. Fortunately the hills north of us gave shelter from the wind.

31.1.32

I woke at moonrise somewhat cold and cramped and was conscious for the rest of the night of champings and chewings in the neighbourhood, but took no notice till after dawn I suddenly heard a noise as of rain falling on an umbrella and looked up to find two camels right up against my groundsheet, one couched and the other standing up. With the appropriate shout I threw my shoe at the standing one, who ceased fire and moved off. An Arab then came and drove them away. The poor brutes had been sheltering from the wind under the same tree as myself. 150 mins. trotting, 220 mins. walking.

Rode 7.40 to 10.10 a.m. Bitter wind straight in one's eyes. Rode pretty fast but got colder and colder in the legs. Nimr made me go out of the way to see "El Hosh",[34] a large ancient fort of unknown origin up against the side of a hill called "Kab". The fort is built of stones in a semicircle running up the hillside. In the middle of the sector is a gate, well and strongly built. The wall at this point is 3 metres thick and still stands as high as a man.

I was too cold to bother about it when Nimr took me to it, but after we had got to camp about 2 miles further on among other hills and I had had breakfast (Fleming's sardines turned out, alas! to be anchovies, good for hors d'oeuvres but useless to a single hungry man) I walked and ran back—to get warm as much as with the object of having a nearer look at El Hosh, and then returned a different way over a pass in the hills. I found

---

[34] "The enclosure".

nothing of interest. Tingle said he and Watt found a pre-historic drawing of a giraffe, but I didn't find it (and I hadn't taken him with me or I couldn't have run or walked so fast). 83 mins. trotting, 120 mins. walking.

It was 1 p.m. when I got back. Shaved, washed, lunched, and then the hamla went on. Hills to the west are called Hizamiya.

Rode 3.17, arrived El Bir El Gedid in the Wadi Mugaddam again, 4.40. Good going but grazing ordinary "toghar"—no gizzu.

This evening was quite appreciably warmer and there was no discomfort in sitting over a fire. Left my trousers off when I went to bed and felt quite warm in pants and pyjamas all night. In fact a pleasant night, if I hadn't wakened at 2 a.m. and continued with rheumatism till dawn.

1.2.32

About 7 a.m. the cold wind began again. Looked at the well, about 90′ deep. Rode 7.17 to 9.28 approx. Arrived Jebel Abu Jahra. Perishing cold, and pleasure not increased by its being Ahdim's turn for being ridden. Going good along bed of Wadi Mugaddam. The depression of the wadi is very wide here, about 1 to 2 miles—with gebels at intervals on both sides. Went out of the wadi-bed onto sand hills to camp. Very few trees, only dry grazing. 131 mins trotting, 222 mins. walking. Fed to the teeth with this journey. Generally typical fifth-week-out feelings prevalent—difficult not to be snappy, and everlasting politeness slightly on my nerves. Part of it is due to lack of sleep due to cold. Felt too tired to read, simply sat most of the time till lunch. Hamla moved about 2 p.m.

After they had gone, Tingle came and told me that Nimr had found news of Arabs near at hand and proposed that we should move to them and stay the night and next morning. Asked how many Arabs and how far, he said about 3 tents and the other side of the jebel. Um Tob well would be only about 1½ hours from where we were. This appeared to me really a little hard on all concerned, to have to rope up and unrope ¾ hour away for 3 tents. Typical of this journey—every place except Um Gawasir, where Nimr says there are Arabs none or practically none are to be found. Also now they say that there is only one Howari in Wadi Abu Gia.

When we came to ride therefore at 3.30, I said plainly to Nimr, "If there is work either for the doctor or me here or anywhere else I have no objection to stopping for it and not getting to Korti till 7 February. But if there isn't, then let us get on." I don't think one Howari knows where the next is to be found. 45 mins. trotting, 60 mins. walking.

We rode round the jebel, over a sand dune and into a valley among hills, unfortunately none to the north, so the wind blew keen. After we had arrived (there were three small tents in the distance), I had a think and looked at the calendar and decided that, as Nimr and I want to see

Purves in his office on a working day, and I want at least one working day in Khartoum, and since Sunday next to Wednesday are all holidays—the Ramadan Bairam[35]—we had better make certain of being in Korti on Thursday and ask Purves[36] for his steamer to take us to Merowe on Friday. I would then aim at taking Tuesday's train from Kereima to Khartoum— if we aren't dead of frost bite before we get to Korti. I sent and told Nimr this.

It seems to me that, with this tribe, it is no use, as with the Kababish and Kawahla, leaving arrangements to the chief who is with one. The best thing is to say, "I am going to see such and such a well or gebel", and chance finding Arabs on the way. Felt much better now I had made a decision right or wrong.

The scattered nature of this tribe and its habit of sitting down in tiny groups of two or three or 1 tent by themselves resembles similar traits in the Bega tribes. It might be worth asking Young if he (who knows both Bega and Howawir) agrees and can suggest any hints for getting at them from methods of administration found useful among the Bega. For one thing, as they are proud of themselves as camel-masters, tribal meetings with bulls and nagas for slaughter, provided by government, with camel races to be held at the same time (prizes provided by government), might be of great assistance. Such meeting could be held once a year at Elai or at Um Gawasir, on the lines of the Hadendowa meeting at Aegir in the Gash. I put this (i.e. the suggestion of camel races—saying Howawir always won the races at Soderi—wouldn't it be a good thing to have more of them?) to Nimr, who said the thing would be to hold meetings at Um Gawasir, since there are always at least a few Howawir there, and if the wadi runs there are a good number there. He seemed quite keen on the notion.

Nimr drank coffee from 7.30 to 8.30 and he looked so cold and scratched his great body so much that I sent him to bed and soon retired myself also.

The wind blew sand under the tent flaps and the night became colder and colder. I lay awake or half-awake (with ridiculous dreams . . .) from 2 a.m., and my shoulder gave me gyp. Semi-paralytic and covered in dust. For some unknown reason Tingle sent the hamla off before sunrise.

2.2.32

Rode ¾ hour from 7.35 to Um Tob. Coldest morning yet, I think colder than any of those at the end of December. I had to run up and down as fast as

---

[35] That is, the *'Id al-fitr*.
[36] W. D. C. L. Purves, SPS 1913–38; governor of Dongola, 1930–32; of Halfa, 1932–34; of Berber, 1934–35; and of the Northern Province, 1935–38. *SPS*, 25.

I could go, when I had dismounted, in all the clothes I had on (vest, pants, two sweaters, two jackets and great coat) to try and get warm.

Um Tob well resembles that at Bir Gadid. 45. mins trotting, 90 mins. walking. Went to see the well and to see my own camels being watered. Nobody here has ever thought of using animals to draw water.

It remained very cold all day. But the wind dropped towards evening and it was like a frosty night in England. I planned to go to bed early, as I felt very weary, but Nimr arrived, all dressed in clean clothes and having shaved his head, at 7.30 when I was just in the middle of supper. So I had to leave the supper to get cold and deal him out coffee over the fire.

He said that the Habasab Howawir who are here are "Awlad Ghareyb" and near relations of his, their mother having been his great aunt. Taiallah Ghareyb discovered this well. The present head of the house is Ata El Manaan.

Gave myself my remaining pink pill, which kept me asleep till nearly 5 a.m.

3.2.32

Rode 7.20 a.m. and rode fast. Not so cold this morning and the wind didn't start blowing till about 8 a.m. Going very good. Fewer trees to be seen—generally very barren—sellim bushes in wadi bed. Arrived near the wells of the Omda Omar Rabbah at 9.48 a.m. Here there were some sheep and goats and green grazing for the camels and a few sellim bushes. In a normal year this country must be desert. Ruined my office hat by trying to clean it with soap. Pity, as I almost never wear the thing, it is practically new. See what Koko can do with khaki blanco later.

This is one of the signs of fifth-week-out loupiness—that the sense of proportion goes temporarily and one gets worried about most unimportant things. Queer. After another week or so of trek the said sense of proportion returns more or less.

It remained fairly warm till 3 p.m. Then cold wind began again. Rode 3.20 till 5.28. Going bad—mostly over gravel and stones. Pace therefore slow. Wind dropped at sunset; calm, cold, starlit night.

Read some more of *Hadith Isa*. Slept none too well owing to rheumatism.

4.2.32

Cold at dawn but not too cold, and calm. Some Sowarab Arabs had turned up in the night, coming from Korti. So we exchanged news, shivering, of prices of sheep and corn against "where the sons of so and so are just now".

Rode 7.15 to 9.15. The going was stony and my camel Zurzur, who had started like a small whirlwind, suddenly went lame: so I stopped and a Howari had a look at the foot in question. The pad had been pierced by a thorn—nothing serious, thank God. Asked Nimr who the notables of Korti are and whether one addressed them as "Bey" or "Pasha" (it is a medium-sized village only). He laughed. About 8 the cold wind began again and colder, it seemed, than ever.

Then over the gravelly hills and below a low range of rocky hills to the N.W., the date-palm groves of Korti began to appear and we all felt better. On these occasions I always feel I can understand the Arab raiding spirit. After weeks of desert and short rations a man, hot-eyed from the wind and sun, and hot-blooded by nature, sees the dark green of the settled villages in front of him, and his camel automatically quickens its pace.

We went down the gravel hills and came to the upper village of mud huts built back from the river on the "hill" as they call it. Rows of villagers turned out to look at us—a sort of raggamuffin army arriving. Then we went through a forest of ushur[37] bushes and into the lower village among big trees, and so to the rest house by the river—and a very fine rest house too. Behind it is a curious step-like wall which looks like the tiers of a bull-ring. Tingle said it was begun as a fort but either part demolished or never completed. And so one looks at the Nile again.

The Omda of Korti, Omar Kimbal, and numerous relations came to greet me with "empressement" in the riverain style of very flowing compliments delivered in flowery, carefully-pronounced language. Pleasant bloke. As he is fasting, he could not come to take tea and insisted on our accepting a bull (*sic*—smallish size calf) and a sheep as guest gifts, which the chaps promptly slaughtered.

I then had breakfast (after pushing Sheikh Nimr off to be comfortable in his family's house here—his polite protests that he ought to attend on me were disposed of firmly) and proceeded to a bath—out of the wind, thank God—and stoutness exercises to get warm, and civilised clothes (tweed suit). Before I had dressed, however, Koko came to say the governor wanted me on the telephone. The news of our arrival had already been passed on. I sent word that I apologised, was in my bath and would come immediately. And so to the queer little post office among the date palms.

Purves's steamer is away. Nicholson[38] has gone on tour with it. So we ride to Merowe tomorrow. He would like me to stay over the Bairam till Tuesday and he has my mail *in large quantities*. I then went to see the little market—very dead as it is not market day—where I found my cook having his best clothes mended, and returned to the rest house to send Tingle with a note to the Omda who had said he would cash a cheque for me.

---

[37] *Calotropis procera.* BM, 251.
[38] H. A. Nicholson, SPS 1923–49. *SPS*, 42.

All the police with me have been away from Soderi over a month, so I have got to provide their pay or part of it. I feel like a bandit chief paying his brigands—only we haven't sacked Korti yet!

Thank goodness to be out of that wind in a pleasant place among trees and birds and farm-yard noises with the Nile and its narrow green banks to look at. All pretty shoddy really—but there is no such thing as pleasure except as contrast to pain. Were it not for contrasts and comparisons and relief (the higher the relief the better) life would be, in my opinion, not merely a rather poor show, but unendurable.

4 p.m. When I had written the above there arrived messengers and donkeys from the Omda to say that he thought it would be better that I should go to see him now rather than after dark, as his house was some way away. Accordingly I rode with Muhammad Effendi downstream, as it were, between sagiya-watered fields of green wheat and cotton. It seemed strange to see wheat—I of course have never seen it in the Sudan before.

Arrived at the Omda's house, we "salaamed" a number of worthies of his family, the Awlad Kimbal, and in particular the head of the house, an ancient named Hasan Kimbal. We were received into a large room in the usual flat-roofed mud house, and given date wine, Abri,[39] a lunch of liver and kidney and eggs and wheat kisra (a kind of biscuit) and tea and coffee. It was embarrassing since they were fasting. But after all it was the Omda's choice of time. Talked much and long. At the end one Abderrahman Muhammad Kimbal came in, who is a farmer on a large scale and owns a motor pump for irrigation and a steam flour mill. Typical Dongolawi merchant type. Hard as nails I should say. I didn't like the look of him at first and he started by a sort of set speech saying all the complimentary things he evidently thought he ought to say to a D.C. However, shortly, when he saw that I was talking casually and without the stand-off hands-off English manner, he became more human, especially when I mentioned Clive Young (deputy governor here for some time) and Jackson Pasha[40] (whom they all loved). An amusing and pleasant party. I like the Omda. He rode back with me to the rest house and stayed chatting till it was nearly 3 p.m. Then I had to pay the troops and the camelmen and do my accounts.

The contrast between the Arabs and these suave sophisticated river-people, who have nearly all had a school education moreover, is most amusing, especially when you have old Nimr plumped, all twenty stone of

---

[39] A drink fermented from *dhura*. For a recipe see Richard Hill, *On the frontiers of Islam: the Sudan under Turco–Egyptian rule 1822–1845*, Oxford 1970, 114–15n.
[40] See note 32, chapter IV.

him, in the middle of them. This place is just like a little bit of Upper Egypt between Halfa and Aswan.

Wrote letters to Mamur Soderi. Sunset.

So ends the hardest journey, bar one (that in the rains on the Eritrean frontier to chastise the Lahawiin in 1927) [I] have done yet. And, but for the extreme cold, it would have been as easy as can be this year, for there was plenty of grass and large tracts of the desert are still green almost to within six miles of Korti.

Next time I have to attack the Howawir, I think I shall apply to do it from Omdurman to Um Gawasir, and, if there is grass in that direction, then from Um Gawasir to Fogi and then south to Um Luei Luat and so home.

Purves said he and his wife would ride out to meet me tomorrow afternoon about 4 from Merowe. . . .

It was after sunset by the time I had finished writing. I watched the last of the light from the balcony of the rest house and then went to talk to Tingle about the camels. The evening was chilly. I dined and went to bed early, for I was extremely tired. But the wind got up in the night and its noise (for I slept indoors) did not assist my sleep, and an Effendi who was living in the other half of the rest house and was fasting, rose in the small hours to take the last meal before dawn; and my shoulder ached: so that sleep was not as good as it might have been.

5.2.32

Had breakfast at 6.30 and by 7.30 we had said our goodbyes to the Omda and all and sundry and ridden out of the rest house to take the road to Merowe. I left all but four of the police and four camels of my hamla at Korti. The light hamla was to trot with me and the doctor and Sheikh Nimr and his people to Merowe all together. We set out to take the "upper" road to Merowe, i.e. that back from the river along the edge of the desert. This was reckoned easier for the camels than the lower road among the cultivated lands and irrigation channels and villages. When we started it was calm, but after $1\frac{1}{2}$ hours' riding a strong wind sprang up which rapidly developed into a severe sandstorm, very cold and straight into our faces. We went on but, after another half hour, the doctor's riding camel refused to go on. I mounted him on my spare camel and we made for the lower road, where houses and palm trees would give us some shelter from the wind. To me it was most interesting to ride among the fields of wheat and groves of palms and huddled villages.

By about 11.15 we arrived at a place called Gereir, the centre of a government scheme for irrigation by pump which had brought many additional acres under crops. There is also a steamer station here, the stationmaster of which proved to be a first cousin of Tingle's (very convenient). I was given the now-empty house of the Agricultural Inspector who used to be stationed here (now economised!) to take my rest in. Pleasant house in the Dongola style (mud brick, low, long, nice wide verandah) with a pleasant garden. It was a relief to get out of the wind, and as there was running water laid on, I could wash the sand out of my eyes, nose and ears. The sand storm had given me a headache. I found some ancient novels lying about and whiled away the time by reading a grim story by Agnes and Egerton Castle. After lunch about 3 p.m. we set off again. Tingle's camel had been tired by the sand storm and he borrowed one from his cousin.

The doctor left us at Gereir, as his ancestral home is immediately opposite across the river, and I considered he had much better spend the days we must wait for a train with his own family. He asked me and the English doctor to lunch on Sunday.

The camel borrowed by Tingle had had no work for many days and was pig fat. Within 100 yards of our start it bucked and threw him off. By the mercy of God he was not hurt and with considerable nerve re-saddled and mounted again, refusing my offer of my other camel.

We rode on through cultivations and later desert (the sandstorm had ceased) till we came to Tangassi, a fairly large market only about an hour's ride from Merowe. From here a road runs dead straight among cultivations to Merowe. We were in some doubt whether Purves would have ridden out by this one or by the desert farther back from the river. After following the road among the cultivations for some way, however, we saw him and Mrs. Purves at some distance to our right in the desert.

After general greetings, we rode slowly into Merowe over the bridge across the watercourse, on one side of which stands the governor's house in its gardens, and on the other General Jackson's.

The Mamur here, Khalafallah Effendi, at one time served in Soderi (when first that station was built) and knows Sheikh Nimr. This again was fortunate for it meant he would be hospitably entertained.

Merowe is, I think, the most beautiful place I have seen in the Sudan. It is not a remarkable makeshift of quasi-European imitation civilisation like Khartoum, but entirely "sui generis" and intrinsically beautiful, unlike anything I have seen elsewhere in the world so far. The whole town was planned, built, planted by General Jackson. The houses are all of one style and in keeping. The roads are shaded by big trees. But the crown of the work is the vast garden which contains the Mudiria offices and the governor's house on the bank of the river. Here one forgets the Sudan and might well be in what I imagine the West Indies are like. The grounds are luxuriant with big trees and grass and rose beds and flowering shrubs.

There is a large portion given up to orange, tangerine, and grapefruit trees, now full of fruit. There are mango trees, now in blossom. There are guavas and bananas and pawpaws, and, of course, numerous date palms and a few coconut palms. In the centre of the garden is a vast tree under which 50 people could sit in shade—it has in fact been specially grown and trained for that purpose. Roses of all kinds are grown; but General Jackson's speciality and delight was fruit trees.

To the south of the governor's house, across the watercourse already mentioned, General Jackson, when he retired from government service, built himself a house and planted a garden like the governor's, but on a smaller scale. There he lived till he died last year. It is now empty and none will buy from his sister who inherited.

Purves had, with great kindness, made all arrangements for my camels and men and for Sheikh Nimr and his people. He put me into his guest house, a complete suite separate from and beside the governor's house. This is my ideal of staying with anyone, for one can spread one's things out, see one's servants, and not be in the way or worry one's hosts. One can also read and write at ease and without interruption.

The D.C. and A.D.C. were on tour and only the doctor (Wallace whom I had met before, in Khartoum and going on leave) was in the station. He came to play bridge and dine with the Purveses. I enjoyed my evening thoroughly, and by no means least a large hot bath in my luxurious suite.

A large mail in two packages forwarded from Khartoum was waiting for me and I read some of it before I slept, in spite of the lateness of the hour.

6.2.32

Purves very kindly let me sleep late. I rose about 7.30. After breakfast he took me to the Mudiria office where we did business with Sheikh Nimr. After that I took Nimr to the guest house for final advice and instructions and thereafter went with him to the merkaz and to the Museum.

The Museum here has two parts: one mostly devoted to ancient monuments and remains discovered at Napata (the ancient town whose site is just outside modern Merowe), at Kawa near by, and in the pyramids and tombs at Barkil, opposite Merowe across the river; the other contains not only more Napatan and Meroitic remains, but also trophies captured at the battle of Omdurman. Some of the ancient carvings are exceptionally fine—to my entirely inartistic and untrained eye at least—especially two rams and the reliefs inside a large sarcophagus. Purves has a short note on the history of Merowe in English and Arabic displayed, giving a brief account of the conquest of these parts by the ancient Egyptians and of

Egypt (at one point in history) by kings from here, and also referring to the Christian Kingdom of Dongola which did not fall before Islam till about 1200 A.D.

Nimr said he wished to start back to Korti next morning and would send me word of his time of departure.

After lunch we played tennis—an amusing four with the doctor. There is a small zoo here and the tennis court is next door to it. The zoo contains one or two ibex, oryx and gazelles and some monkeys. After tea we went to play bridge with the doctor and stayed to dine. The weather is still perishing cold.

7.2.32

This day, being the last of Ramadan, is a public holiday. The doctor was to leave to visit Col. Jackson, who, a retired Sudan officer, has a farm at Mansurkatti (Ganettu) down stream from Korti.

Nimr of course was late in starting—the morning was very cold—but I rode a little way with him, having been lent a horse by Purves and given permission to be late for breakfast by Mrs. P. The rest of the morning was spent going round the garden, being instructed in the grafting of orange trees by Dessuki, the head gardener, and being shown over General Jackson's house by him. I then read my mail.

After lunch, tennis again. Both Mrs. Purves and Purves were much too strong for me of course, but it was not bad fun, as tennis goes. I don't now-a-days become incapable of hitting the ball at all after not playing the game for long periods as I used to do.

Spent part of the evening arguing with Mrs. Purves on Art with a large A and discussing the Sudan with both of them. Went to bed at 10 (they are late birds).

8.2.32

This day was the Ramadan Bairam, i.e. the feast after the month of fast. As servants go to pray at 6.30 a.m. we all stayed in bed till 7.30. After breakfast Purves took me with him to assist at the distribution of corn and clothes provided by the Lee Stack Indemnity Fund[41] to very poor persons. Exceedingly pitiful some of them were. We then visited the hospital, and then the Effendis' Club (ginger beer, coffee and Turkish delight and small talk) and went into the museum again.

In the afternoon we rode—all three for an hour—out in the desert, and at 5 p.m. an exceedingly pathetic couple came to tea. They were a

---

[41] A fund endowed by the Sudan Government with the indemnity paid by Egypt after the assassination of Sir Lee Stack, governor-general of the Sudan 1917–24.

Dane and his wife. He was formerly a business man of sorts in the Sudan who made no money, and, after the failure of his ventures, bought a house and a garden on the river here. They are exceedingly poor. He is almost blind, and they have not been to Denmark for about a dozen years. They speak remarkably good English and were pleasant conversationalists. I wrote letters before dinner and sat talking after dinner till 10.30.

9.2.32

The Purveses took me for a ride to visit Hasan Dikeir, the Omda of Merowe, whose house and village are a little way up-stream. A pleasant man—he had in days gone by fought Goraan at Bir Natrun and Nakheila in the desert. On the way back they took me into the ruins of the ancient temple on the site of the city of Napata. Most of the archaeological work on the site has been done by Reisner and Prof. Griffith.[42] Purves told me that the last time Griffith was here the only museum which could afford to buy his funds was that at Copenhagen, which has the endowment of the profits of a brewery—value £60,000 a year!

Spent the remainder of the morning writing a note for Purves, and discussing it with him, and writing diary.

The train leaves Karima across the Nile tomorrow morning at 9 a.m. I have the loan of the doctor's launch to cross the river (5 miles) but shall have to get up early. The train does not connect with the Express for Khartoum, and doesn't reach Khartoum till 6 p.m. on Thursday. A gloomy prospect, but I have plenty to read.

The rest here in peace and charming surroundings with just enough and not too much society and entertainment (and marvellous fruit to eat) has done me a power of good and I feel fit to face Khartoum, the dentist, and the desert again.

---

[42] F. L. Griffith conducted excavations in Nubia between 1910 and 1914. G. A. Reisner worked in the Karima region in 1916–20.

Chapter IX

A Homicide Case

[Bara—El Obeid—al-Nahud—Umm Kaddadah—near Qadaydim—Umm Qawzayn—Umm Badr—Hamrat al-Shaykh—Umm Khirwa']

15.9.32

After eight weeks of office work in Bara and Soderi, with a brief interval of four days (20th to 25th August) out with horses and camels to see a land case in Bara District, I have at last begun the normal round of trekking.

I left Bara at 1 p.m. on 13th September pretty tired. I rounded off a three days' visit there, mainly to try a case of murder, by working till 10.30 p.m. on the 12th, taking the weekly town ride at 6.30 a.m. on [the] 13th, and the usual office till 1 p.m.

Aglen, who had been visiting Bara with me, and I set off by car. We stopped for lunch at Rakooba, otherwise known as "The Chayter Arms", a rest house half way to El Obeid, and there Aglen left me to trek through the north of El Obeid District by camel. We let loose there the unfortunate secretary bird which, to Charles de Bunsen's embarrassment, had been given to him by a native. These birds are fully protected against killing or capture, and anyway I could not bear to have the thing caged in the garden of the house at Bara (nor did Charles like it either).

Soon after leaving Rakooba I ran into the heaviest storm of rain I have met since my return from leave. The road was mostly a running river. However, I reached Mayall's house about 3 p.m. The rain continued till about 8 p.m.

There was so much to clear up that, with intervals for tea and dinner, I continued writing till 10.30 p.m. and retired dead beat. . . .

On the morning of the 14th I left El Obeid at 7.30 with the Mechanical Transport convoy going to El Fasher. Hunt Bey, whom I had known in Kassala, and who is now in the Western Arab Corps, was returning from leave and travelled with me. We were in luck, as two touring cars belonging to the Darfur Province were being sent back to Fasher with the convoy after re-painting in the workshops in El Obeid. More comfortable seats than the Thorneycroft six-wheelers provide.

The road was vile—much water lying in pools after the rain. Hunt and I in the touring cars reached Hoij, the first station, at noon, but one of the lorries had stuck in a pool and they did not arrive for us to have our lunch till 3.30 p.m. Meanwhile we found the Shartai of Dudia, the local Hamar chief called Muhammad Rashid, employed in having the landing ground at Hoij cleaned of grass. He chatted a good deal but I had a headache, felt very tired and empty, and was in poor form.

After another vey jolting and tiresome stage, we reached Nahud at 8 p.m.

Bill Henderson,[1] of my year, was at home there and gave us a very good dinner. He was in very good form, saying he had had the best leave so far. He appeared to have narrowly avoided getting engaged to some five young ladies, and reduced his golf handicap to 15.

The lorries were sent on ahead on the morning of the 15th to allow me to talk some business with Bill, and Hunt and myself to take breakfast with him. We left about 9.30.

The next stage to Wad Banda (where I had come with the Vicars-Mileses in March), [was completed] by noon, and [we] had lunch and a rest. The road had not been too bad. We went on at 2 p.m. and the road became vile—extremely sandy. The cars swayed from side to side in great ruts. We overtook a party of Western Arab Corps soldiers with remount mules, one of which was sick (alleged "nigma", i.e. horse sickness). Hunt was carrying medicines for this animal and stopped and inspected it—and the whole bunch. We reached Dam Gamad, the halt for the night, about 5.30. The country on the way was dull. Big sand-dunes covered with grass and trees, gum trees and other thorns and the queer tebeldis common in these parts. These tebeldi trees are hollowed out by the natives and used for storing water. Water is very scarce in this part of the world and there are hardly any wells. On the road there are government-bored wells, worked by donkey-engine pumps at Wad Banda and Dam Gamad.

16.9.32

Slept well. Expected rain did not fall in the night. Rose at 6 and had breakfast at 6.30. We started again at 7.30.

The road was not quite so bad as yesterday evening, for we did not actually stick in the sand, but it was exceedingly bumpy and caused the car to sway a great deal. I felt a bit sick at one time. After some 15 miles of sand dune, hills began to appear in the west. These hills are much eroded, like the hills of the desert in Dongola, and present extraordinary shapes. We climbed an enormous sand dune at Gebel [*sic*] El Hilla and after that came into more open country and better going. The hills also made the scenery less dull.

About 11 a.m. we reached Um Kedada. This is a small place—large

---

[1] K. D. D. Henderson (see note 14, Chapter II).

village and small market in a hollow among hills of the flattish-topped eroded kind. The rest houses are mud brick and grass-thatched buildings, very cool and comfortable, which were formerly the two D.C.'s houses. There is now only a police officer stationed here. Moore was already here and my hamla had arrived intact. The camel belonging to the lance-corporal of my escort is lame, otherwise all are fit.

Long talk with Moore. He seems pretty strongly critical of the Native Administrations in Darfur and of the Fasher Court—the so-called Mejlis El Muluk—in particular. He said this last court, which had looked so well on paper and been so much "puffed", had recently developed a system whereby the clerks did all the business and the chiefs who are members and president, practically never saw the plaintiff or the defendant and sent their seals round weekly to [be] affixed to the judgments to make the register look nice. This he has put a stop to.

We talked for a while after lunch and then Hunt went to rest, Moore and I to write. About 4.30 we went for a walk to look at the market (Friday is market day) and the government post. In the market there were some stray animals out of the government pound being sold. I saw Nurab Kababish brands on some of them and asked Moore to hold up the sales, as I knew Sheikh El Tom Ali was due in Um Kedada that evening or next morning. We also looked at the Native Court House—rather a good one —mud-brick and thatched roof, like all the buildings in Um Kedada. What I like about the court house is that it is all open portico on one side. The fewer doors the better, in my opinion.

We returned at 5.30 and Moore had the three local Shartais, Dho El Bait Abd El Daim, Yusef Torjok and Mahdi Sabil, to tea. While the tea party was going on, El Tom Ali and his train arrived, having done, according to themselves, a remarkably swift ride from Gedeidim, which is a long way to the north. Moore seemed much impressed with them. I did not manage to get to bed till 10.10 because I had to stay up after dinner to finish mail which Hunt had said he would post in Fasher.

17.9.32

Hunt left at 7.30 a.m. for Fasher. I had a look at my camels and the police camels, and, after breakfast, spent some two hours talking to El Tom about the various points outstanding between the Kababish and the local people of Um Kedada District (a macedoine of Dar Hamid, Awlad Agoi, Nawahia, Zayadia and Berti). The main points were:

(1) The death of Ali El Tom's horses last February. Thieves from a village called Haada in Um Kedada District stole camels from Ali El Tom's camp near Um Gozein, and Ali El Tom's people killed six horses in overtaking the thieves and recovering the camels. He wants the price of

his horses, which he calls at a very high figure. Unfortunately, soon after the theft, his brother, Muhammad El Tom, was sent to Um Kedada and met Mahdi Sabil in the absence of the senior Shartai, Dho El Bait; and Mahdi Sabil, somewhat overawed, light-heartedly proposed to make the Omodia of the thieves pay a collective fine of £E60. When Moore understood this, he could not consent to it, because he considered it would make a very bad precedent for the future and because the crime had been brought home to individuals and those individuals punished with prison. He therefore altered this decision to a fine of £E15 on each of the two persons convicted of theft. The most he would do was to send for the families of the convicts and have the Shartai use moral suasion to make them pay up the fines on behalf of the imprisoned men.

(2) The murder of an Aidi Azrag this rains. The Kababish were south of Um Kedada when their man was murdered, yet they never reported to government except through Ali El Tom some time later. Moore is going that way now and will take the Kababish witnesses with him to investigate the matter.

(3) Strays. I knew this would come up and was glad I had stopped those sales. Nomad custom enjoins that, if one man's strays come to another man's herd, he puts them in the herd, and lets it be known they are there. The strays remain in the herd as long as you like—five years perhaps—till the owner claims them and takes them back. This does not work with settled peoples who have no large herds. Hence there is always trouble where nomads are in contact with sedentaries, and government pounds have been established for keeping the animals 25 days and then selling them. We agreed that a Kabbashi agent should be stationed in Um Kedada during the rains and the winter to take over Kababish strays at once.

(4) Runaway slaves. Moore agreed, when he had heard my arguments, that such should be guaranteed in Um Kedada and kept there till a bunch could be sent to Soderi to have their cases heard (to be sent under escort).

Today morning and afternoon were occupied with discussion of these matters and one or two minor ones. Proceedings ended with a mejlis of all concerned in the evening.

Moore and I sat talking before and after dinner till about 9.30. He was in the regular army and in the retreat from Mons. Afterwards he joined the Air Force and continued in it in Iraq as liaison officer with the nomad Arabs on the Nejd frontier—a political job. He knew Leachman[2] and others and remained at that work till 1928. His experiences were interesting to listen to and must have been exciting to have. He dressed as an Arab and lived as one: apparently that was the only way to get on with those

---

[2] Col. G. E. Leachman (1880–1920), explorer, traveller, and soldier.

people. It is not surprising that he looks down on the mixed pickles he finds in Darfur and even considers the nomads of Northern Kordofan tame—and after all, so they are, half-tame and with a lot of black blood in them.

18.9.32

The bugles blow in one's ear here all too early. I had a morning session with Sheikh El Tom and then pushed him to the office and, after breakfast, went there myself with Moore.

Koko my servant has been having mild malaria, as also have Muhammad and the corporal, Tingle—everyone gets it at this time of year. I had given orders that we were to start this afternoon. Master Koko sent me a message by Muhammad that he was ill and did not want to travel. I replied, "Very well, he could stay behind two days and come on with a policeman who is following me up". His reaction to which was, "Oh no! he wanted to be sent back to El Obeid and come on later to Soderi". At which I laughed and said he had better retire from service. On my return from office I went to see him to persuade him to go and have an injection of quinine from the dispensary, whereupon he turned on me and said he was travelling and would leave my service when we got to Soderi. Agreed. But, my goodness, I wish I had been able to sack him on the spot.

Wrote a note on the meeting between Moore and myself and finished more mail.

Moore returned from the office at 2.15 p.m. After lunch I started—about 3.45. Moore and the police officer and the local shartais rode with me as far as a hill to the N.W. of Um Kedada, where we took leave of each other. I am very grateful to Moore who did me proud and was pleasant company. It was all very restful after Bara and the Fasher road.

Rode among low broken rocky hills gradually rising over sand hills till just after sunset—say 4 p.m. till 6.45, when we arrived at a village called Jakjok. Berti. Sharp shower on the way. Sheikh El Tom caught up about 7.15 p.m. He had been late in starting from Um Kedada because his camels had not come in from grazing in time. Bad night—sandflies got inside my net and also a dog barked incessantly. My camel El Feki, which has been rested now for ages, still will not go well.

19.9.32

Started 5 a.m. Similar country steadily uphill among flattish tors. Camel refused to go. No reason: simply what the Arabs call "refusing the country". El Tom lent me a camel to finish the stage.

Arrived 8.15 at a fairly large village called Bottikha in a picturesque place, [a] hollow among the hills. The sheikh insisted on slaughtering a bull.

El Tom came to talk and discussed the Meidob, saying that they were near the Kababish at the moment and were behaving badly. I said, "Well the Kababish had recently killed a man of theirs", and so the argument started on that case. I pointed out that there had been no order that Meidob *must* keep to the route Ummat Nawir—Um Soneita—Merkh—Safra—Ribda—which I had traversed. I had asked the Kababish what route the Meidob usually took, and they said this one. The Meidob were not utterly in the wrong therefore in going to Baggaria.

He also raised the question of the camels of A.T.'s which were lost in February (?) and which, he says, Melik Muhammad Sayyah refused to help him find. I am informed that the Melik has sent to look for them.

This village was a pretty place amid high tors. I climbed up to the top of one to see what view there was to the west, but I could not yet see the Berti hills in Northern Darfur as I had hoped. About 3 p.m. flying locusts appeared—kaboora—and the villagers, who are Berti, began running out to shout and keep the locusts off their crops.

I rode on about 3.15 and rode till 6.45. The road all the way has been along the southern edge of a high plateau running N.W. and S.E. The Arabs call it Hajaly, and the Kababish leave it to their right, for it is difficult and stony ground with high sand hills, when they come back with their herds from the south in the rains. We passed through a very thick belt of trees—mostly gafala with himada (a tree I had not seen before), which the Kababish call kakamoto.[3] But before we entered this we had a fine view towards Jebel Dirra and El Fasher. By the time we had passed through kakamota to a rather more open place, we had overtaken the hamla and also it was sunset.

The Omda Ali Garoot, our guide, seemed to think it was still a long way to Mejamid, and I debated whether to make another stage by moonlight about 8 to 10 p.m. However, I found our camels so tired that I agreed to start about 3 a.m. instead. Koko was pretty weak with fever.

20.9.32

Rode at 3.15 a.m. by moonlight. There is a well-defined track which goes on to Mellit. By dawn I was pretty weary. There was a heavy dew too, but it was cool and pleasant riding. By sun-up we had emerged onto a very pleasant plain covered with short green grass and scattered trees and bush. Ahead were the Berti hills about 40 miles away. At 6.45 a.m. I reached camp. Mackrell[4] had arrived the day before and with him the Nazir of the Zayadia and the Melik (king) of Jebel Meidob. A large Arab

---

[3] *Acacia suma.* BM, 172.
[4] J. E. C. Mackrell, assistant district commissioner, Northern Darfur.

tent had been erected, [and] grass hoed from a large square and my tent put up under a tree before the Arab tent. Mackrell's tent was farther off behind the Arab tent. Mackrell had only just got out of bed and was in pyjamas.

I felt dead tired, but a shave and bath somewhat revived me. Also Mackrell gave me a very excellent breakfast.

We decided to let everyone rest this day, both in accordance with custom, whereby the first day of a visit should be consecrated to greetings, compliments and entertainment, and business not touched upon, and also because my police and I and the Kababish were very tired with hard riding.

Mackrell and I talked to the Nazir of the Zayadia and the Melik Muhammad Es Sayyah on general topics. Then Mackrell lent me some *Times*, over which I fell asleep. On the other hand when I tried to sleep after lunch I could not. Mackrell is a pleasant lad but rather sleepy, though by no means unintelligent. He is very, very deliberate, and when he has to talk Arabic a certain hesitation in his speech, normal to him in talking English, becomes so pronounced as to be a positive stammer. He is engaged to be married and hit by the five-years rule.

To bed about 9 and slept like the dead.

21.9.32

This is a pleasant place with wide views and grass—so-called bigheil, which is all in blue flower now. But, my godfathers, the mosquitoes! I have not seen so many or so large even at Um Gozein last year. I am solemnly dosing both my servants twice a day with quinine and taking Plasmoquin myself.

This morning after breakfast we called the Nazir of the Zayadia and El Tom Ali and asked them to get on with the mejlis.[5] As soon as they had gone, we started the Magisterial Inquiry into the killing of the Meidobi at Baggaria by the Kababish. This went on, with an interval for lunch from 2 till 3.15, till dusk and was otherwise interrupted only by Sheikh El Tom to say that the Zayadia had, immediately the mejlis opened, refused to consider paying "dia", i.e. blood-money.

---

[5] In a note (dated 3 November 1979) to accompany his MS, Lea wrote:

The Magisterial Inquiry ... on 21st and 22nd September 1932 was ... into the killing of a Maydubi, Adam Sulayman, in a fight with Kababish on Baqqaria wells in March 1932. The inquiry ... showed no possibility, on the available evidence, of a successful prosecution ... before a Major Court. We therefore ... proceeded to suggest a *majlis* to agree payment of blood money. ...

See Caroll W. Brewster, "The Malha agreement of 1964: background and history of recent relations between Kababish and Meidob", *Sudan Law Journal and Reports* 1964, 226–27.

We then closed down pretty weary, and had drinks and dinner. But we did not get to bed till after 10.

22.9.32

Before breakfast Mackrell summoned the Nazir of the Zeyadia [sic] to the tent and I had a talk with him. His point of view was that:

(1) His tribe were perfectly willing to hand over the accused, who is a slave, to the Kababish to kill if they wish, in accordance with Muhammadan Law (this of course the government cannot allow), or to the government to hang. (He realises, of course, that the government would not have put the case before a mejlis if it thought there was a clear case for hanging). His tribe would have no objection to paying "dia" if they were told by government that the accused was undoubtedly guilty (again an impossibility).

I said, pointing out the difference between government methods and Mohammadan [sic] methods, that Muslims had their laws of evidence, and surely they could find out for themselves whether the slave was guilty. I then pointed out the inevitable consequences of refusal to pay "dia", viz. that the Kababish would declare a vendetta on the Zayadia. No doubt he was prepared for that.

He said that if government ordered his tribe to pay "dia" they would do so. I said that "dia" is essentially a voluntary matter and an order to pay would amount to the imposition of a fine. That was not for me to order. He said that his tribe would not agree to pay "dia" without right. I asked him to put the matter before his sheikhs again. He returned later in the day and said they could not agree to pay.

Now, if this was the Zeyadia point of view from the beginning of the case, then Campbell ought never to have allowed me to bring a Kabbashi wakil to meet the Zeyadia, for it is not Arab custom to meet your adversary unless you hope to agree with him. If Campbell had given me any inkling that the Zeyadia would refuse to accept responsibility for the death of the Kabbashi, I would never have brought El Tom to meet them. For a mejlis broken up with angry words only makes relations worse than they were before. The correspondence on the case is fairly clear. I had definitely asked for a mejlis only if the Zeyadia were willing to meet the Kababish. Campbell had replied that they were. I took this to mean that the Zeyadia would be willing to meet and discuss "dia". Now I and El Tom have been made to look fools.

Meanwhile Mackrell and I went on with the Inquiry (into the killing of the Meidobi at Baggaria by the Kababish) which we finished by 1 p.m. We had lunch at 2.30.

The Nazir of the Zeyadia had protested that Kawahla had come with intent to drink up a smallish rain pool near here, to the east. We sent a policeman to hold up any herds coming to drink till we should ride out there. We left camp just before 5 p.m. Mackrell lent me his horse and himself rode his donkey. The place was just under an hour's fast trotting. When we arrived there we found the policeman we had sent and the Nazir's messenger. They said Kawahla of Dar Bahr and Awlad Zaid had appeared and most of them had drunk before they came. There were numerous herds.

I was glad they had gone. We are in Darfur, but the understanding for the gizzu area is that any man may drink the rain water which is owned by none. Gizzu Idris, the Nazir of the Zayadia's contention was that this particular small pool was very near to his people's cultivations and they wanted it kept for their cows, or hardship would ensue. Mackrell has now agreed to do no more about it.

There were duck on the pool at which Mackrell shot, getting two. There were also sacred ibis about, which looked remarkably beautiful. We did not start back till after sunset and got to camp about 7.15. I was for early bed, being tired. The ride had not been a comfortable one, because the sheikh's son, who acted as our guide, rode a mare ahead of me all the time and the horse was hard to hold in consequence. However, El Tom came to talk at 9 p.m. and I did not get to bed till 10.10 p.m.

He talked about the method of breaking in camels for riding. He said that the tribes of the north begin the breaking a year earlier than the Kababish, when the camel is "wad lebuun" [sic] i.e. two years old. The Kababish begin when the camel is "higg", i.e. three years old. Its owner begins by tying the animal's head and mouth with the "bellaam" . . . which appeared to be a long rope tied twice round the snout and under the chin, the ends being passed round the back of the head and brought down in front along the sides of the face. He then saddles and ties the young camel side by side with an old one . . . and lets the old one lug it about among the herd till midday. He then looses it from the old camel and leads it among the herd till evening. The bellaam is not loosed that day.

Next day the process of leading about among the herd on the bellaam is repeated. If the camel is a quick learner, the owner may ride it on the second or even first day. The bellaam is not loosened and the animal is allowed to graze till the third day at evening. The camel is then allowed to graze till morning. Next morning, it is either retied with the bellaam, or, if it is a quick learner, it is roped with a "rasan" and the owner rides it among the herd. I gather the bellaam may be needed for up to 10 days. The owner then uses the young camel hard for herding for about 4 months until he is exhausted. . . . The camel is then rested for another 5 or 6 months until it recovers condition. When the camel has entirely recovered condition, the owner rides it herding again hard till [it] loses condition and is exhausted. Three years of this hard training should be sufficient to show whether the young camel is going to be a good riding camel or not.

23.9.32
Rose late. After breakfast I had El Tom to see me and dealt with one or two small affairs while Mackrell talked to Melik Muhammad Es Sayyah to sound him out about his accepting blood-money. Later Mackrell came and said he had made some progress. It appeared that the Melik, after some explanation that his people were annoyed because they in the past had fairly often had men killed, while the Kababish had never had anyone hanged for doing so, was willing to accept £E300 blood-money.

I then had El Tom in and explained (a) the Zeyadia impasse (b) that, if the Kababish were willing to talk "dia" the Meidob were willing to accept it: but he must be prepared to offer full dia. Other talk I made also in the hope of "rolling the pitch". He said he would go over later and open the talking match.

My camel Zerzur [*sic*] had been ailing before the arrival in Um Kedada. On the way here it became daily thinner. Two mornings ago I gave it a lb. of Epsom Salts, thinking that might do some good. This morning early it refused to get up and go out to graze. I went to see it. There was obviously much pain in the belly. It died about noon. So my best camel is gone.

At lunch time Mackrell explained to Melik Muhammad Es Sayyah that El Tom proposed to go over to his bivouac and open the talk. The Melik appeared to be pleased. After lunch I wrote and slept a little.

About 5 p.m. Mackrell said he was going for a ride and set off with his corporal on a spare horse carrying his gun. I went for a walk a little later to try my luck at guinea fowl in the gloaming after sunset. I stalked some for a long time but missed when at last I shot. I was not really near enough.

When I returned I found Melik Muhammad, the Demlig[6] Ibrahim, El Tom and Muhd. Musa Lawlaw sitting in my camp. I had them come and sit and drink tea, and, after a short while, they said they had come to an agreement: that the Kababish should pay £E300 blood-money for the death of Adam Suleiman, and that the wounds on both sides incurred in the fight should be washed out.

Mackrell was not yet back. I sat waiting for him till 8.30 when I became anxious, and about 9 p.m. told Tingle to make a big fire and send out men to shout and blow whistles. It would be no good searching till morning when we could take up the tracks.

About 9.15 Mackrell turned up perfectly all right. He had ridden to the pool we went to yesterday, stayed till dark to shoot at sand grouse, and

---
[6] *Dimlij*: rank below *shartay*; chief of a sub-district.

lost his way in the dark coming back. Somewhat childish—but youth will be served and all the English are mad anyway. To bed at 10 pretty weary. The trouble is now-a-days that though I get to sleep at once I wake so very early.

24.9.32

Mackrell decided he could not spare the time to come and visit Ali El Tom. I proceeded to write mail for him to take in to Mellit. We finished off the Meidob-Kababish negotiations by fixing 8 months as the period within which the blood-money must be paid.

Sheikh Gizzu Idris, the Nazir of the Zeyadia, raised the question of the Kawahla attempting to drink at the rain pool called Abu Gaid, again. The Kawahla, or rather some of them, had turned up in the camp, so I advised him to hear what they had to say before worrying Mackrell and myself. He went off and did so and all was settled amicably.

I gave the Omda Ali Garoot, who had been my guide to Mejamid, one of my worked wool saddle bags as a present, and also dosed his son for dysentery.

My camels started after lunch and I left about 4 p.m. Mackrell was going to leave soon after to return to Mellit. Rode till 6 p.m. Passed Mejamid village—a very small one, remarkable only for a tame ostrich. Got down near a herd of Howawir Muwalka camels (Awlad Hamid). Camp on the side of a big depression which is called Shagg El Humara.

25.9.32

Rode 6 a.m. till 9 a.m. Country as before—long rolling slopes, much bush; could see Kanju, a hill of the Berti to the west and Taganor in the distance to the east. Spent the noon writing letters. Rode again about 3.30 till 6.25 p.m. Felt very tired and a little sick. Don't know why. Camel riding never agrees well with me.

Had El Tom Ali to drink tea. He expressed himself as doubtful whether there would not be danger to herds in going to the "gizzu" grazing in the far northwest (if any appeared this year) on account of the bandits from French or Italian territory who raided Bir Natrun this time last year and also raided the Zaghawa near Muzbat in Northern Darfur this last March. I tried to reassure him. But I have been told that the Zaghawa, having killed one of the bandits, are certain the gang will return to avenge their comrade; and I have heard from the Zayadia that none of them will go to the "gizzu" this year from fear. El Tom seemed fairly pleased with what Moore had done about the horses Ali El Tom had lost.

Slept from about 9 till 3.30 a.m. when a very noisy argument among the Arabs who were with me woke me up and I could not get to sleep again properly. I don't know what it was about as I was just too far away to catch complete sentences.

26.9.32
Rode 5.45. Yesterday evening we had been near herds and this morning we passed more, including those of the Melik Muhd. Sayyah; to the east was the hill of Gedeidim on the other side of the valley. We left the rain pool also on our left and went down a slope and up another towards a place where one could make out much dust and which El Tom said was where his people were encamped. There was a strong N. wind blowing. Just like Arabs to encamp in the most dusty spot possible.

All the usual crowd of Nurab with Ali El Tom at the head came to meet me, and rode into camp with me. I felt pretty weary and, after compliments and the usual tea and coffee and a vast bowl of camel's milk, I was glad to bathe and avoid any work for the morning.

Ali El Tom came to talk to me at 2.30 and remained till 5.30. As far as possible I kept off contentious topics unless he brought them up. He did. I explained as far as I could the position regarding the Zeyadia case and the Meidob dia agreement. As regards the former I did my best to clear Sheikh Gizzu of blame in accordance with my promise to Mackrell. But Ali El Tom was clearly very annoyed about the business and insisted upon his belief in Rejeb's guilt of murder. I told him the matter had now been referred back to the governors and I would let him know what was to be done in due course.

As regards the latter (a) He tried to ask for the amount of "dia" to be reduced. (b) He asked for longer than 8 months to pay. I gave him no hope, but I propose to open these two questions to Campbell. (c) He also requested that it might be impressed on the Meidob that he had made these "wakils" on the meshras the Meidob pass on the way to Omdurman, and that, if the Meidob would but come in a gentlemanly way and make use of the wakils, trouble would not arise. Ali El Tom says that the Meidob go along in vast parties, most of them cannot understand Arabic at all, and they will deal direct for water with slaves and other irresponsible persons at the wells. (d) He requested that the Melik Muhammad be urged to insist on his people being a little more easy in their manners in the grazing.

I told him that the Meidob had insisted at Mejamid that those of them who live in the north of the Jebel have long been in the habit of going via Baggaria and that this is the more direct route for them than Ummat Nawawir. I asked him if he would consider appointing a wakil for Baggaria. His reply was (a) that they are incorrect in saying that they have been in the habit of going that way (b) that it is not in fact more direct from the north of Jebel Meidob (c) that it would be difficult to find a wakil (d) that Baggaria is not a large meshra at which it is easy to accommodate suddenly an incursion of strangers with large flocks. I said that the road must be made easy for Meidob but otherwise did not press the question. I propose discussing this also with Campbell, and then taking it up again with Ali El Tom.

In this connexion I asked Muhd. El Tom on 27.9.32. what the correct Arab custom is as regards watering at strange wells. He said that, if one were going with one's herds to water them at wells in a foreign "dar" and stay there, then the correct thing to do would be to go and see the sheikh of the tribe of the "dar" or the "Sid El Meshra" and agree with him. If he allowed you to water by "muhamma"—well; if not, you must make him presents or pay him what he asks. But, if one is going with a caravan or with animals for sale through a foreign "dar", one would not trouble to do that, but merely go to the people actually found on the wells. Good people will not refuse water nor demand money (for that is a shameful thing, to sell water) but, if the stranger has no rope or leather bucket, or does not wish to draw the water himself, he often pays hire to slaves or others who draw the water and fill the "hod" (mud tank) for him.

Ali El Tom also spoke of the double homicide case between Awlad El Feki and Dar Um Bakhit of the Nurab Kababish. He hoped I would let it be settled by custom.

I also talked about the "gizzu". He brought the subject up by saying there were rumours that the raiders of last year and of this summer would return and that therefore he was anxious to know whether it was safe for Arabs to take their herds to the far northwest this year. I did what I could to reassure him and said that I ought to get news of raiders, if any, by 15th October, and I would give him whatever news I had, whether negative or positive. His view is that only hunting this gang down to where they live (which incidentally is almost certainly in French or Italian territory) [would solve the problem]. He suggested of course that this could best be done by an armed party of Arabs. This of course the present government policy will not allow.

I said that his Remington rifles were allowed to him largely for the purpose of herd protection in the "gizzu" and that I proposed now to conclude the account of their tally and to issue ammunition.

After he had gone I went for a short walk and watched the herds of sheep come in. I was desperately tired. But I had to conclude my mail to get it off by the party starting for Soderi with prisoners and sick camels this morning.

27.9.32

There are, thank goodness, hardly any mosquitoes and few sand flies here, but a wind blows at about 3.30 a.m. Rose late.

Ali El Tom came and discussed business from about 9 a.m. till 1 p.m. N.B. I have omitted that I discussed with him yesterday the Um Kedada affairs. I have a large number of men wanted in connextion with slavery. It is always very nearly impossible to get such out of the Kababish, and consequently I proceeded with caution. I also discussed arms and also another visit by either Ali El Tom or El Tom Ali to Kajmar.

About 3.30 Muhd. El Tom turned up with a slave girl (a buxom and not unattractive lass) whom a Bertawi from Um Kedada, who had followed me from that place, claimed as his cousin. She mocked him and insulted him and said she wanted nothing to do with him. There remained the question of the Bertawi's alleged aunt, said to be at Hamrat Esh Sheikh. I took guarantee from the aunt's master for her production and promised to see the old lady at Hamra.

Then Ali El Tom came and most of his household and elders and the parties in the Dar Um Bakhit—Awlad El Feki case. I heard what they had to say and said I would give my decision next morning. The Hakiim (doctor) Muhd. Eff. Ahmad came after dark and drank tea with me.

The country up here is parching very rapidly: a dry wind blew most of the day from the north. It is very hot at noon, but cool at night. Slept better.

28.9.32

Mejlis all morning. In the afternoon El Tom turned up with three magnificent camels for me to choose two—one for the hamla and one to ride. One of the two riding camels he brought is as smooth as a railway train, smoother than that I have lost. Decided to buy this one and the hamla camel.

Meanwhile a Kahli sheikh of the house of El Eaysir arrived and we adjourned to drink coffee. Then Ali El Tom arrived with a crowd to hear what I had to say about the Dar Um Bakhit case.

In the course of preliminary conversation, which was very merry, Ali El Tom let drop that the water in the pool here is getting scarce. I shall therefore hasten my departure. It is pretty certain from what the Kawahla say that their Nazir will have moved back to Um Gozein by the time I can get there.

After the meeting in my tent had broken up, I sent for the corporal and suggested we had better get away tomorrow afternoon. He said he must water camels then and so I suggested he find out if Sh. Ali intends moving tomorrow or the day after. I then went in the dark to see Muhd. Eff. and consult about starting.

The bugs are bad—read in bed under the mosquito net. The usual wind awoke me about 3.30 a.m.

29.9.32

The Kawahla who are visiting Ali El Tom arrived to pay their respects. They appear just a trifle vexed with the Zeyadia about their being refused water for their herds at Um Nigeira Abu Gaid pool. I said that was my doing and the D.C. Kuttum's in whose merkaz the place lay. Muhammad Fadlallah has been west of Taganor drawing water from Um Higeyliga, Omda Ali Garoot's well. They say the country is still green there—camels watering every 15th day and sheep every 5th.

Ali El Tom did not come to see me all the morning and only for a short time in the evening. I shall start tomorrow afternoon if nothing occurs. Muhammad Ahmad El Ayaisir [*sic*] arrived to take me to the Nazir of the Kawahla's tents.

30.9.32

I wanted to spend this morning talking to Ali El Tom, especially about the question of blood-money. Very soon after he had come to see me, however, 7 Kawahla arrived, the spokesman of whom was a certain Ahmad Suleiman Arbab of the Dar Hamid section. He said he had lost two camels and had tracked them and the thieves that morning into the herd of the Melik Muhammad Es Sayyah of the Meidob. Also he said that a Meidobi had refused to help take the track out of the herd and had threatened him with a rifle. He had brought the rifle in to me.

The Meidob followed before I had finished taking down the statement of Ahmad Suleiman and I had to struggle with their version. They denied everything and said the rifle had been taken by force for no good cause and that it was one of the rifles issues to the Melik Muhammad Es Sayyah by government for Native Administration purposes.

I sent two police to go and look at the tracks and try to take them out of the herd. By this time it was 1 p.m. After lunch the hamla moved off.

Ali El Tom came to talk to me again. He made a very strong appeal for the amount of the blood-money to be paid to the Meidob to be reduced —asking that the governor be consulted in the matter.

Then I asked him for his opinion about reduction of blood-money in general. He said he was for all payments to be made in animals. I said that was easy as between camel-owning nomads, but how about the Nuba, Meidob, and other tribes who had no great numbers of camels? He said that in that case the tribe of the slayer should pay to the tribe of the slain animals to the value of the money last paid on an occasion of a blood-money settlement by the latter tribe to the former. *E.g.* if a Kabbashi now killed a Nuba, since the Nubas last paid £E250 in cash for killing a Kabbashi, the Kababish should now pay animals to the value of £E250.

I then told him of the opinion of Niama Sirkatti, Gumaa Sahal and Nimr Hasan, viz. that it should be £E200 cash. Ali El Tom said he thought £E200 too much for Nuba and such to pay still—£E160 or £E170 would be about right. He then gave it as his final opinion that all camel-owning tribes should, in these hard times, pay 100 camels as was the ancient custom. If a non-camel-owning tribe were involved, then the payment should if possible be animals to the value of £E200, or preferably a lesser sum of about £E160. Then he went off and various relatives of his came to talk to me.

Then I rode off about 3.45 p.m. Ali El Tom and the rest escorted me some way as usual. We went south past the hill of Gideidim and got down to sleep on the ridge of a big sand dune, to the east of which was a valley between sand dunes running from the Gideidim hill.

I slept none too well—had very vivid dreams, in one of which I committed a murder by shooting a man with a shot gun. This was clearly the outcome of talk with Ali El Tom in the morning about the Sudan Penal Code and its failure to coincide at most points with Arab law and custom, e.g. especially they consider a man who kills an adulterer taken with his wife as guiltless, likewise the slayer of a thief.

1.10.32

Rode from 6 a.m. till 8.30. Country uniformly dreary—gafal and mearab bush and grass on sand-dunes. Left the hill of Taganor to the east and came upon the Nazir of the Kawahla's camp in the W.S.W. of the hill. I was met by him and his relations. Had a short talk with him after I had breakfasted and washed.

Then I had to take the statements of the police who had gone with the Kawahla to track Ahmad Suleiman's camels, as they had caught up again this morning.

In the afternoon rode with Muhammad Fadlallah on horses to see the well Um Higliga [*sic*] S. of the hill. The Arabs could not produce a saddle to fit me, and so I rode with a blanket and leather pad strapped on the horse's back and no stirrups. It made me a little sore but was better than a narrow Arab saddle. It took about an hour to reach the well. The Kawahla at the moment are very short of water here. They sent to Gedeidim to fetch water and also are drawing from this very deep rock well. The well water is not good and has strong smell of sulphurated hydrogen. It took about $\frac{3}{4}$ hour to reach the well. We spent about 20 minutes to $\frac{1}{2}$ hour there watching men draw water. N.B. They were all free men—Arabs—drawing water, which is rare and shows they must be pretty thirsty. The well is about 156 feet deep. On the way back we passed a herd of camels and Muhd. Fadlallah made a boy milk me a naga. The milk went down very well for I was exceedingly thirsty. The afternoon had been very warm and rain had been falling to the south. Slept well.

2.10.32

These Kawahla are going to move tomorrow. As they will not let me stay behind them I must start tomorrow morning.

I interviewed this morning the brother of the Cairo merchant Ahmad Ibrahim Abu Bateen, who is here buying camels, and also Wad El Hammadabi, the Kawahla guarantor in Nahud, who is here with him. The merchant was a nasty-looking little yellow man. He had a note from Hamilton. He said the Kawahla would not sell at reasonable prices.

Muhammad Fadlallah had previously told me that the merchant would accept only the best and fattest camels. Also Muhd. Fadlallah said that he wanted leave for some of the Kawahla to go down to Egypt and see for themselves what prices they could get there. He said that one or two had gone as far as Debba with camels for Egyptian merchants—as guides.

Muhd. Fadlallah, his uncle Fadl El Mula and one or two others and also Muhd. Eff. Ahmad Hamid spent a long time sitting in my tent and talking. Meanwhile I wished to get letters about the Meidob case written and the Meidob sent off with them. At length by 2.15 I got this done and then was free to have lunch. . . .

I was left alone most of the afternoon. It was exceedingly hot and I slept on the floor of the tent after lunch. Later, when it was a little cooler, I tried writing in this diary. Then came to me a slave of Muhammad Fadlallah's who said he had been cheated of his hire by a Kabbashi for whom he had herded two years. Later came a Kahli called Gadallah El Meleih, who brought an incomprehensible letter from Pumphrey[7] of Nahud about a camel stolen from one Muhd. Hamad who, Gadallah said, is ill. Gadallah himself has a case about another camel. I discussed this with him also and told him I would see him in the morning before I started.

The heat of the afternoon had ended in a very slight shower of rain. Rain had been falling further off.

The evening was warm and damp. I sent for Muhd. Fadlallah to drink tea with me. (a) According to him, Munim Mansur dealt with and finally settled the case of Abu Saida. (b) M.F. referred to the Soghry Barok business and the Feki's complaint to Reid in Dueim which is also settled. (c) I asked him about "dia" and he appeared in favour of animal payments, although he foresaw difficulties in getting parties to agree on the individual

---

[7] M. E. C. Pumphrey, SPS 1930–48. *SPS*, 59–60.

animals. When he heard Ali El Tom's opinion, he said he would not disagree with that, but agreed that £E200 was still high. On the whole it appeared that Muhd. F. had not really made up his mind but, in view of the question of the Nuba and other non-camel-owning tribes, would favour a fixed money sum, whether paid in actual cash or animals. (d) He complained about the number of merchants in his tribe and especially of the number who have settled at Um Badr. I suggested that he should send a wakil with me to bring them before me and I would then ask the governor for leave to expel five out of seven.

I dined off Ovaltine made with camel's milk, cold and very good too. But I spent a bad night. It was hot and damp, and after 3 a.m. when the starting of my hamla woke me, I could not sleep properly again because Arabs were moving about and beginning to pack up.

3.10.32

Started 6 a.m. in a very beautifully coloured dawn. Some Arab families had already begun to move, the women's covered utfa litters swaying about on the slow baggage camels; others more tardy or slothful were pulling down their tents. Rode through the usual dull monotonous rolling bush till 9 a.m. It became very hot and I developed a slight headache. The country soon became absolutely parched. It is extraordinary how this year rain has fallen so patchily: half an hour's ride takes one out of green pastures into barren dry lands.

Camp in a poor place—no grass for camels. Breakfast revived me and then I slept for a little, after doing what could be done about washing in a quart of muddy water. The heat became very great, clouds appeared. At noon I heard the Sheikh's drum being beaten in a valley to the north, showing that the moving Arabs had caught us up at last. They go on all day without resting during these "rahlas" (moves of camp).

Muhd. Fadlallah arrived and drank some tea and departed again. Meanwhile a thunderstorm broke to the S.E. The afternoon may therefore be a little cooler. My godfathers I shall be glad when this next month and a half are over! When the cool weather comes I should revive a little. At present I feel exceedingly limp and depressed.

I tried drawing for a little in the afternoon. One of the hireling camels with my caravan had gone sick—sat down and refused to move. We arranged to leave the lance-corporal, who knows the country, with it. He has a skin of water and some food and will stay by it. If the camel does not either get better or die before tomorrow morning, he is to shoot or slaughter it and catch up on foot. He cannot wait longer as there are now no Arabs behind him and there is no water.

Rode on at 4.30. The countryside is most depressing—everlasting bush and dry as a bone. It looks as if no rain had fallen here this rains.

About sunset we began to catch up with the Arabs again. At first, herds of camels moving through the bush slowly, then herdsmen alternating short songs with shouts of "Hoitch—hee hee—prrrr" to drive the herd. Later in the dark we came upon camels carrying litters and men shouting for straggling families, and then in the dark we saw camp fires ahead and passed through a muddled confusion of herds and pack animals and Arabs huddling round fires, their camels' loads dumped beside them and the camels couched at hand. My camp was pitched just ahead of all this confusion of fires and families.

Rain had fallen and some of the more thirsty Arabs had run to the shower and collected water in skins as it fell, to eke out their insufficient supply.

Muhd. Fadlallah sent his young brother Muhammad Ahmad to talk to me, bringing with him a large bowl of camel's milk. Meanwhile a thunderstorm broke to the west and looked like coming up. The police put up my tent and by the time I had got inside my bed rain was falling fairly fast.

Slept poorly because I was hauled out at 2 a.m. to move my bed for the police to take down and pack up my tent. The hamla moved off at 2.30.

4.10.32

Rode 6 a.m. till 8.45 a.m. Same desolate country until we came to Um Gozein. The sky was overcast most of the morning and the weather, thank goodness, much cooler. The Arabs were left well behind. Also Tingle and Koko got lost because they stopped to adjust the load on Koko's camel and meanwhile a passing herd of camels wiped out my tracks.

They arrived by about 11 a.m. By then it was pretty hot. I had a wash, put on my pyjamas and went to sleep. My thigh muscles are terribly stiff and my tail very sore from that bareback ride of the other afternoon.

About 1 p.m. Tingle woke me to say that a policeman with post had arrived. This was most unexpected. Read my mail and had lunch.

About 4 p.m. I got up and went out. I found Muhd. Fadlallah here. I had been told he had gone back to his Arabs or I would have got up sooner. He wanted to go off. They had made camp some way from here, which is rather a poor show on his part, for he might have brought me to where his people intended to camp. Now he wants me to move back in my tracks tomorrow. My camels are tired and have gone down to water at the lake of Um Gozein. I let him go off and then went for a walk with my gun. This place is not so bad—there is some green grass and good trees. I found two little girls picking berries on the top of the ridge running towards the lake and talked to them. They were herding goats and gathering berries to make scent meanwhile. Pleasant little things and quite unafraid.

On the way back I met an entirely deaf old man and several herds of camels coming back from the water. With one herd was an elderly man on a young camel, who insisted on dismounting and walking with me to my camp. He proved to be Gumaa Ahmad El Aeysir, an uncle of Muhd. F.'s. I gave him tea. He was quite unlike his nephew—real good backwoods Arab.

Long talk with Muhd. Eff. the doctor. Felt very tired—revived myself with milk and whisky. Resolved to borrow a horse and ride to Muhd. F.'s camp tomorrow, stay till the afternoon and come back. A nuisance, but I refuse to tire my camels for his sake: they all need rest and I want to leave here the day after tomorrow.

5.10.32

Rose about 6 a.m. feeling fairly well rested—borrowed Muhammad Effendi's horse "Um Badir", which he wants to sell to me, and set out for Muhammad Fadlallah's camp. Muhammad Effendi went with me as he proposed to spend some days with Muhd. Fadlallah's people. The horse is so thin (I think because he left it behind at Um Gozein in the charge of Arabs) and it has been ill—consequently I said I could not consider buying it unless it got better.

The Arabs proved to be not far away. Spent quite a pleasant day with them. It was not too hot. I had a long talk with Suleiman [*sic*] Ibrahim Abu Bateen, the Hedjazi camel-merchant who is with them, about the Hedjaz and Nejd and Ibn Rifada.[8] I also talked with Feki Fadl El Mula about songs and singers.

Found the Giheimabi Muhammad Ahmad who is witness in the impossible case of that tiresome Bertawi Abdel Majid Muhammadein. His story is different from Belal Ali Belal's and I'm sure Ali Belal did the Bertawi down. But it is all so long ago now that I don't think there can be any result. Rode back on one of Muhd. Fadlallah's horses—a pleasant ride.

The place of my camp is pleasant, with large trees and green grass, and the herds of camels come by morning and evening as they go to and from water.

Spent the evening finishing mail, including a letter to Souper, and sent mail off by Isa El Dho. He should catch the post out of Soderi of 13th October.

---

[8] Hijazi chief whose revolt 'Abd al-'Aziz al-Sa 'ud put down in 1932.

6.10.32

I had intended to go on from here today. Sheikh El Tom Ali arrived in the morning and said his father's people had arrived and that I must stop with them on my way. This I agreed to do. Also he brought a note saying that bovine pleuropneumonia was reported among cattle of certain Zeyadia from Um Kedada who had just arrived to drink at Um Gozein. I found the rumour not true, thank God. But I must remember to enquire of Moore whether there is bovine Pl. pn. in his district.

Muhammad Fadlallah arrived to take leave of me. I moved off about 3.30.

The extraordinary thing here is that, while the immediate neighbourhood of my camp has green grass, yet west of this spot, e.g. Muhd. F.'s camp, is dry and east and north is likewise bone dry. We rode for about an hour and came to Ali El Tom's camp. He has squatted in the water course near where his camp was this time last year when I stayed with him. It is a grim spot this year—yellow and burnt up. And the mosquitoes were terrible.

I determined to get away as soon as possible but agreed to stay till tomorrow afternoon. Had a chat with Ali El Tom in the evening. He is quite agreeable about his school being taken onto government budget.

7.10.32

A long and hot morning's work. I had not slept too well the night before on account of dogs barking. Ali El Tom asked me to lunch.

When at last our jobs were ended and El Tom came to call me to lunch, some Meidob came to say that the Melik Muhammad Es Sayyah had arrived at Muhammad Fadlallah's and wanted to see me. I had therefore to postpone my departure a day. The trouble which had brought him was of course the case of the Kawahla camels and the rifle at Gedeidim.

Ali El Tom left me to eat his lunch alone in a green canvas tent—which was a relief, as I was thereby enabled to eat little of it. We had a talk over coffee and tea about the earlier history of the Kababish.

As we were going towards my tent after I had taken my leave, the Melik Es Sayyah arrived. Ali El Tom took possession of him. I had then to wait patiently in the heat reading a book till Ali El Tom came back, when we dealt with the Bertawi's case and Muhd. Ahmad the Geheimabi. Not a great success.

At sunset the Melik came to see me and we explained mutually about the rifle and the theft of the camels. I handed him back the rifle and bandolier but kept certain obviously illegal rounds of ammunition. I also told him of my decision to approach Campbell about a reduction of the "dia".

Ali El Tom came after dark and talked for a while.

This was a terrible night. It was warm and there was a dance going on. I could not get to sleep till about 1 a.m.

8.10.32

Felt awful and the day was hot. Ali El Tom had evidently (and so I discovered for certain afterwards) taken the Melik into mejlis to pour out all his grievances against Meidob.

Ahmad Gismallah of the Kawahla arrived to accompany me to Um Badr. He is one of the world's most silent men. When he had left me after drinking coffee, I sat wearily and meditated upon Ali El Tom's talk of last night.

He had ranged over a number of topics, but mainly we talked about the educated class. I found him strongly opposed to the educated Sudanese not employed by government going to Egypt and being given jobs there. I rallied him about having his sons educated if he considered the results of education so disastrous: and he said that if they learned to read and write and do sums, that was enough for him. He wound up with a peroration about the need for government's keeping an eye on Sayed Abderrahman El Mahdi.

Also he said, as he has done once or twice lately, that he would like to be visited by his D.C. more often. The answer is, "I do so as often as circumstances permit". By lunch time I felt extremely done.

The Melik Es Sayyah came to take leave of me soon after my hamla had moved off. Then Ali El Tom came with all his Nurab and most of them rode out to put me on my way. Young Fadlallah the Sheikh's son did a joy ride on a horse—and he's only 10, so he has some nerve: seemed quite at ease at the mad gallop they do.

Rode mostly alongside the Wadi Gadab till sunset. Found the camp just to the east of an encampment of the Kawahla—Awlad Hammad. They gave me camel's milk to drink when their herds came in. I felt absolutely dead beat and thought for a little I was in for a go of fever. Retired to bed and slept fairly well.

9.10.32

Long ride from 6 a.m. till 8.30 largely through open bush and over patches of stony ground. This is the southern end of Um Kuhl, the thick tract of bush running N. and S. here. In front of us a hill arose called Garanzaid, to the south one could see Zein El Rowiana and Zein El Atshana and Sikanju hills in Kaja Seruj.

I had hoped for a sleep, but a man with a small girl, daughter of a runaway slave woman, and, so he swears, himself, turned up to see me. I let him keep custody of the child after swearing him to his paternity. Also Teirab, one of Ali El Tom's slaves, arrived with a letter from Ali El Tom and an ex-slave of his, lately released from Port Sudan gaol, who had turned up with an unlicensed rifle and a possibly stolen camel.

It was abominably hot and oppressive, with banks of cloud about. I was constipated and had a headache for the third day running. Altogether I am tired of this trek, and have got to the stage where all food makes me feel slightly sick and I dislike the sight of my best riding camel.

Rode 4.30 to 6.30, mostly over up-and-down stony ground with a number of water courses cutting it. Very oppressive. Camp on a hard dry hill—no grass but bushes. Felt very tired at first and the air was thunderous; but later a wind got up about 9 p.m. and I felt better. Wrote, and slept well from about 10.30 to 5.30 a.m.

10.10.32

A long, and, towards the end, very hot ride to Um Badr. When we got into the hills round Um Badr (El Bahm) everything became greener and soon we passed cultivations. Arrived camp 9.45 a.m. and I told off the lance-corporal for making such a long journey of it. Mail arrived.

My camp at Um Badr was in the wadi to the west of the lake, the flow of which, when there is enough rain to make it flow, fills the lake. The place was pleasantly green. I spent a good deal of the day until about 4 p.m. reading my mail and then writing mail and sleeping.

The afternoon was exceedingly stuffy. A storm came up and rain was falling about 45 miles to the south.

One or two slaves came to see me and I dealt with them in the presence of Ahmad Gismallah. None of those I saw wanted to leave Um Badr. Their grain is good this year and they are all more contented than last year.

Some merchants for whom I had sent came to see me and I questioned them to find out how long they had been in this place. There are too many merchants here.

The night was pretty warm.

11.10.32

Rose about 6.30 and went for a walk with my gun to the lake. There were any number of geese and duck, but I could not get near any. Also there were innumerable sand grouse drinking, but I had walked in a different direction when the sand grouse appeared, and, by the time I returned to the part of the lakeside where they were drinking, practically none were left. The most pleasant sight was the pelicans, of which I counted about 60, and the ibises.

I spent the morning writing mail which left about 4 p.m. by Muhammad Mahmoud.

About 5.30 old Farajallah, Muhammad Fadlallah's slave agent, came to see me. He suggested trying for geese and duck on Um Dabib, one of the subsidiary pools of Um Badr, which was only about 400 yards to the S.W. of my camp. We went there. At sunset I was able to stalk a large number of geese and duck on a mud flat by the pool, but I failed to keep concealed quite long enough and then missed my shot. Returned in the dark to camp.

It appears that PT 75 was paid out this last year for cleaning the landing ground at Um Badr and that Farajallah, instead of dividing it out among the men who did the work, ate it all himself. He complained of the Meganin coming too close to the "dammar"[9] again.

My two walks today did me good. Camel-riding does gradually destroy one's insides and is no good as exercise at all. Fairly large number of mosquitoes here.

12.10.32

Rode off about 6 a.m. and said good-bye to Ahmad Gismallah. Our road was over the dune to the west of the lake (which looked quite beautiful in the dawn) and so among the hills on the way to Gashda. There is no green grass on the sand hills round here—only in the wadis. Reached Gashda about 8.45.

While I was trying to bear the heat and read some Arabic, a runaway slave arrived and poured out his woes that he had been savagely beaten by his master, a Kabbashi, some 5 days previously.

I have had a stupid headache in the eyes for the last two days. Tried to draw a camel—no enthusiasm for this now-a-days.

The afternoon was terribly hot, preliminary to a thunderstorm. Clouds everywhere. After we had started on the afternoon ride, there was thunder to the south of us and rain fell all around. Only a few light drops fell on me. The air cooled a little. When I got into camp I felt wretched and thought I might be in for fever. It was in reality only the result of thunder and constipation. Camp was beyond the place known as El Tamad El Afin, where there are curious upended rocks.

Two Kababish concerned in an alleged slaving case came to meet me on the way and I had to pull myself together to hear what they had to say.

13.10.32

About 3.45 a.m. a thunderstorm broke. The hamla had gone on by this time and I had no tent. Fairly heavy rain fell on us for about 20 minutes

---

[9] Dry-weather watering quarters.

to half an hour. After that the rain stopped and I was able to unwrap my bed and doze for about an hour.

Rode 5.45 till 8.15 when I arrived at Hamrat Esh Sheikh. Dead tired, but steps taken to deal with the constipation had been effective and the pain in the eyes was better. Camp under large trees in the wadi. There appears to have been little rain and certainly none recently. Grass outside the wadi bed is all parched and mostly last year's. Corn poor.

As Tindil, Ali El Tom's slave agent here, was some time about producing certain people I wanted to see, I went to bed and slept for an hour or so, which did me good. After lunch talked to Tindil and saw the people he had produced. Tindil shows the good side of the institution of slavery. He and his father and his father's father have been honoured servants in Ali El Tom's family. Tindil says he was born in the same year as Ali El Tom and brought up with him. Tindil's father carried "the Bey's" keys and went with him to Egypt. (Fadlallah Bey Salim, sheikh of the Kababish in Turkish times.)

When I had finished with Tindil I went for a walk down by the four great wells here. The wells were, of course, at this season deserted, since there are rain-pools to drink from. There is indeed a rain pool at Hamrat Esh Sheikh itself in which there is some water, but not a great deal.

Went to bed at 8 p.m. and slept very well. Neither the full moon nor the start of my hamla made any difference to me.

14.10.32

Did not start till 6.45 for some reason unknown. Tindil accompanied me on a donkey as far as the rain pool at the end of the wadi. Rode till 9.15 by which time it was pretty hot. There is more grass in this stretch of country (we are now going S.E.) although for the most part everything is yellow and dried up. Very hot morning—slept most of it.

The afternoon ride took us by evening to somewhere short of Abu Zaima. I began to feel much better. The weather is infinitely drier now and that makes a lot of difference. Also I am nearing the end of my journey. Drank a large whisky and felt much better for it. In fact felt strong enough to overcome my pride and tell my servant Koko that I should like him to oblige till the end of the month instead of leaving me immediately we reach Soderi. He evidently intends to leave. Slept well.

15.10.32

A real nip in the air before dawn this morning. We rode early and at dawn watered our camels in the Wadi El Milik [*sic*] where there are still a few pools of standing rain water. We crossed the wadi just north of Abu Zaima and then came on to the motor road from Abu Zaima to Soderi (so-called motor road—it means merely that a track was cleared through the bush in 1919).

One is now in familiar country of sand hills and rocky "tors" all over the place. Camel flies now appear in large numbers on the camels—it is strange that, out in the west, scarcely any are to be found. The country here is entirely empty of people and herds but the grass is not bad. Camp under the hills "Galaat Um Zabad".

Lay down to go to sleep. To my surprise, my cook, under pretext of asking me what I would have for lunch, came to ask me what I was doing about this fellow Koko. I said, "Nothing—he said he wanted to go and I merely asked him to stay until the end of the month". Muhammad Sadig said he and the others had been trying to persuade him to stay and he had refused. It appears my camelman, who is a pleasant bloke, would like to become house-boy. He is a nice lad and I don't think he would let me down, but he has no training. I personally would like to have him and train him rather than have some conceited and probably dishonest blighter from Khartoum. But Sheila's arrival is now so close that I am in doubt. Said so. But the conversation cheered me up, for evidently Muhammad Sadig and the camelman have some rudiments of faithfulness and esprit de corps. After he has left I shall find out what really is making Master Koko want to leave.

Did some writing. Pretty hot day. Rode in the evening. My watch has stopped and won't go. Camp on a high sand-hill. Pleasant cool night.

16.10.32

Rode at 5.15 a.m. easy going and cool. Plenty of light from the setting moon till dawn. Two enormous morningstars above the dawn. Passed Um Khirwa' village and reached camp about 7.30.

Chapter X

The Governor of Kordofan[1] Visits Soderi District 12.1.33—25.1.33

12.1.33

Sheila and I had arrived from Bara last night about 6.30. I had been exceedingly tired and we firmly declined to dine with the Mayalls, who very kindly invited us. I did not, however, manage to get a very good night's rest, as I could not get to sleep as early as I wished (El Obeid always seems to have more than its fair share of cocks) and the sounds of men taking their Ramadan meal before dawn [disturbed me].

I got up at 5.30. We were staying in the rest house adjoining the hut which is the English Church. Particularly handy because the governor's house was just round the corner. A lorry arrived about 6.30, and I was considerably perturbed because it already appeared very nearly fully-loaded with the governor's luggage, and I was afraid of sticking in the sand of the Soderi road if it were overloaded. I found him ready so we returned and our luggage was piled into the lorry till it looked like a haystack.

We got away about 7.15. I had understood that Sheila was to stay in a rest house and have meals with the Mayalls. However, it appeared from Mayall's talk this morning that he wants her to stay in his house. It was kind of him but I don't envy her if he insists, because the house has only two bedrooms, a small dressing and a bathroom besides the dining and sitting rooms, and already contains two Mayalls, their baby and a nurse.

Newbold drove the tourer himself and I sat in front beside him. The morning was cool, but not so cold as to be unpleasant driving. The lorry was rather slow going over the sandhills near Abu Sinoun (the first big rock hill out of El Obeid). When we reached the dry rain pool at Abu Sinoun we stopped, talked to a native who had been resting under a tree after fetching water from a rock hole up on the top of the hill, and waited for the lorry. On its arrival we had breakfast.

Took to the road again after about three-quarters of an hour, and passed a party of large red monkeys who scampered towards the hills. The

---

[1] Douglas Newbold (SPS 1920–45) succeeded Gillan as governor of Kordofan in 1933. He was civil secretary from 1939 until his death in 1945. A biography is K. D. D. Henderson, *The making of the modern Sudan: the life and letters of Sir Douglas Newbold . . .*, London 1953.

day soon became fairly warm, but not unpleasant. We ploughed through the sands. Newbold drove as far as just beyond Gleit hill and then made me drive. We reached Mazroub wells about 12.30 to 1.00 p.m. and stopped by the rest hut under a tree. It appeared at once that Sheikh Gumaa Sahal, the Nazir of the Meganin and lord of the wells, had left for Soderi to meet the governor there. Newbold and I walked down towards the wells and saw coming towards us an aged figure who proved to be Sheikh Ali Ajabna —a charming old man, and a great and influential character among the Meganin. He and Newbold greeted each other with great affection, and went to the wells. Several herds of camels were being watered (they are watering here just now in the cold, we gather, about once in 60 days) and we were given a large bowl of milk to drink. After a short talk, however, we went on. About five miles further on we saw some people sitting under trees and waved at them. A little beyond this I suggested stopping at a sand dune for lunch and Newbold agreed. When the lorry arrived, Sheikh Gumaa Sahal was on board of it—it had been his bivouac we had passed. We congratulated him on the robe of honour, which had been granted him and with which he was to be invested next day. He talked for some time and then Newbold dismissed him and we had lunch (Gumaa was, of course, fasting).

From the place where we lunched to Soderi is not very far by car, especially as the going was fairly good. I always feel better when I arrive among the hills and open spaces near Soderi, and the same effect was evident on Newbold. At the top of the first hill, from which one can see the hills of Soderi, I stopped and had the hood put down, so that we could admire the view.

We reached Soderi about 4.30 p.m. As soon as the car came in sight a posse of people with Sheikh Niama Sirkatti at their head started riding towards us at full speed. Meanwhile, farther off, were the police camels being fed at "stables". To the right of our path the women of the police were beating drums and setting up a yell. We stopped in front of Niama's posse and very warm greetings were exchanged between him and Newbold.

Beyond these men who came to meet Newbold were women and slave girls of Niama's people making song and dance. Newbold waved a whip over them and then we went on with Charles de Bunsen, who had come up from the police stables, to the house. I am glad to find that Newbold loathes these dances as much as I do and is entirely in favour of one's politely stopping them when they are got up in one's honour (or in the hope of cash from one).

Charles and I shared a room in the house, and Newbold had the guest room. The house looks much as it was with me in it—but Charles has many more and better books than I have.

We sat and chatted over tea and drinks. Newbold talked exceedingly amusingly and interestingly. We had dinner early, and were all in bed by 9.30. Charles is not looking too fit and has his everlasting cold. I slept like a log after taking two pink pills, and awoke at 6.30 a.m. feeling better than I have done for a long time.

13.1.33

Newbold talked to the Mamur before breakfast. I looked over some papers Charles wanted me to see, and I handed some to him.

After breakfast we went to the office, and Newbold inspected the offices, stores and prison. I got away from the office as soon as I reasonably could. I found the way back to the house encumbered by three separate groups of dancing women. Niama insisted that the rewarding of these dancers was "on" himself and his Omdas. I went to see Newbold and took his leave politely but firmly to disperse the dancers, who were making a terrible noise.

I took one of the Nuba Omdas, an old man who is a great friend of mine, and we went and saluted the dancers and made speeches to them, saying, "The governor is highly delighted with your dances and the honour you do him. But his is exceedingly busy, and so cannot come himself to see you. Moreover, it is Ramadan, and he is afraid that these exertions, while you are fasting, may do you hurt; so he thinks it would be better if you rested now and danced later on. And thank you very much". They dispersed gradually after that.

I went to the house to write letters, and then returned later to the office to deal with a few things with Charles de Bunsen.

Akib Effendi's wife is seedy, and he wants to send her to Omdurman. Newbold granted him local leave to go down to El Obeid, taking his wife in the lorry, which is to return the day after tomorrow to El Obeid, i.e. 15th January. Newbold also took up the question of Akib's transfer.

Newbold very sensibly insisted on having no lunch—only taking sandwiches and tea in a thermos.

I therefore sent off the lorry to go to Abu Zaima (57 miles to the west) at 12.30 p.m. We left in the tourer at 2 p.m. Newbold made me drive. The road is, of course, exceedingly rough and I tried not to bump the passengers. I love this western country and the hills all around. . . .

We arrived at Abu Zaima about 5 p.m. and found the tents up and the escort of camel police all under the trees of the Wadi El Melik in the place where I camped with the Gillans in April 1932 and with Hamilton in June 1930. Sheikh Ali El Tom had sent three magnificent camels for us to ride.

We had dinner fairly early. The talk both before and after dinner was exceedingly interesting. Charles talked of Greenland and Newbold of the

Western Desert,[2] and both of the shortcomings, lack of sympathy, and stinginess of the Royal Geographical Society towards explorers. Newbold also talked of tours he had made in the Near East and especially of Palestine and Trans-Jordan. He talked of Kerak and Petra, and filled me with envy and desire to go there. He said the trip costs about £23. He told the story of Saladin and Renaud de Champigny[3] at Kerak.

Then he turned to administration in the Sudan, and to the attitude of nomad Arabs towards Native Courts in sedentary areas such as Dar Hamar, and how we must propagand to persuade the nomads of the wisdom of the govt. in making these Native Administration embryos. The talk was so interesting that it went on till 11.15 over a roaring log fire without our noticing. We then turned in. I was very tired, and Charles, who admitted to not having slept the night before, looked worn out.

14.1.33

Rose at 5.30 a.m. Newbold rode my camel Abu Zumam. I was mounted on Akib Effendi's lent for the trip; but it was so fat the saddle won't sit on it, so after a few yards I changed onto one of Ali El Tom's camels. The cars returned to Soderi.

We rode west out of the Wadi El Melik towards the ridge of hills by Adhat (pool) El Gawad (of the horse). The morning was cool, and there was a dust haze. The wind sprang up about 7.30 and the haze deepened. We crossed the ridge of Adhat El Gawad and found our camp near the Adhat about 9 a.m.

After breakfast Newbold returned to his tent with a number of Soderi files on the Kababish tribe. Charles and I are sharing a tent. We spent the morning arranging his next trek. He is to go up to Um Rumeila in Dar Howawir by camel via Um Dam, Id El Merkh, Safia, Hobaji, Elai: and later, after the Howawir tribal meeting, trek up the Wadi Mugaddam and into Omdurman, whence he goes on leave about 15th March. . . .

About 3.15 p.m. we rode on. I had fallen asleep in my chair about 2.30, after the hamla had moved, and was rudely awakened by the greeting of a Kabbashi lad, who proved to be one involved in an accusation of kidnapping. He had turned up with the boy he is alleged to have bought. But the boy gave evidence that he was hired to the Kabbashi as a herdsman, and was very happy in his job.

We rode through sparse bush and over another ridge of hills and found camp about 5 p.m. Just as we were taking our boots off, Sheikh Ali El

---

[2] See, e.g., Newbold's "A desert Odyssey of a thousand miles", *SNR* VII, 1924.
[3] That is, Reynald de Châtillon.

Tom arrived. Enthusiastic greetings between him and Newbold. Newbold sent him away to rest until the sun should set and he could eat.

We had dinner at 7 p.m. and Sheikh Ali came to talk at 7.30 p.m. We talked round a fire till about 9, and then went to bed. I slept like a log till 4.45. Sheikh Ali had ridden off in the night.

15.1.33

Rose 5.30, rode at 6.15. A pleasant morning. Neither too cold nor too hot. Passed the wells at Hamrat Esh Sheikh about 8 a.m. Some twenty minutes farther to the northwest we came in sight of Sheikh Ali's people all lined up on the ridge of a sand-hill. Horsemen in front and camelmen behind—some 200 men in all. As we came in sight the horsemen (about 40) in a body descended on us at a gallop. We made our camels kneel, and greeted them; El Tom wad Ali and Muhammad El Tom (Ali's brother) and all his cousins and uncles and young sons.

We rode again and met Sheikh Ali on the crest of the hill. Then the governor had to ride between two long lines of camelmen drawn up on either side of his path, who all gave the queer Arab scream, which denotes joy or sorrow, and waved their whips. We followed with Sh. Ali and his crowd of relatives mounted on horses. The camelmen broke ranks behind us and followed in a great body which tended to break into a gallop, and was restrained by the members of the royal house on their horses shouting, "Get away, you—Muhammad", "Get back, Omar", and so on. The wings of the cohort of camelmen, however, broke round beyond the restraining horsemen and dashed in confused galloping groups towards the Arab tents ahead. By this time our own camels were excited and going fast, and we had to ride with some care to prevent ourselves from being run away with. Horsemen beside us would every now and then break away at a gallop. Thus riding fast we came down upon a vast black pavillion which had been erected for the governor's reception—an enlarged goat-hair tent, decorated with the queer "ganati" (triple cones of leather tufted with ostrich feathers and ornamented with cowrie shells) at either horn of the tent, and with "adwat", a kind of banner, at either side. Beside this tent were placed the official drums of the tribe (which incidentally have a strange history),[4] which two slaves seated on the ground were pounding in syncopated rhythm. Beyond the drums was a semi-circle of some 30 slave girls all laden with gold ornaments and bright raiment, clapping their hands and singing and dancing. The camelmen drew up all round the drums and the dance. The dust, the yelling and the drumming in the bright clear sunlight contrasted with the dignified ranks of the men sitting [on] their camels and looking on.

---

[4] See "The nahas of the Kababish", *SNR* XI, 1928, 213–15.

Newbold went round the semi-circle and admired the drums and waved his whip at the dancers. We then all three proceeded to withdraw to our appointed places in the camp and the gathering broke up.

Ali El Tom had put up three large booths for us in front (i.e. southeast) of his camp—a large one for Newbold in front and two in a line some distance behind for Charles and myself. These booths were made of a black Arab tent with other black tent cloths stretched upon poles in front of it to enlarge the tent before. The sides were made of similar tent cloths. The whole was lined with white cotton cloth and carpeted with "zigafat", i.e. white and black tent cloths. All three were left unfurnished and Newbold's alone was decorated with the leather-work hangings of a woman's litter. After we had drunk tea and coffee (brought to us by the Sheikh's son) we had breakfast.

Breakfast lasted some time, as Newbold held forth after it. He then went to his tent and sent for Ali El Tom, to whom he talked for over two hours. Charles in his tent was talking to El Tom, and I was left alone to my relief. This is the first pleasant and idle rest I have had for some time.

We had lunch about 2.30 and went for a walk up the hills at 4.30 till sunset. Then we sat and talked again and had dinner early. Ali El Tom arrived just after dinner and sat talking till about 9.15 and we got to bed before 10 p.m.

16.1.33

Got up about 6.45 and did nothing except have a bath before breakfast. Newbold talked long after breakfast and Ali El Tom arrived. Charles took him off to do business and then Ali El Tom came back and Newbold and I talked to him about the reduction of the customary amount of bloodmoney and the effect upon it of the new order about the trying of homicide cases. Newbold after Ali El Tom's withdrawal explained to me that he did not intend the new order to be entirely inflexible. In fact we may carry on in Soderi (and, so I gather, but less elastically, in Bara) on the lines we have been pursuing viz. always holding a magisterial inquiry and then proceeding either to hold a Major Court, or to refer to the governor for permission to make a customary settlement, as may seem best to suit circumstances of the case and best to ensure that a vendetta will not arise. Newbold promised to give us something in writing on the point.

We all went to see the school which is kept in Sh. Ali El Tom's camp. He has made a very small grass house for it at the back of his camp. The writing and work of the eldest boys seemed to me very good. Hasan Nagila has about 15 small boys and there are said to be others with a feki . . . [which] acts as a sort of preparatory class. Ali El Tom asked me to impress upon Hasan Nagila and advise him that he must try and approximate himself to the ways of the Arabs. Before we left we had the small boys run races for sweets.

When we got away from the school, Newbold interviewed all the sons of Fadlallah (Fadlallah Bey Salim was Ali El Tom's grandfather). They were some thirty persons and most of them fine and intelligent looking.

Ali El Tom had asked us to lunch with him. We went and found the usual magnificently cooked chicken followed by doughnuts. Ali El Tom, with characteristic politeness, left us alone to wrestle with the food. We had an amusing conversation with him after the meal mainly about the place of women in Arabian life. He said that no man of worth ever consulted a woman about anything. This he was bound to do: but we know of course that women cause trouble with them just as they do with us.

After lunch Ali El Tom pressed Newbold to stay in his camp longer. However, excuses were made since we had a programme to keep to.

Ali El Tom came to see us after dinner, and, in the course of conversation, we talked about (1) dreams (2) the "gizzu" (i.e. grazing on green grass in the winter in the far N.W. desert). Ali El Tom said the young men in the gizzu play many games in the evenings, partly to keep warm. Especially they wrestle (I had not know before that wrestling was a Kabbashi sport) and play a game like prisoner's base.

17.1.33

After breakfast Newbold and I sat talking a long while about Soderi district and about marriage as it affects D.C.s in general and A.D.C. Soderi in particular. Charles was doing business in his own tent.

I had intended going to the school and sitting for a long while to watch the teaching. But, before I could get away, I was caught by Ali El Tom and Charles who wanted to discuss with Newbold and myself: (1) What more to do about the Zeyadia-Kababish murder case about which I had had a meeting with Mackrell in September without any result. We decided that we would try to arrange another meeting between the tribes next rains. (2) Whether a suggestion of Ali El Tom's was acceptable to government—that he should be allowed to deal with homicides inside the Kababish tribe, in which none but Kababish were involved. It was decided that such cases should be dealt with on the lines on which I had dealt with the fight between the Awlad El Feki and Dar Um Bakhit in the last rains, viz. when such homicides occur, Ali El Tom must send a letter explaining the facts and circumstances of the case to A.D.C. Dar El Kababish by hand of a responsible man of good understanding who can be questioned about the case. A.D.C. Dar El Kababish will then question the messenger to satisfy himself that the case is homicide and not rank murder, and then write an answer to Ali El Tom allowing him to settle the case by tribal custom. If other tribes object, the answer is that A.T. is not an exception, since he is *not* allowed to deal with homicides on his own, but has to refer each case. This was all explained to A.T. Newbold said he would give us something in writing about this.

When this was over I made to go to the school, but was again caught over some rifle licences in Charles's tent. By the time that was over it was 1.30 and the school no longer sitting.

Sheikh Hasan Ahmad El Nagila came to see me and was tiresome in conversation. I tried to explain to him again that, in view of the government's Political and Educational policy, viz. Native Administration and more rustic Education—he was in on the ground floor, as a young lad beginning his service, by having been appointed to create this Kababish school. He replied by asking if his transport would be paid for and so on. I told him, "Yes". He shows no enthusiasm or intention to try and stick in Dar El Kababish. In fact, Sheikh Ali asked for a "miskeen" (i.e. poor spirited) fellow and has got more than he wanted in that way.

After lunch poor Charles had to do more cases and so on. It was pretty warm and I took the opportunity to lie outside my tent and read a book. I watched the waiting sheikhs and people outside Charles's door, which was instructive. Ali El Tom does not allow unimportant matters to go to the D.C., but sifts the complainants. I slept for a little. Then the camels came.

We rode out with the usual accompanying crowd on camels and horses. We went down to the big wells in the valley, because these had all been built since Newbold's day as D.C. When we had looked at these, we took leave of Sheikh Ali and rode off in the direction of El Gashda (south of Hamra). Thus ended a very pleasant visit to Sheikh Ali El Tom. Newbold had clearly enjoyed himself thoroughly. So had I.

We rode on till about 5.30 when we came to that pleasant wadi near "El Tamad El Afin" (i.e. the "Stinking Wells"), where I usually make camp on this journey. Ahmad Gismallah of the Kawahla was with us. N.B. I had had an interesting talk with Ahmad Gismallah on the economics of the average Kahli household while we were at Hamrat. We made out that, now that the price of camels has slumped, the average Kahli householder, with say 2 wives and 4 children and 3 slaves, has to sell 4 camels a year to provide for his wants, while a she-camel's period of gestation is 12 months. Thus:

		£E m/ms
Grain	6 camel loads of 4 reikas each	4.800
Clothes	3 suits for himself and each son (shirt, drawers, robe & turban) a year at about 50 PT a suit	3.000
	3 suits of one robe and two petticoats for each of his wives a year @ 40 PT each	2.400
	2 suits for each slave, say 40 PT in all	400
		£E 10.600

Say £E11.000—but this does not allow for onions, pepper and salt (for men and animals), and luxuries such as tea, sugar, scents and gold ornaments (for the women), and *taxes*. Now a very fat camel will fetch only about £E4 at present prices; say average price £E3.

Ahmad Gismallah said that nearly all Kawahla sent their animals to market and sell to buy their needs for the year at the end of the rains about November. They do not buy much after that, unless, say, clothes wear out.

Newbold, Charles and I sat late over a fire this evening talking about travel and exploration. Newbold talks a great deal, but he is so interesting and entertaining that usually I listen most willingly until a very late hour. He was extremely amusing this evening about English country and *Tatler* snobbery, which he loathes.

18.1.33

Rose 5.30 a.m. and rode 6.30 a.m. The police put me on the Mamur's camel, which is like an elephant—an enormous fat brute, like the camels one sees in zoos and fairs, all woolly at the neck. We have three camels of Sheikh Ali El Tom's with us to ride on as spare camels.

Cool morning. Rode pleasantly, chattering at intervals, through El Tamad El Afin (there are some very strangely shaped rocks there) and across a wooded valley and over the spur of a hill to Gashda. I felt tired and we did not get anything much done this morning. A fairly high wind blew.

Rode about 3.30 p.m. over high goz and then broken ground. This elephantine camel's saddle kept slipping and I found that I had to get police to alter it.

Below the first sand dunes of Um Badr, Sheikh Muhammad Fadlallah met us with a large concourse of Kawahla on horses drawn up in line. Muhammad Fadlallah is a young man with a sycophantic manner and it was evident to me at once that he made an unfavourable impression on Newbold. The Kawahla did joy gallops to and fro wherever there was open ground. We went over sand hills and past the lake (the bottom of which is filled with trees). The lake is much emptier than a year ago. I doubt if it will last till the summer.

Muhammad Fadlallah had set our camp near the landing ground and south of it, that is, beyond the first sand dune east of the lake. A new well had appeared at this spot about a year ago, after the lake had been filled to record depth.

N.B. I have omitted one of my conversations with Ali El Tom on 17th January. I explained to him about my proposed trek to Gebrat Esh Sheikh northeast of Bara (a Kababish centre) and to Abu Tineitin, Um Sayala and the eastern side of Bara District; and explained how I proposed to have Muhammad Timsah with me at Gabra and to cast out of Gabra all bad non-Kababish. I asked A.T. to send a representative to help me with this, and he agreed to do so. I said that provisionally the date would be 20th Fatar El Awal, but I would confirm from Bara.

He spoke of Homara wells and I explained again all that had happened there regarding the Awlad Oan and the Guamaa. He said he quite understood but he would like to have a meeting personally about next November with Omda Muhammad El Feki Suleiman, whom he knows as a friend.

Muhammad Fadlallah had put up two large black Arab booths—one for Newbold and one for Charles and myself (and three admirable "conveniences"), but had ruined the appearance of Newbold's booth by a horrible sort of triumphal arch over the entrance made of poles and frightful cheap cotton tartan cloth (Stuart I think). Newbold was adversely impressed.

After we had got rid of the dancing women and general crowd and greeted Muhd. Fadlallah's uncle Fadl El Mula warmly, we chatted till after an early supper. Then Muhd. Fadlallah and Feki Fadl El Mula came to talk over coffee.

Early bed and a good sleep but not long enough. We had agreed to stay all next day at Um Badr to allow Charles and myself doing some work with the Kawahla and their slaves and of Muhd. Fadlallah's holding a race-meeting in the afternoon of the 19th.

19.1.33

A really trying morning. Charles had a worse time than I did. The weather started coldish and then got hot.

There are various odd sheikhships and men of several Bara tribes—Beni Gerar, Hababin and Ferahna—watering with camels and cattle at Um Badr. Their sheikhs in Bara say these are failing to pay taxes. I had to arrest whatever men I could find and arrange to move these Arabs back into Bara District by means of police action. This is a horrid task anyway.

Charles had a number of cases, mostly between Kawahla and their slaves. Muhd. Fadlallah was slippery and annoying. His manners are deficient and his lying transparent. The business went on till after 2 p.m., and then I more or less drove the people from Charles's door so that they could have lunch. Charles had had to see 19 sheikhs one after another about arrears of taxes, and then all these petty and piddling cases. Complainants and people returned about 3.30 and we carried on again till 4.30 p.m. Then Muhammad Fadlallah arrived and said the races were ready. In fact, as we left the tents, the leaders of a long camel race he had sent off came over the sand hill to the east.

There were then four horse races—two about a mile long and the other two about six furlongs. They were quite good fun. The course had been arranged so that horses ran down hill towards us and one could see everything very well. There was a large crowd of Arabs watching. Several amusing incidents occurred—old men riding and so on—and there were some fearful purlers on the course, man and horse rolling over in the sand. I lent my binoculars, and so did Charles his, to one or two sheikhs who looked through them with much amusement and gratification. The races went on till near sunset. Sheikh Mardi Imam, the Shartai of Kaja Seruj, was here and at the races. His cattle are at present watering at Um Badr.

I have forgotten to mention that before lunch that fat and pursy Kahli, Abdallah Ali Abu Sheikha, of the Awlad Gadein (the man whose camp was accused of murdering several Hamar in 1931) came to see me and I sat under a tree with him. Newbold and Charles de Bunsen also came and sat with us. He started saying that the Kawahla did not want Muhd. Fadlallah but wanted to be under the Kababish. Now some twelve years ago the Awlad Gadein had made a great commotion and conspiracy against the ruling Kahli House—that of El Aeysir. We therefore said good-bye to Abu Sheikha and went to lunch without more ado.

I had arrested 11 men in all today, including a merchant who is trading without a licence and against my orders that he should move from Um Badr. Muhammad Fadlallah (who incidentally had been ordered by me to turn out most of these Bara tribes from Um Badr and had failed to do so) sent Ahmad Gismallah to me to ask to guarantee these people. I refused.

After sunset I told off four police to move the Bara tribesmen eastwards bag and baggage. These Arabs must be east of Mazrub within 15 days.

We discussed the shortcomings of Muhammad Fadlallah and of the Kawahla and then had an early dinner.

The evenings and nights are cold, although the afternoons have become rather warm. We made a fire as usual and then Muhammad Fadlallah and Mardi Imam arrived to talk. I had Mardi Imam sit next to me and questioned him about Kaja Seruj and about his family, ancestry and history. He said he is a Bedeiri but not of the same origin as Nadhif

Mukhawi and not of recent Dongola origin. He said that Kaja Seruj and the Kajas of Soderi District are one people and not of the same origin as the people of Abu Hadid, Um Durag and Haraza. Katul, he says, are of the same origin, and the name Kaja comes from a king (Mek) of Katul in former times, Kaja being the name of Katul mountain. He said that his own forebear had held headship over Katul and the Kajas. He was amusing about the "nouveau-venu" origin (in this government) of El Niama's authority in the Kajas of Soderi. He said that the people of Seruj have kujurs (magicians) as do those of Soderi. It might conceivably be a solution of the problem of succession to El Niama (provided El Mardi continues a good chief) to get the Kajas all united under him. He is "persona grata" with Ali El Tom.

We went to bed about 9.30.

20.1.33

Rode about 6.30. My saddle was askew and I stopped within a few yards to have it put right. This disturbed the good order of Muhammad Fadlallah's procession escorting us out, for Newbold waited for me. Then, when we had gone a little way, it appeared that the camel Newbold was riding was lame. Consequently he had to be changed onto a camel belonging to Ahmad Gismallah. Muhammad Fadlallah and his party took leave of us and said they would catch us up later. The morning was pleasantly cool and we rode until about 8.30 and up into the low hills at Qurun El Ajeimi. This is a pleasant place. After breakfast and a shave we all three climbed the highest hill in the neighbourhood. From the top Newbold took bearings on certain fixed points to discover where on the map Khor Es Sunt is. We stayed on top some time to admire the view. The country around looked extremely dry. To the west were the hills of Um Badr and the east the hill of Senagir. When we had descended the hill, we found Muhammad Fadlallah had caught us up. He wanted to go on to Khor Es Sunt and left us immediately. By now the day was hot. Had lunch and became very sleepy. Rode on about 3 p.m. and arrived Khor Es Sunt about 5.

We spent the evening as usual in talk, interrupted only by a visit from Muhd. Fadlallah after dinner. The following topics came up in the course of Newbold's talk: travel, Tennyson's "Ulysses", the sentiments of which he says he greatly admires, Herbert Hogarth as the scholar-traveller, Administration in the Sudan, Effendia and the attempt to make them continue to wear native dress. I left Charles and Newbold talking and went to bed.

21.1.33

Spent this morning at Khor Es Sunt. It was a very busy morning for Charles: but I had quite a slack time. Newbold had a long talk with Muhd.

Fadlallah and Charles with Ali El Nur, the Omda of that very small independent tribe the Dueih. Muhammad Fadlallah had Charles write for him the "permits" for certain Kawahla to take camels to sell in Egypt—45 days' journey from here.

I had a chat with Newbold about Muhammad Fadlallah. He was not so depressed about him as I had feared. He says he thinks he must be considered a bad Nazir, but not so bad as some people in El Obeid have made out. We must attempt to tutor him and in particular try to devise words to express to him that we want him to be less of a sycophant of the government. But can you make a man by nature insincere into something of worth? I don't know.

Newbold is much taken with Muhd. Fadlallah's uncle Muhammad Ahmad, as I was, and with Faki Fadl El Mula's son Ahmad, who runs the small Quran school here.

Left Khor Es Sunt about 3 p.m. Charles rode the Mamur's elephantine camel. The afternoon was hot and I had something of a headache. A pleasant ride. The country here is open. As you pass over the low hills of Zalat Um Khusus you get a good view.

We camped on fairly hard ground among sparse kittir bush where there was plenty of "bigheil" grass. Cloud to the west at sunset and a very beautifully coloured sky. The view after sunset towards Senagir hills was magnificent, but the colours, if reproduced in paint, would have been incredible.

I left the other two still talking about Native Courts at 9.30 and went to bed and to sleep. But I woke about 4 a.m. and could not get to sleep but watched the moon and stars and the first signs of a very magnificent dawn ("the dawn's left hand") and the servants waking and making tea round a bright fire.

22.1.33

Rode at 6.45. A very pleasant cool morning. Not too long a stage. Crossed the pass in Senagir hills (which are very high) and arrived in camp on the other side of the sand hill beyond the valley in which the wells are —8.45 a.m. The view here is of extreme beauty, to my mind. The hills just to the west are very steep and pink in colour. Trees, dark green, and saffron grass throw strong relief against each other. A Sheikh of the Ghazara Kawahla and an old man of the Awlad Barok came to talk after breakfast. However, they did not stay long. When I had shaved, I tried, without much success, a pencil sketch.

Lunch 1 p.m. Hamla left 2 p.m. No more easy going over flat ground but steep sand hills. We left Senagir about 3.15 p.m. and rode for $2\frac{3}{4}$ hours. The afternoon was exceedingly hot and, as we were heading east, we naturally had the sun on our backs. The going also was thoroughly bad over these very high sand hills. When we reached camp we found that the corporal in charge of the escort was not with us. He had fallen behind almost at the start of our ride. We spent some time drinking tea to slake our thirst, and the evening become pleasantly cool. No signs of the corporal, so the L/C with us—Fadl—lit large beacons and arranged to send a policeman in the morning with water to look for him.

Newbold talked till 9.30 and was extremely interesting. The talk was first of soldiering in the Yeomanry, and then of his campaign against the Senussi and of the capture of Jaafar Pasha[5] and of Newbold's subsequent experiences in hospital.

Slept only indifferently because I have contracted a tiresome habit of waking up at about 3.30 when the hamla moves and failing to sleep properly again. Also this morning "my reins chastened me" twice—cold work and prickly in the haskaneet.

23.1.33

Rode 6.15 a.m. Yesterday Newbold rode my camel; Charles, the Mamur's; and I, Charles's. This last is a bad camel. This morning I had all mounts changed because my camel had a sore fetlock. I got a more comfortable mount. The hamla had gone somewhat off the direction of Abu Ajaja about 8.45 to find the cars and also the corporal, who had lagged behind because he had trouble with Charles's deck chair, which he was carrying, and then had missed our camp and signal fires in the dark, owing to the high dunes, and so had slept alone and ridden on in the early morning.

Abu Ajaja means "place of dust" and is so called because the wells are in a depression, the soil of which is of lime. As a result, the herds coming to water powder the soil to a fine white dust, like that of a chalk lane in Sussex in a dry summer. If a wind blows, you cannot see for dust. Fortunately today was calm. We chatted to one or two men at the wells and watered our riding camels as we did so.

We dawdled over breakfast and a mail which the cars had brought to us. I found out that Newbold had got the O.B.E. in the New Year's Honours, which I had not heard of before, so offered congratulations.

Finally we left about 11.30, having written to Sheikh Ali El Tom thanking him for hospitality and the loan of his camels (and also sending their hire money). We had determined to visit Jebel Bakalai on our way to Soderi because there is a report of ancient villages and wells on its top.

---

[5] See Henderson, *The making*, 7; and E. E. Evans-Pritchard, *The Sanusi of Cyrenaica*, Oxford 1949, 125, 128.

We drove there without difficulty, and disturbed a herd of camels grazing at its foot. They were of the Awlad Agoi. Then after talking to a rudely-awakened herdsman, we made to ascend the hill. It rises about 500 feet out of the plain, very sheer at its southeast end and less so at the north-west, where there is a fairly gentle slope ending in a high sand dune. However, Charles and Newbold decided to climb near the southeast end, where we had fetched up in the cars. It was a stiff climb needing hands and feet and almost teeth about half of the way. I like rock-climbing but here not only were the rocks so hot they burned one's hands but there were thorny bushes which tore one's clothes and skin. Charles was first up and I next. When I reached the top, I felt I could easily have been sick. Newbold had given up and descended.

However, the view was magnificent. Also we examined the whole of the top of the hill and found nine big pits in the rock. About six of these had well-constructed stone walls round one side of them in a semi-circle. The walls were ramped with earth and small stones on the sides away from the pits. We found no pottery or stone instruments or weapons—only one single oryx horn.

I cannot of course tell, but it looks as if these holes were "gelti", i.e. hollows in the rocks which hold rain water and store it. There were walls, or rather the remains of their foundation, all over the southeast end of the jebel top: well-built, but they did not seem to be obviously ancient houses. These wells were built in square pattern, not round (as huts are built). Charles and I drank most of the water we had carried up. It was exceedingly hot, but at least there was a breeze on the summit. Then we descended by the easy route to the northwest.

When we reached the cars, we found Newbold half asleep on the ground in the shade. It was by then 3 p.m. and we had been away two hours. He provided for us a tin of pineapples and some biscuits as lunch. We felt that any man who will climb Everest deserves a V.C.

About 3.30 we started again for Soderi. There is of course no motor road here. I acted as guide. After we had gone round the hills at Seleya to avoid sand dunes the way became very easy and we bowled into Soderi about 4.30 p.m. I felt dead tired. It had been so hot. Much tea was needed to quench our thirst and then a bath and clean clothes made me feel better. . . .

24.1.33

Spent at Soderi. Newbold and Charles in office. I sorted a file and maps and little else. Niama came after dark and talked scandal.

Chapter XI

Dar Hamid

[Bara—Zirayqa—Nabalat—Humara—Abu Tinaytin—Umm Qirfa—Bara]

20.2.33

This was the ninth of nine of the most over-worked and tiresome days I have ever spent in the Sudan. Their tiresomeness was aggravated by depression in myself which was not the fault of Bara or of its litigious natives.

It was absolutely necessary to leave this evening, if I was to be certain of being at my rendezvous with Maclaren at Homara wells about 90 miles E. by N. of Bara on the 25th. I was busy till 11 p.m. on the night of the 19th and started again 7.15 a.m. on the 20th. I dealt with papers and giving out stores and arranging clothes for trek; and then back to the office at 12 noon. I had agreed with the Corporal Dardiri before I went to the office that, as I knew there would be difficulty in my getting away, the hamla should go off about 4.30 and I about sunset. The day was, thank goodness, cooler as there had been a northerly wind in the night. I was busy in the office from 12 till 3 p.m. The Province Qadi is here. I called on him and found him at noon-time prayer; and chatted for a very short time. The schoolmaster called on me and then blamed me for not visiting the school oftener. How the deuce can I? The Omda and Chief Merchant came about the appointment of agents, to whom we hope Oakley will allot stalls in the new zinc barn in the El Obeid Vegetable Market, put up recently to help Bara vegetable growers.

I talked to the Omda about a marriage case he had heard (contrary to the rules of his Court, since the Qadi had already heard the case and had not referred to the Bara Native Court—I had already pacified the Qadi) and about a case of a drunken brawl in which a friend of his—that swine Abdallah Yasin—was involved. . . . Then, while the hamla was loading, I had to hear on the verandah of my house a case of assault upon a lance-corporal of the police. My servants also complained that the watchman on my house, while I am on tour, will sleep on the canaba on the verandah and, as he chews tobacco, his spittle indelibly stains the wall of the house, the canaba (settee) and the tiles all round. I hadn't noticed this before; it looks very pretty—also rather "sick-making". . . .

Rode off at 5.45 on Rouse (the white horse) with Dardiri on Furnace (the brown one). All camels had been sent ahead. Rode half at a canter and half walking and talking, out eastwards from Bara by the road leading between the sagias and then the fields, which goes ultimately to Helba and El Dueim. . . . The vegetable season is in full blast and the onions about 2 inches high and smelling to heaven. . . .

Talked to Dardiri about Himeir Kurkab village, where an age-long row (which MacMichael, Reid, Hillard and de Bunsen all in turn tackled and wrote reams on) has broken out again. Unfortunately Charles de B.'s note on the action taken by him is not too clear: and I have been thereby misled. Dardiri says Charles *did* abolish most of the dues payable to the Awlad Seil by definitely taking away part of their lands, i.e. he applied (unconsciously no doubt) the principle of . . . each man's [having] as much as he can cultivate or tap gum on so as to upset the principle of the inalienable right of the Hamar to this bit of land on which MacMic, Reid, and Hillard had worked. Anyway, it don't matter much—the affair is twopenny, and they will have to raise the deuce of a yell before I'll go and see their rotten village.

Overtook the hamla encamped near Um Dabbus village at 7.10 p.m. The Sanitary Hakim who is with me came and paid respects. An El Obeid product temporarily on duty in Bara. A bit smooth and oily, I thought—may have been mere nervousness. To bed 8.30 p.m.

21.2.33

Rode 4.15 a.m. on Abu Zuman. Fairly warm night, cold towards dawn. Abu Zuman's pace is too much for these heavy police camels. I rode in front of the escort as soon as it got light because I got so tired of pulling his nose out of the backs of their saddles.

Ghastly country, like a nightmare, much worse than that between Bara and Kagmar. Almost flat, no hills in sight, large patches of worn-out and fallow cultivation looking like a war picture—burnt tree stumps and so on.

Arrived Zireiga, seat of the Gawamaa Omda Omar Mahmoud and site of one of the Gawamaa Native Courts, at 7.50. Must have covered about 17 miles. The Omda is away deciding a cultivation boundary about 12 miles south of here. Talked to his nephew.

The Medical Service, having for years made propaganda with injections of 606,[1] are now realising (1) what an expensive drug it is (2) that the people do all they can to obtain it as an aphrodisiac merely (3) (I think) that this injecting of a V.D. patient just once and then leaving him is a

---

[1] 606 : Arsphenamine, an antisyphilitic also used to combat bovine pleuro-pneumonia. (*The Merck Index*, para. 839.)

PLATE 9

S.A.D. 587/1/181

Kaja Saruj, 1907: (l.–r.) Ibrahim Fahayl; the 'old friends' Na'im Sirkatti and 'Ali al-Tum; and Harold MacMichael

PLATE 10

Marakh Wells

S.A.D. 587/1/195

PLATE 11

C. A. E. Lea   Author's photograph

PLATE 12

C. A. E. Lea Author's photograph

waste of money and bad medicine. Elliott has written me a letter complaining of the number of injections given free in Bara District, and requesting me always to give a certificate to the Sanitary Hakim when I recommend a poor person for a free injection. This is going to make more work. Why not take a really strong line and refuse 606 to all out-patients and not allow Assistant M.O.'s to take it on trek? These single injections are—as I have heard doctors say—absolutely useless towards curing the disease.

Left Zireiga about 3 p.m. riding Abu Zumam. Passed the old village of Zireiga (farther east). The country became a little less terrible and the sand dunes higher. Set down on the roadside about 6 p.m. Read *Arabian Nights*.

22.2.33
Poorish night. Woke as usual when hamla started at 2 a.m. and then felt very empty and took a long time to get to sleep again. Rode at 5 a.m. Passed Um Shieyba village at dawn. Abu Zumam has started to "brush", drawing blood on his heels. I rode on the horse Furnace. Abu Zumam must be rested.

Yesterday evening as amusing incident happened. As we were going up a long slope, the police saw a man on a camel a long way off driving two men or animals before him. They made out that he had a tripod and therefore thought he must be a policeman *or* a thief. We gave chase and it proved to be our own lance corporal going to ask for some milk for me from shepherds whose flocks were there. I talked to the shepherds, one of whom was carrying a new-born lamb dropped that day.

Also we keep passing and being passed by a band of "hoboes"—Nuba from Kaderu in the Nuba Mountains beyond Dilling, who say they are "walking to Omdurman to see a friend in the Engineer Troops there"....

By 8.10 on 22nd we reached Um Dam. Here there are three villages: the one where the merkaz was until 1919, another belonging to the Omda Jelli Adam; and a third belonging to Omda El Haj Ahmad Ferah. I got down in Jelli Adam's village. A cheerful bloke and pleasant-mannered. I have had to be very unpleasant to him on various occasions and was glad to be able to be his guest and just polite. A policeman arrived with my mail and a very gloomy mail too. I felt awful but had to chat to Jelli and Haj Ahmad Ferha before I could re-read the mail and write a large number of letters as a result of it to catch the post out of Bara on Thursday 23rd. Felt pretty awful. Difficult not to worry on trek—so much time to one's self.

Two aeroplanes (R.A.F.) went over us in the direction of Khartoum about 3 p.m.

Policeman left for Bara under orders to go all night and be there by noon on 23rd. Hope his camel manages it.

Rode at 3.45. Passed through a large village where the people were very perturbed because one of their two wells had fallen in. Camp at side of road about 6 p.m. Asked the doctor to tea. The fellow did not come until I sent for him and then talked in a rather foolish manner, working the conversation round to asking me to get the ambulance for him from El Obeid, when he is transferred there on our return to Bara, because his wife should have had a baby by then. He ought to put up that request to Elliott through the proper channels and not me. I'm sorry about his wife —he brought her to this district because he thought he was definitely transferred to Bara. I'm glad he is not. I think he is wet. I may be wrong. Very tired indeed. Couldn't face Muhammad's soup (which was bad—he's worried about his young son and is cooking badly). Slept exceedingly badly, in which I was assisted by a large herd of cows which passed with its herdsmen singing about 1 a.m. Also filled with the most gloomy forebodings—overtired generally.

23.2.33

Started 5 a.m., pretty cool morning—felt sick and would have liked to be sick. Passed Abu Shok village. Camp at 7.50 in a village full of bonfires which smelled abominably, and also the smoke of one of them blew right into the door of my hut. Tried to sleep and felt better for rest.

The Omda Osman Ali of the Maagla came to see me, having pursued me from Bara because he had paid off his omodia's arrears of Herd Tax and wanted the "mukaffa"[2] (i.e. the 10% of the tax which goes to sheikhs as pay for collecting it). He also had a case about one of his wives who had run away from him and about a sheikh whom he wanted changed. I talked to him also about the well he is for ever digging at El Gleit (on the road to Soderi) in the hope of finding water for his tribe. This heartbreaking task has been going on for years. His tribe has only one well and has to go to El Mazrub for water by kindness of Gumaa Sahal—a long way for the water caravans. I was glad to meet him because he is one of the Bara chiefs I had not yet met. Also he is one of the few with some pretensions of being a gentleman.

Rode on again about 3.30 p.m. I had decided with Dardiri that, as I was so tired, it would be best to make two long shidds of the next 30 miles to Homara rather than three, and so arrive earlier and have a good long day and night's rest before Maclaren was due. I rode Furnace, the brown horse, and left the escort far behind. The going was over sand and among

---

[2] Ar.:*mukafa'a*.

merkh trees, but fairly hard sand. Cantered a lot, but felt awfully tired. Finally reached a well at Nabalat village and greeted the folk there and got into the village just before sunset. I went to bed almost immediately but it wasn't a great success owing to sand flies and a drink party in the village which went on very late.

24.2.33

Rode at 4 a.m. feeling like death—on Abu Zuman, who had recovered from his "brushing" of the hind feet. Arrived at Homara about 7.45. The going becomes hard and sand ends some way before one reaches Homara. Consequently the nature of the country changes—kittir bush and different grasses. Also there are three nice little hills to the N.E. of Homara wells. The village is south of the wells near a pleasant wadi.

I arrived feeling absolutely exhausted and just greeted old Fish Face (the Omda Muhammad El Feki Suleiman, who is lord of this manor) and spent the rest of the day on my bed in my tent. It was hot and a hot gale blew and I got no sleep. But with the help of aspirin and Eno's and Bovril at 3.30 I felt better by 4 p.m. and shaved, bathed and had a long chat with Fish Face in the cool of the evening.

His face and manner are to me so comic that I can't keep my own face grave while I talk with him and I have to screw my mouth up, twist my moustaches, or look away while he is talking. Some Shueyhat of Helba over the border of the White Nile came and accused certain Awlad Oan Kababish of stealing sheep. It looks like a cert., especially as a sheikh of the Baghadda gave evidence of the accused's confessing. Fish Face and I continued chatting till evening prayer time.

After that I had some tea and wrote a letter and went to bed. Fish Face had been putting up "rakooba" houses of durra stalks for Maclaren to stay in at the end of the village. I had my bed carried right out into the open to avoid any repetition of last night's experiences. Fell asleep after long thinking (an unusual thought hitherto for me) how pleasant it would be to work in England rather than in Africa.

Was awakened in the middle of the night by a dog which bayed at me from a distance of 20 yards for about half an hour. Finally could stand it no more and drove the animal off to the home it belonged to, while I heard the woman of the home tell it to shut up, which, thank God, it did.

Slept again till 6.30 and awoke feeling as if my head would fall off any time and with a sore throat. Felt better however about 9 a.m.—it was effects of pink pills wearing off.

Inspected police camels. Fined Mustafa El Imam a day's pay for a sore back. Waited for Maclaren. Omda El Amin Bolad arrived—drank tea with him. Omda of Sheyhat [*sic*] of Helba arrived—drank tea with him.

He has a game leg and looks disgruntled. No Maclaren. So had breakfast and felt better. Inspected police rifles.

Maclaren and his wife arrived about 11 a.m. Had them into my tent while their servant unpacked, and talked. Mrs. Maclaren appeared a pleasant girl and quiet. She went off to rest and Mac came back and talked for a long time about Soderi and about N.A. Gave them lunch about 1.45. Opened tin of gooseberries.

My complaint is now clear, as I have a hacking cough. What I have been suffering from for the last three days is a chill on the tummy combined with over-tiredness. Felt better and ate all the lunch except the meat. After a rest I took the Maclarens at 4.15 for a ride to the wells. She rode my camel, El Feki; Maclaren, Rouse; and I, Furnace. Fish Face went with us on a donkey. We had a good look at the wells. There are some cows here with rinderpest. I ordered a quarantine and promised to send for the veterinary ghaffir, who is in the neighbourhood. There was fun with one of the sick cows which I sent a man to catch. He caught it by the tail and then it swung round a tree and so did he still on the tail.

We rode a little way further and then returned to the village at sunset. By the time we got to the wells, my voice had gone, and, by the time dinner came, I had no voice and could not eat but drank some hot toddy.

We, and especially I, talked a lot, mainly decrying the Sudan.

There followed for me a rather grim night. I had my bed put right outside the village so as to be away from noise. By about midnight I had the worst sore throat I have ever had, and felt like suffocating. As I was feverish, I decided to move into the tent. I went there via some sleeping camels and donkeys and woke Nur Ed Din to carry in my bed. We then went out with a candle and could not find it for about twenty minutes. Slept after that till morning.

26.2.33

Quite dumb. Breakfasted with the Maclarens. Maclaren and I then spent all the morning talking to sheikhs and dealing with cases. We had an interview with the four Omdas who were present—Fish Face, El Amin Bolad, Abdullahi Babikr, and Ismail Muhammad (this last from Helba in the White Nile). There were not very helpful in suggestions as to how to deal with theft. Only El Amin Bolad was very outspoken, saying that the Omdas themselves are the cause of the trouble—if they wished to clear up their own countryside they could do so.

After lunch I had a rest till 4 p.m. and then held a meeting in front of my tent. I wanted to try a theft case, but Mac. came over to talk about something, and the meeting became a general scream against thieves. The

Omdas abused one another in front of us—an unedifying spectacle. The talk went on till sunset.

Then Mac. and Mrs. Mac. and I went for a short walk and sat to talk. I noticed, after I had been talking rather more than usual, that Mac. was very silent and shortly made excuses to have a bath. He said he had a bad headache. When I returned from my bath, I found he had gone to bed and [I] had dinner with Mrs. Mac. alone and talked about their leave in Cornwall, to which county they propose to go, partly for his health's sake. . . .

27.2.33

Better night but still no voice. Gave the Maclarens breakfast at 7.30. Muhammad produced a poorish breakfast and appalling coffee. Mac. said he felt better.

They left at 8.10 and I settled down in one of the rakoobas vacated by them to a terrific morning's work. First I tried the case of sheep-stealing by the Awlad Sani of the Awlad Oan Kababish from the Shueyhat. Then more and more people arrived with more and more complaints. What little voice I had completely went and finally I became exhausted and sent them away about 2 p.m.

The sergeant left behind by Mac. took over his prisoners and Fadl El Mula Masoor, whom I had that morning sentenced for sheep-stealing, and left for El Dueim. Nafar Ibrahim Muhammad El Feki brought in the Awlad Abu Shura Hisseinat Kababish wanted in connexion with the missing thief, Wad Abu Nijeyjeel.

I rode about 3.30 and took leave of Fish-Face affectionately at his wells. It was a very hot day indeed and practically no wind. The going is very good and firm—the road could easily be motored. Direction N.W. Fairly thick bush. Found hamla about 6.15. Drank a lot of whisky and retired rather tight and full of hot whisky. Woke in the night and mused gloomily but the whisky did me good.

28.2.33

Rode before 5 a.m. and arrived Um Seyala about 8. Met in the cultivation near by (and it looked very good cultivation) by El Amin Bolad. He is a live wire, an outspoken little martinet with a sense of humour. I should think about as honest a man as is to be found in this twisty Sudan.

His house and the rest house he keeps next to it among large trees are built as low and long "kurnuks" of grass thatching, very pleasant to look at and to stay in. He had put down good carpets and had a large "canaba" sofa for me.

Chapter XI

After breakfast and a bath, I rode with him on Rouse (the Omda has a good black horse) to see the place where the market is held and the well and the old locust dump. The market is the usual square of grass booths. Hitherto market day has been Friday. Now we have decided to break up the market at Um Girfa, about 25 miles west, and remove the merchants to Um Seyala and hold the market there twice a week. The moving of these merchants is going to present problems, for they are a slippery folk. Um Girfa was a nest of theft and vice.

The well was crowded with people and animals. So many leather buckets down the well at once that the water comes up all sullied and brown. El Amin pointed out the place where he proposes to dig another well by the site of an old one which fell in and just west of the market place.

Had a look at the locust dump. Practically no bran left and what there is mostly useless, as white ants have eaten the sacks.

By now it was terribly hot. Rode back drenched with sweat. It is about 1½ miles from El Amin's house to the market and well. Had a rest and then he produced various complainants to see me. He brought also 3 Um Girfa merchants who said they had no objection to moving to Um Seyala, provided *all* merchants do so, as otherwise unfair competition would result. This sounded reasonable but, as I had not yet had time to consider the problem all round, I gave them no answer.

El Amin refuses to have the family of Dho El Beit El Ajab,[3] the Nubawi thief, in Um Seyala because they will not consent to reside by his house and be under surveillance. I therefore put the eldest son under arrest again to take him to Abu Tineitin to Muhammad Timsah . . . .

Another Nuba complained that Niama Sirkatti had killed his son. Watt had evidently dealt with this case. Told him I would enquire in Soderi. Gosh! it is an effort keeping calm with no voice in this heat.

Rode on [at] 3.30 having asked El Amin to come into Abu Tineitin to the Native Court next day.

He and his domain appear a sort of oasis of good order in all this welter of shouting complainants, thieves and Omdas and sheikhs, who run with the hare and hunt with the hounds, which constitutes Eastern Dar Hamid.

When I got to Um Deimin well, just outside Um Seyala, I found Muhammad Timsah and his brother Besheiri and a number of their followers. They had come on their way to meet me at Um Seyala and had found my hamla on the way to Abu Tineitin. They all appeared in very good form and said Nurab had arrived: Ali Musa, who is dealing with Gebra, Fadlallah Belal, and Ibrahim Feheil, who had pursued me from Bara about the Zeyadia murders.

---

[3] Ar.: Daw' al-Bayt . . . .

We soon came up with the hamla (still marching) and I arranged to stay the night in some fields which were there and come into Abu Tineitin early next morning. Muhammad Timsah and his company went on. Some women came and demanded the "custom", i.e. when women have a threshing floor in a field in this part of the world and a big chieftain comes and camps near their field, they expect him to give them alms as a rejoicing for the harvest. I gave them three piastres, which pleased them. Slept till fairly late.

1.3.33

Thank God, February is over. Hot morning. Reached Abu Tineitin about 7.30 with El Emin Bolad, who had come up in the night. Abu Tineitin is a fair-sized village. The Native Court House is to the north of it and the rest house just below it. Felt better this morning thanks to long sleep.

Had a long talk with Muhammad Timsah after breakfast about:

(1)(a) prevalence of theft in this part of the world, and the results of my meeting with Mac. I suggested that, as Yusef Habbani of the White Nile Native Administration is going to do a circuit again in May on his side of the border, Besheiri Timsah had better do likewise on his. (b) that only activity and change of heart on the part of these scallywag Omdas of Dar Hamid could effectively put down theft. This had been El Amin's speech at Homara; and so was my corollary suggestion his in origin, viz. that we should seal the Omdas all to a bond—a sort of Magna Carta to put down theft and do right. (I had asked El Amin if it would be any use swearing the Omdas and he said, "No. They'll swear to anything: take a bond of them.") (c) I said further that I would do my best to get Ali El Tom to send a really powerful agent here in the summer.

(2) Um Girfa Suk. Here we agreed that all merchants known to have frequented Um Girfa market should be listed, and all these and all in the neighbourhood of Um Seyala ordered to move to Um Seyala. If there were to be any exceptions they must be few, and they must be agreed to in mejlis by all chiefs concerned, e.g. the Nurab. We would collect Feki Osman, Mirghani Wad Aif, and El Amin Bolad and settle the business. I also suggested making an order that no trading should take place within an hour's camel-ride of Um Seyala unless it took place in the market itself.

(3) Gebra. I explained again that, as there were so many complaints about Gebra of theft and assault by Awlad Oan, I had agreed with Ali El Tom that all elements which Maarufiin Sobah El Kheir could not be responsible for must be removed from Gabra [*sic*]. Ali Musa had come to effect this and Muhammad Timsah should consult with him as to how it is

to be done. (Nothing will result of course, but, as I cannot get to Gebra at the moment, this is the best I can do.)

We then went to the Native Court and I sat for an hour. It did not impress me greatly—such a lot of shouting and the members and president did not seem to get a move on at all. Most Native Courts get through business pretty quick and rough and ready. Nearly everyone in this neighbourhood shouts till I am deaf and weak. The natives round here strike me as a foul crowd.

Returned to the rest house when I had heard the beginning of a case brought by a Lahawi from the White Nile about stolen nagas—which case I had brought for the court to inquire into, as it seemed to me that the Wakil/Omda of the Baghadda had taken no steps to try and find the thieves.

I then had a long talk with the three Nurab about the Zeyadia and about Gebra. Then people came in and shouted at one another and at me. Also I concluded the theft case of the Awlad Sani. About 3 p.m. I was tired out and sent everyone away and had lunch.

Then I composed a bond for the Omdas, as Muhammad Timsah's clerk was quite incapable of doing this alone. I had the clerk (Sirdar) write my draft out in Arabic at my dictation. Fuss and clamour went on till sunset.

I went to bed very early and much depressed by the state of things in general. This is a futile job.

2.3.33

One long forenoon and afternoon of clamour. I have never met such natives or such ridiculous complaints. No one will go straight to his Omda or Nazir and, when sent, many won't accept their judgement.

However, in spite (as I learned) of protests and great fear, all Omdas present thumbed my bond, which I explained carefully to them.

A rumour came that Maarufiin of Gabra was dead—since found to be false. I wish I had time to get to Gabra. I shall have to try to go in April. I wonder if Newbold would get me cars.

Also we fixed up about the merchants—in theory. I gave Beshuri two orders—one with a long list of merchants, all of whom must go to Um Seyala; the other about the one-hour limit. Ali Musa is to send to me at Um Girfa tomorrow two merchants from Gabra, of whom one is to be chosen to stay there. In future there will be no unofficial market at Shidera (Gebra). N.B. When I get back to Bara I must arrange for a strong patrol to go and carry out these orders. Nothing will be affected otherwise.

Shoutings and screamings—especially about the sheikhship of Um Kuhl village (Baghadda) went on till 3.30.

At 4 p.m. I rode. Very hot still. Rode till 6.15 when we found the hamla in fields. We had passed south of Fadliya and through villages of Awlad Himeir (Agoi) and were near Jebel Atmur. Had supper. Rode again 8 p.m. till 10.20 p.m. (on Rouse this time). Feki Osman and Ibrahim Feheil were with me and they chatted together all the way. Slept like a log in a patch of cultivation till 6 a.m.

N.B. on 1.3.33 Abderrahman (Hakim Sahha) arrived Abu Tineitin and I sent Muhd. Ibrahim back to Bara.

3.3.33

Rode 6.30 and arrived Um Girfa 7.30. A good thing, that moonlight ride. I feel much better for sleeping late. These early morning rides from 4 to 8 wear me out. Um Girfa has many trees and is pleasant. To the N.W. one can see the hills north of Kagmar—Atshan and Shuwaff (Rowyan) not far away.

Mail waiting for me. News not very encouraging. Letter from Newbold who seems to have liked my annual report.

Hot today; but a strong wind cools it a bit. Wrote for a while and then sent for the young Omda Mirghani Wad Aif and Feki Osman. They had collected one or two of the Nuba who reside at Um Girfa, are listed with the Nuba of the Northern Hills, and have failed to pay their taxes. There have been many orders and agreements in the past about Nubas at Um Girfa, the last one being in 1931. Some are listed with the Northern Hills and some with Wad Aif. Each time a new tax listing is made the trouble and complications crop up again over sons who have grown up and over intrigues by Niama Sirkatti and Wad Aif. Today I took it as an axiom that sons follow their fathers, and, if I find a father listed in the Northern Hills, his sons must be too and vice versa. That runagate Nuba Sheikh Muhammad Fadlallah turned up.

Feki Osman had also collected various persons wanted by Um Ruaba in a camel theft case of (so it seemed to me) some complexity.

I had the usual string of shouting complainants. Also merchants about Um Seyala market. I am not at all sure that what I am doing in the matter of ordering merchants to move to Um Seyala is legal. I am sure that it is a good thing, and I must discuss it with Newbold and see if I can get his sanction before I do anything more.

Very hot afternoon. Mirghani arrested a suspected thief. My roll of prisoners is now 14.

The cows coming home in the evening raised a dust which tickled my throat up and I had a fearful fit of coughing. However, I soon read myself sleepy and slept well.

4.3.33

Rode at 6 a.m. Feki Osman and Mirghani Wad Aif saw me on my way for quite an hour's ride to the first village of Meramra. I then rode with Ibrahim El Feheil (Nunky) who was quite chatty most of the way. Arrived Dakhla village (Meramra) about 8 a.m. Quite a comparatively cool morning with a pleasant breeze—sky overcast with dust. It remained fairly cool all day.

The sheikh of this village (Meramra) had been concerned in a lawsuit, the hearing of which at Abu Tineitin I had listened to. The woman who was the defendant in it (a good-looking piece, but an awful little termagant) tried to appeal to me, but I refused.

I spent the morning reading and feeling rather weary. About 1 p.m. the villagers started to make a dance. I left them for about a quarter of an hour and then went and thanked them and asked them to stop till I should be about to leave. Various men had various complaints. The dance started again, so this time I sent and stopped it a little more peremptorily.

Had a talk with Ibrahim Feheil, who condemned the immodesty of the women of these parts and their drinking of too much tea.

A messenger came from Omda Abdel Majid Hamid (who hates me like hell and so do I him) to say he is ill. I arranged to send the doctor to him.

Ibrahim Feheil says that the people in Bara are afraid of me and that he and the other Nurab there had said they were my friends and liked me well and that the fault must be with the people of Bara. It is true I dislike the Bara folk and have not been too easy and cheerful with them since my transfer, but then it has been such a wretched time—tax arrears and so on, and general economic depression.

Rode about 4 to 6.30. Ordinary goz and merkh bush country—some fine haraz[4] trees. A high wind from the north got up and the sky became overcast and it was cold. Talked to Ibrahim Feheil about Ali Wad Belal. It appears he still refuses to go to Hamrat Esh Sheikh. Ali Belal is running up bills with merchants.

Camp 6.30. High wind and dust. Cool night. Coughed a lot and couldn't get to sleep. As soon as I did it seemed to be time to get up.

5.3.33

Cool, almost cold, morning. Sky overcast with dust. Rode Furnace. Passed Jebel Meleisa. Arrived Omda Salih Hakir's village about 7.30. On the road Ibrahim Feheil had been in great form keeping the police laughing with stories of his experiences in the Mahdia.

---

[4] *Acacia albida.* BM, 172.

Points for action on return:
(1) Eastern Dar Hamid and theft and the problem of the Kababish thieves in that part.
(2) Um Seyala market.
(3) Gabra.
(4) My next tours.
(5) Telegraph Bolton re (a) El Amin Akkam, (b) Yahya (c) Case involving Tigani Aif.
(6) Go through cases and papers of all prisoners now with me and see that they are in order.
(7) Herd Tax of the men at Dakhla—see diary.
(8) Nuba at Um Girfa—what to do about them.
(9) Zeyadia murder case.
(10) Government Experimental Convoy dates . . . .

6.3.33
Arrived Bara (on Abu Zumam) at 7 a.m. Found Maxwell-Darling, the locust-hunter, here. Also telegram from Elliott the doctor that he and a parson called Guiness would arrive 8.30. They got here early and found me shaving. Gave them breakfast.
Bara as usual.

Chapter XII

"The Biggest *Shaykh* in the Sudan"

3.6.33

I left Soderi at 4 p.m. on the afternoon of 31.5.33. The day had been slightly cooler than those just past owing to dust in the air which overcast the sky. I was set on my way by the Mamur and the usual merkaz staff and local notables. Probably my last view of Soderi. The journey to Hamrat Esh Sheikh was along a road which I have travelled many times and was uneventful. A cold I had caught in the night of 30–31st May developed, and the doctor, who was travelling with me produced mentholatum and a medicine which rapidly got it under control. The weather became terribly hot again. My camel stumbled and fell with me at one place, without damage. At Um Khirwa I talked to Naieem Fereih and left a freed slave woman for settlement by Belila, the slave agent of the Kababish. At Abu Zaima it was so hot that I just lay and panted all day and did not even go round the wells to chat to the Arabs. We paused that evening for dinner in the middle of the hills near Adhat El Gawad and there was a very fine sunset. I tried to photograph the camp and the hills in the evening light. A couple of caravans passed us going west. We rode again from 8 till 10, and then, after chasing and killing a persistent camel fly, I got to sleep . . .

Rose at 4.30 and reached Ali El Tom's ferik at 7.30. The country all the way is bone dry and lacks grass. Just near Hamrat Esh Sheikh rain has evidently fallen, for shoots of green grass and of leaves on the trees are appearing. The news is that rain fell west and made a pool at Um Hatob which the herds have just drunk up after a fortnight.

I arrived pretty tired, but revived after a bath. Beautiful water, clear and cold here—a great contrast to the filthy stuff at Soderi.

Long session with Sheikh Ali 9.30 to 1.30. The talk came round to the Kababish in the east and then to what to do to control them, and I went on to obey instructions and "create an atmosphere" that government wants Ali El Tom to have powers of imprisonment. I attacked it (1) from the point of view of neighbouring tribes who have become big Native Administrations and whose tribal spirit has thereby increased. It is necessary to the Kababish way of life to be on good terms with them, yet the heads of these tribes see the Kababish out of control and by questioning find that Sheikh Ali's legal powers are very small compared with their own and draw the conclusion that he does not or cannot control his tribesmen. Also they wonder whether there is one policy and law for their tribes and another for the Kababish—this increases envy and malice. (2) From the point of view of his own personal honour—he is called the biggest sheikh in the Sudan, yet surrounding sheikhs lesser than he have bigger legal powers. (3) From the point of view of the future of his tribe and of his sons holding the chiefship after he is gone. The Kababish, and especially the Kababish in the east, are bound to become more sophisticated. Sheikh Ali runs them by means which are, we hope, just, but are not legal. We wink at this. His tribesmen do not complain. If they did complain it would be exceedingly embarrassing. Very likely they won't complain so long as he, who built up the tribe and is adored by them, remains. But it will be a different matter when his son succeeds and the old men (who knew the woes of the Mahdia and war, and compare these with the blessings Sheikh Ali's rule has brought) are gone.

He listened to all I had to say and then said that he realised that the government had put Omodias together and Nizaras together all round Dar El Kababish . . . until there had been built up large Native Administrations with Courts and so on. He did not want a state of affairs to arise whereby the Kababish would be on one line and the other tribes on another . . . . For he realised that this would cause envy and unfavourable comment and comparisons. But the Kababish were in fact not as these other surrounding sedentary tribes. The Kababish were nomad Arabs whose only desire was grass for their camels and markets in which to buy grain. I pointed out that these two very things inevitably brought them into contact with other tribes. He said that he would willingly accept whatever the government wished. I tried to point out that it was not so much a question of that as of trying to regularise what he actually does now. If he would come into the open and say what he wants, an agreement could easily be arrived at.

But my speech was interrupted first by the arrival of El Tom and then by that of a big dust devil which covered us in filth and took the top coverings off the Arab tent in which we were.

He talked also of the Zeyadia troubles, but I, while listening, reserved my observations on this.

He went at 1.30 and I lay outside in shade and a fitful hot breeze and flies, panting till 3.15 when I called for lunch and ate a little of it. Tingle came and we discussed the route via the Heitan to Anyoro and plans for the march (as much as possible by night) and for water economy (three waterless days' march).

Ali El Tom returned at 4.30. Slave case. Queer story of the Ma'alawi who is searching for a lost and sold Dinka girl and got separated from the police and arrested by the Awlad Tareef (who are suspected of having bought the girl) as a suspected thief. I think (1) the police have either been bribed or been negligent (2) Ali El Tom has properly put it across us—not my fault as I arrived too late to prevent this.

Ali El Tom also started his old game of playing the innocent fool about licenced rifles and Native Administration rifles. I am quite good at this game and usually return him to baulk.

Took down the Ma'alawi's statement after sunset. All very fishy. Had another bath to remove sweat and the effects of the dust devil. Dined. Ali El Tom did not return, and so to bed. Ali El Tom has a wretched cold.

4.6.33

Wrote till 10 p.m. on the 3rd. and then slept well till 6 a.m. Very still night. Inspected rifles of the police at 7 a.m.

Kawahla—Muhammad Ahmad El Aeysir and Muhammad Jangai—who are going with me to Mellit, and Haj Meheimid, came. Haj Meheimid is still on the job about the naga which he says a Shenbali has. The Haj is the richest man in the Kawahla—extraordinary how he fusses about one naga of all his hundreds.

Liver for breakfast. Felt much better today.

Long session with Ali El Tom from 8.30 till 1 p.m. A fair amount of business done. Took the opportunity of pointing out, with reference to one case, what a lot of trouble his lack of control of the east of his dar causes.

He says he has a case on with the Nurab slaves who are accused of stealing one of his camels. He says he burned down all their huts the other day and now proposes searching out the thief. Rough methods. I hoped that it would not lead to a large number of demands for removal from the dar and freedom.

He proposes to take three enormous water-skins (cow skins) on this trip, giving the third to be put under guard of my police, as he says they are more careful about water than the Arabs.

Had lunch and slept till 3.30. Wrote various notes for Akib. Went for a walk and observed how terribly burnt-up everything looks now compared with what it did in January or even March. Not a leaf nor blade of grass on all the hill sides. Much cooler today: quite a pleasant breeze—not yesterday's simoon. El Tom came while I was having my tea and we dealt with one or two minor matters. I have looked at the police camels. After dark, Muhammad Effendi and Hasan Nagila, the schoolmaster, came and chatted, mainly about the Arab view of what is pleasant and beautiful.

Bath, food and letters till bed.

5.6.33

Hot night till early morning then cold. Bilal Abdallah, sheikh of Awlad Tareef, accused of buying a slave girl, arrived about 7 a.m.

I went at 7 to see the school. The Arab camp is very well-built this summer. I noticed, passing through it, that they had found plenty of mahareib grass.[1] The school appeared to be doing quite well. I looked at the exercise books and made a list of names of the small boys there— about 24. I heard them on history and geography. They seem pretty well up in the history of their tribe and also the master is teaching them tribal songs. Geography is (and should be) of the simplest local places and how to find your way, and the elements of mapping. We made a map on the sand. They wanted races for sweets at the end, which I let them have. Spoke to the master, impressing the need of ensuring that they understand the stories they read and write as dictation. Returned to breakfast about 9.30.

Long talk with Sheikh Ali. After much talk he agreed that the government, in its relations and policy towards the many tribes of the Sudan, is like a house of one design with many different rooms. The design of each room is different, but they fit into the design of the whole. If the Kababish remain outside the scheme of the whole they will be like a separate house and their close understanding and relations with the govt. and other tribes will be broken. The Kababish wish to remain nomads and retain their traditions and conditions, but they cannot live within a ring fence. They need grass and grain from the lands of other tribes. If they remain outside the scheme of policy for all other tribes they are bound to become regarded as outsiders. The outsider is not regarded as any easy person to understand and be friendly with. Government wants Sheikh Ali to come under the Native Administration scheme:

(1) Because, while he has an administration of his own which close observers, such as his D.C.s, can see works, yet those not in close touch cannot realise. Govt. wants his position regularised so that all can know and understand how he runs his tribe, especially high govt. officials and neighbouring N.A. chiefs.

(2) Change must come. He cannot keep out change because he must have contact with the outside world through traders and officials. He himself has shown he realises this by asking for a school for his sons so that they may have knowledge to protect themselves and the tribe from what is upsetting in change. Outside influences are bound to make his tribesmen more sophisticated—they are already becoming so in the east, and I could point an object lesson in the Awlad Oan rapscallions I had

---

[1] *Cymbopogon proximus*. IT, 19.

brought to Hamra and who addressed him as Sa'adat El Bey[2] and wanted to know what charges there were against them and so on. As tribesmen become more sophisticated they will become vocal and not mutely submissive to irregularities and illegalities in his patriarchal autocratic system of administering his tribe. Some day some of them would complain in Khartoum and, if he had not the law on his side by having his powers regularised and brought up to date, it would mean trouble for him.

(3) The situation outlined above might not become acute in his day, especially as he was the hero of his tribe, who had raised it from poverty at the end of the Mahdia to power and wealth now. But it would surely become acute when his son El Tom succeeded. El Tom is a good man but he is the son of a hero. There is a difference between Odysseus and his son: between the warrior who established the state and the successor who must maintain it in peace.

(4) There is acute need for him to have more power and to delegate that power to control the distant eastern units of his tribe. This power must include imprisonment.

(5) The government considers he is the biggest sheikh in the Sudan and [it] has shown that by making him a K.B.E. It is difficult for neighbouring chiefs to understand that they are lesser men while they can imprison and fine and hold wide powers, while he in strict legality can only fine to £E25.

He said that he realised that this hanging behind . . . of the Kababish from the general scheme would in the long run do them no good. He wished to come into it and wished me to report all our conversation to Newbold.

I said that I had a note from Hamilton written at Abu Zaima about 3 years ago from which it appeared that Sheikh Ali, when first the N.A. schemes had started and he had not been given new powers but had been left outside it, had been puzzled and wondered if his honour and position were affected; and later had come to the conclusion that these Mahakim[3] were not suited to the nature of his tribal system.

But the government's own N.A. scheme had widened much since then. A new law last year had widened the basis of the policy and made the scheme much more elastic so that he need not fear that his system would be distorted to fit in with the govt.'s policy if he asked now to be included in the general picture. His system as it stood could probably be now included without alteration, or only slight alteration, but he would have to explain his system definitely and clearly. I would return to this subject again because, although he might accept in principle, the details of the actual agreement would need much working out.

---

[2] The title of a *pasha* or other high official: "His Grace the Bey".
[3] Courts; sing.: *mahkama*.

He said that I was going, but, as I was becoming a school inspector, I should still have a "leg in his camp" so long as a school was there, and I must not forget him but assist him in Khartoum.

He then began to talk on the Zeyadia, which I turned aside, saying that I had much to say on that, but had reserved it all for our journey.

Dealt with the Awlad Oan, serfs, and a merchant's debts.

Hasan Nagila came and brought me copies of a number of very good Kababish songs he had collected and these he explained to me. Haj Meheimid came again about his perishing naga. Wrote a facetious note for him to show to Charles later.

A gale had been blowing a duststorm all the morning and everything was covered thick and hands and eyes and face all muddied. The cook could not light a fire. Lunched off Bovril and figs and completed the mail. Hamla left at 3 and then pretended sleep. Rode at 4.35, direction 292°.
Camp No. 1 at 6.30   (Dirrat Bajjar   278°) [sic]
                    (Top of Kajkoj   12°) [sic]
This makes it look as if these are too far north as placed on map. Pace about 4 m.p.h.

We were seen off by a vast crowd with drums and singing and dancing and were accompanied by a large crowd on horses and camels some way. The going was good over hard sand dunes, Wadi Sadaf to the north below the rise over which we rode. Passed Sh. Ali's hamla of heavy water skins: one vast camel with two enormous skins on it towed by a small black slave on a small white camel. Like a tug towing a tanker. Sheikh Ali has a terrible cough. Wind dropped a good deal after sunset.

6.6.33

Hamla left at 1 a.m. I was awakened at 2.30 and rode at 3.10 a.m. direction 278 approx. Bright moonlight till the moon set about 3.45 a.m. The night was balmy. The ground was not too easy going—khors and screes of stone. At 4.30 a.m. it was getting light and we stopped for the dawn prayer. I found that the east end of Dirrat Bujjar hill was at 348° and quite near, say 2 miles. Went on over good hard sand through rolling country with fairly thick bush. On our right the hills of the Heitan rose. They are a curious broken line of ridges rather like a sort of great wall broken in parts. At 7.10 overtook the hamla and made camp in thick bush. I climbed a neighbouring tor of black stones and found east end of Dirrat Bujjar 75° and En Nueiga hill 235°. Very hungry. Breakfast and read and sleep till 11 and rest till 12. I find the book of G. K. Chesterton's essays which Jumbo Leicester lent me very entertaining.

It is depressing to think that this small trip is probably the last time I shall experience even the ghost of an adventure or the pleasure of going where few whites or none have gone before. It is a pity not to be able to grow out of that childish desire to see what is round the corner or over the next hill.

High wind again since 8 a.m. and fairly hot. Hamla went on at 2 p.m. Sheikh Ali then came to talk to me where I sat under a tree. He came almost immediately to the point of the relations between the Kababish and Darfur: said that of course I must have talked with the Governors about the question, and asked me to give him either the government's view or, failing that, my own. I said that I would return to the subject again and was now talking without the book. But in the main the government's views were as follows: Good relations between the Kababish and the Darfur tribes were important to the government so long as the Kababish did, and were allowed to, graze across Darfur. He himself had admitted that he was . . . [greedy]—for grass from the Zeyadia. Good relations had from time to time since the reoccupation of Darfur been broken. The government, judging from the records of these cases which it possesses, was of the opinion that, on the whole, the Kababish had been more to blame in these troubles between themselves and Darfur than the Darfur tribes. As to the present situation between the Kababish and the Zeyadia there was:

(a) The case of the alleged killing of Fadl El Mula Belila. He could hardly blame the government over this case or the Zeyadia. Mr. Gillan and I had explained to him carefully in April 1932 that the charge of murder against Rejeb, the Zeyadi slave, was extremely doubtful, and Gillan had given him the choice of taking his chance with a government court or with a Mejlis Ahli.[4] He had chosen the latter and it seemed to me that the Kababish had behaved tactlessly at it.

(b) The killings of two Zeyadia at Teiga this year. In this case there were 3 aspects from the government's point of view: (i) The killings. Government had tried the case by Major Court and had hung one Kabbashi and imprisoned another for a long term. The government was of opinion that the Kababish were definitely the aggressors in this case and to blame for the occurrence. However, so far as the crime was concerned, the government had taken its pound of flesh and would be favourable to any agreement which the two tribes might come to in order to "cool the blood" and restore peace. (ii) Abuse of arms given to Sheikh Ali for "haras"[5] purposes. The evidence showed that the killings had been committed by at least one of the government Remingtons on Sheikh Ali's N.A. permit. The other rifle was said to be a .303 and had not been

---

[4] Native council.
[5] Defence.

produced. These rifles had been given to Sheikh Ali with ammunition on his personal responsibility that they would be properly used. Khamis and Kurru had used at least one of them for first hunting contrary to the Game Laws, and second, murder. Government took a very serious view of arms and their use by natives, and govt. proposed to take away from him some of the rifles he now has on N.A. permit as a sign of displeasure and as a punishment. (iii) Breaking of the Game Laws. This, government did not take so seriously. In Northern Kordofan we do not make a fuss if an Arab kills an occasional gazelle. But govt. considered that it was definitely a "bad thing" when large hunting parties go out to kill numbers of gazelle outside their own dar.

Finally, I knew that government did not wish to exclude the Kababish from Darfur, but it would probably insist on excluding the Kababish from Teiga. I did not think Sheikh Ali would find the Zeyadia so difficult about Fadl El Mula's case as they were last September.

Sheikh Ali, expressing general willingness to submit [to] whatever government demanded, protested at length against: (i) The blame in general being placed upon the Kababish. He took the line that, when the Kababish do even a small thing, outside tribes and chiefs magnify it and the government takes it at their valuation and lays all the blame on the Kababish. In the present case: every tribe has bad or hasty men, in any tribe an unfortunate incident such as that at Teiga might occur. He had immediately investigated the complaint, traced the culprits through the name of Kurru, and sent them to government confessing. If there had been denial or concealment on the part of the Kababish, he would have admitted that they ought to be blamed. But here he did not consider blame lay. I have heard this line both on the general and the particular before. I do not sympathise with him in the general but secretly I do somewhat in the particular Teiga case. However, I refused to accept his arguments. A tribe is a tribe and must accept responsibility for its members and their actions.

(ii) He protested more strongly and at length about the threat to remove Remingtons. He said he had warned Kababish to whom he had issued Remingtons that they must be used only for haras purposes. How could he help it if men abused them without his knowledge or authority, far from him? If government made a public example of the Kababish because two of its tribesmen erred, it would be serious and would greatly lower the tribe's prestige before its neighbours. If a man in Bara stabbed another, did I hold all Bara responsible and call upon them for exemplary punishment? I said, "No, the men of Bara are not a tribe. You cannot have it both ways. Either you are, as you have always said, a tribe and Arabs of The Arabs [sic], in which case you must accept responsibility tribally, or you are townsfolk or de-tribalised folk, and, in that case, government will administer you with "tafteesh" and "tarteeb"[6] and "police" and so on.

As to the particular matter of arms, I consider he would be most ill-advised to make an uproar. Since 1928 government's policy regarding arms had been very "hot" indeed. He had cause to be very grateful to govt. since he had been trusted in the matter throughout and his tribe had had no "tafteesh" I knew of one case, the Rashaida in Kassala, where the govt. had ransacked the Arabs' tents with troops. (I omitted to tell him—and must do so—that this is the first case, so far as I know, where a Nazir's N.A. firearms have been abused to commit murder or any other crime of violence.)

The argument than ceased as my camel arrived. Rode at 3.50 p.m., direction 303°. We rode with the Heitan on our right looking more like walls than ever. We were quite close to them. A hot simoon blew all the afternoon and the sun ahead tried my eyes.

We got down at 6.30 and I rather collapsed. I had a dreadful thirst and could not quench it. Every time I drank (tea tried first, then whisky) I felt dreadfully sick. Finally I went into the bush and tried to be sick and failed. So I countermanded dinner and went to sleep—stomach full of dirty water but still thirsty. The water is very foul, unlike the water I had in Ali El Tom's ferik. They say the day we started a large number of camels had been watered and dust had blown down the wells. But I think there is also tar off the "delu" (buckets) and the water skins in it, for the water is the colour of tea.

An evening like this makes me despair and long never to see the Sudan again.

7.6.33

Awakened at 2.30 and had a tin of apricots and a cup of cocoa. Felt better. Rode 3.10 a.m. [At] 3.35 a.m. crossed Wadi Hamoora—deep and almost precipitous sides. This runs from the Heitan to Abu Bessama Fula. Rode away from the S. end of the Heitan over rolling gozes. [At] 7 a.m. came up to the hamla by Gereywit es Singit and passed hamla. Got down under trees below small kopje at 7.30. Sheikh Ali insisted on my taking the only large tree in the neighbourhood and on giving me his "barda" (saddle pad) to lie on. I fell asleep as the police were putting up my tent.

Breakfast and then slept from 9 till 12.40. I then broke my own rules and sent for water to wash in, as I was so covered in salt from dried sweat

---

[6] *Taftish*: supervision, inspection, investigation; *tartib*: organisation, order.

that I wished to reduce my thirst. High simoon blew all the morning and it was very hot.

Hamla left at 2 p.m. Tingle and I then climbed the kopje to see if there was anything on which I could take a bearing. There ought to have been one or two hills but the dust fog was so thick that they were invisible . . . .

At 5 p.m. we came over the top of a goz and saw an enormous goz before us and beyond it the jebels . . . . We finally climbed over a lower goz, up the high goz and camped just beyond the ridge of it. Slaked my thirst very carefully this evening. The thirst wasn't so bad anyway as there had been no wind all the afternoon and the dust slightly obscured the sun. Tingle, moreover, said that there was plenty of water and suggested that I wash. I therefore relieved much of my thirst by washing arms and legs before I started tea-drinking. Tingle says we may reach Anyoro wells tomorrow morning. I hope we do as I am becoming very done from heat and this turning of night into day.

8.6.33

Could not get to sleep until 10.45 after I had taken a pink pill. Rose 2.30 very sleepy. Full moon still well up in the sky. Rode 3.25, straight ahead on former line. It seemed as if this shidd would never come to an end. The high hills of Meidob appeared very dimly seen through the dust on our right front. The place has much more the air of Exmoor or Dartmoor all dried up than anything in Soderi district. Low ridges of hills like cliffs along the Devonshire coast come first, and behind are piled up real high mountains.

We saw at the time of the dawn prayer some gazelles and Ali El Tom asked me whether, supposing they saw more, they might shoot. I said, "Yes"—entirely illegal of course but I know they are short of meat and so am I. Soon we saw more gazelle and Ali Muhammad El Tom took Sheikh Ali El Tom's rifle and tripod and went hunting. He shot one but wounded it and went in pursuit. Later, after we had gone on, we heard him shoot again—also the wounded gazelle came our way and was caught and slain. "Gralloched" is, I believe, the *Tatler and Field* word. I'm not partial to this hunting at all. I don't mind shooting for meat (as we were doing) when hard up, but I prefer it done by an expert shot. I myself wounded one or two (as well as killed some out right) when I was a "snotty" and don't want to do any more. But all this is in the Arab blood.

Arrived at camp in the wadi running down from Anyoro at 8.15 a.m. Personally I was dead tired. Plenty of large trees in the wadi. Hills rose to the N.E. and N. and a high goz to the S.W. There was nothing to eat, but that did not matter as I was too tired and thirsty to have eaten, so I had some coffee and then slept till noon and read and dozed. At 2.30 I called for a bath—removed three days' beard and bathed and put on clean clothes and lunched. I had intended to go to the well when the camels went to water, but Tingle said they proposed to stay on the water till midnight and also I found myself too tired to walk. I fell asleep at 4.00 p.m. About 4.45 I went for a walk up the wadi, which is in a broad open valley leading N.W. to the hills. I saw some small Meidob boys at play and on my way back passed a group of huts. The Meidob huts appear very primitive indeed: merely logs piled together into a rough wigwam and covered with brushwood and grass. The door openings always face west, for what reason I do not know. As I passed his bivouac, Sheikh Ali came out and made me come and sit and talk and drink tea. He had a large number of his cousins and uncles sitting round and also two Kawahla who are with us. The talk ran on the battle of Omdurman and on the re-occupation of Darfur also. I left just before sunset.

I had come to the conclusion that it was essential for me both to have a good meal and also a long sleep. I therefore sat and drank 3 whiskys in the rising wind and then ate a dinner of gazelle meat and a tin of fruit and went to bed much happier and rather tipsy. At 10.20 p.m. I was awakened by a violent huboob and dust storm from the N.E. I thought perhaps rain would follow and so moved my bed inside my tent. I fell asleep with the duststorm still going on. No rain came and I awoke about 6.30 with everything completely filthy and my eyes and nose choked with dust and mud. It was still blowing.

9.6.33

Got up about 7.30 and made a slow business of getting clean and having breakfast. Felt better for my sleep.

Sheikh Ali El Tom arrived about 10 a.m. I said I had thought of going to see the well, but Tingle, summoned, said the camel-men had reported the distance $2\frac{1}{2}$ hours.

Sheikh Ali sat and talked till 1 p.m. Apart from mere conversation on Arab likes and dislikes and the origin of the English race, he talked, led on by me, about the "new sulta",[7] i.e. government's N.A. scheme. He appeared to think that, if he accepted a "new sulta", he would have to write down and treat as a "case" every small fault which occurred even in his own household and among the Awlad Fadlallah. This would put him in the wrong with them. On the other hand, if he let them off and yet dealt with all other Kababish, the latter would see the injustice of it. I asked him to explain further. He then said he would frankly explain his methods. Frequently when fights occurred, and the like, he would find an offender

---

[7] Literally, power.

was a poor man and he would let him off or make a peace ("sulh") or perhaps take the man and make him draw water and hew wood (slavish occupations) for a while. He was afraid that, if he took a "new sulta", he would have to "hukm" everyone who erred with fine or imprisonment . . . .

I let him go on and then took him up . . . . I said that all he had explained about his way of doing justice was acceptable to government. And the government wanted nothing better than to leave the Kababish to be dealt with according to their customary justice. If he pardoned people who committed offences within the tribe because they were poor and so on, the government would not object so long as his methods kept crime down and the tribe contented. But if Kababish committed crimes against foreigners, i.e. men of other tribes, then a punishment must be inflicted, and, if the man had no wealth to pay a fine and his people would not make the damage or blood good to the complainant, the offender must go to prison. He said he agreed with that, as otherwise it would make bad blood between the Kababish and other tribes.

I went on to say that the government's own scheme of these "sultas" had altered and widened since first it began, so that now it could embrace many tribal customs and practices which formerly it could not. I did not think the government would insist on violent or great changes in his methods. It did not want to make him into anything different—a "sultan tarabeza"[8] and so on—and it realised that methods and schemes of N.A. suitable to, say, Hamar would not be suitable to the Kababish. I thought the govt. would have to insist on his writing down his judgments. That was necessary as a protection to him. I did not fear that people would complain of his judgments any more than they did now. But I am afraid, and every D.C. Dar El Kababish must be afraid, for the future. The Kababish were becoming more sophisticated. Sheikh Ali cannot do all the work himself. The agents who went from him now "hukm" and we all know it. Their "ahkam"[9] were entirely illegal and it was only a matter of time before some sophisticated Kabbashi complained. The danger might not be great now while Sh. Ali was strong and here, and while he had powerful friends like MacMichael in the government high up. But MacMichael would go soon and, if anything happened to Sh. Ali, the position would be extremely difficult for El Tom. The government must insist (1) on his regularising his position and the administration of his tribe (2) on his increasing his power to deal with offences affecting men on other tribes.

The matter was just the same and just as serious as regards the money "awaid". We all knew these existed, and nobody complained, so we

---

[8] Literally, a "table-sultan".
[9] Judgements; sing.: *hukm*.

winked at them. But, if the Kababish in the east, say, became sophisticated and complained, a very awkward situation would arise. From what I heard as I travelled around, I was pretty sure that, while the Kababish did not refuse what the Sheikh "ate", they objected to what the Nurab took. If such complaints arose now there would be "mulama".[10] Sheikh Ali's good name would suffer and neighbours would point at him, possibly he would be fined. But, in view of his services and length of service, no doubt the govt. would find excuses for him. But if he had died and El Tom taken over it would be much more difficult for government to make excuses, and misfortune would result. And I thought that, if he died and El Tom took over, the danger of complaint and of a general complaint would be acute. From what I heard on all sides, he was known for generosity and his hand known to be light, but the Nurab and Awlad Fadlallah were known for rapacity and their hands were heavy. If El Tom were to take over, the tribe would say that the counsels of these rapacious uncles and cousins was bound to prevail and things would become worse (in fact the story of Solomon and his son).

By telling the story of my meeting a Hamar Shartai and discussing with him "awaid" of corn among the Hamar—how the Nazir had his "ood"[11] and the Shartai his "ood" and so on, and how this system was really not mere "eating" by Nazir and sheikhs, but a system of insurance against bad years, I showed him that govt. could understand there may be sound reasons of public benefit behind "awaid".

He immediately rose to this and explained how he and Sheikh Muhammad El Tom had originally had only one herd of camels between them and they had made the "'ada" of one sheep a murah;[12] and how from this things had grown; and how he made the "awaid" collected by him to help the tribe to pay its taxes, to assist poor persons with food and clothes, and to run the administration of the tribe by rewarding all his numerous manadib and agents and messengers.

I said I understood this perfectly and so did everyone who had served as D.C. Dar El Kababish, but the facts were imperfectly known outside both to English and to natives. One heard people say, "Sheikh Ali eats everything and his relatives eat what is left", and so on. Why would he not come into the open and make all this clear so that his methods should be explainable to outsiders and both he and his friends (native and English) free from fear of consequences? If I, when questioned, could say, "Yes, Sheikh Ali takes "rial ed Dho" and gets £E1,000 a year by it—but then he

---

[10] Reproofs, reproaches, blame; sing.: *malum*.
[11] Share.
[12] Ar.: *murah*: flock.

expends that on grain for poor tribesmen", and so on, then there is a plain answer to his detractors. Why would he not make a "Beit El Mal"[13] and keep an account and show it to his D.C. and say, "Look here, this is how the finances work. I want government to regularise this position for me so that both of us—you, the govt. and I the Sheikh, may be at peace of mind"? I went on to explain by way of example the way the Shukria N.A. worked, carefully pointing out that the same methods would not apply here though the principle might be one. The govt. wanted to preserve his honour and position vis-a-vis govt. and vis-a-vis other chiefs. I knew that it would mean some extra trouble for him to keep accounts, even of the simplest and so on, but the government would help him to keep things simple and I did not think it would be difficult for him to agree with the government. And his coming to terms would be a great insurance for the future and for his sons. He said again that for the future he wanted the Govt's. relations with the Kababish to be like its relations with all other tribes.

I am myself convinced that Sheikh Ali will refuse to cooperate at all if he is told he must pay in fines to government and give up "awaid" and so on. Or, if he does not refuse, he will cooperate with his tongue in this cheek. I am convinced that there are only two ways, either (1) leave the Kababish as they are or (2) accept Ali El Tom's system of administration both *judicial* and *fiscal* (as the two are not divided in his mind and those of his tribesmen) "en bloc" and legalise them with as slight modifications as possible e.g. insisting that he have powers of imprisonment, write down his judgments in a book, and keep accounts of fines and awaid. This is to say the Kababish, who are now really a Native Administration judicially and fiscally, but a N.A. illegal and unofficial, must be made into a full-fledged N.A., as fully-fledged as that of the Shukria. Otherwise I think all attempts to extend the govt. scheme to them will fail.

He left at 1 p.m., and the sky became a little cloudy. Will it rain? Had lunch and the hamla moved off.

Sh. Ali then appeared to say that Belula Fadl El Mula the Tareefy [sic], who is wanted in Mellit, both as being father of the lad alleged murdered by the Zeyadia slave 2 years ago, and also as accused of being in illicit possession of a .303 rifle, was ill and could not be moved. He asked me to come and see him, which I consented to do. News of this kind at this late moment seemed to me suspicious. I found the man lying on a goat skin under a tree, all wrapped up in a tob. He complained of swelling of the testicles followed by pain exactly like appendicitis pain. He may conceivably have appendicitis. In any case I had no means of telling

---

[13] Treasury.

whether he was really ill, and what was the matter with him if so. Accordingly I told Sh. Ali to leave someone with him but bring on all the other witnesses summoned to Mellit.

I rode off about 4 p.m. southwards across the wadi-bed and up the very high sand hill on the far side. If the Meidob knew how to cultivate, this wadi would yield wonderful crops.

Set down on the goz at about 5.45. Good grazing (that was why we had come here). The clouds had materialised into showers of rain falling on the hills and to the north of us. The hills looked extraordinarily like parts of Dartmoor and very British in the sunset. The Awaida who have been at Muzbat were some of them encamped south of us and their herds could be seen in the distance. Also we passed a herd of meagre Meidob cows. Muhammad Sadig came for a drink of Epsom Salts.

The night was alternatively stuffy and cool and I slept fitfully after 3 a.m., merely dozing and dreaming very vividly.

10.6.33

Rode at 5.15 over goz country with plenty of grass. Direction S.W. Jebel Meidob behind. Found hamla already in camp at 6.45. The L/Corporal in charge said they had stopped because Muhammad Sadig was ill. All that is wrong with Muhammad Sadig so far as I can tell is constipation. The fool lets it go on for 3 or 4 days instead of complaining at once and taking medicine. Gave him the necessary.

I felt exceedingly tired. Since dawn I had been having a terrible stitch in my right side under the ribs, which did not get better after I got off my camel. Also the day was one of those gusty and intensely glaring days with cloud which precede a thunderstorm. Thunder broke over the hills to the N.W. at noon.

Hamla went on about 1.30. Rain was then falling N.W. but none came to us. Rode 3 p.m. and it was very hot and trying, also the pains in my tummy got worse although I tied the belt of my shorts as tight as possible. By sunset we had got near to the Taqabo Hills of the Berti. They are really beautiful, standing in queer cathedral-like peaks out of the surrounding high sandhills. Rain had fallen all round us, but none near at hand. The evening was very sticky and warm. I felt like death and, having taken rather gingerly steps to quench thirst, took two pink pills and went to bed. I suppose I must have slept from about 8.30 p.m. to 4.30 a.m. By that time a strong and very cool wind had sprung up.

11.6.33

Rode 5 a.m. Clear, cool, rain-washed morning. My tummy, tightly strapped, still hurt me but not nearly so badly. What I really need is a good meal, including milk (other than tinned milk) and plenty of it. My belly is so empty that it is wobbling all over the place: that is the trouble. Possibly in Madu we should find milk as it is a well-centre for animals.

Rode and rode and rode. Got right up to and among the hills by 6.30. Took photos of them. Tingle fell back and started to look for the hamla's tracks. The well was described as being not far: "by that hill". The result was we rode for 4½ hours in all, the last two hours being very hot. Towards the end all among the hills was found a definite government-made motor road and [we] came down this from the hills to camp—at last—near the well of Madu. Muhammad Sadig still pretty poorly. However, he found me some milk and I had a meal and felt better, though weary. Also had a bath. This place is distinctly attractive: high mountains behind and the wadi with trees below. But it is all dry and barren as a bone and very fly-bitten. Likewise a hot simoom blew all the forenoon from the north. Clouds banked up but too light to do much good. I shall rejoice to get this journey done. I tried reading but the flies worried me too much. Lunch at 2.15. I then went out to look at the well. Some of Kababish were still getting their camels watered and their water-skins filled. I took a photograph of the scene. The next moment a violent blow of wind and dust came on, followed by a few drops of rain. The dust storm continued at intervals for about a quarter of an hour; evidently it was raining farther to the west over the hills. This marvellously cleared the air. The atmospheric effects were very striking. I returned to my tree and the two Kawahla sheikhs came for a chat.

We rode at 5 S.W. up a high goz along a wide road and past a Berti village. The evening scene from the top of the goz was so beautiful as to deserve a picture. We were riding over a big down of fairly hard sand of the queer North Sudan colour between terracotta and beige covered with saffron-coloured grass. The goz curved down to the west to a dark line of bush and trees beyond which rose range after range of hills for some twenty miles. These high rocky hills were of the fantastic shapes of spires and pinnacles and castles which the imagination of mediaeval Italian painters put into the backgrounds of so many of their pictures, and in the evening light they took on the same blue tints. Behind and beyond the southern limit of the hills rose a great dark mass of cloud up into the clear blue sky, and behind this the sun sank behind the hills, throwing a final splash of rose upon distant banks of cumulus cloud towering faraway on the eastern horizon. The cloud above the sun took on more pearly tints. Below us as we descended the other side of the down the bright flames of our camp fires already lit by the hamla were points like stars or a distant forge when the door is opened. Then the hills stood out dark as if cut in fret-work on a stage against a cyclorama of afterglow which turned from gold to pearl of the clearest and most translucent, and so to glowing grey fading into dark azure and ultramarine above. Men off-saddled and prayed while the camels went to graze. A native passed up the road behind me singing and breaking his song to cluck at his camel and abuse its unspeakable birth. Later in the dark followed another whom I took (since I could not understand his words) to be a Meidobi singing an incomprehensible song in slow, wavering, syncopated rhythm. Then all was dark and quiet except for the noises of the camp and the laughter of Arabs round a fire some little way off.

12.6.33

Rode 5 a.m. till 7.30. This pain under my ribs and in the right shoulder seems to have become a permanency. The going was over gozes with the hills away to the right. The day became very fiercely hot. Clouds collected and then rolled away from us again. Would give anything for a real drench of rain to cool the air and take the electricity out of it. Slept part of the morning—not feeling too well . . . . [Shaykh Ali] unburdened himself of the complaint concerning the Zaghawa at Muzbat: that they had taken far too much off the Awaida who went there. He admitted that the Awaida were in the wrong to go there at all and he proposes to punish them therefore. But he said that the Omda of the Zaghawa agreed at first to water them for the season for a present of two hunting dogs and a camel. These Abdel Kheir's son took to him in due course. But then, when the Awaida Nas Hasan went to Muzbat, the Zaghawa "aggal"ed[14] naga after naga. Apart from this they had lost 50 nagas stray, which they are convinced the Zaghawa stole. I asked had they evidence and he said he thought not but they had told Moore.

Rode about 3.30. Very hot. We passed a Berti village where all the women, damnably ugly all of them, rushed out at us with drums and demanded "the custom". The Kababish were vastly amused. As we had not stopped anywhere near their village, we said if one of them liked to come on to where we were spending the night (Sayyah) we might give her something. She did not appear, of course: Sayyah was some way.

After that village we began a steep descent through broken and rocky ground and "kerrib". Away to the southwest across the valley in which Sayyah lies, one could see more hills and mountains. We met large numbers of folk coming up the hill from Sayyah, for this had been market day there. Sayyah itself is a long valley between rocky sides. To the north the valley side is steep escarpment out of which jut jagged rocks and piles of stones. To the south the slope is much gentler over sand hills. The valley

---

[14] Ar. *'aqala*: to hobble.

resembles a very shoddy replica of one of the kheiran. All but two palm trees (folk told me there had been many) have died. No one troubles to cultivate the soil in the valley. There are no shadoufs. Consequently there is nothing but a small Berti village with a little market on the slope to the north of the wells and the wells themselves. We crossed the valley and camped on the goz to the south beside the Mellit road.

The local Omda and two others appeared on horses to greet us, and I gave them tea. They were not very chatty, except one of them who had taken drink: and I was tired, stupid and in pain. After their tea they pushed off to see Sheikh Ali.

Just after sunset a terrific gale and dust storm began. Nur ed Din and I rushed my bed and the rest of my luggage into the tent and police appeared to prop it up. Rain immediately followed. I being afraid of the results of a chill on Sheikh Ali, who already had a bad cold, sent to him to take shelter. He arrived under a carpet held by slaves. So we shut the tent and sat amid a pile of trek kit and chatted while I smoked. He insisted on sitting on the floor with his back to the driving rain, so I made him wear my burberry. We discussed mainly the unemployment problem and that of poverty generally. He said obviously our dole system merely means that the poor live on the rich and the ultimate result will be that soon both will be in poverty and want. He said again clearly as the English government had so many countries in its possession, it should make its unemployed emigrate to them. I explained that the folk in these dependencies would not accept immigrants except skilled men, and that, on the other hand, most of our unemployed had each some one job or skill for which they were any use, and that could not be found outside England. His opinion was that this was ridiculous. If the govt. was a govt. the colonials ought to be compelled to accept their poorer brethren and train them to the work they wished to get out of them.

Now a well-organised Arab tribe like the Kababish arranges for its poor. Sheikh Ali said that, when men in a section become poor and come and say to him, "Divide out to us our portion . . . from our wealthier brethren", he refuses because for sure the poor men receiving their portion of animals would simply sell it or waste it in improvident buying. He therefore takes the poor men and insists on their working either as cultivators or hired herdsmen till they can restore themselves to sufficiency. I asked of widows and orphans in a tribe and he said that the nearest male relative was by custom bound to make himself responsible for them.

I made hot coffee for him so soon as the storm was over and then he left. I immediately felt very sick and had a bad pain between the shoulders and at the back of my neck, and so went supperless to bed. It blew hard in the night.

13.6.33

Woke feeling frightful. Sent Tingle to buy sheep and wrote letters to Mellit which I sent by a policeman. It was a beautiful cool morning and the sky overcast. Unfortunately my temperature steadily rose and I kept to my bed. Milk was obtainable here in small quantities for a price, and so I sipped milk and took aspirin and hoped that my temperature would go down and various aches and pains cease. They did not. So in the afternoon I took 30 grains of quinine, declined all visitors and composed myself to wait for morning, since willy nilly I must ride on then.

14.6.33

Rose 5 a.m. weak and deaf but willing. Pains in chest and shoulders almost gone and temperature down.

Rode 5.30 till 7. Arrived Wadi Kibrin. Only about 8 more miles to do. The road sandy but among hills and steep in parts.

Sheikh Ali and the two Kawahla came to see me and chat. The talk turned on the Zeyadia. One of the Kababish riding camels disappeared in the night and some of them have gone to look for it. Of course they think Zeyadia have stolen it, especially because, so I hear, the Zayadia [*sic*] abused them on the wells at Sayyah. We went on to talk of theft, and I tried to get out of them whether they thought: (1) that imprisoning the thief or securing compensation was the more important. They avoided my question by saying that, if the thief was imprisoned and his people made to pay up, undoubtedly theft would be stopped. (2) that imprisonment was any good? They said that a nomad Arab feared it, and his people would do anything to get him out of it. He is a milk-and-meat man and used to open spaces, so prison life does not suit him. But a grain-eating peasant comes out of prison like a camel on heat.

On the whole it appeared to me that they definitely consider that compensation, if strictly enforced, is a better deterrent (apart from the natural strong desire of the Arab to obtain his lost animal *or* compensation by fair means or foul) than prison, and that they did not much believe in prison as a punishment. Sheikh Ali pointed out that the more people the govt. puts in prison the more for prisoners has to be paid for by innocent taxpayers. He also instanced the latest case of Kababish going to Dar Hamar and having their case heard by Munim, who gave sentence of imprisonment and fine, the accused being Kaja of Seruj. They then went to Mardi El Imam, who said, probably with technical truth, "They have no animals". And I refused to interfere when they came to me.

I strongly incline to the view that we ought to concentrate on compensation and not imprisonment. Now this Native Administration, which is so much more British Administration than Native Custom, has made Courts and told them to judge according to native custom, but also insists on their approximating their methods and decisions to [the] Penal Code, rather than to tribal custom, so as at any rate to cut out collective responsibility such as I have found to exist in all Arab tribes I have come into contact with—either nomads or Bara sedentaries. It is on this principle—collective responsibility—that govt. itself acts when it levies a collective fine on a village.

I cannot understand why there should be two laws in the Sudan, one for sedentary N.A. and one for nomads. When nomads do anything wrong, Govt. says, "The tribe is responsible", even if the tribe produces the guilty men confessing. But when a sedentary from a N.A. steals—"Oh! he has no animals and cannot pay a fine."

I may be entirely wrong. It may be that Hamar and Darfur tribal customs do not include anything but individual responsibility. But I doubt it.

I mean to write a tract called "Vox clamantis in deserto" setting out "the dying thoughts of a dying man to dying men" as old Pridgeon once said in the pulpit.

THE ANGLO-EGYPTIAN SUDAN

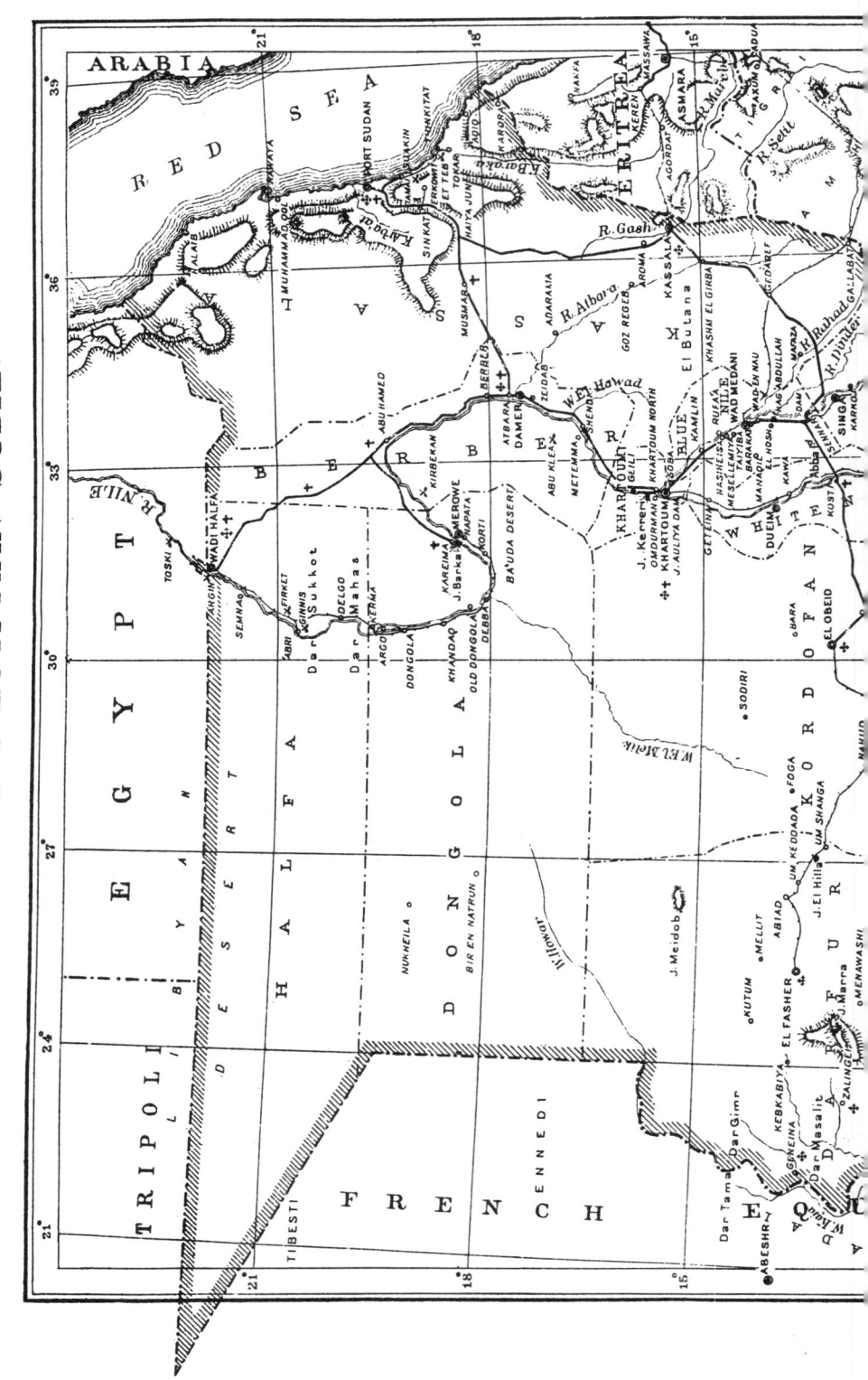

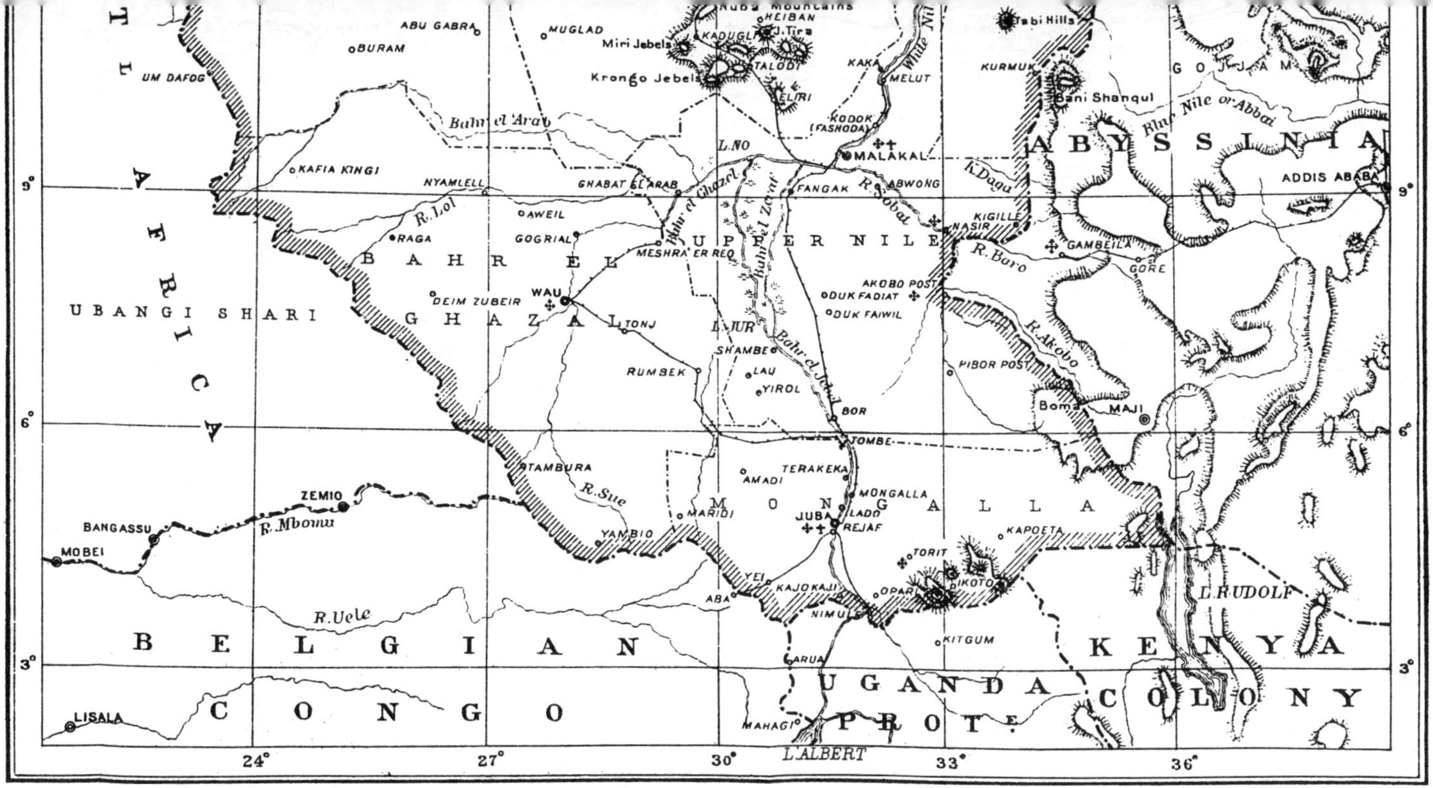

Reproduced by Sudan Survey Dept., Khartoum, Topo. Nº S. 507-33. (Oct. 1933)

Scale 1 : 8,000,000

Miles 100 50 0 100 200 300 400 Miles

REFERENCE

International Boundaries	Railways
Province Boundaries	Telegraphs or Telephones
Motor Roads	Wireless stations
Battle fields	Landing ground for Aeroplanes

Northern Kordofan and surrounding areas
showing general tribal divisions

Part of a map of 'The Anglo-Egyptian Sudan (Tribal)', printed at the Ordnance Survey Office, Southampton, 1928, to accompany a *Military Report on the Sudan, 1927*, prepared by the General Staff, the War Office. Crown copyright, reproduced with the permission of the Controller of Her Majesty's Stationery Office, from a copy in the Sudan Archive, University of Durham Library.

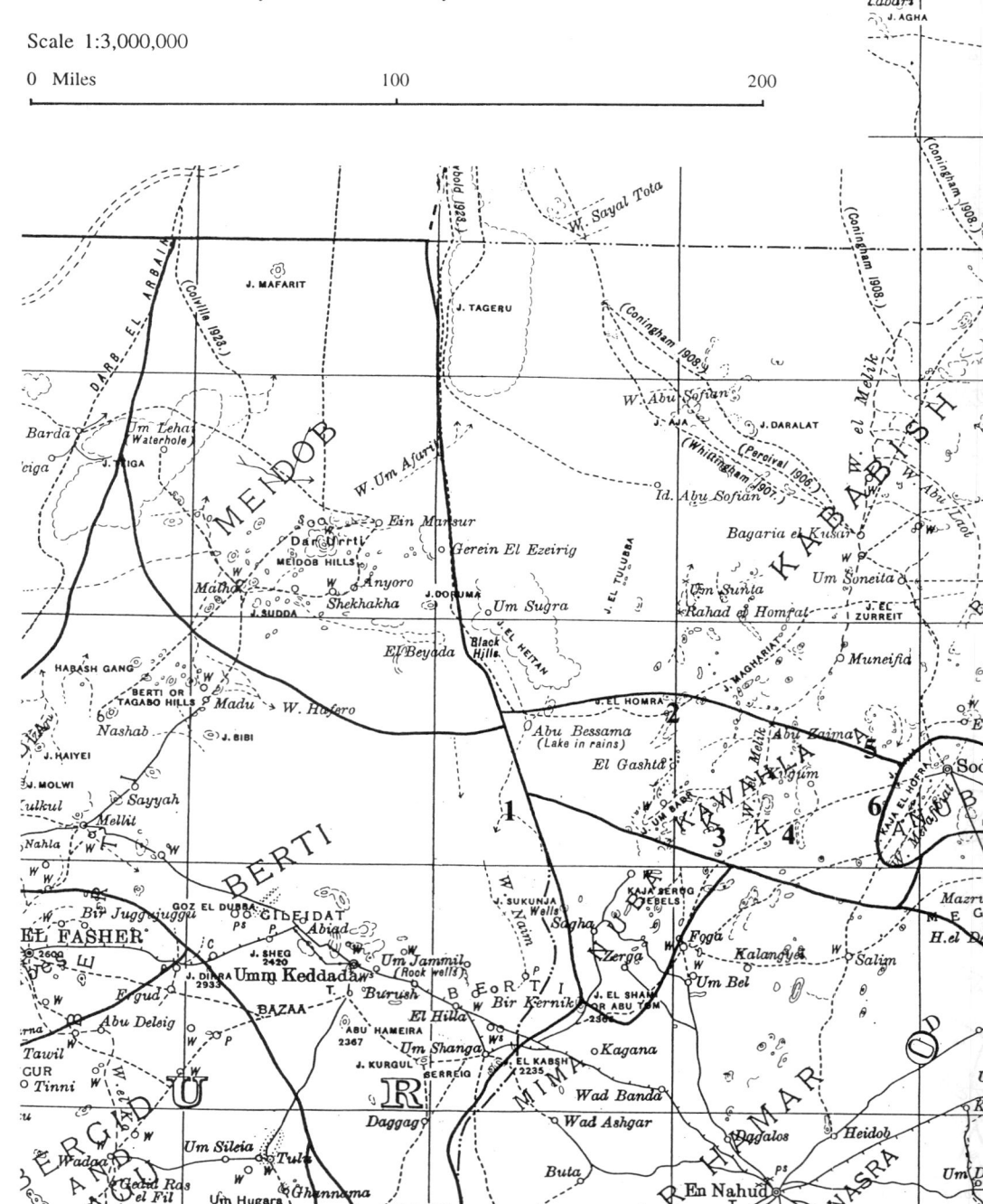

Scale 1:3,000,000

0 Miles 100 200

Additional place-names

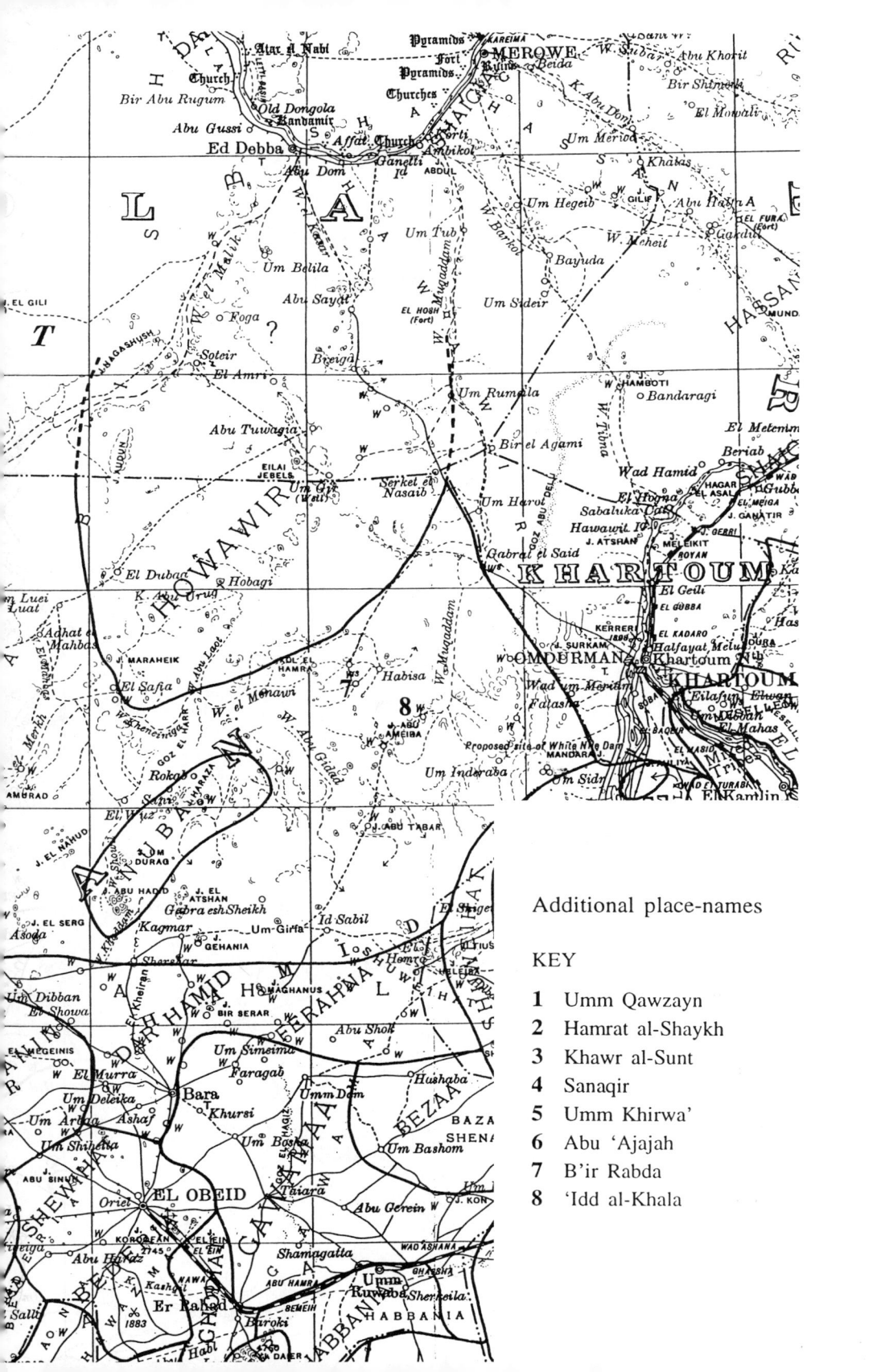

KEY

1. Umm Qawzayn
2. Hamrat al-Shaykh
3. Khawr al-Sunt
4. Sanaqir
5. Umm Khirwa'
6. Abu 'Ajajah
7. B'ir Rabda
8. 'Idd al-Khala

Appendix

Family Tree of Shaykh 'Ali al-Tum of the Nurab Kababish

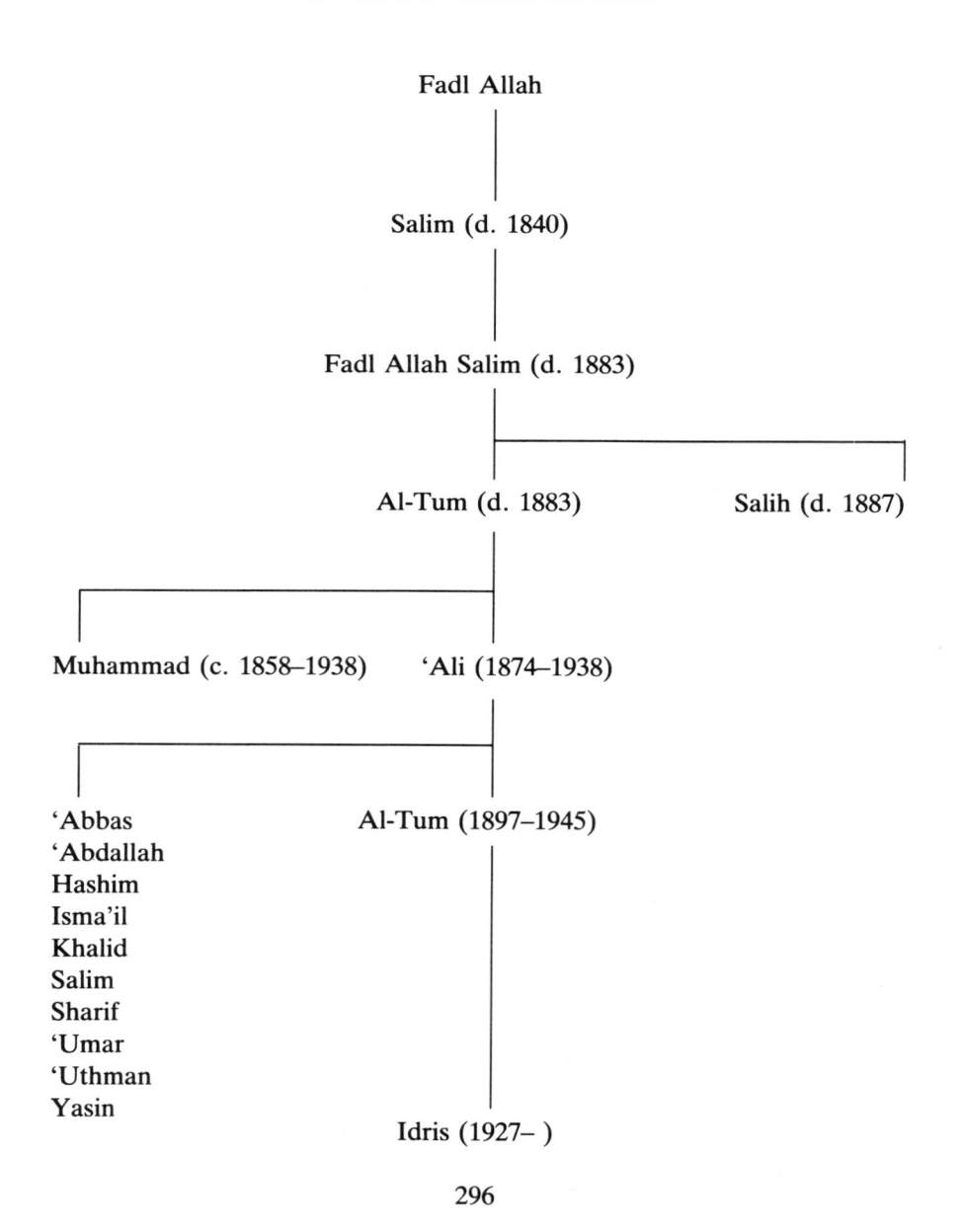

Fadl Allah

Salim (d. 1840)

Fadl Allah Salim (d. 1883)

Al-Tum (d. 1883)   Salih (d. 1887)

Muhammad (c. 1858–1938)   'Ali (1874–1938)

'Abbas
'Abdallah
Hashim
Isma'il
Khalid
Salim
Sharif
'Umar
'Uthman
Yasin

Al-Tum (1897–1945)

Idris (1927–)

Index

'Abd al-'Aziz Ibn Sa'ud, 39, 55, 104, 204–5, 237
'Abd al-Hadi Dulib, 138, 149
'Abd al-Qadir 'Awad al-Sid, 50–1
'Abd al-Qadir al-I'aysir, 125
'Abd al-Rahman, Faki, 189, 190–1
'Abd al-Rahman al-Mahdi, 158, 171, 239
'Abd al-Rahman Muhammad Kimbal, 212
'Abd al-Rahman Wad al-Nujumi, 34
Abd El Gadir, *See* 'Abd al-Qadir
Abdallah Abu Chieyba, *See* 'Abdallah Abu Shiyaba
'Abdallah Abu Shiyaba, 45
'Abdallah 'Ali Abu Shaykha, 254
'Abdallah Fadlallah Na'im (Niama), 84
'Abdallah Muhammad, 89
'Abdallah Sulayman, 85–6, 87
'Abdallahi, Khalifa, 1, 64, 65, 129, 142
Abu 'Ajajah, 51, 93, 94, 95, 257
Abu Bassama, 120–1, 122, 206, 280
Abu Fa's al-Mufattih, 46
Abu Hadid, 66–7, 135. *See also* Jabal Abu Hadid
Abu Hashim, 144
Abu Sinun, 244
Abu Tabr, 141
Abu 'Uruq, 71, 137, 140, 199, 201, 203, 206
Abu Za'imah, 28, 29, 30, 131, 242, 246, 272, 276
Acland, P. B. E., 11
Adam 'Abdallah, 71, 73, 74, 83
Adam al-Dish, 83
Adam al-Nur 'Ubaydallah, 151–2
Adam Hasan, 87
Adam Murdas, 117
Adat al-Jawwad, 131
Aglen, E. F., 164, 218
Ahamda, 200, 201, 202
Ahmad Duwayna, 62, 69, 74, 76, 78
Ahmad El Aisar, *See* Ahmad al-I'aysir
Ahmad Farah, 261
Ahmad Gismallah, *See* Ahmad Qasmallah
Ahmad Gumaa, *See* Ahmad Juma'
Ahmad al-I'aysir, 88, 89
Ahmad Ibrahim, *Shawish*, 78
Ahmad Ibrahim, *Shaykh*, 109
Ahmad Ibrahim Abu Batin, 234, 237
Ahmad 'Izayri, 103, 104
Ahmad Juma', 181, 184

Ahmad Juma Abu Gideiri, *See* Ahmad Juma' Abu Jidayri
Ahmad Juma' Abu Jidayri, 146, 147
Ahmad Jibril, 73, 74
Ahmad Kabjerak, 46
Ahmad Okair, *See* Ahmad Ukayr
Ahmad Qasmallah, 47, 48, 107–8, 109, 114, 129, 251–2, 255
Ahmad al-Sharif, 83
Ahmad Ukayr, 68
al-'Ajab, '*Umda*, 66–7, 149–51, 182, 184
'Ajabna Jamid, 140, 141
Akib, *See* 'Aqib Effendi
Alfa Hashim, 113
'Ali 'Ajabna, 156, 158, 188, 245
'Ali Babikr Badri, 121
'Ali Bilal, 39, 270
'Ali Dinar, 36, 50, 64–5
Ali El Tom, *See* 'Ali al-Tum Fadlallah
Ali Garoot, *See* 'Ali Qarut
'Ali Hasan Khalifa, 207
'Ali Ibrahim Dulib, 188
'Ali 'Izayri, 102, 103, 106, 107
'Ali Khayrallah, 80, 82, 88–90, 91, 160
'Ali al-Mirghani, 206
'Ali Muhammad al-Tum, 185, 186, 281
'Ali Nasir, 88, 90
'Ali al-Nur, 46–7, 256
'Ali Qarut, 223, 228, 232
'Ali Salih, 36
'Ali al-Tum Fadlallah, 3–5, 13–14, 15, 17, 19, 25–8, 31–9, 44, 47, 53, 59, 60, 65, 67, 70, 76–7, 79–80, 83–7, 91, 92, 99, 108, 110–12, 115–20, 122–31, 136, 142, 144, 145, 147, 148, 160, 171–84, 204, 206, 220–1, 228–33, 235, 238–40, 242, 246–51, 253, 255, 267, 272–80, 282–6, 288–90, 292
al-Amin Baruda, 90
al-Amin Bulad, 264, 265, 266, 267
al-Amin Rahih al-Amin, 89
Anaj, 138, 140–1
'Aqib Effendi, 52, 132, 133, 155, 160, 161, 246, 274
'Arabi Dafa'allah, 64, 141
Arabic, 8, 31, 33, 47, 50, 63, 76, 82, 102, 104, 118, 153, 157, 161, 164, 176, 191, 224, 229, 268
'Ata al-Manan, 210

Atawia, *See under* Kababish, Atawiyya
Atawiyya, *see under* Kababish, Atawiyya
Atkey, O. F. H., 23
Athat El Gawad, *See* 'Adat al-Jawwad
al-'Atrun, 14, 75, 120
Audas, R. S., 38
Awad El Kerim Abu Sinn, *See* 'Awad al-Karim 'Abdallah Abu Sinn
'Awad al-Karim 'Abdallah Abu Sinn, 11
'Awad al-Sid 'Abd al-Hadi, 83–4
'Awad al-Sid al-Kabis, 114
Awaida, *see under* Kababish, 'Awayda
Awlad Kimbal, 212
Awlad Sulayman, *See under* Kababish
Awlad Tarayf, 34, 43, 58
Awlad Ugba, *See under* Kababish, Awlad 'Uqba
Azande, 65

Ba Naga, *See under* Ban al-Nuqa'
Bahr El Ghazal (Bahr al-Ghazal), 64
Baily, R. E. H., 11
Bakalai, *See* Jabal Bakalay
Bakhit Jadallah, 89, 91
Ban al-Nuqa', 75
Bani Jarar, 46, 102, 104–5, 107, 109, 155, 186
Bara, 6, 23, 50, 59, 62, 64, 66, 75, 99, 106, 169, 174, 186, 218, 222, 244, 249, 253, 254, 259–60, 262, 270, 271, 279–80, 291
Barara, *See under* Kababish
Bence-Pembroke, R. A., 163
Beni Gerar, *See* Bani Jarar
Berber Province, 11
Bethell, D. J., 165
Bija, 209
Bilal 'Abdallah, 273–4, 275
Bilal al-Mahbas, 118, 119
Bint Kobi, 142, 144, 184
B'ir al-Hasanawi, 197
B'ir al-Jadid, 208, 210
B'ir Natrun, 172, 176, 217, 228
B'ir Rabda, 58, 78, 80, 83, 86
B'ir Shanqul, 139, 141, 188
Birti, 120, 223, 228, 287, 288, 289
Bishariin, 40
Bredin, George, 36, 206
Bolton, A. R. C., 166
Boustead, Hugh, 16, 17
Britain, British, 1–2, 3, 33–4, 39, 63, 65–6, 76, 108, 110, 147–8, 163–8, 172, 199, 281

Cambridge, 21
Camels, 37–8, 40, 44, 50, 60, 82, 99, 102, 103, 104, 106, 107–8, 109, 110, 111, 112, 118, 122, 124, 126, 135–6, 157, 199, 220, 221, 226–7, 230, 232–3, 234, 235, 238, 251–2, 274
Campbell, Ewan, 33, 225, 229, 230
Campbell, Mrs Ewan, 33
Circumcision, 68–9
Clapham, John, 63
Clarke, W. P. D., 206
Clarkson, Thomas, 35
Cromer, Lord, 2

al-Dabba, 198, 202, 204, 234
Dahr al-Himar, 139
al-Damir, 38, 189
Dar Hamid, 5, 80, 102, 174, 266, 267, 270–1
Dar Omar, *See under* Kababish, Dar 'Umar
Dar Zunqul, 144
Dardiri, Corporal, 259, 260
Dardiri Muhammad al-Khalifa, 31, 99
Darfur, 4, 5, 15, 17, 36, 37, 50, 54, 64, 100, 119, 172, 206, 218, 220–1, 226, 278–9, 291
Darling, Inspector, 136, 137, 271
Darwil, 54
Davies, Reginald, 50, 56, 63, 67, 144
De Bunsen, Charles, 16, 131, 150, 164, 218, 245, 246–58, 260
Devolution, *See* Indirect Rule
Dhu al-Bayt 'Abd al-Daym, 220, 221
Dinkas, 118, 120, 129, 273–4
Dongola, 14, 59, 62, 160, 161, 162, 172, 184, 186, 200, 203, 204, 214, 216, 219, 255
Dualib, 64
Duayh, 43, 46, 49, 130, 256
Dueih, *See* Duayh
Dulib family, 137–8, 142, 144, 145, 149, 176

Egypt, 1, 2, 3, 206, 234, 239, 242
El Atrun, *See* al-'Atrun
El Amin Bolad (El Emin Bolad), *See* al-Amin Bulad
El Damer, *See* al-Damir
El Fasher, 28, 36, 65, 99, 120, 122, 147, 152, 175, 206, 218, 220
El Gadab, *See* al-Qadab
El Gleit, *See* al-Jalayt
El Haj Saiied, *See* al-Hajj Sa'id
El Obeid, 6, 13, 17, 18, 23, 24, 61, 68, 94, 99–100, 103, 131, 157, 162, 163–8, 169, 218, 244, 246, 259, 262
El Tom Ali, *See* al-Tum 'Ali al-Tum
El Wuzz, *See* Hamrat al-Wazz
Elliott, A. V. P., 164, 260–1, 262, 271
En Nil Sahal, *See* al-Nil Sahal

Ennedi, 14, 172, 205
England, English, *See* Britain
Ez Zakhufa, *See* Jabal al-Zakhufa

Fadil Murjab, 104–5, 106
Fadl al-Mula, Faki, 111, 113, 114, 116, 124, 224, 237, 253
Fadl al-Mula Bilula, 117, 278, 279
Fadl al-Sid 'Ali Hashim, 58–9
Fadlallah 'Ali al-Tum, 239
Fadlallah Ahmad 'Abd al-Qadir al-I'aysir, 13, 49
Fadlallah Bey Salim, 242, 250
Fadlallah El Eaysir, *See* Fadlallah Ahmad 'Abd al-Qadir al-I'aysir
Fag Gumur, *See* Fajj Jumur
Fait 'Ali, 72
Fajj Jumur, 197–8
Farajallah, Shartay, 99–100
Farid Bey, 33, 53, 204
Fattasha, 92
Ferid Bey, *See* Farid Bey
Fleming, M. H. V., 206

Gadallah Abu Qurain, *See* Qadallah Abu Quran
Gafala, *See* Qafalah
Galaa El Tin, *See* Qal'at al-Tin
Galaat El Gumur, *See* Qal'at al-Jumur
Gashda, *See* Qashta
Gambir, *See* Qambir
Gannetu, *See* Qannatu
Gawamaa, *See* Jawama'a
Gedeidim, *See* Qadaydim
Geleit, *See* Wadi al-Jalaytah
Gereir, *See* Garayr
Gillan, Angus, 18, 53, 160, 163, 164, 169, 246, 278
Gizzu Idris, *See* Jizzu Idris
Golaat El Jihadi, *See* Qal'at al-Jihadi
Gordon (Memorial) College, 6, 55, 121, 128, 164
Goz Regeb, *See* Qawz Rajab
Griffith, F. L., 217
Gum, 16, 51
Gumaa Sahal, *See* Juma' Sahal
Gumuiya, *See* Jamu'iyya
Gumuwiya, *See* Jamu'iyya
Gurun Abu Ajaama, *See* Qurun al-'Ujaymi

Hababin, 19
Habaji, 78, 192, 193, 202, 247

Habisa, 78, 82, 83
Hadandua, 209
Hadarat al-Sudan, 120, 191
al-Hajj Khidr al-Dukri, 65, 141, 142, 194, 198
al-Hajj Sa'id, 68, 112, 113
Hamad Muhammad Hamad, 109
Hamadallah Tamar, 134
Hamar, 13, 25, 94, 103, 108, 109, 111, 126, 130, 158, 161, 166, 219, 254, 284, 290, 291
Hamid Ajur, 116, 120
Hamid 'Ali, 69, 134, 135, 136, 142, 144
Hamilton, J. A. de C., 12, 13, 15, 16, 18, 21, 28, 29, 32–4, 36, 39, 41, 42, 43, 45, 53, 64, 65, 75, 77, 96, 105, 113, 115, 119, 130, 134, 137, 147, 150, 151, 165, 167, 168, 169–74, 176–7, 178–81, 199, 234, 246, 276
Hamrat al-Shaykh, 80, 130, 134, 144, 145, 242, 248, 272
Hamrat al-Wazz, 14, 30, 39, 62, 67, 69, 135, 137, 140, 146, 148, 160, 161, 174, 176, 177, 178, 181–5, 190, 199, 206
Hamza al-Malik, 59
Haraza, 27, 66, 67, 68, 94, 132, 136, 140, 141, 142, 143, 145, 148, 188
Hasan Ahmad Nagila, *See* Hasan Ahmad Najila
Hasan Ahmad Najila, 17, 18–19, 27, 29, 30, 31, 116, 120, 128, 129, 183, 249–50, 251, 274, 277
Hasan Dulayb, 67, 68, 72, 75, 137
Hasan Khalifa, 14, 27, 67, 68, 71, 72–3, 74–5, 76–7, 85, 188–9, 190, 192, 199
Hasan Kimbal, 212
Hasaniyya, 89
Hatan, *See* al-Hitan
Hataan, *See* al-Hitan
Hawawir, 5, 12, 14, 25, 53–92, 143, 155, 156, 185, 186, 187–92, 193–4, 197, 198, 199, 200–4, 208, 210, 213
   Atawiyya, 77, 82
   Barara, 77, 82
   Fazzanab, 202
   Fazarab, 74
   Habasab, 210
   Khamasiin, 62, 206
   Rubab, 25, 71, 73, 74, 83, 92, 186, 188, 191, 199, 201, 202, 247
   Sulhab, 74
   Taxation of, 72, 73, 74
   Umm Suray, 82, 83
Headlam, Tuppy, 22
Heitan, *See* al-Hitan
Hejaz, *See* al-Hijaz
Henderson, K. D. D., 25, 42, 219
Herd Tax, 14, 16, 50, 63, 73, 97, 107–8, 109, 110, 112, 114–15, 119, 156, 186, 189, 262, 271

al-Hijaz, 39, 113, 237
Hilaire, General, 205
Hillard, John, 51, 82, 260
Hillat Ban Jadid, 159
Hillat Maraykha, 152
Hishayb, 146
al-Hitan, 121, 122, 206, 273, 277, 280
Hobagi, *See* Habaji
Howawir, *See* Hawawir
Hufra, *See* Hufrah
Hufrah, 94–5, 133
Humphry, John, 89
Hunt Bey, 218–19
Huskisson, 35

Ibn Rifada, 237
Ibn Saoud, *See* 'Abd al-'Aziz Ibn Sa'ud
Ibrahim, *Dimlij*, 227
Ibrahim Adam, 66
Ibrahim Fahayl, 34–5, 119, 179, 266, 270
Ibrahim Faheil, *See* Ibrahim Fahayl
Ibrahim Farayh, 28–9
Ibrahim Fereih, *See* Ibrahim Farayh
Ibrahim Musa Madibbu, 68
Id El Kheil, *See* 'Idd al-Khala
Id El Merkh, *See* 'Idd al-Marikh
'Idd Abu 'Ajajah, *See* Abu 'Ajajah
'Idd al-Khala, 58, 84
'Idd al-Marikh, 58, 62, 65, 69, 76, 154, 155, 186, 202, 247
'Idd Sumayn, 94, 96
Indirect Rule, 2–3, 4–5, 6, 11, 12, 14–5, 171, 199, 202, 203–4, 220, 232–3, 247, 249, 251, 256, 259, 267, 268, 272–3, 275–6, 278–80, 282–8, 290–1
Italy, Italians, 172, 173

Jaalin, *See* Ja'aliyyin
Ja'aliyyin, 81, 84, 192
Jabal Abu Hadid, 64, 133, 135, 143, 146, 147, 149–50, 176, 179, 182, 184
Jabal Abu Sinun, 18
Jabal al-Akhdar, 75, 205
Jabal al-Arbad, *See* Jabal Arbit
Jabal Arbit, 61
Jabal 'Atshan, 175
Jabal Bakalay, 51, 94, 95, 157–8
Jabal Baruk, 92
Jabal Haraza, 64, 65, 67, 80, 133, 137, 138
Jabal al-Hilla, 219
Jabal Kaja Soderi, 27, 51
Jabal Katul, 19, 20, 21, 95, 133–4, 151, 153, 255
Jabal Kaylum, 138

Jabal Maydub, 33, 50, 58, 104, 121, 139, 172, 223, 230, 286
Jabal Murabba, *See* Jabal Umm Ruaba
Jabal Nasib al-Husan, 67, 70, 75, 187
Jabal Nasib al-Sumugh, 70
Jabal al-Nihid, 135, 176, 178
Jabal Sanaqir, 96
Jabal Shau, 54
Jabal Shikayb, 46
Jabal Shikhab, 46
Jabal Shuwaf, 185, 195
Jabal Sikanju, 105
Jabal Sumugh, 186
Jabal Tajiru, 121
Jabal Turuk, 61
Jabal Umm Dabi, *See* Jabal Umm Zabi
Jabal Umm Duraj, 133, 135, 137, 145, 146, 176, 177
Jabal Umm Karus, 139
Jabal Umm Ruaba, 152
Jabal Umm Sunta, 134
Jabal Umm Zabi, 29, 30
Jabal al-Zakafa, 71
Jabir Taqa, 61, 69, 155
Jabir Tugga, *See* Jabir Taqa
Jackson, Col. 216
Jackson, Sir Herbert, 73, 212, 214, 215, 216
Jad al-Rab al-Nur, 147, 148
Jad al-Sid Muhammad, 51
Jadallah Abu Qurun, 104, 105, 111
Jakdul, 201, 202, 203
al-Jalayt, 18, 19
Jamal al-Din al-Afghani, 55
Jamu'iyya, 29, 89, 90, 91, 183
Jangai, 118
Jawama'a, 87, 260
Jebel, *See* Jabal
Jebel El Turk, *See* Jabal Turuk
Jebel Sheikheib, *See* Jabal Shikayb
Jebel Sheikhab, *See* Jabal Shikhab
Jerusalem, 185
Jima'a, 51
Jizzu Idris, 226, 228, 229
Juma Sahal, *See* Juma'a Sahal
Juma'a Sahal, 14, 19, 26, 76, 96–7, 133, 155–6, 157, 158, 163, 233, 245, 262

Kababish, 1, 3–4, 7, 12–15, 23–4, 29, 31–9, 42, 56–8, 62–3, 65, 69, 70, 76, 81, 84, 101, 108, 111–29, 131, 134–7, 144, 166, 172–3, 188, 192, 194, 204, 209, 220–1, 223–4, 226, 247, 248, 250–1, 253–4, 263, 265, 271–3, 275–86, 289–90
'Atawiyya, 121, 142, 147–8
'Awayda, 36, 58, 121, 122
Awlad Sulyaman, 58

Awlad 'Uqba, 34, 69, 84, 89, 91, 92, 104, 134, 135, 136, 142, 144, 146–7, 148, 160, 178, 188
  Barara, 40
  Dar 'Umar, 62, 69, 148
  History of, 33, 37, 63, 67, 119, 129, 238
  Kibayshab, 104, 136, 142, 144
  Nurab, 4, 5, 79, 80, 81, 121, 123–4, 125, 126, 144, 185, 220, 229, 230, 231, 239, 250, 267, 268, 284, 292
  Rawahla, 54, 58
  Relations with Hawawir, 69
  Relations with Kawahla, 24, 30, 32, 39, 41, 42, 44, 47, 116, 119, 120, 121, 122, 123, 124, 125–9
  Relations with Maydub, 22–3, 32, 33, 59, 75–6, 116–7, 118, 223, 224, 227–8, 229, 239
  Relations with Nuba, 31, 66, 76–7, 121, 136–7, 142, 144, 145, 147–8, 153–4, 160, 174–5, 176–84, 232–3
  Relations with Zayadiyya, 117, 128, 224–5, 229, 250, 278–9, 285–6, 290–1
  Ribayqat, 62, 68
  Sarijab, 58, 62
  Shilaywab, 56, 58, 62, 68, 69
  Taxation of, 25, 28, 29, 42, 63, 70, 79–80, 81, 204
  Zanayqa, 29
Kaja, 37, 42, 49, 94, 108, 254, 255, 290
Kajmar, 124, 131, 171, 176
Karabat al-Sarir, 61
Karima, 209, 217
Kassala Province, 11, 12
Katool, Jebel, *See* Jabal Katul
Katoul, Jebel, *See* Jabal Katul
Katul, *See* Jabal Katul
Kawahla, 5, 12, 13, 24, 26, 28, 29, 35, 40, 43–50, 59, 89, 98–9, 101, 102, 103, 104, 105, 106–32, 156, 161–2, 166, 199, 209, 225–6, 228, 231, 232–4, 239, 251–2, 253–8, 274
  Ababda, 98
  Amara, 105, 106, 113–14
  Awlad al-Faki Sadiq, 114
  Awlad Hamad, 239
  Baruk, 105, 113–14
Khalafallah Effendi, 214
Kennedy-Cooke, B. 177, 178, 180
Khamis Tamar Agha, 134, 152–3, 154
Khartoum, 6, 12, 19, 30, 152, 162, 163, 209, 217
Khartoum Province, 11, 29
Khashm El Girba, *See* Khashm al-Qirba
Khashm al-Laban, 184
Khashm al-Qirba, 11, 186
Khawr Abu 'Uruq, 70
Khawr Jadayn, 138

Khawr al-Sumit, 69
Khawr al-Sunt, 45–9, 97–8, 106, 130, 225–6
Khor Es Sumiit, *See* Khawr al-Sumit
Kibeishab, *See under* Kababish, Kibayshab
Koko (C. A. E. Lea's servant), 17, 48, 75, 136, 210, 211, 222, 223, 236, 243
Koko Mafa, 117, 118, 119, 123
Kol Zurga, *See* Qal'at Zurqa
Korti, 204, 207, 208, 209, 210, 211–13, 216
Kufra, 37, 173
Kuttum, 112, 123

Lammens, Henri, 31
Lee Stack Indemnity Fund, 216
Leicester, "Jumbo", 17, 20, 21, 22, 23, 66, 169, 277
Locusts, 44, 64, 112, 136

Mackrell, J. E. C., 223, 224, 225, 226, 227–8, 229, 250
Maclagen, T. A., 152, 206
Maclaren, J. F. P., 22–3, 67, 102, 108, 110, 134, 177, 259, 263, 264, 265, 267
MacMichael, Harold, 7, 12, 28, 38, 54, 57, 64, 67, 84, 91, 137, 139, 163, 201, 260, 283
Macphail, J. G. S., 163–4, 165, 167, 169
Madden, John, 100
Madjdub, Faki, 189
Mahdiyya, 1, 2, 4, 33, 54, 56, 76, 127, 129, 141, 142, 152, 194, 198, 215, 270, 273, 276, 282
al-Mahi Ahmad, 93
al-Mahi Jibril, 73, 74
Majamid, 223, 228
Majanin, 12, 14, 19, 64, 94, 241, 245
Mardi Imam, 254–5, 290
Marfa'ibat, 67, 185
Marien Balila, 152, 154
Marjoribanks, Edward, 22, 48, 49, 123
Masarin, 144
Maxwell-Darling, *See* Darling
Mayall, R. C., 17, 135–6, 160, 161, 163, 164, 165, 166, 168, 218, 244
Maydub, 5, 23, 32, 33, 56, 59, 60, 62–3, 106, 225, 227, 229–30, 232, 234, 281, 282, 286
Mazroub, *See* Mazrub
Mazrub, 18, 19, 26, 155, 156–7, 158, 163, 245, 254, 262
Mecca, 19
Meganiin, *See* Majanin
Mellit, 223, 274, 286
Merafa'ib, *See* Marfa'ibat
Merkh, *See* 'Idd al-Marikh

Merowe, 209, 211, 213, 214–15
Milner Mission, 3, 11
Mitchell, Dicky, 146, 170
Moore, Guy, 35, 165, 220, 221–2
Muhamma, See *Muhanna*
Muhammad 'Abduh, 55
Muhammad Abu-l Qasim, 112
Muhammad Adam 'Abdallah, 188
Muhammad Ahmed, Shaykh, 56
Muhammad Ahmad Abu Sinn (al-Hardallu), 59, 76
Muhammad Ahmad Effendi (Dr.), 58–9, 60–1, 62, 65, 67, 68–9, 70, 71–2, 76, 77, 121, 126, 128, 183, 184, 186, 189, 191, 195, 198, 212, 213, 231, 234, 237, 274
Muhammad Ahmad Fadlallah, 114
Muhammad Ahmad al-I'aysir, 233, 274
Muhammad Ahmad al-Mahdi, 1, 13
Muhammad Ahmad Salih, 104
Muhammad 'Ali, Shaykh, 53–4
Muhammad 'Ali Da'ay, 186
Muhammad 'Awad al-Sid, 107–8 109, 110, 113, 115, 126
Muhammad Fadlallah, 13, 14, 26, 30, 32–3, 39, 40–1, 42, 43, 44–5, 46–7, 48, 49, 50, 51, 59, 97, 98, 100–2, 104–28, 156, 158, 161–2, 168, 232, 233–5, 236, 237, 238, 241, 252–3, 254, 255–6
Muhammad al-Faki Sulayman, 263, 264, 265
Muhammad Hasan Khalifa, 72, 77, 185–6
Muhammad Jad al-Rab, 19
Muhammad Jangai, 46, 274
Muhammad Kaddad, 256
Muhammad Musa, 53, 56, 57, 58, 59–60, 61, 62, 63, 65, 68, 69, 71, 72, 76–92
Muhammad Nasir, 156
Muhammad Rashid, 219
Muhammad Sadiq, 50, 56, 70, 78, 90, 97, 184, 243, 262, 286, 287
Muhammad Salih, 17, 222
Muhammad Sayyah, 223, 227, 229, 232, 238, 239
Muhammad Sirkatti, 65, 66
Muhammad Timsah, 266, 267–8
Muhammad al-Tum, 30, 32, 33, 36, 39, 56, 79, 115, 119, 126, 127, 136, 142, 143–4, 221, 230, 231, 248, 284
Muhanna, 13, 14, 145, 177–8, 180, 181, 182, 184, 230
Mun'im Mansur, 168, 234, 290
Murah Ribah, 113
Musa Fadlallah, 89
Musa Gelli, See Musa Qalli
Musa Kurfis, 81–2, 83–4, 85–7, 88, 119
Musa Qalli, 84

Nadeef, See Nadif
Nadif Mukhawi, 51–2, 93
al-Nahud, 25, 94, 99, 103, 117, 129, 152, 160, 161, 219
Na'iim Fereih, See Na'im Farayh
Na'im Farayh, 28, 158–9, 272
Na'im Fereih, See Na'im Farayh
Na'im Surkatti (Niama Sirkatti), 5, 14, 20, 24, 25–8, 31, 62, 63–5, 67, 76, 121, 132–4, 135–9, 141–3, 147–9, 151, 154, 155, 158–9, 160–1, 163, 174–5, 176–85, 188, 233, 245, 246, 255, 269
Nakhila, 120, 172, 186, 217
Napata, 215, 217
Nasb El Husan, See Jabal Nasib al-Husan
Nasb Es Sunugh, See Jabal Nasib al-Sumugh
Nasir Muhammad al-Shaykh, 108, 126
Native Administration, See Indirect Rule
Newbold, Douglas, 203, 204, 244–58, 269, 276
Niam-Niam, 64
Niama Sirkatti, See Na'im Surkatti
Nicholson, H. A., 211
al-Nihid, 137, 142, 146, 147–8
al-Nil Sahal, 19
Nile, 2, 7, 211
Nimr, Shaykh, 71–8, 83
Nimr 'Ali Arti, 117
Nimr Hasan Khalifa, 155, 186–9, 190–2, 194, 196–9, 201–9, 211–16, 233
al-Nuayqa, 122
Nuba, Nubas, 5, 12, 14, 20, 31, 37, 42, 51–2, 53–4, 65, 67, 78, 94, 111, 133, 135, 136–7, 138, 142, 144, 147–8, 149, 152–62, 176–85, 188, 246, 254–5, 261–6, 269, 271
Nurab, *See under* Kababish
Nyala, 99

Oakley, A. S., 166
Omaara Kawahla, *See under* Kawahla, Amara
Omdurman, 4, 26, 34, 57, 58, 90, 91, 92, 102, 103, 118, 128, 142, 185, 198, 206, 213, 229, 246, 247
Oxford, 21

Passports and Permits Ordinance, 23
Penn, A. E. D., 88, 206
Powers of Nomad Sheikhs Ordinance, 3, 11, 14, 145, 187
Pumphrey, M. E. C., 234
Purves, W. D. C. L., 208–9, 211, 213, 214, 215, 216, 217

al-Qadab, 100
Qadaydim, 220, 229, 238
Qafalah, 137
Qal'at al-Jihadi, 91
Qal'at al-Jumur, 197
Qal'at al-Tin, 129
Qal'at Zurqa, 67, 139–40
Qambir, 73, 83, 194, 200, 202
Qannatu, 153
Qashta, 37, 39–40, 91, 115, 241, 252
Qawz Rajab, 11
Quraan, 14, 33, 75, 111, 120, 172, 173, 205, 217
Quran al-'Ujaymi, 45

Rabih Safi, 93
Rahad al-Dabib, 151, 152
Rahma 'Udaylha, 29
al-Rajjaf, 64, 141
Rakuba, 218
al-Rasan, 78
Reid, J. A., 34, 67, 118, 190, 260
Rejaf, *See* al-Rajjaf
Ribayqat, 58, 81–2, 84, 97
Ribda, *See* B'ir Rabda
Rifles, 35–6, 37, 38, 64, 71, 75, 77, 106, 117, 156, 181, 189, 230, 238, 251, 274, 278–80
Royal Geographical Society, 247
Rufa'a, 11
al-Rukab, 139

al-Saddat Umm Kuhl, 100
Safia, *See* al-Safiyah
al-Safiyah, 58, 62, 67, 75, 144, 185–6, 202, 247
Sa'id 'Abd al-Baqi, 103
Salim 'Ali al-Tum, 44
Salim Bilal, 92
Salim Fadlallah, 63
Salim Ibrahim Dulib, 136, 141, 143, 144, 180, 188
Salmon, R., 164
Sanaagir, *See* Sanaqir
Sanaqir, 50, 96, 256
Sandison, P. J., 172
Sanusiyya, 172, 173, 205, 257
Savile, R. V., 159
Sayyah, 288–9
Scott, G. C., 167
Seligman, B. Z., 56
Seligman, C. G., 56
Shaw, *See* Jabal Shau
Shukria, *See* Shukriyya
Shukriyya, 11, 60, 61, 77, 79–80, 285

Sifaya, 176, 182–3, 184
Simon, Lady, 43
Simons, John, 23, 51
Skander Effendi Tadros, 101
Skeet, C. H. L., 165, 166
Slatin, Rudolf, 37, 65, 142
Slavery, slaves, 6, 15, 32, 33, 34–5, 36, 37, 38, 42, 43–4, 47, 49, 59, 88, 90, 97, 98–9, 106–7, 117, 123, 126, 130, 161, 240, 241, 247, 253, 272, 273–4, 275
Soderi, 4, 12, 14, 17–27, 39, 41, 52, 79, 93, 99, 117, 123, 132, 152, 160–2, 163, 177, 206, 209, 212, 213, 218, 249, 258, 272
Sudan Archive, 7
Sudan Medical Service, 260–1
Sudan Political Service, 1, 6–7, 11, 59
Sulayman Arbab, 101

Tamar Agha, 95, 134, 154, 155
Tangassi, 214
al-Tarabil 67
Thabit Murjab, 102, 105–6, 107, 109, 113, 120
Tichu, 51, 94, 96
Timsah Simawi Jarajir, 175
Tingle, Corporal, 26, 27, 30, 32, 41, 49, 51, 52, 73, 96, 98, 100, 101, 110, 112, 125, 129, 136, 146, 153, 154, 158, 161, 184, 189, 191, 195, 202, 208, 211, 213, 214, 222, 236, 273, 282, 287, 290
al-Tum 'Ali al-Tum, 32, 36, 37–8, 39–42, 44, 45, 76–7, 79, 116, 121, 122–4, 126, 148, 171, 175, 181–2, 185, 206, 207, 220–9, 231, 238, 248, 249, 273, 274, 276, 284
al-Tum Fadlallah Salim, 4, 13, 144
al-Tum Hasan, 77
Turkiyya, Turks, 2, 3–4, 63, 129, 144, 149, 242

Um, *See* Umm
Um Badr, *See* Umm Badr
Um Botatikhat, *See* Umm Batatikh
Um Gawasir, *See* Umm Qawayz
Um Gozein, *See* Umm Qawzayn
Um Jawasir, *See* Umm Qawayz
Um Kedada, *See* Umm Kaddadah
Um Meiroos, *See* Umm Mayrus
Um Seyala, *See* Umm Sayala
'Umar Kimbal, 211
'Umar Yasin Dulib, 190
Umm Badr, 30, 32, 35, 39, 40, 41, 45, 48, 58, 98, 99, 106, 123, 130, 134, 235, 240, 241, 352, 253, 254
Umm Batatikh, 121

Umm Dabi, 37, 175
Umm Dabus, 260
Umm Dam, 69, 247, 261
Umm Danun, 134
Umm Duraj, 64, 66, 94, 141, 143, 148–9, 150, 153, 160, 178, 179, 181, 182, 184
Umm Hatub, 130, 272
Umm Haymi, 101, 102
Umm Indaraba, 34, 80, 87, 88, 89, 124, 160, 183, 206
Umm Kaddadah, 35, 36, 219–20, 221, 222, 231
Umm Khirwa', 27–8, 131, 243, 272
Umm Kuhl, 97, 239, 268
Umm Mayrus, 32, 33
Umm Qawayz, 73, 201, 202, 203, 206, 208, 209, 213
Umm Qawzayn, 100, 105, 119, 224, 236–7, 238–9
Umm Rumayla, 198, 200, 247
Umm Sayala, 265, 266, 267, 268, 271
Umm Shidara, 19
Umm Sidr, 90
Umm Sunaytah, 56–9, 60–1
Umm Tub, 208, 209–10
Umm Zabad, 131
Ummat, 37
Upper Nile, 1–2
'Uthman Adam Janu, 54

Vicars-Miles, A. L. W., 113, 161–2, 166, 168, 219

Wadi Abu Kitr, 91
Wadi Abu Sunayt, 177
Wadi Abu 'Uruq, 78, 187
Wadi El Gadab, *See* Wadi al-Qadab
Wadi El Geleita, *See* Wadi al-Jalayta
Wadi El Gelta, *See* Wadi al-Jalayta
Wadi Hamid, 207
Wadi Hamra, 14, 26, 31, 65, 176, 177, 178
Wadi al-Hasanawi, 196
Wadi Hawa, 14, 205
Wadi al-Jalayta, 192, 194, 195
Wadi Jumur, 196, 197
Wadi al-Malik, 200–1, 202, 242, 246, 247
Wadi Masarin, 67, 185
Wadi Mugaddam, *See* Wadi Muqaddam
Wadi Muqaddam, 190, 197, 200, 202, 207, 208, 247
Wadi al-Qadab, 101, 102, 105, 239
Wadi Shau, 172, 173, 176
Wadi Umm Hayaya, 130
Wadi al-Wazz, 64, 76, 121
Watt, Hector, 12, 13, 19–25, 26, 50, 67, 72, 73, 74, 131, 133, 147, 152, 169, 187, 190, 195, 203, 208
White Nile province, 34, 50, 89
Winder, John, 166
Wolff, Mabel, 57
World War I, 2, 4
World War II, 7

Yasin Muhammad Jayli, 68, 70, 74, 75–6
Young, Clive, 12, 67, 118, 212
Yusuf Idris, 77

Zaghawa, 173, 174, 176, 183, 228, 288
Zalatah Umm Khusus, 49, 97, 256
Zayadiyya, 13, 111–2, 120, 123, 140, 223, 224, 225–6, 227–8, 232, 266, 268, 271, 273, 277, 278, 290–1
Zeyadia, *See* Zayadiyya
Zolot Um Khusus, *See* Zalatah Umm Khusus